REHABILITATION, MUSIC AND
AND
HUMAN WELL-BEING

Edited by

Mathew H.M. Lee

MMB
MMB MUSIC, INC.
CONTEMPORARY ARTS BUILDING
3526 WASHINGTON AVENUE
SAINT LOUIS, MISSOURI 63103-1019 USA
314 531-9635; 800 543-3771 (USA/Canada); Fax 314 531-8384
http://www.mmbmusic.com

REHABILITATION, MUSIC AND HUMAN WELL-BEING

Edited by Mathew H.M. Lee

ISBN 0-918812-59-3

CONTEMPORARY ARTS BUILDING
3526 WASHINGTON AVENUE
SAINT LOUIS, MISSOURI 63103-1019 USA
314 531-9635; 800 543-3771 (USA/Canada); Fax 314 531-8384
http://www.mmbmusic.com

Cover artwork: Sandra Stanton
Printer: Thomson-Shore, Inc., Ann Arbor, MI USA

TABLE OF CONTENTS

THE BROAD VIEW

THE SHARP FOCUS

ABOUT THE AUTHORS

Howard A. Rusk, MD
Distinguished University Professor, Rusk Institute of Rehabilitation Medicine, New York University Medical Center

Mathew H.M. Lee, MD, MPH, FACP
Acting Director, Rusk Institute of Rehabilitation Medicine, New York; Professor, Clinical Rehabilitation Medicine, Adjunct Professor, Music, Clinical Professor, Behavioral Sciences and Community Health, New York University; President International Association of Music for the Handicapped

Rosalie Rebollo Pratt, EdD
Professor of Music, Brigham Young University; Co-founder Music Education for the Handicapped; Executive Secretary, International Association of Music for the Handicapped; Chair, ISME Commission on Music Therapy and Music in Special Education

Masayoshi Itoh, MD, MPH
Associate Professor of Clinical Rehabilitation Medicine, New York University; Associate Director, Rehabilitation Department, Goldwater Memorial Hospital, New York

Frank Wilson, MD
Associate Professor of Neurology, University of California/San Francisco; Author, *Tone Deaf and All Thumbs?*; Board, International Association of Music for the Handicapped; Board, Performing Arts Medicine Association

Barry R. Dworkin, PhD
Department of Behavioral Medicine, Pennsylvania State College of Medicine

Bhagwan Shahani, MD, Ph.D (Oxon)
Director, EMG and Motor Control Clinic, Department of Neurophysiology, Massachusetts General Hospital, Harvard Medical School

D. Cros, MD
Harvard Medical School

Steven Halpern, PhD.
Composer, Performer, Producer; President, Sound R_X Productions

John J. Kella, PhD
Assistant Professor, Music, New York University; Board, Center for Occupational Hazards; Violist, Metropolitan Opera Orchestra

Ralph Spintge, MD, PhD
Chair, Department of Psychophysiological Research, Pain Therapy and Rehabilitation, Sportclinic Hellerşen, Lüdenscheid, W. Germany; Founding member and Executive Secretary, International Society for Music in Medicine

Heinz Lippmann, MD, FAPC, FACA, FRSH
Professor, Department of Rehabilitation Medicine, Albert Einstein College of Medicine; Chief, Peripheral Vascular Clinic, Bronx Municipal Hospital Center

Hunter J.H. Fry, MS, FRCS, FRACS
Plastic Surgeon, Epworth Hospital, Kew, Victoria, Australia; Scientific Convenor, Performing Arts Medicine Society

Mary Elinore Boyle, EdD.
Director, Music Therapy Program, The College at New Paltz, NY

Fred Kersten, EdD.
State University of New York, Potsdam

Dale Taylor, PhD, RMT-BC
Chair, Department of Music, Director of Music Therapy Studies University of Wisconsin at Eau Claire; Board, International Association of Music for the Handicapped

Wilbur J. Gould, MD
Founder/Director, Vocal Dynamics Laboratory, Lenox Hill Hospital, New York

Pi-Tang Lin, MD
Chief, ENT Department, Metropilitan Hospital, New York

François Haas, PhD
Associate Research Professor, Department of Rehabilitation Medicine, New York University School of Medicine

Horacio Pineda, MD
Assistant Clinical Professor, Department of Rehabilitation Medicine, New York University School fo Medicine

Kenneth Axen, PhD
Associate Professor, Department of Rehabilitation Medicine, New York University School of Medicine

Shirley Harris, Dip., Teacher Certification
Director, Harbor Conservatory for Musical Growth, E. Burwood, Victoria, Australia

Joan E. Edelstein, MD
Senior Research Scientist, New York University Post Graduate Medical School; Clinical Assistant Professor, Orthopedic Surgery, Professor, Physical Therapy and Prosthetics and Orthotics, School of Education, New York University

Joseph C. Nagler, MA, CMT
Director, Center for Electronic Music MIDI Research Center for Music Therapy, New York University; Faculty, New York Public Schools

Myrtha Perez, MA, CMT
Director, Child Life Department, Children's Memorial Hospital, Chicago

Corrie Van Hugten
Faculty, Foundation for Wheelchair Dancing, Netherlands

Ondine du Hullu
Physical Therapist, Netherlands

Peter F. Jampel, MA,CMT-BC
Director, Baltic Street Day Hospital, South Beach Psychiatric Center, New York

FOREWORD

Howard A. Rusk, M.D.

Since the establishment of the first rehabilitation medicine service at New York City's Bellevue Hospital forty years ago, we have witnessed the exponential growth of all phases of comprehensive rehabilitation medicine.

The aim of rehabilitation medicine is to restore a disabled person to maximum capacity - physical, emotional and vocational. Medical care cannot be considered complete until the patient with the residual physical disability has been trained "to live and work with what he has left."

I have known Dr. Mathew Lee for the past 25 years and he has guided Goldwater Memorial Hospital's Department of Rehabilitation Medicine into one of the largest, most innovative departments in the world, addressing the total rehabilitation needs of the chronic long-term disabled patient. He holds professorships in the Schools of Medicine, Dentistry and Music at New York University.

As President of the Fourth International Conference on Music, Rehabilitation and Human Well-Being held at Goldwater Memorial Hospital in 1985, Dr. Lee noted the tremendous ground swell of interest worldwide and nationally in this field. The late Senator Jacob Javits and I had the pleasure of speaking at and attending this magnificent conference.

This book, *Rehabilitation, Music, and Human Well-Being,* introduces a new concept of physical restoration through music. It also covers the rehabilitation of musicians, a neglected area of medical care.

Contributors with special expertise in the field of medicine and music have been chosen to explore a wide array of significant literature. Most of them are pioneers in their field of expertise.

This book should appeal to musicians, music therapists, physicians and health personnel.

To rehabilitation medicine it adds a new and vibrant dimension; and to patients, a holistic approach to care.

FOREWORD

Mathew H.M. Lee

"Art established the basic human truths which must serve as the
touchstone of our human judgement."
– President John F. Kennedy

The exponential worldwide interest in music and rehabilitation medicine shared during the Fourth International Symposium on Music: Rehabilitation and Human Well-Being, held in 1985 at Goldwater Memorial Hospital, was the driving force toward the conceptualization of this unique book.

From the expressions of the attendees and patients it was clear that such a volume would serve as a central rallying point for those interested in the area of music and health in its broadest dimensions.

An array of authors, recognized in their respective fields of endeavor, have contributed chapters ranging from the history of music and medicine and the biology of music to musicians' neuromuscular disorders and the application of music therapy to the treatment of the severely disabled patient.

Some of the material is at the so-called "cutting edge." If these issues evoke discussion, further interest and study, this book will have served a major function.

This book is divided into two major sections: The *Broad View* and the *Sharp Focus*. Chapters in the Broad View section deal with music on a universal level; chapters in the Sharp Focus section deal with specific topics in music and medicine.

Since the beginning of time, the therapeutic effects of music on the general population have been utilized by various cultures. During the past decades, greater concern, interest and focus have been directed to the medical problems of the musician, the application of music therapy for the severely disabled, and the neurobiological study of the brain.

The greying of America, the increase of leisure time, the advent of new tools to study the neurophysiological effects of music, and the passage of federal legislation have now converged to re-establish the historic bond between music and medicine.

Goldwater Memorial Hospital has established a music therapy center for the severely disabled, including a center for electronic music in conjunction with the Department of Music of New York University. We have produced a videotape, *Rehabilitation, Music, and Human Well-Being* to demonstrate that music and the arts can improve the rehabilitation of an individual in the areas of mental functioning, breathing capacity, pain, socialization, vocational skills, and self expression. We hope that this film will encourage other health facilities to pursue these types of clinical observations and research so that appropriate data can be gathered to delineate the neurophysiological value of music. We are grateful for the grant from the Arnold and Marie Schwartz Fund for Education and Health Research for making the film possible.

Editing an international multi-authored book requires the wisdom of Solomon and the tenacity of a bulldog! However, this volume was a pleasure to produce and I wish to express my thanks to each contributor personally.

I would also like to thank Dr. Rosalie Pratt, Professor of Music at Brigham Young University and Executive Director of the International Association of Music for the Handicapped, for her inspiration and leadership in the field of music and medicine; Andrew McKinley, Founding Director of the Usdan Center for the Creative and Performing Arts; and Dr. Howard Rusk, the "Father of Rehabilitation Medicine."

Thanks also to the staff of the New York University School of Music, especially Dr. Lily McKinley, Dean Jerrold Ross, Dean John Gilbert, Former Dean Roger Phelps and Professor Barbara Hesser.

To my former student, now colleague, Joe Nagler, Director of the Center for Electronic Music, who has grasped modern technology and applied it to the field of music and medicine, it is a pleasure to watch his professional and personal growth.

Many thanks to Norman Goldberg for his patience, counsel and belief in this project and to Sandra Stanton for her administrative efforts and editorial assistance.

I also want to express my deep gratitude to Fortune and Catherine Pope for their loyal and staunch support of my ideas and their humanitarian concern for the disabled.

And finally I am grateful to my parents who gave me early exposure to music; to my wife Mary Lou for her steadfast support to complete this vision; and to my son Randall, a graduate of the New York University School of Music for an insight into the complexity of a young musician's life.

THE BROAD VIEW

A BRIEF HISTORY OF MUSIC AND MEDICINE

Rosalie Rebollo Pratt

> This variable composition of man's body hath made it as an
> instrument easy to distemper; and therefore the Poets did well to
> conjoin Music and Medicine in Apollo, because the Office of
> Medicine is but to tune this curious Harp of man's body and to
> reduce it to Harmony.[1]

These remarks, addressed to King James I by Sir Francis Bacon, describe an alliance between music and medicine that has been perceived since the time of the ancient Greeks. The concept behind this union is simply that health is a matter of concordance or harmony in the body. The restoration of health, therefore, is a matter of tuning the body back to this harmony. From earliest history until today, the claim continues to be made that music and medicine enjoy a natural bond, and that music can indeed heal. How was this idea conceived? And why has it continued throughout the history of the two arts?

The ancient Greek and Roman cultural traditions provided the foundation for the concept that music is a component of physical and mental harmony. The partnership of music and medicine was clearly affirmed in Greece. Of all the gods, Apollo appears to have been among the busiest. In addition to his jurisdiction over the musical arts, another of his many duties was to cleanse man of disease, guilt, and evil. The Greeks believed that this cleansing process restored harmony to the body and soul. The harmonic balance, in turn, bore a direct relationship to the health of a human being. Apollo was certainly one of the most influential of the gods, and titles such as Musagetes and Iatros attest to his leadership in both the musical and medical arts.[2] The bond between the two arts was then forged completely through the union of Apollo and his son Aesculapius.[3] As far as the Greeks were concerned, Apollo was the inventor of medicine and Aesculapius was the enlightener of the art. Temples were erected to Aesculapius to which both the sick and the healthy were brought. Stories of cures may in part be due to the iatromantic nature accorded the two gods, who were gifted with the qualities of physician and seer.[4] The patients and pilgrims who came to the temples to be cured may actually have been healed because of their implicit faith in the gods and in the ritual involved. And so, there was actually a psychotherapeutic aspect to the temple rites and the healing ritual done in the name of the gods. The idea that a physician might have certain connections with deities was continued by the Neo-Platonists and is manifest today in cultures with medicine men and shamans.

The concordance of health and harmony within the body was an idea shared by prominent Greek philosophers. The sixth century B.C. philosopher and scientist Pythagoras saw the human soul as a harmony within itself. He believed that daily singing and playing helped one achieve emotional catharsis, and that health could be developed through a regular routine of music.[5]

There were also certain very blessed human beings chosen by the gods to share music and poetry with lesser creatures. Orpheus, for example, was a legendary musician who could charm the beasts with his music. One of the Greek legends describes him as a discoverer of cures for diseases as well as one who could calm the anger of the gods. Homer, another of these blessed mortals, noted that music can prevent anger, sadness, and disquiet, in addition to promoting health. One of this great poet's accounts is the story of Ulysses being cured of a profusely bleeding wound by means of an incantation.[6] The words incantation and chant have a common root, and both have been an integral part of healing ceremonies throughout history. And, before the Greeks, Egyptian physicians understood the efficacy of music as part of the treatment of diseases. Egyptian medical

1

papyri dating back to more than four thousand years ago show that various diseases of the time were treated with music and drug therapy.[7]

Both Plato and Aristotle believed in the unity of the soul and body as well as the need for harmonic balance between the two. Plato saw music as the medicine of the soul. He believed that melody and rhythm helped restore order and harmony.[8] Aristotle's hypothesis that music may influence the soul and body is an idea that recurs again and again in the history of music and medicine.[9]

The Romans took much of this thinking to heart. Men such as Cicero, Lucretius, Celsus, and Seneca pursued the Greek positions on philosophy and medicine, although the application of their thinking was more social and political. The Greco-Roman concept that health was a matter of balance between the mind and the body was reflected in the well known maxim attributed to Juvenal: "mens sana in corpore sano."[10] Both Macrobius and Quintilian described music as an educational tool and a means of developing good health. Lucretius went on record about the power of flute music to aid the digestive process and that such music should be played after meals. He also spoke of the power of music to affect the mind, behavior, and emotional state of a man.[11]

Theophrastus, Aristotle's most important disciple, claimed that music played on the flute has a powerful somatic influence. He said that persons subject to sciatica would always be free from its attacks if a musician played flute music over the part affected.[12] The Greek physician Asclepiades was reported to have used some sort of trumpet to cure deafness. Actually, the method probably involved a kind of amplification device inserted in the ear.

The Platonic-Aristotelian belief in the affective power of music continued to hold the attention of future thinkers. Throughout the history of ancient Greece, Rome, and the Europe of the Middle Ages, there was an insistence that music held some awesome power capable of influencing character, health, and behavior. The Greek physician Herophilus is often credited with the idea of regulating the arterial pulse by means of the principle of the musical scale. Much later, the eighteenth century French physician Marquet based his theory of understanding the human pulse on principles of music theory.[13]

Many of the early Greek and Roman thinkers had theories about the specific effects of music on the human mind and body, effects that have been studied and evaluated continually throughout the history of both Eastern and Western cultures. Although we do not know how the ancient modes sounded, it was not the mode alone that caused the character and mood changes claimed by the Greeks. Aristides Quintilianus, the music theorist, made it clear that rhythm was a vital factor and that the use of more than two rhythm patterns could affect the heartbeat.[14] Quintilian had declared earlier that knowledge of the principles of music could enable one to excite or assuage the emotions of mankind.[15] The Roman physician-historian Celsus understood how music could be used to combat the problems of mental disorders. He prescribed music – cymbals and other sounds – as a treatment for melancholia induced by mental illness.[16] During a pestilence in Rome, circa 364-362 B.C., music, dancing, and poetry were used to combat disease.[17] The same remedial approach appeared much later in Apulia, Italy, where a mysterious disorder was supposedly caused by the bite of a spider. In both cases, the remedy did not effect a cure. In addition to the stories of Pliny and Varro about sprains and gout being cured by music, there is a most unusual tale of music therapy mentioned by Plutarch. He described an account (allegedly given by Aristotle) of a punishment meted out to Etrurian slaves. It appears that these slaves were often punished by flogging. As they were being whipped, however, flute music was played. It was believed that flute music alleviated the pain of the beating.[18]

Hippocrates, who lived around 400 B.C., was responsible for one of the most dramatic changes in the theory and practice of medicine. Hippocrates finally separated the science of

Rosalie Rebollo Pratt

medicine from the study of philosophy.[19] The body of writing ascribed to him, however, was almost certainly a collection of early Greek medical treatises compiled by Alexandrian scholars in the third century. The famous oath traditionally taken by medical students at their graduation was most probably written long after the death of Hippocrates.

Galen, born in the second century in Pergamum, Asia Minor, is a significant figure in medical history. He held medicine as the highest art, although he also recognized the liberal and honorable nature of music and recommended its inclusion in the educational curriculum.[20] Galen's major work *On The Natural Faculties*, is a strong defense of what he regarded as the Hippocratic position of diagnosing and treating the "whole" man. Much of the three books in this opus is a vigorous argument against the mechanistic and atomistic approaches advanced by the physicians Asclepiades and Erasistratus.[21]

In the Middle Ages, there was a tremendous effort made by the Christian Church to free itself from the pagan influences of the Greeks and Romans. Augustine, one of the leading Christian thinkers of the time, saw the value of the Greco-Roman legacy and tried to keep much of it in the educational system. In the sixth century, Boethius maintained that music could have an effect on moral development. He also commented on the physiological effects of music on infants by contrasting the calming effects of a lullaby with the excitation of a "shrill and harsh" melody.[22] The Middle Ages in Europe was a time when disease was often attributed through granting absolution and thereby helping the sinner regain his relationship with God. However, the old belief that music had power to change mood still persisted.

Much of the writing and thinking of Galen and Hippocrates might have been lost to us during the Middle Ages had it not been for the Arab world. During the eighth and ninth centuries, the Arab culture reached its apex. Much of the Greco-Roman tradition and, in particular, the writings of Hippocrates and Galen were preserved. Many of these Greek books were translated into Arabic, the intellectual language of Islam. It is certain that the preservation of certain works by Hippocrates and Galen is due to the scholarship of Arabs in these two centuries. There is also little doubt that European medicine in the later Middle Ages was directly influenced by the Arabs. The medical tradition of Greece had passed to southwest Persia, thence to Baghdad, and secured its position in the Islamic culture.[23]

It was during the Middle Ages that the interdependence of all branches of knowledge was recognized and, from that start, there emerged the basis of an integrated liberal arts curriculum that dominated higher education through the Renaissance. Of course, the body of knowledge of the time was still within the grasp of a human mind, and it was not unusual for a medieval physician to have studied astronomy, astrology, music, and mathematics, as well as ethics, metaphysics and politics.[24]

Rhazes, a major medical writer of the time, was chiefly interested in music as a youth and appears to have been a skilled lutenist.[25] Ibn Hindu, an important physician and medical theorist of the eleventh century, stated that music was one of the disciplines needed by a doctor in order to be a well-rounded professional. Ibn Hindu then went on to discuss the psychic effects of different Arabian musical modes and their applications to the art of music therapy. Once again, we note the belief in the power of music to heal, and a physician's attraction to the art.[26]

A few more points about the Arab culture of the Middle Ages are germane to this history of music and medicine. The Arabs believed in four basic elements: earth, air, fire, and water. This concept was rooted in theories that had been proposed by the Greek thinkers Empedocles and Pythagoras. The idea was reconceived later in the Renaissance and molded into a theoretical base upon which music and medicine met.[27]

The system of vigorous oral examinations, theses, and dissertations in modern colleges and universities is modeled on the Arab tradition. Here again, these dialectic contests were yet another meeting ground for music and medicine. It has been said that the development of medical science in European schools of the late Middle Ages and Renaissance is, in large part, the history of the impact of Arabian scholarship on medieval Europe.[28]

The early university curriculum was based on a pattern of the seven liberal arts, articulated by Martianus Capella in the fifth century. Martianus was a native of Carthage and a Neo-Platonist. In his books of allegory describing wedding activities, the seven liberal arts appear as bridesmaids to Philology, the most learned virgin.[29] Undoubtedly influenced by Plato's ideas concerning music's high position in learning, Martianus placed music above the other arts. This pattern of the seven liberal arts proved to be a most important one in the history of music and medicine because it formed the basis in European universities of the Middle Ages and Renaissance. Since the baccalaurate in the arts was a prerequisite to admission to the higher faculties of theology, medicine, and law, it is entirely logical to assume that medical students first had to master music as part of the quadrivium, which included arithmetic, astronomy, geometry, and music. Nan Cook Carpenter's research has shown that musical problems were investigated in medical courses, and, occasionally, there were men teaching music along with medicine.[30]

Carpenter also found that in universities having strong traditions in medical studies, such as Padua and Vienna, one finds much documentary evidence for musical studies allied with medicine, a parallel to which is seen in the close connection between music and bodily health in philosophical writings from the time of Plato onward.[30]

The tradition was then established that, before going on to the higher study of medicine, one needed first to be a master of music. In the Renaissance, there are many examples of medical men who were poets, musicians, philosophers, as well as scientists. Many of them were ardent lovers and supporters of music. For example, the sixteenth century surgeon, Paré, claimed that music cured spider bites, sciatica, and gout. John Case, another Renaissance physician, defended the use of music in church. The best known medical doctor of the time, however, was Samuel Quickelberg, who served at the Bavarian Court with Orlando Lassus. Quickelberg's knowledge of music was quite extensive and his commentaries on the problems of "musica reservata" are an important part of music history.[31]

The Renaissance made its own statement about the number four, the importance of which goes back to Pythagoras and Empedocles. To the concept of the four elements (earth, water, air and fire), the medical theoretician from the time of Hippocrates added the idea of four bodily humors: blood, phlegm, yellow bile, and black bile. Although the concept has now been discarded by medical science, the humoral theory held up through the Renaissance and apparently added a musical analog, the design of soprano, alto, tenor, and bass.[32] Zarlino, one of the most important music theoreticians of the Renaissance, devoted a segment of the third book of his *Institutioni* to the relationship of the harmonic components with the theory of the four cosmic elements.[33]

Zarlino proposed that bass corresponded to earth, tenor to water, alto to air, and soprano to fire. He described musical harmony as a correct relationship among the four musical elements already mentioned. He then carried the analog a step further to the medical theory of four humors. Finally he proposed that the physician must have a correct knowledge of music in order to prescribe medicine accurately, to judge proportions between cold and warm, to measure the human pulse – another theory that was picked up two centuries later by the French physician Marquet – and to acquire the sense of rhythm necessary to judge the regularity of the heartbeat.[34]

Rosalie Rebollo Pratt

Zarlino's judgments about the harmony of the mind and body and the relationship between the two are similar to those of the anatomist Vesalius. And they were only two of the many Renaissance writers who noted the effects of music on disease and mood. It was clear to these men that there was an interrelationship between mind and body, and some of them even noted that music has a direct effect on the spirit and body via the passions. Zarlino's view was directly traceable to the position of the Greeks. He made one other point that indicated a direct correlation between the medical and musical theories of the period. Zarlino wrote about the motion of the heart in connection with the rhythmic pulse of music. With reference to the theories of the physicians Galen and Avicenna, Zarlino then compared the heart's systolic and diastolic motion to the thesis and arsis of music.[35]

Philosophers, physicians, and writers of the seventeenth century carried on the idea that music and medicine are related. Pellegrini, for example restated the time-honored belief that music drives away madness, sorrow, and quiets the passions of the mind. Descartes summed up the purpose of music by stating that the object of musical art is sound, and the purpose is to delight and to move the various affections in man. In 1634, Mersenne said that health is so musical a matter that disease is simply a matter of dissonance to be corrected or at least eased by music.[36]

Robert Burton's *Anatomy of Melancholy* is a three-volume work in which this extraordinary man discussed the causes and cures for melancholy. One of the sections of the work, entitled "Music Is a Remedy," reveals the writer's cures for depression: "a cup of strong drink, mirth, music, and merry company."[37] Burton was eloquent in describing the powers of music. He claimed that music affected the ears, the arteries, and strengthened the mind. In the same section of the work, he went on to say that music "ravisheth the soul and it hath power to expel many other diseases. It is the sovereign remedy against despair and melancholy and will drive away the devil himself."[37]

From the seventeenth century on, discussions about the effects of music continued to emphasize benefits that had been claimed by the Greeks. However, the most intriguing example of music and medicine was undoubtedly the relationship of music to the disease of tarantism. Works about this mysterious disease appeared from the sixteenth to the nineteenth centuries. The musicologist Armen Carapetyan has named fourteen different publications on the subject.[38] The dancing mania, as it was known, occurred in northern Europe where it was known as St. Vitus's Dance, or St. John's Dance, and then appeared in Apulia, Italy, a southern region that had originally been a part of Magna Grecia and had maintained a strong Greek tradition. Fragments of strong, rhythmic dances known as tarantellas were played for the dancers. The legend was that the music alleviated the distressing symptoms of the disease, supposedly caused by the bite of a spider. The twentieth century physician-historian Sigerist has posed an interesting theory about tarantism. He hypothesized that orgiastic rites and violent dances were a part of the original culture in Apulia. When the Christian religion came to the region, certain accommodations had to be made with the old pagan ways. Sigerist believed that the people simply continued the rites of the cult of Dionysius behind the backs of their Christian teachers. By the time of the Middle Ages, the old dances had lost much of the original meaning and the movements themselves became symptoms of the disease of tarantism. The clear sexuality of the dance was simply excused as part of the illness. Sigerist described the Apulian population as basically inbred. He also believed that much of the behavior of victims of tarantism could be classified as neurotic.[39]

Physicians of the eighteenth century were intent upon using music for curative purposes and tended to base their observations and results on a more scientific basis than had their predecessors. Desbout, Craanen, Nicolai, and Browne (physicians of the time) looked specifically at the benefits obtained with each patient. In 1748, Joseph Louis Roger wrote a treatise explaining how musical vibrations helped the body rid itself of unwanted humors and obstructions.[40] Physicians were now aware of specific physiological effects of music on heart rate, circulation, as well as the influence of music on the emotions. Roger's treatise went into great depth to explain how sound affected the liquid and solid properties of the body. He claimed that excessively ornamented music enervated the basic force of the sound.[40]

Another eighteenth century physician, Robert James, wrote a three-volume history of medicine in which he had something to say about the use of incantation in healing. James claimed that the use of incantation went back to the fourteenth century B.C. Greek prophet and physician Melampus, who allegedly learned from the Egyptians to use this method in the cure of diseases.[41] James also presented an account of how the technique actually persuaded the patient that the practitioner was a cut above the ordinary:

> Incantations and charms were coeval with Physic and seem to have been originally introduced artfully in order to impose a belief upon those not in the secret that the person who exercised them was particularly favored by some superior being. This was attended with a very good effect upon the Practitioner, as it excited a veneration for him in the minds of the vulgar; and in consequence of this, the patient was more easily persuaded upon to submit implicitly to whatever was directed. Meantime, the cure was performed as a part of, or only in aid of the charm or incantation, as the patient was made to believe. . . I must confess that the solemnity of the ceremony might possibly have some effect on the person upon whom it was performed, as it might exalt the faith of the patient in his physician, a circumstance of no small moment and, besides, might give in some degree a turn to the distemper as the body in manifestly influenced by the affections of the mind.[41]

The nineteenth century was especially important in the history of music and medicine because there were so many physicians who were convinced of the role music could play in overcoming mental and emotional illness. The French physician Hector Chomet wrote a book in 1875 about the effect of music on health and life.[42] Chomet was convinced of the importance of music when, as a medical student, he witnessed the illness of a relative who also happened to be a medical doctor and a lover of music. The relative had suffered a stroke that had apparently rendered him unconscious for two days. When he regained consciousness, half of his body was paralyzed and his speech was affected. When the condition did not improve, the man asked to hear some music. His response to the music was immediate. He smiled and remained content as long as the music was playing. Gradually the musical style was changed from grave and serious to compositions of an entirely different nature. A piano was brought into the sickroom. Chomet wrote: "The improvement was more marked every day, and the convalescence continued without interruption. The cure was rapid and complete."[43]

Like his predecessor Dr. Roger, Chomet also held a theory concerning the actual effect of musical sounds upon the system. He said that "the action of sound and the influence of the sonorous musical fluid seem chiefly useful in nervous diseases, especially among women."[44] Chomet's most interesting and rather passionate book is filled with cases of music-related cures of catalepsy, fever, and emotional disorders. He has given us some fascinating accounts of people such as Georges Sand, who wrote to Meyerbeer, thanking him for the music from the opera *Robert le Diable*. Sand credited the music for her cure of a deep depression. She evidently felt that the opera was real therapy for her and told Meyerbeer: ". . . and why should I believe now that music is an art purely for pleasure or mere speculative enjoyment when I remember the surprising influence it had upon me, and that its eloquence was more convincing than all the philosophy taught in books."[45]

Rosalie Rebollo Pratt

In 1849, Warthin, a medical doctor, presented his results on experiments with the physiological and mental effects of music on hypnotized patients. He noted specifically that both pulse and respiration rates of hypnotized subjects were significantly altered when excerpts of Wagnerian operas were played for them.[46] This same experiment produced little if any change in these functions when the subjects listened, under normal circumstances, to the identical music. Warthin advised great caution in further experiments since one of his subjects had experienced transient hyperesthesias during a performance of the Overture to the opera *Tannhäuser*. Next, Dr. Warthin gave an account of another experiment with a physician who, upon being hypnotized, listened to the "Ride of the Valkyries."

> . . . the subject's pulse became at once more rapid, fuller, and of increased tension. As the music continued, the pulse rate rose from 60, his normal rate, to 120 per minute, becoming very quick, full, and of low tension; at the same time, the rate of respiration was increased from 18 to 30 per minute. The subject's face showed great mental excitement; his whole body was thrown into motion; the legs were drawn up and the arms tossed in the air; at the same time, the whole body was bathed in profuse sweat.[47]

Upon being awakened, the subject declared that he had perceived the music as feeling rather than sound.

In 1899, Corning, another medical doctor, wrote of his experiments conducted before and during sleep with the use of musical vibrations. Lying on a couch, the subject was stimulated with music introduced into a soft leather hood placed over his head. In addition, colored slides were presented on a screen directly in front of him. Corning claimed that this form of treatment mitigated symptoms associated with melancholy, neurasthenia, and other neuroses.[48]

Another report in 1899 described the frequent use of music as group therapy. Davison, a British physician, reported the benefits of piano music in a hospital ward. Pain was reported to be either markedly reduced or entirely eliminated and fevers were reduced in seven out of ten cases. Davison also said that Chopin waltzes cured the insomnia of a child, while flute music was effective as a remedy for yet another insomniac child. He also claimed that harp music had finally reduced a fever that had persisted for eighteen days. In the same report, Davison also mentioned experiments conducted by Dogiel, who had discovered that music influenced blood circulation and pressure as well as cardiac contraction and respiration. Davison believed that the human organism vibrates synchronously with music and that music influences the body without the intermediary of the nervous center. He stated further that it was important to match the patient's mood and gradually bring him to a healthier condition – a point of view supported by another medical doctor, Altshuler, nearly half a century later. Davison said that painful vibrations from disease could be replaced by the pleasant vibrations of music and that this procedure was important in restoring a patient to physical and mental health. He expressed faith in the power of music to achieve physiological gains and a prophetic statement about music therapy and its partnership with medicine. "Pharmacological therapeutics will not lose any of their efficacy in the treatment of disease when, side by side, mental therapeutics in the form of music . . . pursue the same end."[49]

Theodor Billroth was a leading surgeon, scientist, and musical amateur of the nineteenth century. His pioneer work in surgery of the larynx and digestive tract are well known to medical doctors. What is perhaps less well known is Billroth's close friendship with the composer Brahms. Billroth's letters, published in 1895, offer warm and personal insights into Viennese medical and musical life. We are indebted to the physician-historian Feilding J. Garrison for his research in 1948 into Billroth's life and writings.[50]

The March 1929 issue of the British medical journal *The Lancet* published an article by Swale Vincent, a professor of physiology at the University of London. The account was entitled: "The Effects of Music Upon the Human Blood Pressure."[51] Vincent experimented with three groups of patients: musical, moderately musical, and nonmusical. His findings were that the greatest effects of music on blood pressure were apparent in the first two groups. Melody produced the most marked effects in the musical group while volume effects were most apparent in the moderately musical subjects. Vincent commented:

> There are corresponding difficulties with the type of music selected for the experiment. It is not to be expected, for example, that a musically sophisticated person will be roused to any very great emotion by the rendering of a Strauss waltz, even if he hears it directly from Vienna! On the other hand, it is not much use to try Holst's *Planets* on a gentleman who can go into raptures over "The More We Get Together."[52]

Music therapy as it is known today began around the time of World War II. In 1948, Ainlay described the overcrowded conditions of military hospitals and the need for programs to occupy the time of convalescing soldiers. Ainlay, a physician, was largely responsible for musical materials developed and published by the U.S. Army and War Department.[53]

From the military hospitals, music therapy found another home in the developing mental hospitals. It soon became apparent that music therapy would have to become more organized. In 1950, the National Association for Music Therapy was established in the United States. The Society for Music Therapy and Remedial Music was founded in Great Britain in 1958. Organized music therapy began in South America in 1966. Since that time, music therapy organizations have begun in countries throughout the world.

In 1948, Altshuler urged music therapists to spend more time researching music itself and the relationship between man and music. He also advocated a stronger relationship between psychiatry and music therapy. Altshuler believed that this bond would help raise the level of music therapy to that of a certified science.[54] Five years later, in 1953, Cholden, a resident in psychiatry at the Menninger Foundation, cautioned therapists: "First you must educate yourselves by study and research into the things that music therapists can do; then you must educate the public, the hospital administrators, the patients, and, most important, the physicians, who may be the least educable of all."[54]

Altshuler proposed the theory that the thalamus is the seat of esthetic reactions. He claimed that music appeals directly to this center, bypassing the cerebral interpretive relays. Severely disturbed patients can, therefore, be contacted through music. Altshuler presented two principles: his "iso" principle, which states that the therapists must begin with music that matches the mood and condition of the patients; and his "level attacks" theory, which begins with the musical elements of rhythm and progresses sequentially to melody, harmony, mood, and, finally, pictorial-associative music.[55]

In 1961, Blanke claimed that music becomes therapeutic when it bypasses the intellectual function and goes directly to the unconscious level. He described the process whereby the healing power of music reaches the psyche of a sick person and how this connection restores the patient to health and harmonious well-being. The philosophy of this twentieth century physician is remarkably Neo-Hellenic.[56]

In 1979, Pierre Rabischong, a French psychiatrist, Meg Peterson, an American music educator, and the writer conceived the plan for bringing medical doctors, music educators, music therapists, special educators, psychologists, and any other interested professionals together for an interdisciplinary symposium on music for the handicapped. The first symposium took place in August 1980 at the University of Montpellier, France. Jointly sponsored by the Montpellier Faculty of Medicine and Music Education for the Handicapped, the conference brought together more than two hundred teachers, therapists, physicians, and psychologists from all over the world. The interdisciplinary discussions were quite lively and reminiscent of the Renaissance university forums. Indeed, it was most appropriate that this first symposium took place at the University of Montpellier, one of the oldest medical schools in Europe, and alma mater to the Renaissance physician-historian Felix Platter. The University of Montpellier medical school also has a historical link to the Arab medical tradition. Until the middle of the seventeenth century, the school used Avicenna's *Canon* as a primary medical text.

Musical Education for the Handicapped (MEH) was founded as a nonprofit, international, and interdisciplinary organization in 1979. After the Montpellier symposium, MEH presented three more conferences: the 1981 symposium at Brigham Young University, Utah; the 1983 conference in Ebeltoft, Denmark, under the patronage of Her Majesty, Queen Ingrid of Denmark; and the fourth symposium in 1985 at Goldwater Memorial Hospital in New York City, under the Honorary Chairmanship of Itzhak Perlman.

Medical doctors of this century have and are taking a serious interest in research about the importance of music in healing and ameliorating the quality of life for handicapped people. Some physicians who are leaders in this field include Mathew Lee, Director of Rehabilitation Medicine, Goldwater Memorial Hospital, and President of the Board of Directors of MEH; Frank Wilson, Associate Clinical Professor of Neurology, University of California School of Medicine at San Francisco; Ralph Spintge, International Society for Music in Medicine, Lüdenscheid, West Germany; Hunter John Hall Fry, plastic surgeon and internationally renowned specialist in overuse injury in performing musicians; Richard Lederman, The Cleveland Clinic Foundation; and Richard Lippin, founder, the International Association for the Arts in Medicine.

Dr. Lee was Chair of the symposium held at Goldwater Hospital in August 1985. As President of the Board of Directors of MEH, Dr. Lee has guided the organization toward a closer alliance with the medical world. His brilliant direction of the 1985 symposium brought music therapists, music educators, and all delegates into a hospital facility that is one of the most prominent of its kind in the entire world.

Dr. Wilson has toured the country, presenting his unique perspective on the effects and benefits of music in terms of neurological and cognitive development. His 1984 Biology of Music Making Conference in Colorado is considered to be a milestone in medical and musical research. Music educators have invited Dr. Wilson to address national and international conferences. His book, *Tone Deaf and All Thumbs*, is an important contribution to this area of research.[57]

Dr. Spintge is a young German anesthesiologist who has clinical proof that music does in fact offer an alternative to the usual methods of anesthetizing patients. Dr. Spintge is one of the directors of the International Society for Music in Medicine, and editor of two books of proceedings of symposia presented by the International Society for Music in Medicine, Lüdenscheid, West Germany.[58]

Dr. Fry is currently an attending plastic surgeon at the Epworth Hospital in Melbourne, Australia and is the Scientific Convenor for the Performing Arts Medicine Society of Victoria. In his research on overuse injury in musicians, he has already surveyed members of six symphony orchestras and nine music schools. Dr. Fry is continuing his research in this area and has already contributed an article to the *MEH Bulletin*.[59]

Dr. Lederman is a neurologist with the Cleveland Clinic Foundation, Ohio. The Foundation was formed for the purpose of enhancing the diagnosis, treatment, and understanding of a variety of occupationally-related disorders among musicians. The majority of specialists in the group are either musicians themselves of have a major interest in the arts. Observation of the musician-patient in performance with the instrument is a very helpful part of the diagnosis and assessment procedure. Dr. Lederman is renowned for his insight and expertise in this increasingly important area of medicine.

Dr. John Diamond is a psychiatrist who has evidence that a certain kind of music rhythm pattern can actually cause muscle damage to listeners. He cites a particular rhythm pattern: short-short-long-pause, or, using the more technical terminology, stopped anapestic rhythm. Dr. Diamond's research involves the testing of muscle weakness and strength in situations involving subjects listening to this rhythm pattern. His research indicates that these listeners can experience muscle weakness, and that the stopped anapestic pattern can actually confuse the body and weaken the muscles. His book, *Your Body Doesn't Lie*, discusses this problem and other reasons for muscle weakness and general illness.[60]

There are signs that physicians and musicians are seeking out each other. The writer, a music educator, was recently invited to address a symposium conducted by the International Society for Music in Medicine. Dr. Wilson, a medical doctor, has recently addressed conservatory audiences and national music education meetings. Throughout the world, there is an awakening, a renascence of dialogue between the arts of medicine and music. The International Association of Music for the Handicapped, for example, publishes the *JIAMH*, *(Journal of the International Association of Music for the Handicapped)* a scholarly journal to which medical doctors as well as psychologists, therapists, and educators contribute research articles. It appears that Apollo and Aesculapius are once again together. The conversation they began so long ago has been renewed, this time with new vigor, more information, and the cameraderie of old friends.

REFERENCES

1   Bacon, F.: *Advancement of Learning.* 2.10.2.
2   Aeschylus, Supp. 263; Aristoph. *Pl.* 11; Aristoph. *Av.* 584.
3   Pind. *Pyth.* 3. 40 et seq.
4   Eum. 62
5   Iamblicus. *De Vit. Pyth.* 25; Aristot. *Pol.* 1341b.38.
6   Hom. *Od.* 19. 457
7   Treves, N.E.: Study effects of music on cancer patients. *Hosp Soc Serv,* 1927, **16**, p. 123.
8   Plato. *Tim.* 47.
9   Aristotle. *Pol.* 8. 1340a. 5
10 Juv. 10. 356.
11 Lucr. 5. 1384-91.
12 Athen. *Deip.* 14. 624.
13 Marquet, F.N.: *Nouvelle méthode facile et curieuse pour connoitre le pouls.* Amsterdam, Didot, 1769.
14 Arist. Quint.: *De Musica* 2. 15. 304.
15 Quint. *Inst. Or.* 1. 10. 31.
16 Celsus. *De Med.* 3. 18. 10.
17 Livy. 7. 2. 3.
18 Plut. *De Cohib. Ira.* 458.
19 Celsus *De Med. Proem.* 8.
20 Galen *Adhort. Ad. Art. Addisc.* 1.

21 Idem, *On the Nat. Fac.* 1-3. Translated by A. Brock.
22 Boethius *De Inst. Mus.* 1. 1. 13-15.
23 Campbell D.: *Arabian Medicine and Its Influence on the Middle Ages.* London, U.K.: Kegan Paul, Trench, Trubner, & Co., 1926.
24 Carpenter, N.C.: *Music in the Medieval and Renaissance Universities.* Norman, OK.: University of Oklahoma Press, 1958.
25 Browne, E.G.: *Arabian Medicine.* Cambridge, U.K.: Cambridge University Press, 1921p. 44.
26 Shiloah, A.: Ibn Hindu, le médecin et la musique. *Israel Oriental Studies*, 1972, **2**, pp. 447-462.
27 Carapetyan, A.: Music and medicine in the Renaissance and in the 17th and 18th centuries. In: Schullian D., Schoen, M. (eds): *Music and Medicine.* New York: Henry Schuman, 1948, pp. 117-157.
28 Campbell, D. *Arabian Medicine and Its Influence on the Middle Ages.* London, U.K.: Kegan Paul, Trench, Trubner, & Co., 1926, pp. 58-59.
29 Martianus Capella *De nupt. Phil. et Mer.*
30 Carpenter, N.C.: *Music in the Medieval and Renaissance Universities.* Norman, OK.: University of Oklahoma Press, 1958, p. 117.
31 Carapetyan, A.: Music and medicine in the Renaissance and in the 17th and 18th centuries. In: *Music and Medicine* Schullian D., Schoen, M. (eds). New York, Henry Schuman, 1948, p. 140.
32 Zarlino *Inst. harm.* 3. 58.
33 Ibid., 58-59.
34 Marquet
35 Zarlino 2. 8.
36 Carapetyan, A.: Music and medicine in the Renaissance and in the 17th and 18th centuries. In: *Music and Medicine* Schullian D., Schoen, M. (eds). New York, Henry Schuman, 1948, pp. 138-140.
37 Burton. R.: *The Anatomy of Melancholy.* 2. 2. 6. 3.
38 Carapetyan, A.: Music and medicine in the Renaissance and in the 17th and 18th centuries. In: *Music and Medicine* Schullian D., Schoen, M. (eds). New York, Henry Schuman, 1948, p. 153.
39 Sigerist, H.E.: The story of tarantism. In: Schullian D., Schoen, M. (eds): *Music and Medicine.* New York, Henry Schuman, 1948, pp. 96-116.
40 Carapetyan, A.: Music and medicine in the Renaissance and in the 17th and 18th centuries. In: Schullian D., Schoen, M. (eds): *Music and Medicine.* New York, Henry Schuman, 1948, pp. 146-151.
41 James, R.: *Medical Dictionary*: Volume 1. London, U.K.: T. Osborne, 1743; iv.
42 Chomet, H.: *The Influence of Music on Health and Life.* Flint L.A. (transl.). New York: Putnam, 1875.
43 Ibid., pp. 215-217.
44 Ibid., p. 217.
45 Ibid., pp. 226-227.
46 Warthin A.S.: Some physiological effects of music on hypnotized subjects. *The Medical News,* 1894, **65**, pp., 89-94.
47 Ibid., p. 90.
48 Corning, T.L.: The uses of musical vibrations before and during sleep. *Medical Record,* 1899, **55**, pp. 789-86.
49 Davison, J.T.H.: Music in medicine. *The Lancet.* October 1899, **28**, p. 1162.

50 Carrison, F.H.: Medical men who have loved music. In: Schullian D., Schoen, M. (eds): *Music and Medicine*. New York: Henry Schuman, 1948, pp. 190-217.
51 Vincent, S.: The effects of music upon the human blood pressure. *The Lancet*, March 1929, **9**, pp. 534-537.
52 Ibid., pp. 535.
53 Ainlay G.W.: The place of music in military hospitals. In: Schullian D., Schoen, M. (eds): *Music and Medicine* . New York, Henry Schuman, 1948, pp. 322-351.
54 Gleanings from the Topeka meeting. *NAMT Bull*, 1953, **2**, p. 4.
55 Altshuler, I.M.: A psychiatrist's experience with music as a therapeutic agent. In: Schullian D., Schoen, M. (eds.): *Music and Medicine*. New York, Henry Schuman, 1948, pp.266-281.
56 Blanke, K.F.: Music therapy experiences in the practice of internal medicine. *NAMT Bull*, 1961, **19**, pp. 17-23.
57 Wilson, F.R.: *Tone Deaf and All Thumbs*. New York: Viking-Penguin, 1986.
58 Droh, R., Spintge, R. (eds.): *Angst, Schmerz, Musik in der Anästhesie*. Basel: Roche, 1983.
    Spintge, R., Droh, R. (eds.): *Musik in der Medizin*. Basel: Roche, 1985.
59 Fry, H.J.H. The physical injury overuse due to music making. *MEH Bull*, 1985, **1**, pp. 22-49.
60 Diamond, J.: *Your Body Doesn't Lie*. New York: Warner, 1979.

EPIDEMIOLOGY OF DISABILITY AND MUSIC

Masayoshi Itoh
Mathew H.M. Lee

The history of mankind is a tapestry in which the silken threads of peace and artistic and scientific achievement are intertwined with the harsh threads of innumerable wars and perpetual human suffering. The agonizing struggle of man against famine, starvation, flood, earthquake, fire and the loss of loved ones through disease and trauma has been documented in the written and oral history of every culture. As disease, trauma and subsequent death became more frequent and universal, a continuous search was undertaken for preventive and/or curative interventions. In many instances, when these measures failed, religion offered various mystical or philosophical interpretations to sustain the suffering believers.

Today, literally thousands of disease conditions, including trauma, are recognized and are neatly organized and classified according to causation, symptoms, body organs involved, etc. Preventive and/or therapeutic methods are known for most of these conditions. Even if there is no known curative method, some means of controlling progression and/or suffering are known for most diseases. However, this vast accumulation of knowledge in medical science did not come easily. Many theories were advanced; trial and error continued. Pathologists' findings were correlated with these clinical findings. After centuries of effort, adherence to scientific methodology, and the advancement of scientific technology, medicine has developed the current understanding of disease conditions.

The concept of "Epidemiology," which has developed into a branch of medical science, was born of this effort. The literal translation of "Epidemiology" is a study among people. As the name suggests, epidemiology, from its inception, was the branch of medical science concerned with the study of epidemics. Understandably, an epidemic of any disease creates great concern in any population. The fear of the populace toward the plague many centuries ago is not much different from that toward acquired immune deficiency syndrome (AIDS) today. During the period when epidemics of plague were being recorded in history, the cause, mode of transmission and method of treatment were unknown. In the past, and most certainly in the future, epidemiology has been and will be a science that explores diseases of unknown entity.

However, Welch[1] later defined epidemiology as a study of the natural history of disease, which traces and delineates when, how, what, why and which people are subjected to a given disease. Lilienfeld[2] further broadened the definition to include the study of the distribution of a disease or condition in a population and the factors which influence this distribution. Utilizing investigative techniques developed over centuries of experience with contagious diseases and epidemics, it is now possible to analyze any given disease condition within a relatively short period. Legionnaire's disease in the seventies and AIDS of the eighties are examples of the rapid unmasking of the nature of previously unknown diseases.

Although epidemiology is one of the specialties of medical science, its approach is quite different from that of clinical specialties. While the subject of clinical medicine is an individual person who suffers from an ailment or disease condition, epidemiology deals with numerous individuals. Because of this unique approach in epidemiology, it is necessary to establish fundamental concepts of health and causation of illness and to apply such concepts to the actual situation.

13

HEALTH

When a child is born, death is inevitable in the distant future. Birth and death are the two extreme ends of human life. Leigh Hunt, a nineteenth century writer, wrote "The groundwork of all happiness is health." George Gissing, Victorian novelist and crusader against the brutalizing effects of poverty, stated, "For the man sound in body and serene of mind, there is no such thing as bad weather; every sky has its beauty, and storms which whip the blood do but make it pulse more vigorously." Although people encounter various health problems during the course of life, (Figure 1a), ideally they should have perfect health from the time of birth up to the moment of death (Figure 1b).

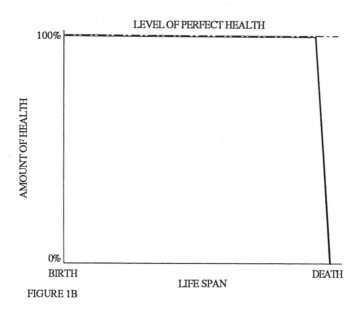

FIGURE 1B

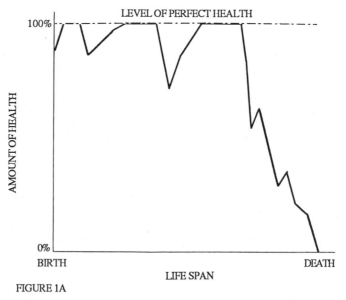

FIGURE 1A

Masayoshi Itoh, Mathew H.M. Lee

In order to advance the above thoughts on human life, it is necessary to define health. The most commonly quoted and most comprehensive definition of health was provided by the World Health Organization of the United Nations: "Health is defined as a state of complete physical, mental and social well-being and not merely the absence of disease or infirmity."[3] This definition is quite broad and dynamic. If total health must fulfill the above definition, it is no longer the sole domain of medical science since medicine cannot improve, maintain or change the social well-being of a population. These are areas for which the social and political sciences must take responsibility. For example, the famine on the African continent in the 1980s has had a great impact on the health of the population, particularly young children. Although many nations contributed food, in order to solve the problems related to the famine in this region, sociopolitical and economic reform are necessary. Improvement or reformation of socioeconomic well-being would greatly influence physical and mental well-being.

The most striking aspect of the W.H.O. definition of health is the recognition that "mere absence of disease or infirmity" does not constitute health. It follows that there is a gradation in what we refer to as "health." It is important that this area be explored further so that a clearer understanding of health can be obtained. Health is the general condition of the body. Thus, one may use a phrase such as, "A person is in poor health," or "A person is in good health"; "poor" and "good" indicating quality. However, it should be noted that health may be viewed in quantity as well. Assume the sum of an individual's health is 100. There can be 100% presence of health or good health and 0% of ill health or absence of health. Another person can have 75% good health, or presence of health, and 25% ill health or absence of health.

Rogers[4] developed the Health Status Scale and the idea of presence and absence of health. His scale is divided into five categories: Optimum Health, Suboptimum Health, Overt Illness or Disability, Approaching Death, and Death (Figure 2). Optimum Health is perfect health as defined by the W.H.O. While everybody wishes to maintain Optimum Health all of the time, it is not humanly possible.

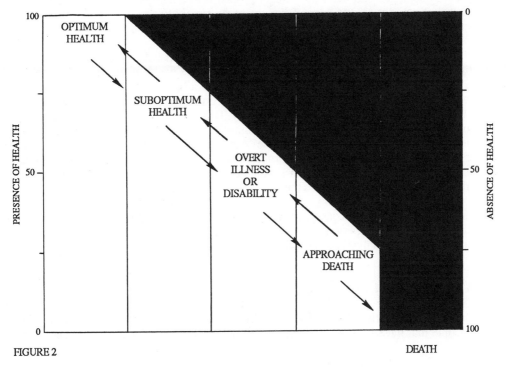

FIGURE 2

Epidemiology of Disability and Music   15

Optimum Health and Overt Illness or Disability are easy to understand and visualize. Suboptimum Health is a state characterized by the incubation period of an infectious disease, latent diabetes mellitus or even extreme fatigue. Those who are in a state of Suboptimum Health do not necessarily progress to Overt Illness since the various defense mechanisms of the body may fight the indisposition and restore Optimum Health.

Those who are in a state of Overt Illness or Disability can be recognized by various clinical symptoms. However, the onset of Overt Illness may be different. Some diseases, such as acute appendicitis, manifest a very abrupt onset while other diseases, particularly chronic progressive neurological disease or degenerative disease, are quite insidious. The course of health for an individual in this state is one of the following: 1) recovery to Suboptimum Health and eventually to Optimum Health; 2) remaining in this state (as in nonprogressive chronic disease); or 3) progressing to Approaching Death or even to Death.

Even though an individual is in the Approaching Death state, death is not inevitable. Various organ transplantations may successfully return the individual's health to at least Suboptimum level. The most important concept of Rogers' Health Status Scale is the demonstration of the dynamic aspect of an individual's health. Throughout life no one remains in a particular health status since it constantly changes until death. This concept of health can readily be applied to any disease condition and its eventual outcome. For example, an *apparently* perfectly healthy 45-year-old man experienced crushing chest pain and collapsed in his office. The man was brought to a hospital and a diagnosis of acute myocardial infarction or heart attack was made. Let us observe this episode up to this point. The key word is "apparently." He did not have any symptom whatsoever prior to this episode and he might have thought he was in "Optimum Health." A heart attack is usually caused by a blood clot closing off one small branch of blood vessels feeding the heart muscles. Although the onset of a heart attack is sudden, the growth of a blood clot is a very slow process, possibly taking days, weeks or even months. During the growth of the blood clot this man was indeed in "Suboptimum Health". At one point, however, this blood clot dislodged and the blood stream pushed it to a narrower part of the blood vessel through which it was not able to pass. Thus, the blood supply to a part of the heart muscle was obstructed by this clot and severe chest pain occurred. His status became "Overt Illness."

What may transpire next is death or necrosis of the heart muscle due to oxygen and nutrient deprivation in this part of the heart. The outcome of this man's health status depends largely upon the size of the blood clot. A large blood clot indicates that a large blood vessel is obstructed and, therefore, a large part of the heart muscle becomes necrotic. In this case, he rapidly proceeds through the status of Approaching Death, and finally, Death. On the other hand, if a small blood clot is involved, only a small part of the heart muscle becomes necrotic. In this case, proper treatment prevents the man from passing into the "Approaching Death" status. The affected part of the heart muscle would eventually heal by forming a scar. Appropriate treatment and rehabilitation can restore his health even to "Optimum Health" as there are certain types of treatment which prevent the formation of blood clots and thus prevent a recurrence of the heart attack.

Medicine, in general, is concerned with maintaining good health and, if one becomes ill, curing him/her in as short a period of time as possible. This concept of an individual's health is vitally important to any analysis of the various activities of medicine.

CAUSATION OF ILLNESS

Illness has been with us long before recorded human history began. Skeletal remains of prehistoric people that have been scientifically examined have revealed arthritis, cancer and other

Masayoshi Itoh, Mathew H.M. Lee

debilitating diseases and illnesses. Later, knowledgeable people began formulating theories on the causation of illness. These individuals were in the learned professions, and as philosopher, astronomist, mathematician, religious leader, or healer, competed for prestige. Depending upon their background, their interpretation of the causation of illness varied from very primitive to somewhat sophisticated. During the latter part of the twentieth century, due to developments in scientific technology, the natural history of a previously unknown disease can be uncovered in a relatively short time. Legionnaire's disease and acquired immune deficiency syndrome (AIDS), etc. are recent examples.

In the absence of advanced technology and knowledge of disease processes, many theories on the causation of illness appear to be far-fetched. However, careful examination of these theories reveals that although the rationality of each theory may not agree with present day understanding, there is always some degree of correlation between the old beliefs and the proven facts. Thus, it is interesting to analyze some of the old theories.

BALANCE

In ancient Chinese medicine and, to a certain extent, in modern Chinese medicine, the belief exists that the imbalance of two polar elements, yin and yang, is the cause of illness. In all aspects, these two elements are completely opposite, i.e., positive vs. negative, masculine vs. feminine, active vs. receptive, and so on. However, in theory, nothing is pure yin or pure yang. Within yin, there is a certain element of yang and, in yang, vice versa. The "order of nature" is in complete harmony when the balance of yin and yang is maintained.[5] This is the theory behind acupuncture, which aims to restore balance and, thus, cure an ailment or control pain.

American Indians also believe in the balance theory of good health and that herbal medicine from certain mushrooms maintains or restores balance, thus maintaining health or healing illness.[6]

The idea of yin and yang was advanced by Taoist philosophers. There is a profound philosophical basis for their theory that is sometimes difficult for occidentals to comprehend. Both the Chinese and American Indian theories stress "balance." All scientifically minded people today acknowledge the importance of balance. The order of our whole universe depends on the balance of universal gravitation. The jet plane that flies and the large ship that navigates the ocean both depend on balance. Unchecked logging or farming disturbs environmental balance and rich green land may turn into a desert.

Likewise, imbalance in certain elements of the human body may cause certain illnesses and even death. The most commonly known balance needed for human health is a balanced diet. Consumption of an unbalanced diet for a prolonged period, particularly in early childhood, may cause mental retardation and various other diseases due to a lack of specific nutrients in the food.

Medical practitioners are always concerned about electrolyte, (i.e., sodium, potassium and chloride) balance in a patient's blood. As its name indicates, electrolyte is a vital element for the conduction of electricity. Many human body functions are regulated by electric charge, i.e., metabolism of cells, heart beat, brain function, etc. It is well known that retention of too much sodium in the body can lead to fluid accumulation and may result in weakening of the heart; and an excess amount of potassium in the blood may cause cardiac arrest. Thus, the electrolyte balance must be maintained in order to insure proper body function.

Vital functions of the body such as metabolism, growth, body temperature, heart beat, brain function, etc. are regulated largely by various hormones that are stored in specific cells and secreted as needed. One group of hormones may complement each other and another group of hormones may cancel each other. A lack or absence of a particular hormone or an abundance of another hormone in the blood stream causes various metabolic diseases. In order to maintain proper health, hormones in the blood stream must be balanced.

These are just a few examples of the balance that is required for maintenance of health. The unproven theories of the yin and yang balance in Chinese medicine, "balance" as the American Indians refer to it, and various ideas of balance in modern medicine are all synonymous. Nevertheless, it is a proven scientific fact that maintaining the proper balance of certain elements in the body is a prerequisite for health.

GOD, SPIRIT AND SIN

In many primitive societies, ancient and contemporary, there is a belief that offending or angering a god causes an illness. The sufferer may not always be the person who offended the god but the god must be appeased if the patient is to be cured. Prescriptions include material offerings, elaborate rituals of prayer, music, singing and dancing. If these ceremonies have not proven effective, a belief that the illness is a punishment often develops. Though there is no scientific basis for this idea, it persists today in cultures throughout the world.

It has long been believed that an evil spirit can possess a person and, consequently, cause illness. Believing that a witch could cast a spell on a person, many innocent victims accused of witchcraft were burned to death. Churchmen engaged in exorcism to drive out these evil spirits and cure the illness. These stories have been told for centuries and are good subjects for thriller novels and motion pictures. In many cases, those who were supposedly under the spell of an evil spirit appeared to have symptoms of convulsive and/or physical disorders, often giving very mystical and bizarre impressions to those who observed them. Therefore, it is quite understandable that some supernatural force would be reported as the cause of these illnesses.

Evil spirits rising with the stench from sewage and stagnant water were thought to be the cause of plague epidemics. Plague is an infectious disease caused by a microorganism called *Yersinia Pestis* that is transmitted to men from infected rodents via fleas. Airborne droplets or household pets with plague pneumonia are also responsible for spread of the disease. The lack of sanitation and poor environmental hygiene, characterized by the presence of foul odorous sewage and stagnant water, drew and sustained numerous rodents. Since microorganisms or airborne droplets are invisible and unknown, they were interpreted as an "evil spirit".

It has long been believed that committing sins results in illness. In Webster's *Seventh Collegiate Dictionary*, "sin" is defined as "transgression of the law of God." All religions prohibit certain types of behavior and encourage others, setting forth examples such as the Ten Commandments. Sins are actually transgressions of contemporary social norms as declared by a prophet of a given religion. Such social norms are usually universal when they relate to ethical and moral issues. Hence, it is rather difficult to conceive that a man becomes ill when he deviates from those norms.

However, even today many still firmly believe venereal disease is a sign of immorality, and sexual promiscuity is frowned upon by some religions. The question of sin aside, an increase in the number of sexual partners itself increases the chance of exposure to sexually transmissible disease organisms.

Masayoshi Itoh, Mathew H.M. Lee

Some religions prohibit consumption of pork, regarding those who ignore this guide as unclean. There was certainly a great danger in contracting trichinosis, which may be fatal or severely disabling, by eating pork. Then what was the best way to prevent followers from becoming victims of trichinosis? Perhaps, the most effective way was to make consumption of pork a sin. Some religions emphasize the value of moderation and it is well known today that excess of almost anything can cause ill-effects contributing to illness.

CURRENT UNDERSTANDING OF CAUSATION OF ILLNESS

Using superstition, evil spirits, sins, etc. as the cause of ailments, gave succor to the populace when no logical explanation existed. The fundamental flaw of these simplistic approaches is that they ignore the fact the the human body is an extremely complicated electrical, chemical, mechanical and biological machine. Illness is the failure of this delicate machine, the causes of which may be numerous, and a single explanation completely insufficient.

The modern epidemiological model of the causation of all illness holds that the simultaneous interaction of three causative factors: host, agent and environment, is responsible.

"Host" in this case is a human being characterized by such factors as sex, age, race, occupation, marital status, education, nutritional status, genetic variations, body constitution, habits, custom and psychological and/or emotional status.

One of the important aspects of the host's characteristics is susceptibility, a word derived from the Latin word *suscipere*, meaning to receive or undertake. The classic definition of susceptibility is "The quality of a person presumably not possessing resistance against a particular pathogenic agent and for that reason is liable to contract a disease if exposed to such an agent."[7] However, the word "susceptibility" is now more broadly used and is synonymous with the term "high risk." For example, all humans are susceptible to variola virus, the causative microorganism of small pox, unless the individual has been vaccinated recently. Vaccination provides the person temporary immunity which is security against a specific illness or poison, sometimes called resistance. Those who have hypertension, arteriosclerosis or rheumatic heart disease are susceptible to stroke or cerebrovascular accidents. There is no effective means to increase immunity to stroke; therefore this group can be considered "high risk."

As the above examples show, susceptibility and immunity are two extreme reactions of the human body. As susceptibility increases, immunity decreases and vice-versa. Susceptibility and immunity are heavily influenced by various host characteristics.

The second causative factor is the agent, which may be classified into biological, chemical, genetic and physical elements. Biological elements include a variety of bacteria, viruses, fungi, parasites, insects, animals, etc., which are self propagating. Chemical elements may encompass all industrial, household and pharmaceutical products or chemical substances in plants which may be inhaled, ingested or have direct contact with the skin surface. Mechanical elements often affect a human body in the form of force such as pull, push, twist, hit, friction, etc., resulting in various injuries or trauma. Genetic elements may be the agent for so-called hereditary or congenital anomaly or genetic disorders. High or low temperature, atmospheric pressure, etc. are considered physical elements of the agent. Although these agents are often erroneously considered the cause of ill-health, the agent alone cannot cause illness.

The third causative factor is environment. Bad air and/or bad water, particularly stagnant water, have long been considered a source of illness, a stench often being identified as an evil spirit. In order to protect themselves from such malodor, the upper classes carried smelling salts. In religious ceremonies over the centuries, incense has been used to purify the air.

Biologically or chemically contaminated water is a well-documented source of illness. Minimata disease was caused by mercury contaminated water in a salt water bay from which fish were caught and ingested. Continuous and prolonged consumption of the fish, particularly by children, caused chronic mercury poisoning among the populace.

An indirect consequence of bad or stagnant water is malaria, which is transmitted by a specific species of mosquito whose breeding takes place in this type of environment. Thus, the current steps toward irradication of malaria do not include killing mosquitoes with pesticides, but rather draining pools of stagnant water so that the breeding ground is eliminated. Aside from water and air, atmospheric conditions (e.g., humidity, temperature, wind, etc.), soil, home, work place and the sociopolitical /economic conditions to which people are exposed constitute environmental factors.

The application of these three causative factors to an actual situation is not as simple as it appears, requiring an in depth analysis of each factor involved in their simultaneous complex interaction. Let us take the seemingly simple case of an automobile accident which resulted in quadriplegia of the driver. The investigation of the accident revealed that it occurred at 11:00 p.m. on a rainy night, the car skidding at the curve of the road and hitting a utility pole. The driver was on his way home. A witness said the car was moving at very high speed in an erratic fashion. At the hospital, physical examination and blood test revealed that the driver was highly intoxicated and police found the seat belt had not been in use. The facts described above are very common findings in accidents involving driving while intoxicated but can one conclude that an excess intake of an alcoholic beverage caused quadriplegia?

Although acute alcoholic intoxication does not produce quadriplegia, alcohol intake is one of the host characteristics. Examine the host factor, i.e., why he consumed alcohol to a point of intoxication, and why he drove an automobile while intoxicated, etc. In order to answer both questions, many social and psychological factors must be investigated and examination of his pattern of behavior is necessary. It is most likely that this was not the first time he operated a motor vehicle while intoxicated. He might not have realized how intoxicated he was or he might have had false confidence in his ability to operate a car under the influence of alcohol. When an individual is intoxicated, judgement is impaired, attention span shortened and reaction time increased; thus susceptibility to an accident increases.

Visibility at night is limited and a wet road is always slippery when driving. While environmental factors such as darkness and rain could not be controlled by the host, the driver certainly failed to create a safer environment by wearing his seat belt. It is important to note that there are both controllable and uncontrollable environmental factors.

One may assume the automobile or the utility pole was the agent, since the agent can be defined as a force or energy and the automobile is a machine which creates energy or force. When a subject at high velocity collides with a stationary object, there is a tremendous momentum - a force of a burst of energy. This force is the agent factor in this instance.

It is now clear that if one of the above factors had not been present, or all factors did not interact simultaneously, this person would not have had the accident and would not be suffering from quadriplegia. The above example illustrates the application of the three causative factors theory to an actual situation and also shows the complex analysis of each factor.

DISABILITY

Disability is a state of deprived physical, moral or intellectual strength. There are many words which are sometimes used interchangeably with "disability" such as handicapped, crippled, invalid, lame, maimed, etc. "Handicap" is a disadvantage that makes certain achievement difficult, usually a physical disability that limits the capacity to do specific work. On the other hand, "crippled" is defined as the loss of a significant amount of use in the limbs, particularly the lower.[8] "Invalid" refers to a state of being sick or diseased. Note that there is a certain subtle nuance and a difference in feeling among these definitions as they appear in the dictionary.

In medicine, disability is a state of deficiency in physical and/or intellectual function which may be transient or permanent in nature. "Physical function" refers not only to neuromuscular and skeletal function but to almost all organ systems including sensory organs. The degree of deficiency in function may differ from a total absence of function to a slight impairment, depending upon the organ system involved. For example, there may be total blindness or deafness but not total absence of cardiac function, which would mean death.

An individual with a disability is not necessarily disabled. For example, a person with myopia can function normally with a pair of eye-glasses or contact lenses. While myopia is a permanent disability, it can be easily corrected to functional vision.

There are a variety of causes and diseases which result in disability (e.g., genetic abnormality, intra-uterine acquisition of biological or chemical substance by a fetus, or a birth related injury or infection). Any acquired disease or trauma is more prevalent among those who are in the second and third decade of life. Diseases closely related to gerontological degenerative processes such as stroke, hypertension or arteriosclerotic heart disease are frequently observed in the population of mid-forty and older. Fracture of the hip is more common among elderly females than among any other groups.

In general, those who are in the same age and cultural group expose themselves to a similar degree of risk to a given disability or disability causing disease or trauma. However, this generalization cannot be sustained when one's host characteristics differ greatly from his/her peer group as in occupation or hobby. Professional athletes and dancers may be subjected to a certain disability which is unique to them. Some conditions are so frequently observed that they have telltale names such as tennis elbow, baseball shoulder or even jogger's nipples.[9][10] Injuries to the knee among football players and ankle disorders among dancers are additional examples of occupation-related disabilities. Common disabilities among professional musicians are described in detail elsewhere in this book. It should be noted that there are certain physically demanding professions and hobbies that, if followed seriously and consistently over a period of time, will result in a disability peculiar to that particular profession or hobby. This selectivity in the development of disability can be understood through careful epidemiological analysis of causation of illness, i.e., host, agent, and environment.

In order to describe the degree or quantity of disability, adjectives such as slight, moderate or severe are often used. In describing the performance of activities of daily living (ADL), one may use descriptions such as "totally independent", "partially independent" and "totally dependent", or "needs total care." When a person is graded as partially independent, it also means partially dependent, requiring further explanation as to what type of ADL the individual can perform independently. When a descriptive term is used to express the degree of disability, there is always an element of subjectivity in the determination.

The most commonly used method for grading muscle strength is either 0 to 5 numerically or words Zero, Trace, Fair, Good and Normal. Each grade is further expressed in terms of + (plus) or - (minus). In simple terms, this system uses two types of resistance: gravity and manual resistance. While there is no controversy with regard to gravity, the amount of manual resistance to be applied in testing may differ from one examiner to the other. Over the years, many clinicians and researchers have developed various methods of grading or measuring disabilities.[11] [12] [13] [14] [15] [16] Some methods are cumbersome and time consuming while others may require certain degrees of experience and, at times there is a certain degree of arbitrariness. It is important to recognize that each such method of measurement has its own purpose and consequently, there is no universally acceptable simple and objective method to express degree of disability. Thus, it may be concluded that the present day knowledge and technology of grading disability is more of an art than science.

Disability cannot be equated with deformity or disfigurement. While deformity and disfigurement are always visible and are sometimes associated with disability, other disabilities cannot be recognized visually unless one has to perform a certain task that requires the lost function. Just seeing a deaf person, one cannot recognize the disability until this person does not respond to audio-stimuli. Similarly, a mute person does not have any overt sign of his disability until he does not initiate speech when it is appropriate for him to speak. On the other hand, a person whose leg was amputated is immediately recognizable, as walking is impossible without an artificial limb or a pair of crutches.

Duration and intensity of disability vary. An elderly woman had a fall in her house, experienced a sharp pain in her right hip, and could not stand up. The x-ray examination revealed a fracture of the neck of the right femur. She is now disabled because she is not able to walk. If all goes well, after surgical reduction and a prescribed period of a rest and rehabilitation regime, this woman is expected to resume all her previous activities within a few months, and will no longer have a disability. In this case, her disability was transient or temporary.

The outcome of the rehabilitation of a person with a hip fracture is not always as successful as the above example. For various reasons, a patient may fail to achieve full ambulatory capacity and must use a wheelchair for locomotion. In this case, the disability, i.e., inability to walk, becomes permanent. Paraplegia and quadriplegia due to spinal cord injury are considered, in most instances, permanent. A person who has had a stroke resulting in hemiplegia may regain full use of the limbs through spontaneous or natural recovery and rehabilitation treatment. However, if there is still a functional deficit after a sufficient amount of time for these processes has elapsed, the residual disabilities must be considered permanent.

Most disability does not progress further, but in certain instances, the intensity and variety of the disability may increase. This is particularly true in progressive diseases such as multiple sclerosis, amyotrophic lateral sclerosis (Lou Gehrig's Disease, or ALS), muscular dystrophy, etc. For example, at the onset of ALS, a patient may experience slight weakness of the leg muscles but as time goes by and the disease progresses, the patient will lose muscle strength in all extremities and major parts of the body. Thus, the patient may eventually use a respirator for breathing due to weakness of the respiratory muscles.

In general, there are two types of disability: Primary disability is the direct consequence of a disease or condition,[17] as in the above examples. A secondary disability is that which did not exist at the onset of the primary disability but subsequently developed.[18]

The secondary disability does not have a direct relation to the disease or condition which caused the primary disability. For example, traumatic paraplegic or quadriplegic patients lose skin

Masayoshi Itoh, Mathew H.M. Lee

sensation and when they lie or sit in one position for an extended period, a decubitus ulcer or bedsore develops where the skin is compressed by the weight of the body. Due to the lack of skin sensation, these patients cannot feel the discomfort that normal individuals experience under the same circumstance. Therefore, a normal individual would change body position to ease the discomfort, thereby restoring blood circulation to the compressed skin area. While paraplegia or quadriplegia is the direct consequence of spinal cord injury, decubitus ulcer is the consequence of paraplegia or quadriplegia.

A common occurrence in the stroke patient is the contracture of the elbow and fingers on the paralyzed side with complete loss of extension. Hemiplegia is the direct result of the stroke. One of the symptoms of hemiplegia is the imbalance of muscle power between a set of antagonistic muscles due to spasticity and weakness. Joint contracture, which is the inability to extend or bend a joint, is the result of hemiplegia rather than stroke and is not present at the onset of the stroke.

One of the most important treatments for a person who has an illness or injury is bedrest. Before surgical techniques for hip fracture reduction were developed, a patient was placed in a plaster of Paris cast from the pelvis to the tip of the toes and remained in this position for a period of months. Such patients often developed secondary disabilities such as pneumonia, and decubitus ulcers on the back of the pelvis and leg. Prolonged bedrest causes disease atrophy of muscles (wasted muscles), osteoporosis (bones becoming brittle due to loss of minerals), contracture of joints, decubitus ulcers, etc., which are secondary disabilities that did not exist at the onset of the primary disability.

The progressive disabilities mentioned previously are not secondary disabilities. For example, during the very early stage of multiple sclerosis, a patient may experience transient incontinence of urine and/or blindness. Later the patient begins to have difficulty in walking and balancing due to muscle weakness. All of these disabilities are primary disabilities. However, in the very late stage of multiple sclerosis, severe flexion contractures of the joints or decubitus ulcers may be observed, which are indeed secondary disabilities.

The onset of a primary disability is usually sudden or abrupt and development of a secondary disability is often insidious. The primary disability can be either totally eliminated or remain as a partial or total permanent disability. Secondary disabilities are preventable and reversible when they are treated in the early stages of development. However, if secondary disabilities are neglected, they become permanent disabilities. A combination of primary and secondary disabilities has a devastating effect on a person's functional status.

The effect of disability on a person's functional status and vocation differs greatly. A well-known great statesman and a world renowned violinist are both known to be paraplegics. However, the same disability might well prevent a pianist, organist or timpanist from playing their instruments. Laborers in the situation would change their occupation. Blindness is a very severe disability for any person. Those who operate motor vehicles, trains or planes would no longer be able to perform their occupation without sight; however, there are many great musicians who are blind. Thus, ADL may be tedious and inconvenient, but people in occupations such as musicians can continue to maintain a high standard of performance with or without vision. The stereotype of a person with a disability being less capable is discriminatory and wrong.

PREVENTION

Medical science may be classified in many ways. From the view point of health care, it can be grouped into two broad categories: clinical medicine and preventive medicine. Aside from these categories, there are basic medical sciences or basic sciences such as anatomy, physiology, biochemistry, microbiology, pharmacology and so forth. While basic science does not directly involve health care, it is the fundamental element in the development of both clinical and preventive medicine.

The objective of clinical medicine is to restore to Optimum Health status an individual who is in the state of Overt Illness or Disability or Approaching Death. This is accomplished by means of establishing a correct diagnosis and providing appropriate definitive treatment. Since there are many diseases which mimic totally different diseases, and incorrect diagnosis leads to incorrect treatment, the results could be catastrophic. For example, it may be difficult for an inexperienced physician to differentiate ectopic pregnancy (tube pregnancy) from urinary tract infection, acute appendicitis or pelvic inflammatory disease. If any of these diseases are incorrectly treated, the consequence will be either death or prolonged disability.

Preventive medicine is a part of public health and its objective is to maintain an individual or a given population in the Optimum Health status without allowing them to slide down to Suboptimum Health or Overt Illness or Disability status. Examples of preventive medicine for an individual are vaccination against small pox, immunization against various infectious diseases such as influenza, typhoid fever, yellow fever, poliomyelitis, pneumonia, or prenatal care and so forth. Fluoridation of drinking water, enriched flour or iodizing table salt are examples of preventive medicine aiming to prevent specific diseases in large populations.

While preventive medicine does not have the curative component of clinical medicine, clinical medicine contains, in many instances, the preventive aspect of public health care. The characteristics of cancer and malignant tumors are fast growth, and rapid spread to other organs which, in many cases, is fatal. Therefore, early diagnosis and proper treatment of cancer prevents its spread and thus prevents Death. Antibiotic treatment for urinary tract infection prevents development of sepsis which can also be fatal. The goal of rehabilitation medicine, one specialty of clinical medicine, is the restoration of a lost function and/or compensation for the primary disability. However, a major part of a rehabilitation team's effort is devoted to the prevention of secondary disabilities.

Let us again consider the example of the elderly woman who sustained a hip fracture after a fall. The goal of rehabilitation, for this woman, is to walk out of the hospital independently. Since she was walking before the fall, there is no reason why she should not be able to do so again. Although surgical reduction of the fracture was successfully performed, she is not yet ready to start walking. In the rehabilitation service, she will be placed immediately on a wheelchair for as long as can be tolerated and will stay in bed only for sleep in order to *prevent* pneumonia and decubitus ulcers or bedsores. Exercises for all joints except the involved hip will be started right away so that joint contracture is *prevented*. Exercises to strengthen the muscles in all extremities but the involved leg *prevent* disuse atrophy or wasting and weakening of muscles. These preventive rehabilitation [19] [20] [21] measures must be started as soon after surgery as is practical. By failing to institute these preventive measures, the outcome would be prolonged hospitalization, and the patient unnecessarily becomes wheelchair-bound or perhaps even dies.

In recognition of various preventive aspects of health care, a concept of the Level of Prevention which encompasses the entire health care program has been developed. Depending on the investigator, [22] [23] there are some differences in the interpretation of health care activities but there is no major controversy in its concept. All agree to three levels of prevention: primary, secondary and tertiary. Table 1 and Figure 3 show the Level of Prevention by Itoh and Lee[19] and its relation to Rogers' Health Status Scale.

TABLE 1 Levels of Prevention[19]

Primary	Secondary	Tertiary
Health Promotion	Early Diagnosis	Disability limitation
Specific Protection	Proper treatment	Custodial Care
	Rehabilitation	

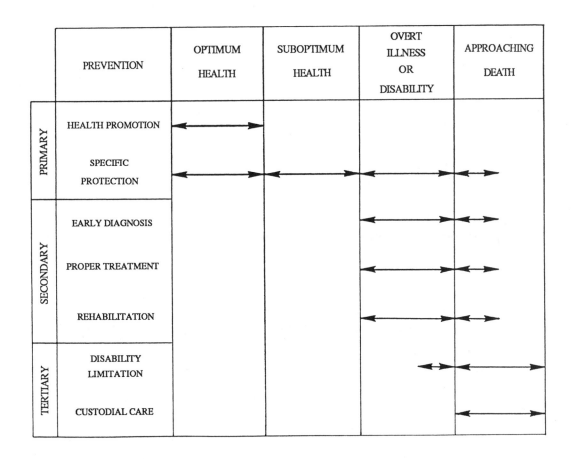

Figure 3

The purpose of Primary Prevention, Health Promotion and Specific Protection is to maintain an individual in the state of Optimum Health for as long as possible. By definition, a person in this state of health cannot be made healthier. However, by various means it is possible to increase functional reserve and immunity as well as to decrease susceptibility. Some may mistakenly believe that athletes are healthier than the general population. The only difference between these two populations is that athletes have far greater functional reserve than nonathletes. Types of functional reserve differ according to the type of sport.

Health Promotion aims to maintain general health, without focusing on any specific disease condition, largely through education and training. For example, the importance of a balanced diet is taught in school as well as through the multi-media public education system. However balanced the diet may be, over-eating on such a diet may result in obesity. Thus, various dieting methods have been publicized. Another example of a program of Health Promotion is driver safety education. Reckless driving of an automobile is not only dangerous to the driver but it also endangers the life and property of others. Prenatal guidance, mental health, genetic counselling and sex education are all a part of Health Promotion. The value of exercise as a part of Health Promotion is now widely recognized, but physical exercise in any form must be preceded by a warming up and conditioning period and it should be moderate in duration. The ill-effects of excessive exercise overshadow its benefit.

The education and training provided by Health Promotion increases public knowledge and skill. However, knowledge and skill combined do not promote health unless they are put into practice, which can be accomplished only through motivation, self-discipline and sustained effort on the part of the individual. Sporadic exercise is not only ineffective but sometimes harmful. When public compliance cannot be guaranteed, a seemingly effective program, such as driver safety education, may have disappointing results.

Specific protection is offered by vaccination for acquired immunity against a specific infectious disease, but the duration of such immunity varies. Fluoridation of drinking water against dental decay, enriched flour against pellagra or iodizing table salt against thyroid dysfunction are other examples of Specific Protection. Industrial or occupational medicine has developed various safety standards to protect workers from specific disease conditions or trauma. Safety education programs are one of the most important activities of labor management in industry. Helmets or hard hats, masks, goggles, ear plugs, special shoes, and gloves are some examples of protective devices for workers brought into the workplace as a result of safety education.

In a democratic society, voluntary compliance with primary prevention is the ideal but, sadly, this is not always the case. Thus, from time to time, it has become necessary to legislate such measures such as immunization for school children or use of an infant automobile seat in certain states. However, there are many laws which have aided promotion of Primary Prevention but their purpose promoted something else. Lowering the highway speed limit to 55 miles per hour has reduced highway accident rates greatly but the purpose of the law was conservation of petroleum. The Occupational Safety and Health Administration (OSHA) is empowered to enforce its safety standards (OSHA standards) with the threat of monetary penalties, so that the motivating factor is not primarily the welfare of the workers, but cost containment.

Primary prevention is not only for those who are in a state of Optimum Health but also for those who are in Overt Illness or Disability and, in some cases, Approaching Death. For example, dietary counselling and foot care programs are given to a diabetic person. Most diabetic patients are controlled with insulin injection and/or oral medication, the daily amount of medication being carefully adjusted according to prescribed food intake. Therefore, poor compliance with food intake

Masayoshi Itoh, Mathew H.M. Lee

may result in many serious complications. Unless meticulous foot hygiene is maintained, a diabetic person may develop an infection and/or ulcer which could eventually result in the amputation of the leg. An elderly person who has a respiratory disease, diabetes mellitus, heart disease or hypertension is urged to be vaccinated against influenza in the fall.[24] Although its efficacy is not conclusive, this Specific Protection is designed to lower mortality from influenza in the winter season.

Early Diagnosis, Proper Treatment and Rehabilitation are listed under Secondary Prevention which is applicable to those who are in the state of Overt Illness or Disability and, in some instances, those who are in the Approaching Death status. The preventative components of the activities under Secondary Prevention have been discussed.

Tertiary Prevention is applied to those who are chronically ill and/or disabled in either the state of Overt Illness or Disability or the state of Approaching Death. Individuals who fall into these categories are expected to have various physical limitations and a primary disability. Therefore, the main efforts are directed toward limitation to prevent development of a variety of secondary disabilities. Modern medicine and technology are incapable of improving the physical limitation or primary disability of these individuals to a state of Suboptimum Health. Thus, the focus is on maintenance of the existing condition for as long as possible, i.e., Custodial Care. Custodial Care does not limit its scope to the physical condition but should include psychological and spiritual well-being. Examples of Custodial Care are activities performed in a nursing home or hospice.

Classifying health care activities from the preventive point of view is a relatively new and unique approach. For the past decade, the phrase, "Quality Care" has been used often, meaning good medical care or practice. Good medical care acts on a person's health rather than reacting to a person's health problems. In order to do this, a practitioner must train him/herself to envision the preventive aspects of medicine.

MUSIC IN MEDICINE

The effect of music in human health has been vaguely recognized for a long time. Wilson[25] reported a very interesting incident: After the Vatican Conference, a new young abbot was assigned to the Benedictine monastery in France. He took the recommendations of the Vatican II Conference to heart and started modernization of the monks' way of life. Believing that monks spending six to eight hours a day chanting while they worked were wasting time, he abolished this centuries old custom. Shortly after this new daily routine was implemented, the monks began to feel fatigue, which became progressively worse, until finally a team of physicians was needed to combat this malady. Various medical remedies had no effect on their fatigue, so finally, an expert in psychology and music was consulted. He suspected that termination of the chanting might have resulted in this symptom. After the hours of chanting were reinstated, the monks' fatigue was completely cured. This case study delightfully illustrates the close relationship between music and the health of the individual.

Music or music therapy has been used in psychiatry and for cases of physical and mental developmental disability for quite some time, focusing on the psychological effects and aiding in the development of socialization skills.[26 27] On the other hand, Moog[28] stated, "The use of wind instruments in therapy for speech disordered persons appears to improve their auditory and motor skills as well as their breath control." He also claimed psychological benefit as well as the improvement of social skills. Furthermore, wind instruments were utilized for the improvement of pulmonary function in asthmatic children.[29] Osborn observed an increase in muscle power in the upper extremities of orthopedically handicapped children who played handbells.[30]

Historically music was very often utilized for the developmentally disabled. Frequently, however, music education and music therapy were not clearly distinguished. Utilization of music in medicine or music therapy is not music education or training. Although its purpose is not to train a musician, one who undergoes music therapy may later develop music appreciation as a hobby or play an instrument as an avocational activity. However, as therapy it should be considered a therapeutic modality like physical or occupational therapy. For example, wind instruments and vocalization of music should be beneficial to respiratory function. The use of any musical instrument requires a certain amount or range of motion in the joints, muscle strength and mental and physical coordination. Thus, it is conceivable that the intelligent selection and application of various muscle techniques will have a great impact on the rehabilitation of the disabled.

Music is one of the things that distinguishes the human race from all other animal species. Appreciation of music is universal in all societies, from the very primitive to the very advanced, and is used to mark all the important occasions in a person's life. Appreciation of music is displayed by listening, dancing, singing or playing a musical instrument, and is one of the most common recreational activities. In some cases, music increases spiritual awareness and, in general, provides great relaxation. Whether one listens to the radio or chooses to go to the opera, both lessen mental stress and promote the individual's well-being. If food is a nutrient for the body, music is for the mind. Thus, music earns a definite place in Health Promotion.

As music is closely related to human well-being, it does have therapeutic value. In the total concept of health care, music therapy should be recognized as another modality for Prevention and Health Promotion. In this sense, music therapy is applicable to a person who is in a state of Optimum Health as well as to a person who is in a state of Approaching Death.

Soldiers sing marching songs during their long marches and those who have had such experience testify that by singing, they suffer less from fatigue. Workers sing a variety of work songs in unison. Railroad workers pounding the roadbed with a sledge hammer or fishermen pulling fishnets to the shore sing very unique songs. While doing their work, which requires great strength, the workers move their bodies to the rhythm of the song, the rhythmical motion preventing not only fatigue but also injuries to their backs. Picking tea leaves is very boring labor and thus, Japanese women who engage in this work sing while working to prevent boredom. These various work songs and work chants were designed for a specific reason but are unintentionally a form of primary prevention utilizing music.

There is also no comparable application of music to Secondary Prevention, Early Diagnosis and Proper Treatment. However, music therapy is applicable to preventive aspects of rehabilitation by selection of proper music techniques that prevent various secondary disabilities.

In Tertiary Prevention, the psychological effects of music are readily applicable for prevention of isolation, depression and as an aid to resocialization. Those who are chronically ill and/or disabled, particularly those who are institutionalized, tend to isolate themselves, to feel sorry for themselves and to lose the desire to socialize. For those in custodial care who can participate, group music therapy, such as singing, handbells, or simple music and band activity may dispel loneliness and lessen psychological distress. Even for those who cannot participate, listening to soft music can be very soothing. It is often incorrectly assumed that those who are in a coma cannot hear music, however, soft music is highly recommended for patients in this condition. The value of music therapy in all levels of Custodial Care should not be minimized.

Masayoshi Itoh, Mathew H.M. Lee

In conclusion, music therapy, at the level of Prevention, has a rightful place in the total health care system. However, further research and clinical trials are urgently needed before music therapy can become a mainstream therapeutic modality.

Various music techniques must be classified according to an individual's anatomical, physiological and mental requirements. Music for listening must be identified according to the emotional needs of and possible kinetic effect on the listener.

When studies in the above areas have been completed, the findings must be synthesized with modern medical knowledge of disease conditions in order to transform current music therapy into a vital therapeutic modality.

REFERENCES

1   Welch, W.H.: Institute of hygiene. In Rockerfeller Foundation Annual Report, New York, 1926, pp. 405-427.
2   Lilienfeld, B.E.: Epidemiologic methods and inferences. In: Hilleboe, H.E. and Larimore, G.W. (eds.) *Preventative Medicine*. Philadelphia, PA: W.B. Saunders Company, 1965, Chapter 43.
3   World Health Organization: Constitution of the World Health Organization. Geneva: World Health Organization, 1964.
4   Rogers, E.S.: *Human Ecology and Health. Introduction for Administrators*. New York: Macmillan Company, 1960.
5   Bresler, D., Trubo, R.: *Free Yourself from Pain*. New York: Simon and Schuster, 1979.
6   Kavasch, E.B.: Puhpohwee: the mushrooms of the Amerindians. *Garden*, 1985, Vol. 9, No. 5, pp. 14-23.
7   Salvato, J.A.: *Environmental Sanitation*. New York: John Wiley and Sons Company, 1958.
8   *Webster's Third International Dictionary*. Springfield, MA: G.C. Merriam Company, 1981.
9   Levit, J.: Jogger's nipples. *New Eng. J. Med.* 1977, **297**, p. 1127.
10 Newuin, N.D.: More on jogger's ailments. *New.Eng J Med*, 1978, **298**, pp. 405-406
11 Burns, R.M.: Rating of industrial disabilities. *Lancet*, 1939, **58**, pp. 17-20.
12 Dristine, M.J.: Disability evaluation. Principles of quantative diagnosis. *Northwest Med.*, 1962, **61**, pp. 1041-1042.
13 Knapp, M.E.: Disability evaluation, 1. *Post Grad.Med*, 1969, **46**, pp. 184-186.
14 Knapp, M.E.: Disability evaluation, 2. *Post Grad Med*, 1969, **46**, pp. 201-203.
15 Moskowitz, E., McCann, C.B.: Classification of disability in chronically ill and aging. *J.Chron Dis*, 1957, **5**, pp. 342-356.
16 Price, L. Medical disability standards. *J.Occup Med*, 1955, **8**, pp. 542-547.
17 Itoh, M., Lee, M.: The epidemiology of disability as related to rehabilitation medicine. In: Kottke, F.J., Stillwell, G.K., Lehman, F.J. (eds.) *Krusen's Handbook of Physical Medicine and Rehabilitation (3rd Edition)*. Philadelphia, PA: W.B. Saunders Company, 1982, Chapter 10.
18 Ryder, C.F., and Daitz, B.: Prevention of disability. In: Selle W.A. (ed.) *Restorative Medicine in Geriatrics*. Springfield, MA.: Charles C. Thomas, 1963, chapter 14.
19 Itoh, M., Lee, M.: The future role of rehabilitation medicine in community health. *Med Clin North Amer*, 1969, **53**, pp. 719-733.
20 Itoh, M.: Preventive rehabilitation for leprosy - a new approach to an old problem." *Rehab Rev*, 1968, pp. 13-14.
21 Karat, S.: Preventive rehabilitation in leprosy. *Leprosy Rev*, 1968, **39**, pp. 39-44.

22 Leavell, H.R., Clark, E.G.: Levels of application of preventive medicine. In: Leavell, H.R., and Clark, E.G. (eds.) *Preventive Medicine for the Doctor in His Community.* New York: McGraw-Hill Book Company, 1965, Chapter 2.

23 Division of Epidemiology, Columia University, School of Public Health and Administrative Medicine: *Principles, Methods and Uses of Epidemiology*, New York, 1965.

24 Horman, J.T., Stetler, H.C., Israel, E., Sorley, D., Schipper, M.T., Joseph J.M.: An outbreak of influenza A in a nursing home. *Mer. J. Pub. Health,* 1986, **76**, pp 501-504.

25 Wilson, T.: Chant - the healing power of voice and ear. (Audio Tape Cassette) Dallas, TX, Sound of Light, 1985.

26 Boxill, E.H.: *Music Therapy for the Developmentally Disabled.* Rockville, MD: Aspen Systems, 1985.

27 Madsen, C.K.: *Music Therapy: A Behavioral Guide for Working with the Mentally Retarded.* Lawrence, KS.:NAMT, 1981.

28 Moog, H.: Wind instruments with individuals suffering from speech deficits. *MEH Bull,* 1985, **1**, pp. 35-42.

29 Tateno, K., and Suziki, I.: Asthma music. *British Journal of Music Therapy*, Autumn, 1982, **13**, pp. 2-10.

30 Osborn, M.: A vocal choir and handbell choir for orthopedically handicapped children. Paper presented at 4th International Symposium of Music: Rehabilitation and Human Well-Being. August 8, 1985, New York.

THE BIOLOGY OF MUSIC

Frank R. Wilson

Dr. Lewis Thomas, author of the celebrated New England Journal series, "Notes of the Biology Watcher," recently published a collection of new essays called *Late Night Thoughts on Listening to Mahler's Ninth Symphony*.[1] Dr. Thomas is fascinated with music and writes about it a good deal. In the new book, he says:

> Surely music (along with ordinary language) is as profound a problem for human biology as can be thought of, and I would like to see something done about it. A few years ago the German Government set up a large advisory committee to work on the question of what the next Max Planck Institute should be taking on as its scientific mission. The committee worked for a very long time and emerged with the recommendation that the new Institute should be dedicated to the problem of music – what music is, why it is indispensable for human existence, what music really means – hard questions like that. The government, in its wisdom, turned the idea down. . . I shall take it as a sign of growing-up in the United States when we can assemble a similar committee for the same purpose and have the idea of the National Institute of Music approved and funded.

Was Dr. Thomas being facetious? Or should there, indeed, be a National Institute of Music? It seems to me the case in support of his proposal is a strong one. Music lives the double life of feast and famine in our society; we have more music teaching in conservatories and universities than ever before; more professional musicians and composers; superb and regular music performances of virtually every musical form; and such a prolific recording industry that we live out lives bathed in ubiquitous musical accompaniment – it is almost *too* much! At the same time it is the rarest of musicians who can make a living at performance alone; it is an unusual musician – even if successful – who does not labor under extraordinary strain and pressure in order to satisfy audiences and his or her own standards; it is a remarkable adult who enjoys music making as a form of personal recreation; it is an exceptional public school that provides music as a basic component of its curriculum; and it is a rare hospital that employs a music therapist.

What is the cause of this paradox? I suspect that either we have forgotten, or perhaps never fully understood, why music is part of the natural fabric of human life. As we have become accustomed to the achievements of the exceptionally gifted musicians in our midst, and inclined to let them do our music making for us, we may have unwittingly put them, and the musical experience itself, in a glass cage. Doing so certainly makes for better ambient music, on the whole, but it may ultimately be a bad thing, especially if the roots of our musical inclinations are physical as much as they are cultural. Perhaps we are *all* equipped to compose and play music, (just as we are all equipped to write letters to the editors of our newspapers), and possibly even at risk for neurologic decline if we suppress or neglect this particular aspect of our personal potential. If so, the perspective and authority of the biologic and behavioral sciences might help restore music to its proper place in our lives.

In this chapter I would like to suggest something of the shape that serious inquiry into human musical responsiveness and ability might take. And although I agree that this pursuit holds great promise for improving the musical lives of us all, there are other reasons for making the effort. In particular, and reflecting a neurologist's peculiar bias, I would argue that there are very likely things to be learned about human biology through the investigation of musical behavior that cannot be learned any other way.

Historically, neurologists have been most interested in the study of cognitive impairments discovered in musicians after brain injury or illness – Ravel and Gershwin are well-known examples– hoping thereby to approach a more comprehensive understanding of higher cortical function in man. A recent illumination of this topic is to be found in John Brust's paper on loss of musical ability in association with neurologic disease.[2] But neurologists also share in the public's joyful amazement over the more brazen examples of mental capacity found among musicians. Composers and conductors are generally held in awe for their remarkable auditory prowess, and in some cases for their display of incomprehensible feats of memory. The composer Felix Mendelssohn, best known for his popular violin concerto, was also a pianist, both a contemporary and close friend of Franz Lizst, and there is a wonderful story about the two playing at a dinner party. Lizst proposed that a Hungarian dance be played, and the two would improvise short pieces, or variations, based on the dance theme. With customary bravado Lizst ran off nine or ten of these, and then turned to Mendelssohn to proceed. No one was quite prepared for what happened next. According to the report of a musically sophisticated audience, Mendelssohn sat down at the piano and proceeded to play, note for note, the entire series of variations Lizst had just played, despite the fact that no one in the room, including Lizst himself, had ever heard the music before.

Had there been an embryonic science of brain function at the time, it is possible someone would have tried to explain Mendelssohn's feat. The neurosciences have matured sufficiently now that we *know* we would not be able to explain it. For the truth is, we know very little about the neurologic organization and control of musical behavior.

As a neurologist, my own interest had tended to center on questions having to do with the technical mastery required for performance of music. That is, one may ask what are the anatomic and physiologic features of the human brain and muscular system that account for the refinement of muscular control observed in finished musical performance? If we listen at all carefully to music, we cannot escape the conclusion that the brain mechanisms involved must be of a very high order and among the most complex found in biologic control systems.

Musicians understand the patient and concentrated effort required to polish even the most modest piece of music. For those who are advanced, technically difficult music may present obstacles that are all but insurmountable. And yet we routinely encounter examples of nearly flawless technique in performing musicians. Perhaps that is so because genuine virtuosity tends to be highly rewarded. The virtuoso, like the trapeze artist, is revered for his or her ability to bring an audience to its feet in a frenzy. Paganini, the best known of the violin virtuosi, finally became so adroit that he would deliberately break strings during performance to demonstrate that, unlike mere mortals, he did not need four strings on his instrument. There are instances on record of his having worked his way down to one string before he was through! Many people regard sheer virtuosity as overrated in performance, but that is another matter; whether virtuoso or amateur, the serious musician must perforce be exploring certain special boundaries of human mental and physical capacity.

I would probably not be far wrong if I guessed that most readers of this volume have had their hands on a piano, or some other keyboard instrument, at one time or another in their lives, and the chances are excellent that some people have spent and continue to spend a significant amount of time relaxing with or working at an instrument, or singing. Anyone left out of that group has surely sat at a typewriter or computer terminal. Everyone with such experience has been exercising a unique human capacity for controlling what are called fractionation movements of the digits – these are the separate, discrete and highly practiced movements of individual fingers on which keyboard skills depend. Other instruments require the precise regulation of other elements of the musculoskeletal system: the organ demands skilled movement of the feet as well as the hands and arms; wind instruments demand control of the facial and intraoral muscles to provide a pleasing tone. Wind instrumentalists of course share with vocalists the obligation to acquire, as well, exceptional control of the air stream used to set up vibrations in the oscillator on which their sound is built. This is true, no matter what one might think, even for the sweet music of the bagpipe.

And so we may ask: How is this done? As might be expected, no one has any basis for a comprehensive answer about anything, but it *is* possible to formulate some intriguing hypotheses about some of the critical neurophysiologic processes in musical execution. Here I lean heavily, if not entirely, on a reading of the extraordinary work that has come from laboratories such as Tom Thach's at Washington University, and Mahlon DeLong's at Johns Hopkins, and the free extrapolation that it occurs to me to make because of what happened to me in the process of beginning to study the piano as I approached my fortieth birthday.

The advances in our understanding of the control processes involved in skilled movements have come about as a result of the recent collaboration of physiologists and psychologists. Primates have been trained to perform patterned movements, mainly of the upper extremities, and were then studied with recording techniques that permit description of the activation of single cells in cortex, basal ganglia, all regions of the cerebellum, and nuclear structures in the brain stem. In most cases simultaneous single unit EMG recordings of active muscles are also obtained. This approach, used extensively since the early 1970s, has made it possible to specify parameters of activation of single brain cells in relation to self-initiated and self-regulated movements, and to study the temporal relationships of activation of cell groups controlling these movements. It will never be possible to specify the full electrophysiologic ancestry of even the simplest skilled move, since the complete life history of the animal and the redundancy and recurrency of the brain's circuitry, will always be involved and can be depended on to evade complete detection of description with any sort of specificity. But if one is curious about how things seem to work during an epoch of a few hundred milliseconds encompassing a rather simple, highly practiced self-generated move, the picture certainly seems to be coming into focus.

Let us look at the problem facing the student who is attempting to become technically proficient with an instrument. In the early stages, arm and hand movements are slow, tentative and inaccurate. Velocity, force, and duration of contraction are inconsistent, and a smoothly coordinated balance of activation and inhibition of muscle contraction is lacking; the result is not what we normally call musical. It is only after an extended period of practice (normally measured in years) that we expect to hear what we call an artistic performance. What accounts for the improvement?

Perhaps the best way to envision the process is by regarding musical skill as akin to archery, table tennis, and chopping carrots. The common element is that each requires a great deal of target practice: the body must learn to move in a highly controlled and specific way in order to control the behavior of an external object. The analogy incorporates, as well, the elements of an abstract goal, play, the dependence on speed and accuracy to score (a hit), and sometimes the distraction of competition.

In undertaking this sort of activity in our daily lives (and there are countless examples), we generally succeed according to a principle referred to as "Fitts' Rule,"[3] which proclaims that the faster we move, the bigger the target must be for us to hit it. In music making, one must often achieve high rates of speed in movement without a compensatory increase in target size. So Fitts' Rule cannot help us understand finished musical performance.

In the early 1970s the physiologists found a clue that had been left on a shelf nearly 90 years earlier. In 1895, Paul Richer took a series of rapid sequence photographs of the quadriceps muscle during a kicking motion.[4] After studying the photographs, he said this about the contraction of the muscle during the kick: "It is very energetic and short lasting. It launches the limb in a set direction and ceases long before the limb will have completed its course of action." Because of the similarity of this kind of move and the firing of a gun shell, it was called "ballistic."

After extensive study of the kind I referred to earlier, using animals trained to make rapid moves toward a defined target, it has now been shown that there is something very special about ballistic moves. As required by Fitts' Rule, speed and accuracy of movement are inversely related. Ballistic moves do not follow this principle.

In the studies that have been done, animals approach the problem by going through a trial and error process. The limb moves in small, discontinuous increments, with marked fluctuations in acceleration. Visual and proprioceptive information is required to succeed at this task. Once the move is learned so that it can be done accurately, and if the animal is rewarded for speed, it will come under a ballistic mode of control. There will be a marked increase in the speed of the move, disappearance of the fluctuations in acceleration, and, quite remarkably, a loss of the previous dependence on visual or proprioceptive feedback. Under conditions of ballistic control, the limb can be completely shielded from the animals view, and deafferented, and neither accuracy nor speed will be significantly compromised. Furthermore, the move can be perturbed, or interfered with, and it still will land on target.

By definition, ballistic moves are very brief in duration – not longer than 0.2 seconds – and they terminate against some kind of barrier. Another class of highly skilled movement that is somewhat longer in duration is the self-terminated move which normally requires the braking action of antagonist muscles. Whereas there is just one burst of agonist activity in the ballistic move, without the need of terminal braking, the self-terminated move is driven by two brief agonist burst, with an antagonist burst interposed.

The inference drawn from these findings is that there is a central program for the entire move contained in a command signal that initiates it. Stated differently, the command signal specifies the terminal position intended for the limb. One way this might occur, as suggested by Bizzi and co-workers at MIT,[5] is that the signal appears to specify for each muscle participating in the move the correct length and tension it must achieve in its resting position.

There are at least two lines of evidence suggesting that the cerebellum is critically involved in the regulation of the kind of movements used by musicians in skilled performance, not only movements where ongoing modification is possible, but in ballistic and self-terminated moves where there is no time for correction. First, there is the circuitry itself; Eccles has proposed that the cerebellum – particularly the lateral hemispheres – is ideally situated and functionally competent to receive instructions from motor cortex in the form of successful movement histories, and to store that information in the form of subprograms – a sort of software – which can be retrieved as necessary so that the precentral cerebral cortex does not have to plan and monitor each movement it must execute, each and every time it is called for. The portion of the cerebellum involved communicates with the precentral cortex mainly through the dentate nucleus.

Second, as in the case of basal ganglia, there are now studies of timing in behaving animals that document the activation of cerebello-cerebral circuits in advance of self-generated, skilled movements. Dr. Thach's laboratory has reported results showing that over 80% of dentate nuclear cells changed their discharge frequency before the first EMG changes, some as much as 80 msec sooner;[6] furthermore, when recordings were made of both dentate and precentral neurons in these movements, the changes in activity in dentate preceded activation in precentral neurons by as long as 33 msec.

The obvious question is, what kind of information is being sent from dentate to precentral cortex? It now appears, to distill an enormous amount of work, that the dentate is signalling for

Frank R.Wilson

movement to occur, by triggering the discharge of preset assemblies in the cortex. When the dentate nucleus is removed from the system by temporary cooling, in a technique that was pioneered by Vernon Brooks in Ontario, the result is prolongation of agonist contraction, and delay of onset of antagonist or braking action.[7] Skilled movement *can* occur without the benefit of the cerebellar contribution, but timing and smoothness are compromised.

Sir John Eccles' made these remarks about the cerebellum in a paper he presented in 1977:[8]

> We can say that normally our most complex muscle movements are carried out subconsciously and with consummate skill. The more subconscious you are in a golf stroke, the better it is, and the same with tennis, skating or any other skill. In all these performances we do not have any appreciation of the complexity of muscle contractions and joint movements. All that we are conscious of is a general directive given by what we may call our voluntary command system. All the finesse and skill seems to flow naturally from that. It is my thesis that the cerebellum is concerned in this enormously complex organization and control of movement, and that throughout life, particularly in the earlier years, we are engaged in an incessant teaching program for the cerebellum. As a consequence it can carry out all of these remarkable tasks that we set it to do in the whole repertoire of our skilled movements in games, in techniques, in musical performance, in speech, dance and so on.

I confess to taking great comfort in this particular passage, since it implies that there is some room for cautious extrapolation of the primate studies to humans. I choose to believe that this work is beginning to provide a very solid foundation for at least a rudimentary understanding of what musicians are really up to, and what they are up against physiologically. Moreover, as is the case with all good science, the crop of new questions is larger and more interesting than the answers.

For me, the most interesting question has to do with cerebellar function in the refinement of complex skilled movement by instrumentalists. Is the pianist, or the violinist, spending all those years and countless hours in repertoire in order to stabilize cerebello-cerebral circuitry? Is the speed and suppleness of execution exhibited by the skilled musician a mark of cerebellar ballistic control? And is this kind of performance somehow related to improved antagonist inhibition? Since truly finished performance is marked by precision and economy of movement, it could well be that the cerebellum contributes critically by keeping unwanted contraction "out of the act," as it were.

In discussing subjective mental state with experienced performers, one hears consistently the assertion that success requires the ability to achieve a freedom from concern about the mechanical details of execution (what note, or notes come next? what finger falls on what key?). Does this awareness of the musician during performance that he or she has entered an altered state of consciousness somehow correspond to a shift from current to ballistic control? For there is no doubt that the performer who begins to think consciously about the mechanical details of execution is courting disaster. Is it possible that the mysterious "Self Two" of Gallwey's *Inner Game* books is really the cerebellum?

I have begun to think there is a physiologic basis for the well known precept of Saint Saens: "Practice very slowly, progress very fast." If ballistic programming demands consistency in the reproduction of a complex movement sequence, one would lose time only by practicing at a pace too fast for accurate execution.

And what about muscle spindles and ballistic movements? Is it possible that the gamma system subserves what the musicians refer to as *muscle memory*? Or allows the musician to adapt this laboriously constructed ballistic program to a world full of keys, pedals, strings and valves that never respond the same way twice, or to his own muscles, whose reactivity may vary dramatically with temperature change, or fatigue.

Finally, what does the auditory system have to do with all this? In the final analysis, the musician is striving for control of his own muscular system so that an intended sound will be generated. The connections between auditory and cerebello-cerebral control systems must be both intimate and extensive, and very special indeed in the trained musician. I think the closer we look at musicians, the more astonished we will be at the kind of performance they routinely demand of, and extract from, their neuromuscular systems.

A critical question to settle is whether there is any real prospect for *in vivo* confirmation of the primate studies in human skilled movement. One indirect but nonetheless promising possibility resides in the use of very short-lived isotopes in combination with positron-emission tomography. John Mazziotta at UCLA has recently shown by this technique that basal ganglia are active in "complex overlearned tasks."[9] It is possible that the use of high speed filming of hand movements, with subsequent computer analysis, would help.

Obviously, our understanding of brain mechanisms in musical activities is still only rudimentary. That's the bad news, if your sleep is disturbed by unanswered questions. But the apparent necessity of studying phenomena like these to help us understand how the brain does *anything* is good news. It means brain scientists are going to look more and more closely at musicians in order to understand what it is that makes humans so special. In other words, you can expect the bright light of the scientist to be drawn more and more toward the musician as a wellspring of information about the special nature of the human brain. Working together, musicians and brain scientists could well give us the most exciting developments in human biology of our generation.

REFERENCES

1 Thomas, L.: Things left unflattened by science. In: *Late Night Thoughts on Listening to Mahler's Ninth Symphony*. New York: Viking-Penguin, 1979.
2 Brust, J.: Music and Language: Musical alexia and agraphia. *Brain*, 1980, **103**, pp. 367-92.
3 Fitts, P.: The information capacity of the human motor system in controlling the amplitude of movement. *J Exp Psychol*, 1954, **47**, pp. 381-391.
4 Richer, P.: Note sur la contraction du muscle quadriceps dans l'acte de donée un coup de pied. *C R Soc Biol* (Paris), 1985, **47**, 204-205. (Quoted from Brooks, V.: Motor programs revisited. In: *Posture and Movement*, Talbott R., Humphrey, D., (eds.). New York: Raven Press, 1979, p. 21.)
5 Bizzi, E., *et al.*: Role of neck proprioceptors during visually triggered head movements. In: Cerebral Motor Control in Man.: Long Loop Mechanisms. *Prog Clin Neurophysiol*, 1978, **4**, (Desmedt, J. [ed.]), pp. 141-152.
6 Thach, W.: Timing of activity in cerebellar dentate nucleus and cerebral motor cortex during prompt volitional movement. *Brain Res*, 1975, **88**, pp. 233-241.
7 Brooks, V., *et al.*: Effects of cooling dentate nucleus on tracking-task performance in monkeys. *J Neurophysiol*, 1973, **36**, pp. 974-995.
8 Eccles, J.: an instruction-selection theory of learning in the cerebellar cortex. *Brain Res*, 1977, **127**, pp. 327-352.
9 Mazziotta, J.: Visualizaton of brain metabolism in skilled movements. In: *The Biology of Music Making: Proceedings of the 1984 Denver Conference*, Roehmann, F., Wilson, F. St. Louis, MO: MMB Music, Inc., 1988, pp. 100-103.

COMPUTERIZED THERMOGRAPHY AND OTHER TECHNOLOGICAL AIDS IN THE DIAGNOSIS OF MUSICIANS' NEUROMUSCULAR DISORDERS

Mathew H.M. Lee
John J. Kella

1. INTRODUCTION

Clinical and epidemiological evidence suggests that chronic rather than infectious diseases now constitute the major source of human illness. These findings indicate that health care specialists in the coming decade will be increasingly concerned with the clinical effects of environmental stress and occupationally related disorders, and with their role in determining the health and well-being of men and women.

An out-patient group that serves as a most appropriate target population for the study and treatment of environmental stress and occupations ailments is that of musicians and other performing artists. This group performs highly complex, sophisticated musculoskeletal movements within exacting professional criteria in public settings under potentially anxiety-producing conditions. Clinical reports in journals such as *The New England Journal of Medicine, Journal of Occupational Medicine, Journal of the American Medical Association, Journal of Behavioral Medicine,* and *Biofeedback and Self-Regulation,* as well as the new journal, *Medical Problems of Performing Artists* , all suggest that musicians and other artists present a variety of both physical and psychological occupational stress problems.

Though reports of performers' medical ailments have appeared intermittently since 1874,[1] a computer search[2] of relevant publications revealed a significant increase in the number of related articles from 27 (published between 1966 and 1972), to 56 (1972-1979), to 76 (1980 - 1985). Other evidence of increased interest in the subject includes the creation of several medical centers and institutes dedicated to serving the health needs of performing artists,* and the sponsoring of several national and international conferences and symposia held since 1983 on performers' ailments.[3] [4]

In addition, the high percentage of performers affected by occupationally related disorders is indicated by a recent survey[5] which found that these injuries apparently occur in 5% to 20% of music students and in over 50% of orchestral performers internationally.

From this information, it may be seen that there is an expressed interest in and need for systematic research on the diagnosis, treatment, and prevention of occupational stress and medical problems of musicians and other performing artists.

2. CATEGORIES OF MUSICIANS' PHYSICAL DISORDERS

In her review of relevant literature, Harman[6] cites six basic categories of musicians' physical disorders (See Fry, ref. 5 for further discussion):

---

* Kathryn and Gilbert Miller Health Care Institute for Performing Artists at St. Luke's-Roosevelt Hospital Center, New York, New York; Northwestern Medical Program for Performing Artists at Northwestern University Medical School, Chicago, Illinois; Medical Center for Performing Artists at the Cleveland Clinic Foundation, Cleveland Ohio; other clinics are proposed.

a. nerve compression syndromes:
   viol paraesthesia, paralyzed embouchure, flutist's neuropathy, carpal tunnel syndrome
b. muscular, tendon, or myofascial (soft tissue) disorders:
   occupational cramps, trigger finger, tenosynovitis, and other over or misuse-related disorders
c. dermatitis:
   fiddler's neck, flutist's chin, trumpeter's lip, guitar nipple, clarinettist's chelitis
d. dental and other oral problems:
   velopharyngeal stress incompetence, parotitis, laryngoceles, diverticulosis
e. cardiac irregularities:
   premature ventricular contractions, tachycardia, arterial blood pressure changes, Valsalva-like cardiac maneuvers
f. miscellaneous problems:
   eyestrain, myopia, singer's respiratory and vocal chord problems

This article describes technological aids useful in the diagnosis of the first two categories: (a) nerve compression syndromes, and (b) muscular, tendon, or myofascial disorders. These might be described together as neuromuscular ailments.

Before describing diagnostic aids, it may be of use to review the natural history of disease, and examine the individual and environmental factors that interact to affect human health and illness.

3. NATURAL HISTORY OF DISEASE: THE HEALTH-ILLNESS CONTINUUM

The natural history of virtually all diseases, including occupational stress syndromes, can be charted on a "health-illness continuum" which encompasses several states of health (Figure 1).[7][8] Applicable to all individuals, this continuum extends from complete physical, mental and social well-being (optimal health), to reduced functioning (suboptimal health), to illness (overt illness or disability), and ends in the total absence of health (death). However, difficulties can arise in appropriately identifying health states. For example, individuals in the incubation period of infectious diseases, or young performers functioning under a personal overload of occupational stress, may not yet show overt signs of illness, and may be inappropriately perceived as being in optimal health. Without appropriate diagnosis and intervention, these individuals may decline to a state of physical, mental, or social impairment, with subsequent decrease in mobility, strength, or immunity, and consequently, may experience loss of work status or even occupation.

As can be seen, an important aspect of the natural history of disease is that one does not stay in a particular state of health for an indefinite period. The health of individuals is constantly shifting in either direction, towards or away from optimal health. Medical and psychological interventions are some methods for influencing the direction of change in the health-illness continuum. Attempts to increase the quality of health are considered therapeutic medicine, while efforts to inhibit ill health are preventive. The next section identifies the individual and environmental factors which interact to affect states of health and illness.

Mathew H.M. Lee, John J. Kella

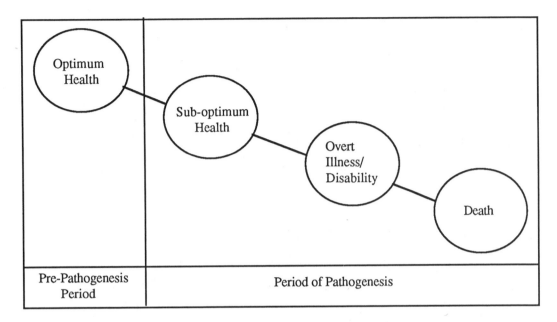

Figure 1: Natural History of Disease: The Health-Illness Continuum

4. A MODEL OF INDIVIDUAL AND ENVIRONMENTAL HEALTH INTERACTIONS: THE INSTITUTE OF MEDICINE'S FRAMEWORK OF STRESS RESEARCH

In researching performers' disorders, it is necessary to consider what personal and environmental elements interact to create states of health or illness. Of several possible interaction models, the most comprehensive and parsimonious is the "Framework for Stress Research" developed by the Institute of Medicine (Figure 2).[9]

This model begins by identifying potential **stressors**, which may be physiological, psychological, and/or environmental. Stressors can lead to **reactions**, which subsequently may produce mental, physical, or behavioral **consequences**. In this model, responses are generally considered to be immediate, transient, or short-term reactions to stressors. Consequences are considered to be more prolonged, long-term, or cumulative effects that may occur after a substantial time lag. Some stressors may produce transient reactions that are not intense enough to produce consequences, while others may be stronger or accumulate sufficiently to change one's state of health. Also of importance is the possibility that the stressor-reaction-consequence chain may in turn become a feedback loop, with the consequences themselves becoming potential stressors.

It should be stated that stressors, reactions, and consequences may not necessarily be considered as negative. Some stressors may produce positive consequences such as socially desirable personality traits, or increased work quality or productivity. Other stressors, though, may create reactions and consequences that are relatively debilitating.

In addition, **mediators** can filter or modify each stage in this sequence, producing individual variations at each state. These variations may refer to the unique characteristics of individuals, or may be other physiological, psychological, or environmental aspects.

Finally, all four elements of this model – stressors, reactions, consequences, and mediators – can vary according to intensity, quantity, temporal patterning, and organizational level (from cell to organ to individual to organizational to societal).

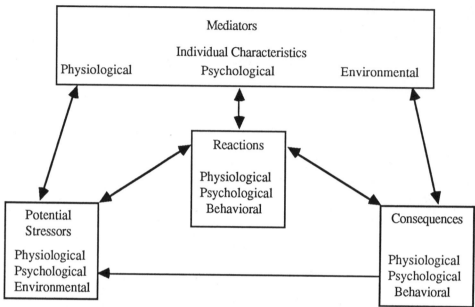

Figure 2: The Institute of Medicine's Framework of Stress Research

Descriptors for each element: Intensity
Quantity
Temporal patterning
Organizational level

In many cases, the specific elements of the stressor-reaction-consequence chain may be easily determined. For example, a dancer, actor, singer or musician may be exposed to stage-fog, smoke, and other "special effects," as well as to air-born pollutants or high decibel sound. Fog and smoke effects (potential stressors) are frequently created by vaporizing or misting organic chemicals such as petroleum distillates. These distillates are flammable or combustible, and can cause eye, throat, and lung irritation (reactions), which in time can lead to pulmonary edema or damage the central nervous system through its potentially narcotic effects (consequences), especially in heavy exposure or among high-risk individuals (mediators). Health problems related to special effects can range in seriousness from Michael Jackson's slicked hair catching fire to the death of Vic Morrow and two children during the filming of a helicopter sequence in *The Twilight Zone*.[10]

In other cases, the identification of the elements in the stressor-reaction-consequence chain may be more difficult. For example, Fry[5] has identified at least three factors (potential stressors) that may be involved in overuse injuries in musicians.

a. individual genetic physical proclivity or unsuitability for performing on particular musical instruments;

Mathew H.M. Lee, John J. Kella

b. individual performing technique that is high or low in degree of coordination and/or muscle tone;

c. intensity of performance multiplied by duration of effort that is suitable or unsuitable for performer's body.

In a situation involving the third possible stressor (over-intensity multiplied by a long practice/performance schedule), a violinist may perform repeated, effortful flexings of the left hand, which in time lead to consequent feelings of weakness or incoordination in the left thumb and fingers. These consequences may be attributed to carpal tunnel syndrome (requiring the surgical intervention of cutting the transverse carpal ligament) or may be attributed to exudation flowing from overused and swollen flexor muscles into the carpal tunnel around the flexor tendons (requiring the behavioral intervention of resting and elevating the arm).[5]

It is clear that an important contribution would be the identification and evaluation of technological aids for diagnosing the cause of occupational pain syndromes, and tracking the process of rehabilitation in work-related disorders of musicians and other performers.

5. TECHNOLOGICAL AIDS FOR DIAGNOSING MUSICIANS' NEUROMUSCULAR DISORDERS

The accurate diagnosis of the category, location, and severity of musicians' ailments must play a central role in all disease treatment and rehabilitation. Diagnostic approaches to musicians' physical disorders include:

a. direct observation:
   through surgery;
   through the insertion of optical instruments into affected areas (as in arthroscopy of diarthrodial joints, including shoulders, knees, ankles);
b. irradiation of anatomical irregularities:
   through roentgenography (X-ray photography);
   through radioactive isotopic up-take as an indicator of skeletal or muscular injury;
c. bioelectrical measurement:
   through chronaxy;
   through nerve conduction measurements (study of evoked potentials);
   through electromyography (study of action potentials);
d. thermoregulatory measurements (computerized thermography).

These diagnostic methods are described below in the order of most intrusive (arthroscopy) to least intrusive (thermography).

6. ARTHROSCOPY

Arthroscopy is the insertion of an optical instrument into affected diarthrodial joints such as the shoulder, knee, or ankle. The instrument is inserted through a small surgical portal while the patient is under anesthesia. Arthroscopy is useful in diagnosing and surgically treating frozen shoulders, dislocations, glenoid labium tears, loose bodies such as cartiloginous formations and bone chips, adhesive capsulitis and rotator cuff tears, and subluxations. Arthroscopy is also useful in diagnosing shoulder laxity, which can cause joint instability without frank dislocation among athletes and arts performers. Shoulder laxity is very difficult to diagnose in clinical or X-ray examinations, and can be misdiagnosed (without direct observation) as subdeltoid bursitis, rotator cuff tendinitis, or bicipital tendinitis.[11] However, due to the intrusiveness of arthroscopy, it is not suggested that this diagnostic approach be used for performing artists except in cases of severe injury or diagnostic uncertainty.

7. ROENTGENOGRAPHY (X-RAY PHOTOGRAPHY)

X-rays provide photographic representations of differences in densities of body tissues, thus aiding in the diagnosis of structural abnormalities such as skeletal misalignments, subluxations, or fracture. These conditions all have the potential for nerve impingement or injury to surrounding soft tissue.[12] However, though X-ray photography is effective in diagnosing disorders of the skeletal structure, it is not generally as effective in diagnosing soft-tissue or neuromuscular injuries. For these injuries, diagnosis can be undertaken through the analysis of the electrical functioning of neuromuscular structures (electrodiagnosis), or through the analysis of thermoregulatory processes (computerized thermography).

8. ELECTRODIAGNOSTIC METHODS

A description of electrodiagnostic methods requires a brief summary of neuromuscular functioning of the body. Human movement is normally controlled in part by means of electrical messages sent by various sectors of the central nervous system, including the cerebellum, motor nuclei in the mid-brain, basal ganglia, red nucleus, and motor areas in the cerebral cortex. Messages sent by the CNS are integrated with one another and coordinated through information received from feedback regulatory loops in many parts of the body, such as the muscles themselves, as well as the sensory systems of the skin, eyes, ears, and the organs of equilibrium in the inner ear. All motor commands for both voluntary and involuntary contractions of skeletal muscles are then routed through the alpha ventral horn motoneuron in the spinal cord, and on to the individual motor units, each of which is comprised of a nerve cell and the muscle fibers it supplies.[13]

When a muscle fiber contracts, its surface membrane undergoes electrical changes (depolarization), which, when measured, are called action potentials. In health, the only measurable electrical activity in muscles occurs when muscle fibers are activated directly by neurons (normal motor unit action potentials). In diseases in which the structure and function of motor units are affected, motor unit action potential may exhibit abnormal configuration, or may demonstrate altered patterning of voluntary movement, such as in the apparently spontaneous contractions of individual muscle units without measureable neuronal activation.[14] Thus, measurements of the duration, intensity, and continuity of electrical activity in neuromuscular structures are useful diagnostic indices of health or illness in our nervous and muscular systems.

Electrodiagnostic methods – including chronaxy, nerve conduction measurements, and electromyography (EMG) – record these various aspects of healthy and diseased motor functioning in different ways. Each method is discussed below.

Chronaxy is a measure of muscle contraction, and requires two phases. The first phase consists of determining the least amount of current which, when applied to a muscle for an indefinite period, is just sufficient to evoke a minimal muscle contraction (rheobase). The second phase is a measurement of the amount of time in milliseconds for a current twice the rheobase to evoke a muscle contraction (chronaxy).[15] While normal chronaxy durations or values are less than 1 millisecond, chronaxy values for impaired neuromuscular structures (denervation) can be over 80 milliseconds.[16] Chronaxy is most useful as a diagnostic tool in following the stages of muscle degeneration (the second category of musicians' disorders), and as a therapeutic aid in analyzing the processes of muscle regeneration.[15]

The second electrodiagnostic method consists of nerve conduction measurements, which can be carried out on either motor or sensory nerves. Nerve conduction tests consist of introducing brief low-level electrical impulses into different nerves to determine nerve and muscle functioning (the study of evoked potentials). These tests can measure:

a. the velocity and time of nerve conduction following stimulation;
b. the amplitude and duration of action potentials of nerves following stimulation;
c. the excitability of the peripheral neuromuscular system;
d. the fatigability of the peripheral neuromuscular system in response to repetitive stimulation.[15]

Nerve conduction measurement are particularly useful in diagnosing injuries and lesions due to local pressure or compression on peripheral nerves (the first category of musicians' ailments).[14]

The third diagnostic tool is electromyography (EMG), which measures and records action potentials arising in contracting skeletal muscle fibers (the study of action potentials). Action potentials are then amplified and displayed in a number of ways: visually on an oscilloscope, aurally through a loud speaker, or recorded by a pen writer or tape recorder.

Healthy, relaxed skeletal muscles generally evoke no motor unit activity (referred to as "electrical silence"). Muscles affected by reduced nerve supply (denervation) can show a degree of spontaneous electrical activity consisting of small potentials (100-200 microvolts in amplitude, lasting up to 2 milliseconds in duration, and referred to as "fibrillation potentials"). Denervation may also be indicated by irregular diphasic waves of variable amplitude and duration, known as "sharp positive waves" because of their similarity to that wave form. During the process of re-innervation, muscles can demonstrate unusual motor unit activity preparatory to visible muscle contractions. This activity consists of single motor units that evoke action potentials distinguished by abnormally increased duration, amplitude, and number of recorded "spikes" beyond the usual number of three or four ("polyphasic motor unit potentials").[17]

Electromyography is clearly an aid in detecting skeletal muscle denervation and re-innervation. In addition, EMG is also useful in:

a. distinguishing between lower and upper motor neurone types of paralyses;
b. diagnosing anterior horn disease;
c. analyzing muscle activity affecting posture (such as in the positions and movements associated with music instrument performance, vocal production, or conducting);
d. distinguishing a neuropathic paralysis from a myopathy;
e. diagnosing diffuse motor neurone disease;
f. distinguishing disuse atrophy with contracture from ischemic muscle necrosis with subsequent contracture;
g. diagnosing myotonias;
h. distinguishing hysterical paralysis from nerve dystonia [17]

It should be noted that all three electrodiagnostic methods described above are interdependent in clinical evaluations. For example, abnormal EMG findings (such as positive waves and fibrillation) are indicative only of muscle innervation pathology, and do not necessarily provide any anatomical localization of the offending lesion itself. Other electrodiagnostic procedures (such as determining motor conduction velocities or identifying the latency of motor response on nerve stimulation at different muscle sites) are necessary for confirming the anatomical locations of possible neuromuscular lesions.[17]

However, though X-rays and arthroscopy are helpful in diagnosing anatomical abnormalities, and though electrodiagnostic measurements are useful in accurately indicating the physiological functioning of individually selected nerves and muscle fibers, some patients may require a nonirradiating and nonsurgical diagnostic approach that can quickly and accurately measure neuromuscular functioning in several contralateral parts of the body simultaneously. This approach is computerized thermography, described below.

9. COMPUTERIZED THERMOGRAPHY

9.1. Introduction

One of the most important parameters of health or illness in humans is body temperature, for "thermoregulatory processes are essential in maintaining well-being and life."[18] A method for measuring temperature changes in the body is the special photographic technique of thermography. Thermography detects and measures surface temperature by sensing invisible infrared heat emission patterns radiated naturally by the body. Variations in these infrared patterns are of diagnostic importance because heat emissions can be indicative of changes in peripheral blood-flow and metabolic activity. For example, thermographic measurements of relatively low infrared emission rates can indicate body areas of lower temperature, reduced metabolic activity, vasoconstriction of blood vessels, or overactive sympathetic nerve function. Higher infrared rates indicate areas of higher temperature, increased metabolism, vasodilation, or loss of sympathetic nerve function.[19]

9.2. Equipment for Computerized Thermography

In practice, computerized thermographic equipment consists of a heat-sensing camera linked to a computer and monitor. The camera, which is sensitive to within O.1°C, detects and amplifies heat-emission patterns within seconds, and transfers them into electronic signals. These signals can be computer-analyzed, displayed on monitors, stored in computer files, and reproduced on color photographic prints of continuous-tone black-and-white pictures (thermograms).

No part of the thermographic equipment comes in contact with the subject, and no potentially hazardous gamma radiation is used during examinations. Computerized thermography is therefore noninvasive, rapid, and painless, as well as safe for children, pregnant women, and chronic pain patients who may have already undergone repeated X-ray examinations or experienced previous invasive procedures.

The accurate reading of a thermogram depends on knowing the range of normal versus abnormal variations in skin temperature. In Uematsu's study[19] of the range of normal skin temperatures in 32 healthy subjects, it was found that the forehead elicited the highest average skin temperature (34.5°C, +/- 0.73°C), while the toes averaged the lowest (27.1°C, +/- 4.03°C). Skin temperature differences from one side of the body compared to the other are not only extremely small but are very stable throughout the body (Figure 3.) The differences between sides of the forehead are normally 0.12°C, and are normally 0.25°C in the thoracic paraspinal area. The temperature of the fingers and toes are not as stable as the other parts of the body, with variations in the fingers averaging 0.38°C from one side of the body to the other and the toes averaging 0.50°C contralaterally. The small temperature differences between sides of the body are apparently unaltered by age, for the correlation coefficient between age and temperature difference is -0.52°C.

Patients afflicted with peripheral nerve impairment exhibited far greater temperature variations. The skin temperature variations contralaterally in afflicted body areas averaged 1.55°C, a difference of six times the temperature variations exhibited by normals. The correlated means t-test between normals and patients on consecutively anatomically matched amples yielded p<0.001 (t=6.6), thus indicating a significant temperature change in the body area of the damaged nerve.

Sensory Area	Number of cases	Temperature Differences (°C)	Standard Deviation (+/-°C)
Head: Forehead	29	0.12	0.093
Trunk: Cervical Area	11	0.25	0.191
Thoracic Area	11	0.25	0.092
Shoulder	10	0.13	0.108
Biceps	10	0.13	0.119
Forearm (lateral)	19	0.32	0.158
Palm (lateral)	21	0.25	0.166
Fingers (average)	–	0.38	0.064
Toes (average)	–	0.50	0.143
Extremities	–	0.20	0.073

Figure 3: Average skin temperature differences between sides of body as measured among normals by thermography [19]

9.3 Differences Between Thermography and Other Diagnostic Methods

It can be seen that thermography differs from the previously discussed diagnostic aids in two ways. First, X-rays, electrodiagnostic methods, and arthroscopy provide images of anatomy by displaying anatomical damage to bones, joints, nerves, or muscles. In particular, X-rays, which are sensitive to differences in tissue densities,[12] provide visualizations of structure abnormalities such as misalignment, subluxation, or fracture. Thermography, however, can be characterized as a window on the internal physiological functioning of the body, and is useful in the diagnosis and prognosis of soft-tissue lesions and associated pain. Secondly, X-rays, electrodiagnostic measurements, and arthroscopy are relatively intrusive compared to thermography, which requires no use of radiation, electrical stimulation, or surgery.

9.4 Uses of Thermography

Thermography can be used to measure changes in body temperature due to a number of possible causes, including muscular effort, inflammation or compression of nerves, joints, muscles, and other soft tissues, abnormal growths such as cancerous tumors, or the healing processes associated with stress fractures,[20] rheumatoid arthritis, and other ailments.

More specific uses of thermography include the diagnosis of inflammatory arthritis and rheumatoid disease,[21] [22] peripheral circulatory problems,[23] benign and malignant breast diseases,[18] deep venous thrombosis and other vascular impairments,[24] musculo-ligamentous injuries,[12] myofascial syndromes, neuropathic syndromes, neurovascular compression syndromes, reflex sympathetic dystrophy, soft tissue injury, thoracic outlet syndromes, burns and grafts, tumors, headaches, and psychogenic pain syndromes. Thermography can also help in evaluating treatment effectiveness in post-traumatic sympathetic distrophy,[25] in following the recovery process of nerves,[19] and in identifying physiological bases for patients incorrectly diagnosed as experiencing psychogenic pain.[26]

The utility of thermography as a diagnostic indicator of soft-tissue may be seen in the special case of reflex sympathetic dystrophy. In soft-tissue injuries, the involuntary sympathetic nerves sometimes remain irritated even after apparent healing. When stressful effort or stimuli reirritate these nerves, involuntary sympathetic signals are sent to blood vessels and other neural pathways (partly mediated by the A delta and C fibers in the tissues), causing vasoconstriction. The resulting reduction in blood flow and tissue perfusion causes the area to become cooler. The reduced blood flow maintains nerve irritation, producing the perception of pain. This process, of reflex sympathetic distrophy, may persist long after the original injury appears healed.[24]

Another use of thermography of particular interest to musicians is occupational thermography. This special application of thermography requires "stress-testing" of the physical exertion a patient usually expends in his or her work to demonstrate graphically whether performance-related activities affect or possibly aggravate the performer's physical condition. It is this use of thermography that is described in Section 9.6, and shown in Figures 4, 5, and 6 below.

9.5 Criticisms of Thermography

Criticisms of thermography include low correlation between clinical evaluations and thermographic assessments;[23][27] higher percentage of false positives in thermographic assessment compared with X-ray examinations;[12] ineffectiveness of thermography in distinguishing normal from inflamed small joints of the hands and toes compared to the effectiveness of thermography in diagnosing inflammatory processes in the larger joints of the shoulder, elbow, knee, and ankle;[28] and the ineffectiveness of thermography in the assessment of breast diseases.[18]

Lindhagen, et al.[26] found low correlation (46.3%) between thermographic assessments and clinical findings of deep venous insufficiency. Wallin, et al.[23] also found low correlation (58%) between thermography evaluation and clinical assessment of deep venous thrombi, suggesting that these diagnostic approaches did not test positive for the same patients. However, when Wallin, et al. combined clinical and thermographic screenings, he found a sensitivity of 97% and a specificity of 41%, suggesting that a combination of clinical and thermographic assessments together can provide diagnostic certainty equal to that of the 99Tcm-plasmic test for deep venous thrombosis (rated at 95% sensitivity by Wallin).

Karpman, et al.[12] in his study of the assessment of soft tissue injuries in the lower back, found that thermography tended to exhibit more false positives than X-ray examinations. Among 34 patients being screened for possible low back disorders during routine pre-job-placement examinations for industry, 23 were found to have normal X-rays, normal thermographic assessments, and were clinically found to be asymptomatic. Six others exhibited abnormal thermograms, normal X-rays, but only one was asymptomatic. Five were found to have both abnormal thermograms and abnormal X-rays, but were also asymptomatic. This study indicated a 30% rate of false positives for thermograms (about 10 out of 34), and a 15% rate of false positives for X-ray examinations (5 out of 34). However, four points are of importance. First, all patients who were symptomatic exhibited abnormal thermograms. Secondly, no patients exhibited a normal thermograph in association with an abnormal X-ray, whereas 9 patients had abnormal X-rays as well as abnormal thermograms. Third, Karpman hypothesizes that symptomatic or asymptomatic individuals demonstrating abnormal thermograms of low back region may be afflicted with what he termed "unstable backs" and may be more susceptible to low back strain than those demonstrating normal thermograms. Lastly, in an additional study by Karpman of 44 patients who had thermograms after an acute traumatic injury of the lower back, Karpman found that 26 symptomatic patients exhibited abnormal thermograms but had normal X-rays. This suggests that thermography can be a useful indicator of low back musculoligamentous injury, if carried out in conjunction with expert clinical examinations.

Rajapakse, *et al.*[27] used thermography to monitor changes in disease activity in arthritic patients. He found that thermography could accurately and reproducibly distinguish between normal and inflamed elbow, ankle, and knee joints. However, he found that thermography could not satisfactorily distinguish normal from inflamed joints in the dorsal hand and fingers in rooms controlled at 20°C. Even among normals, these small joints of the hands exhibited an increase in the thermographic index after the baseline temperature was established. Rajapakse theorizes that this process might have been due to a rebound vasodilation response following initial vasoconstriction, which might be predictable in normal vasculature after entering a cold environment. Rajapakse suggests that the accuracy and reproducibility of thermographic assessment of the small joints of the hand might be improved by using a higher room temperature and thus reduce the rebound vasodilator response in digital cutaneous vasculature.

Gautherie[18] reported the failure of some studies to demonstrate the effectiveness of thermographic assessment, such as in the Breast Cancer Detection Demonstration Project (BCCDP). Gautherie concludes that this and other previous programs did not succeed because they did not require systematic training of the individuals who were required to evaluate the thermographic findings, nor did the programs provide a common and appropriate protocol for evaluating the thermograms. Gautherie, in his own study of the effectiveness of thermography in detecting breast disease, suggests the developments of a computer-assisted interpretation system and computerized protocol that leads the thermographic assessor through a series of specific questions in consistent order that take into consideration both absolute temperature differences between contralateral body parts and changes in thermographic patterns. Numerical scores can then be assigned to each score related to the ultimate thermal class for the patient (5 classes, ranging from TH-1 for normal to TH-5 for highly abnormal).

9.6. An Example of the Use of Computerized Thermography for Musicians With Performance-Related Pain Syndromes

Five musicians (3 violinists, 1 violist, 1 pianist) affected by performance-related pain syndromes were examined clinically by one of the authors (Lee) and photographed thermographically with the assistance of the other author (Kella) at a CT clinic.*

In terms of the health-illness continuum (Figure 1), these musicians self-reported as having an overt injury of the upper extremities, shoulders, or upper back. In terms of the IOM model of stress (Figure 2), these musicians had experienced a potential stressor, namely, Fry's third cause of overuse injury (intensity times duration, due to the perceived demands of an unusually important musical performance).[5] The consequent experiences of pain were of such intensity and duration in each case that the subjects sought medical assistance.

The clinical examination consisted of a complete history and physical assessment prior to the computerized thermographic (CT) examination.

For the CT examination, patients were advised to avoid excessive sun exposure, physical

---

* Computerized Thermography Center, 25, Central Park West, Suite 1R, New York, NY 10023

therapy, and medical treatment of the affected areas for 24 hours. To avoid vasoactive effects of hot or cold beverages, the subjects were required not to eat, drink, or smoke during the last 2 hours before the CT scanning. The subjects were then allowed to equilibrate for 20 minutes to the temperature of the CT examination room, which was maintained at an average of 20.0°C, +/- 1.0°C.

The CT equipment consists of an infrared scanning camera, a microprocessor system, a video display unit, and a color printer. The camera is capable of detecting 15,000 separate thermal measurements during a 5-second scan of body surfaces within its view. The microprocessor can record and display this information in the form of a thermal map, which is color-coded to represent 16 possible body-temperature levels for each individual thermal measurement. The microprocessor can enlarge a selected portion of the video display to show detail, or provide a thermal overview of the entire photographed body area. In addition, the microprocessor can visually bracket selected body areas from each display, and determine the highest, lowest, and average temperature for each bracketed area. This computer-assisted procedure allows for convenient thermal comparisons of contralateral body areas. A modified camera is used to photograph and permanently record the video display and a printer is used to produce a color printout version of the thermal map.

The subjects were photographed under four conditions, described below. Immediately after each condition, the subjects were photographed from four views. The CT examination lasted approximately 60 minutes for each subject. The conditions and views are shown below:

Four Conditions:
a. after temperature adaptation to CT room ("baseline equilibrium");
b. after maintaining for 5 minutes a posture that produces pain syndrome ("static stress");
c. after simulating for 5 minutes the movements of instrumental performance ('active stress");
d. after performing for 5 minutes on musical instrument ("contact stress" or "active performance").

Four Views:
a. anterior view of upper body with arms and fingers extended;
b. posterior view of upper body;
c. right side of torso with right arm flexed;
d. left side of torso with left arm flexed.

The resulting CT photographs were analyzed. Selected contralateral body areas were bracketed, and each was measured for lowest, highest, and average temperatures within the boundaries of each bracket.

Figure 4 indicates the temperature of the contralateral body areas of each musician following the first and last of the four conditions (after "baseline equilibrium" and "active performance"). Figure 4 indicates (a) that CT can accurately measure temperature differences between contralateral body areas before and after musical performance, and (b) that these temperature differences are in some cases significantly greater than the average skin-temperature variations among normals (see Figure 3). The body areas that show the greatest differences post-performance among the violin and viola subjects were the right shoulder (which averaged 1.05°C warmer than the left shoulder), and the left hand (which averaged 1.65°C warmer than the right hand. The pianist exhibited pre- and post-performance temperature differences that were within normal skin-temperature variations.

Violinist 2 measured the greatest pre-performance differences between contralateral body parts (right upper arm warmer than left upper arm by 0.7°C; right forearm, by 0.5°C; right wrist, by 2.3°C; and right hand, by 3.2°C).

Figure 5 depicts the "thermographic profile" in graph form of Violinist 3 following the first and last conditions, and is an example of "thermographic profiling" that could be used to assess temperature differences pre-and post-performance among musicians.

Figures 6a and 6b show the original CT photographs of Violinist 3 taken immediately following the first and last conditions.

The diagnostic evaluations based on the entire CT series of photographs for each of the five musicians are shown below:

Violinist 1: "[In this series of thermograms,] there are areas consistent with a myofascial pain syndrome centered over the insertion of the lateral left trapezius as well as the right T6-T8 parvertebral muscles. With use, there was a normal response to exercise with an increase in the metabolism of the active muscles, including the right deltoid, right lateral epicondylar and right infraspinatus muscles. The right acromioclavicular joint becomes inflamed after use and this may represent a potential area of osteoarthritis. There was a decrease in temperature of the right hand after playing; this may be of vascular and/or neurogenic disorder, most likely at the wrist. Also noted was a decrease in temperature of the fingers bilaterally with continued playing; this may also be of vascular and/or neurogenic origin. There is no evidence of a radiculopathic process."

Violinist 2: "There is a consistent finding of increased heat production of the right infraspinatus and right deltoid. This is consistent with a myofascial dysfunction syndrome of the infraspinatus and the associated paravertebral scapular stabilizing musculature. This can lead to altered biomechanics of the right glenohumeral joint. The right distal bicep demonstrates a consistent increase in heat production compared to the left. This is consistent with a new injury to the right distal bicep or a fibrocytic process in the left distal bicep. The consistent increase in heat production centered over the left cervical region along with a decrease in heat production of the ipsilateral arm at rest is consistent with a root irritation on that side, but may also be indicative of a vascular or peripheral neurologic process. The left forearm muscles demonstrated a marked increase in heat production with use. This may be indicative of an overuse syndrome wherein there is no acute injury in the muscle but it becomes weakened and painful with use."

Violinist 3: [After active performance,] "the posterior upper extremities demonstrate an area of marked increased heat production overlying the right rhomboid and the paravertebral (T-4) region, of 0.5°C. Also noted is an increased temperature in the left posterior fingers (2nd, 3rd, 4th fingers) of 1.0°C compared to the right. The anterior upper extremities demonstrate an increased temperature centered over the right anterior deltoid (0.6°C), an increase in temperature of the left fingers (0.9°C) and an increase in the left proximal thumb of 0.8°C. The view of the lateral upper extremities show the right lateral deltoid with increased heat production of 1.2°C. The right lateral upper epicondylar region demonstrates an increased heat production of 0.3°C as compared to the left. However, the left wrist demonstrates an increased heat production of 0.7°C when compared to the right. These films, over the series of stresses, demonstrate a consistent pattern of inflammation in the right extensor forearm muscles, including the tendons into the wrist. The varying shoulder and rhomboid increases in temperatures may be work-related. Although a palmar increase in temperature may be work-related, this may also be related to a vascular or neurologic process.

Violist: "There is a consistent increased heat production located in the right levator scapulae region. This is consistent with a myofascial pain dysfunction syndrome, and may represent an old injury with current inflammation. There is a consistent area of the left posterolateral upper extremity which demonstrates decreased heat production. This may be of neurologic, vascular, or soft tissue origin, including an old injury with fibrocytis, and needs clinical correlation. An additional region of consistent heat production is overlying the right infrasponatus. This also may be of soft tissue origin encompassing a myofascial pain and dysfunction syndrome. With an applied work load the left hand and forearm demonstrate a marked increase in temperature which is most likely due to a myofascial pain syndrome or overuse syndrome of that arm. There appears as if there is tendinitis of both flexor and extensor mechanisms of the left forearm and hand. Also noted in these series of films was that the right sternocleidomastoid muscle consistenly appears to have soft tissue irritation. There is no evidence of a radiculopathic process in these views."

Pianist: "These films do not demonstrate any consistent pattern of an overuse or an inflammatory process. The increase temperature in the left radial forearm was demonstrated only after the second static stress session. This may be vascular or neurologic origin and should be followed with clinical correlation."

10. SUGGESTIONS FOR FUTURE RESEARCH IN THE USE OF COMPUTERIZED THERMOGRAPHY FOR DIAGNOSING THE WORK-RELATED DISORDERS OF MUSICIANS

Suggestions for future research in the use of computerized thermography for diagnosing neuromuscular disorders of musicians include the following:

a. Determine the range of normal "thermographic profiles" (TP) for student and professional musicians after baseline equilibrium and after active performance, with differentiation of TP according to type of instrument, duration of performance, and type of music performed;

b. Compare the diagnostic effectiveness of computerized thermography versus other diagnostic approaches (i.e., X-ray, electrodiagnostic measurement) in differentiating symptomatic and asymptomatic musicians, and in identifying and locating the work-related disorders of the symptomatic performers;

c. Determine the "thermographic profile" for each stage in treatment and recovery of selected performance-related physical disorders of musicians.

	Cervical	Shoulders	Upper Back	Upper Arm	Forearm	Wrist	Finger
Violinst 1							
(BL) Left	33.0	31.3	31.6	30.6	30.0	29.9	31.5
Right	33.1	31.8	32.4	30.6	30.1	30.1	31.3
Diff.	0.1 Right	0.5 R	0.8 R	0.0	0.1 R	0.2 R	0.2 Left
(AP) Left	31.7	30.3	31.5	28.9	31.9	30.3	31.0
Right	31.1	32.3	31.9	29.3	32.0	29.3	28.1
Diff.	0.6 L	2.0 R	0.4 R	0.4 R	0.1 R	1.0 L	2.9 L
Violinst 2							
(BL) Left	32.5	31.4	32.2	30.7	30.6	26.1	25.5
Right	32.2	31.4	32.1	31.4	31.1.	28.4	28.7
Diff.	0.3 L	0.0	0.1 L	0.7 R	0.5 R	2.3 R	3.2 R
(AP) Left	32.5	30.5	31.9	29.7	32.7	---	32.1
Right	32.2	31.9	32.4	31.4	32.2	---	30.8
Diff.	0.3 L	1.4 R	0.5 R	1.6 R	0.5 L	---	1.3 L
Violinist 3							
(BL) Left	31.6	30.7	30.7	30.7	29.1	29.6	30.3
Right	31.6	30.8	30.4	30.7	29.3	29.7	30.1
Diff.	0.0	0.1 R	0.3 L	0.0	0.2 R	0.1 R	0.2 L
(AP) Left	31.6	31.0	31.4	31.2	30.2	30.6	29.0
Right	31.4	32.2	30.9	31.1	30.5	30.8	27.9
Diff.	0.2 L	1.2 R	0.5 R	0.1 L	0.3 R	0.2 R	1.1 L
Violist							
(BL) Left	33.0	31.3	31.6	30.6	30.0	29.9	31.5
Right	33.1	31.8	32.4	30.6	31.0	30.1	31.3
Diff.	0.1 R	0.5 R	0.8 R	0.0	0.1 R	0.2 R	0.2 R
(AP) Left	31.7	30.3	31.5	28.9	31.9	30.3	31.0
Right	31.1	32.3	31.9	29.3	32.0	29.3	28.1
Diff.	0.6 R	2.0 R	0.4 R	0.4 R	0.1 R	0.3 R	0.4 R
Pianist							
(BL) Left	32.0	31.5	31.2	31.6	31.0	31.0	30.0
Right	32.1	31.6	31.3	31.5	31.1	31..3	30.4
Diff.	0.1 R	0.1 R	0.1 R	0.1 L	0.3 R	0.3 R	0.4 R
(AP) Left	31.6	30.5	30.2	30.5	30.5	30.3	30.0
Right	31.6	30.7	30.3	30.0	30.0	29.2	28.9
Diff.	0.0	0.2 R	0.1 R	0.5 L	0.5 L	1.1 L	0.1 L

BL = Baseline Temperatures AP = After Active Performance Diff. = Difference between Right and Left body areas in each condition (temperature differences greater than average variations are underlined)

Figure 4: Averaged Thermograph Temperatures of Five Musicians (3 Violinists, 1 Violist, 1 Pianist) Under Two Conditions (Baseline Equilibrium and After Active Performance) According to Contralateral Body Areas.

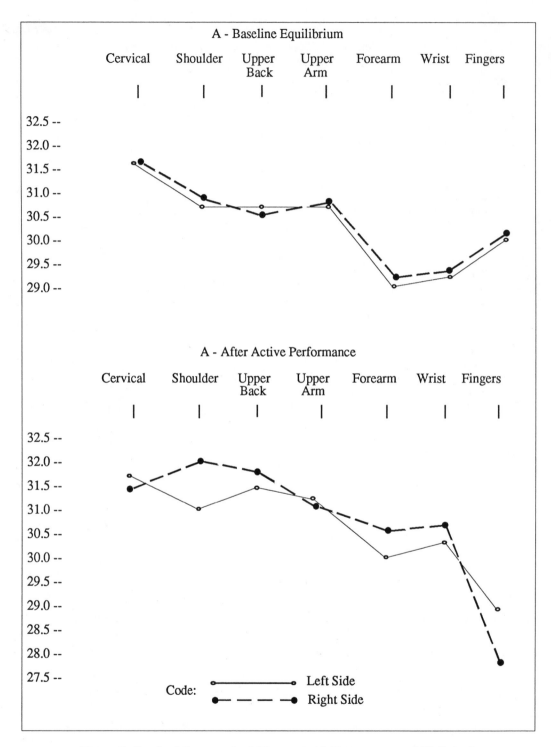

Figure 5: Graph of Computerized Thermograph Temperatures of Violinist 3

Mathew H. M. Lee, John J. Kella

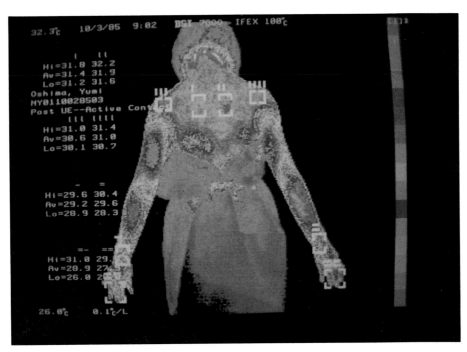

Active Performance Measurements of Posterior Upper Extremities

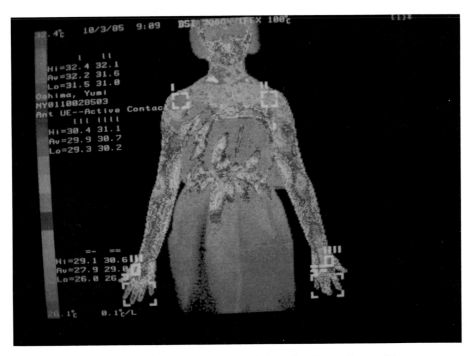

Active Performance Measurements of Anterior Upper Extremities

Figure 6a: Thermograms of Violinist "After Active Performance"

Computerized Thermography and Other Technological Aids in the Diagnosis of   53
Musicians' Neuromuscular Disorders

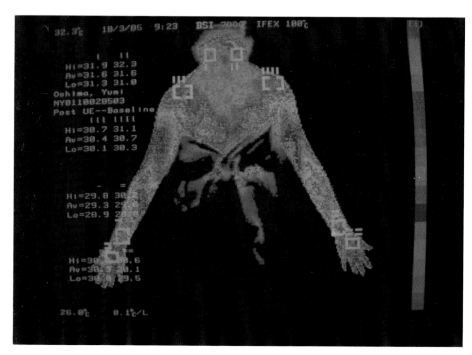

Baseline Measurements of Posterior Upper Extremities

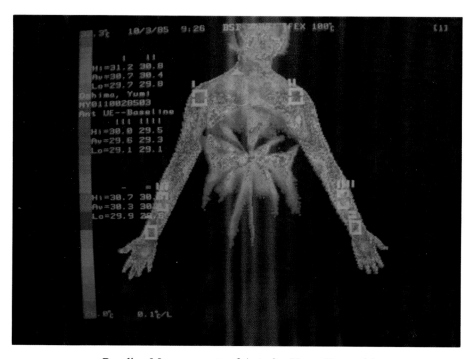

Baseline Measurements of Anterior Upper Extremities

Figure 6b: Thermograms of Violinist "After Baseline Equilibrium"

Mathew H. M. Lee, John J. Kella

REFERENCES

1 Stone, W.H.: On wind pressure in the human lungs during performance on wind instruments. *Philosophical Magazine*, (series 4), 1874, p. 48

2 MEDLINE: Computer search by DIALOGUE of Medline and Psycinfo at New York University on topics related to performing arts medicine.

3 Brandfonbrener, A.G.: To celebrate a new journal. *Med Probls Perf Artists*, 1986, **1**, p. 1

4 Kella, J.J.: Experts study the role of stress in the arts. *International Musician*, October 1985, **84**, p. 20.

5 Fry, H.J.H.: What's in a name: The musicians' anthology of misuse. *Medical Probs Perf Artists*, 1986, **1**(1), pp. 36-38.

6 Harman, S.E.: Occupational diseases of sintrumental musicians: Literature review. *Maryland State Med J*, 1982, **31**, pp. 39-42.

7 Rogers, E. S.: *Human Ecology and Health: Information for Administrators*. New York: Macmillan, 1960.

8 Itoh, M., Lee, M.H.M.: Epidemiology of pain. *Bull LA Neurol Soc*, 1971, **44**, pp. 14-31.

9 Elliott, G.R., Eisdorfer, C.: *Stress and Human Health: Analysis and Implications of Research. A Study by the Institute of Medicine*. New York: Springer, New York Academy of Sciences, 1982.

10 Rossol, M.: *Stage Fright: Health and Safety in the Theater*. New York: Center for Occupational Hazards, 1986.

11 Parisien, J.A.: Shoulder arthroscopy. *Bull of the Hosp for Joint Diseases*, 1983, **43**, pp. 56-69.

12 Karpman, H.L., Knebel, A., Semel, C.J., Cooper, J.: Clinical studies in thermography. *Arch of Environ Health*, 1970, **20**, pp. 412-417.

13 Strand, F.L.: *Physiology: A Regulatory Systems Approach*, 2nd Edition. New York: Macmillan, 1983.

14 Lenman, J.A.R., Ritchie, A.E.: *Clinical Electromyography*, 2nd Edition. Kent, England: Pitman Medical, 1978.

15 Cohen, H.L., Brumlik, J.: *A Manual of Electroneuromyography*. New York:: Hoeber Medical Division, Harper & Row, 1968.

16 Dasco, M.M., Lee M.H.H.: Rehabilitation after major surgery and serious trauma. In: Powers, H. (ed.): *Surgery of the Aged and Debilitated Patient*. Phila.: W.B. Saunders, 1968, pp. 552-579.

17 Menon, M., Lee, M.H.H.: Clinical electromyography: Principles and diagnostic applications. *J Indian Medical Assoc*, 1969, **52**, pp. 369-375.

18 Gautherie, M.: Thermobiological assessment of benign and malignant breast diseases. *Am J Ob & Gyn*, 1983, **147**, pp. 861-869.

19 Uematsu, S.: Thermographic imaging of cutaneous sensory segment in patients with peripheral nerve injury. *J of Neurosurgery*, 1985, **62**, pp. 716-720.

20 Goodman, P.H., Heaslet, M.W., Pagliano, J.W., Rubin, B.D.: Stress fracture diagnosis by computer-assisted thermography. *The Physician and Sportsmedicine*, 1985, **13**, pp. 114-132.

21 Bacon, P.A., Collins, A.J., Ring, F.R., Cosh, J.A.: Thermography in the assessment of inflammatory arthritis. *Clinics in Rheumatic Diseases*, 1976, **2**, pp. 51-65.

22 Bird, H.A., Calguneri, M., Leatham, P.A., Wright, V.: Measurements of temperature in the arthritic hand. *Rheumatology and Rehab*, 1980, **19**, pp. 205-211.

23 Ghys, R.: Thermography in peripheral vascular disorders. *Belgian J of Radiology*, 1974, **57**, pp. 263-272.

24 Wallin, L., Albrechtsson, U., Fagher, B., Lagerstedt, C., Larusdottir, H., Olsson, C.-G., Westling, H., Oquist, B.: Thermography in the diagnosis of deep venous thrombosis. *Acta Med Scand*, 1983, **214**, pp. 15-20.

25 Carron, H., Weller, R.M.: Treatment of post-traumatic sympathetic dystrophy. *Advances in Neurology*, 1974, **4**, pp. 485-490.

26 Hendler, N., Uematsu, S., Long, D.: Thermography in psychogenic pain patients. *Psychosomatics*, 1982, **23**, pp. 283-287.

27 Lindhagen, A., Bergqvist, D., Hallbook, T., Lindroth, D.: After-exercise thermography compared to strain-gauge plethysmography and pressure measurements to detect deep venous insufficiency. *Scand J of Laboratory Investigations*, 1983, **43**, pp. 293-295.

28 Rajapakse, C., Grennan, D.M., Jones, C., Wilkinson, L., Jayson, M.: Thermography in the assessment of peripheral joint inflammation: A reevaluation. *Rheumatology and Rehab*, 1981, **20**, pp. 81-87.

APPLICATION OF LEARNING THEORY TO MUSICAL TRAINING

Barry R. Dworkin

ABSTRACT

The principles of modern learning theory can be used to enhance the effectiveness of musical skill training. A discussion of instrumental, or trial and error learning, with particular emphasis on motivation, delineates these principles and applies them to the conventional teaching situation. The application of learning theory to computer aided musical instruction is described with a sample scenario of how this kind of training could proceed using an electronic keyboard, a microcomputer and a voice synthesizer linked through the industry standard MIDI interface.

INTRODUCTION

The emergence of high quality electronic instruments has revolutionary implications for the production of music, and for the training of musicians. The declining critical enthusiasm for technical virtuosity on the concert stage could be a reflection of a fundamental change in the aesthetics of musical performance. What photography did for painting at the end of the 19th century, digital electronic sound technology may do for music, as we approach the end of the 20th. Conceptualization, expression, and interpretation will be valued more, and actual physical and technical manipulation of the instrument, less. The possibility of a musical career will be open to people with a different range of abilities: handicapped individuals previously limited in developing their musical talents, will be able to make use of special interfaces which will be easily adapted to digital electronic musical instruments.

Historically musicians have availed themselves of technology. At the time of their invention the multi-valved horn, the pianoforte and the pipe organ were among the most technologically advanced mechanisms. Musical reproduction has similarly incorporated the latest technology. The mechanical music box, player piano, gramophone, magnetic tape and high fidelity reproduction have all been examples of the technical state of the art. More recently musicians were among the first professionals outside of the sciences to use analog and digital computers. The Columbia-Princeton Electronic Music Center employed advanced micro-computer instrumentation twenty years before it became commonplace in scientific laboratories on those two campuses. Digital recording technology was employed by musicians almost at the same time that digital storage methods achieved sufficient capacity. The digital compact disk – a technological tour-de-force incorporating the most recent electromechanical, electro-optical, signal processing and microcomputer technology – has been in general use for nearly four years, and only in the past one year has it been adapted for more general data storage requirements. New microprocessors – the hearts of microcomputers – are incorporated into advanced digitally sampling keyboard instruments before they are used in advanced laboratory instruments.

All of this makes good sense. Music is a highly complex patterned signal and the analytical and discriminative capabilities of the human ear are extraordinary. While there is little doubt that the sound of the very best acoustic instruments, such as the Stradivarius violins will be perfectly duplicated by digital electronic instruments in the near future – indeed the technology already exists – this fact is less exciting than the prospect of the electronic "Super-strad" with a potential for extension of tonal quality into realms yet undreamt. Just as the great composers of the 18th and 19th centuries learned to write for the pianoforte, clarinet and bassoon, the great composers of the late 20th and 21st centuries will produce brilliant humanistic compositions for the new opto-electronic instruments.

With music performance pressing to the technological frontier, it is somewhat incongruous that the methodology of teaching instrumental technique has not changed much since the 17th century. The beginning student has at very most an hour or so (and usually less) per week of efficient practice, which is carefully and critically guided by a professional music teacher. The student may work independently without external guidance for an indeterminate number of additional hours, but the usefulness of independent practice depends on a developed critical capability, and most students do not achieve a useful degree of independent judgment until many years into their training. This chapter will suggest new methods for bringing musical training into the 20th century by incorporating the principles of modern learning theory into the teaching situation.

While behavioral theory has important implications for all types of musical training, characteristics of the conventional student-teacher interaction limit the efficient application of learning principles to the traditional teaching situation. The music teacher has limited time available for each student, particularly beginners, and the actual duration of closely supervised practice rarely exceeds an hour per week; the remainder of a student's practice is self-monitored.

Because beginners have a difficult time discriminating correct from incorrect technique, at least from the perspective of learning theory, individual practice without direct supervision is at best very inefficient. The delay between a particular behavior and reinforcing feedback intended to correct or encourage that behavior is a critical determinate of the efficiency of the learning paradigm. With delays in presenting feedback of greater than a second or two the feedback or reinforcer probably is without any direct effect upon the behavior. The minimum time a good teacher requires to recognize a notable behavior and bring it to the student's attention is, under the most ideal circumstances, barely within the critical temporal window of optimal reinforcement. These facts limit the usefulness to conventional musical training of the most critical insights of learning theory; consequently it is neither surprising nor deplorable that pedagogical training of music educators traditionally has been conducted without even the most rudimentary exposure to modern behavioral learning concepts.

INSTRUMENTAL OR TRIAL AND ERROR LEARNING THEORY

Near the turn of the century Edward Thorndike,[1] one of the founders of educational psychology, performed a simple and informative experiment which demonstrated the necessity for relative immediate critical evaluation in the development of skills. He blindfolded groups of students and had them draw a straight line exactly 3 inches long for extended sessions. He found that no matter how much practice the students had they did not improve their performance no matter how numerous the repetitions. This showed very clearly that learning a skill is intrinsically different from developing muscular strength: simple use of the organs of a skill does not improve their accuracy. In order to improve it is necessary that sensory and motor divisions of the nervous system interact with one another in a specific organized manner. In fact, later researchers found that if a person is informed each time after his attempt to draw a 3 inch line whether it is too long or too short, he will improve with repetition.[2]

The sensory-motor interaction has been studied extensively in the 20th century and is usually termed "trial and error"[3] or "instrumental learning."[4] The basic components of this process are (1) the behavior or response, (2) the criterion and (3) the reinforcement or feedback stimulus.

Barry R. Dworkin

The response is the unit of behavior or activity which is to be modified in the instrumental learning procedure. While it can be a very elementary movement like an eye blink or twitch of the thumb, it may also be a relatively complex sequence of movements. However, subsuming a pattern of behavior under the rubric of a single response is only useful if the pattern tends to occur as a coherent unit. Operationally this means that when the first element of the sequence occurs the probability of the second occurring is significantly increased, and that with each additional element the probability of the subsequent element in the sequence becomes greater.

A response pattern can be innate or anatomically determined in the genetic code. The gait or sequence of leg movements involved in walking, running or jumping is probably largely specified at birth. Similarly certain types of coordinated muscle movements involved in grasping objects or swallowing food are necessarily present at a very early age and are probably innate patterns, which can be usefully considered as single responses. But a pattern need not be innate or specified by the genetic code to have many of the characteristics of a unitary response; furthermore the components of biologically innate patterns can sometimes be dissociated by learning. The various bowing techniques used by string players are highly integrated patterns which probably fit the above definition, but it is obvious for several reasons that they are not biologically innate; dancers frequently begin with the common patterns of movement and carefully modify them to achieve special effects.

The second major element of the instrumental learning procedure is the criterion. The criterion is the desired behavior, and the response is always compared to or measured against a criterion. In the usual musical training situation the response is what is actually performed by the student and the criterion is an image, held by the teacher, of a somewhat different, presumably better, response. For example, in violin bow technique the position of the right elbow is very critical, and most beginning students have difficulty consistently achieving a satisfactory position. Every good teacher knows the "perfect" elbow position he would like the student to achieve eventually; however, the "perfect" position is different from the criterion: the criterion lies between the perfect position and what the student is doing. This compromise reflects the experienced teacher's wisdom. Since it is practically impossible for a beginning student to assume a perfect position, the teacher must initially expect less and concentrate his attention on changes that are within reach.

The reinforcer is the last major element of the instrumental learning procedure. When the student performs a **response** which meets the teacher's **criterion**, the teacher gives the student a special signal. This signal, the **reinforcer**, contains important information: It says, "You have done it correctly." While it is informative, the reinforcer is not simply information, more significantly, it is crucial to the student's motivation. The relationship between motivation and reinforcement is the most important yet least understood assumption of any instrumental learning procedure. Motivation is most simply defined as a need, and the reinforcer is an event which in some way satisfies the need.

MOTIVATION AND SKILL TRAINING

There are simple so-called primary motivations such as thirst or hunger which are shared in common by all complex animals. Thirst is the need for water and hunger is the need for food. When thirsty, water is a reinforcer; when hungry, food is a reinforcer. For humans, motivations can be very much more complex and quite distant from readily identifiable biological necessities. For example, humans may have a need for the respect or admiration of others, and some may even have a specific need to create beautiful things or express complex thoughts. These needs, like thirst and hunger, are satisfied by specific activities.

If a motivation or need is present and some procedure, or set of behaviors, is known to satisfy it promptly and arbitrarily the procedure may be useful as a reinforcer. While the ordinary biological function of a reinforcer is to modify those functions which address specific or intrinsic needs, psychologists have found that if certain conditions are met, reinforcers can also modify a variety of behaviors unrelated to the need that the reinforcer satisfies. The most important condition for a reinforcer to work effectively is a specific temporal relationship between the behavior and the reinforcer. This relationship is called contiguity: if a behavior, performed in the presence of a need or motivation, is followed very soon by a reinforcer which satisfies the need, that behavior is typically strengthened. This fact has been demonstrated repeatedly in experiments with both humans and lower animals. For example, children with cerebral palsy can be taught to stabilize their heads using an opportunity to watch television as a reinforcer.[5] In this therapeutically useful procedure the child wears a special hat containing motion sensors. The sensors are connected to an electronic circuit which measures head position and controls a video tape recorder. When the child maintains an acceptable head position for a predetermined time interval, the recorder begins playing an enjoyable program; the program plays as long as the child maintains a satisfactory position. With this procedure the child gradually improves head control.

In this instrumental learning situation the **response** is head motion, the **criterion** is an improved head position, and the **reinforcer** is an opportunity to watch an entertaining video program. A similar sequence of events or process can be identified in conventional musical training except that a music teacher replaces an electronic device to monitor the behavior and deliver reinforcements. The teacher observes the student's behavior while waiting for an improvement; when the improvement occurs the teacher verbally praises the student. The response is the specific activity which the teacher and student are working on, such as shifting position on a cello, the criterion is a noticeable improvement in the way the student performs the activity and the reinforcer is praise. Why is praise a reinforcer? It may be that the student needs the teacher's approval, as a confirmation of ability, or it may offer relief from the anxiety about an upcoming performance. Whatever the need, if it exists and is satisfied by the teachers words, the effects will be to strengthen the behavior that immediately preceded it. In this example that would be a more correct shift. In contrast if there is no need to respond to the teacher's words, then the information content of the teacher's criticism or approval alone will not modify the student's behavior. This point is very important; teachers often complain that they repeatedly correct the technique of very capable students without any effect on their subsequent playing. Intuitively, they know that when the student is not "motivated" the instruction is useless. The role of motivation like many other aspects of behavioral theory is implicitly understood by experienced instructors and have been incorporated into their methods of teaching; however, very few are able to articulate their teaching principles into explicit procedures. Thus motivation is often considered to be a general somewhat nebulous feature of an individual student's personality, rather than a momentary need which should and can be used to further the development of specific technical skills.

Sometimes motivation and the response to be learned are closely related. For example, in animal experiments it has been shown that rats will learn to lick at a water tube for a drink, more easily if they are thirsty; training a pigeon to peck at a key for grain will proceed more rapidly when the birds are reduced to 80% of their normal body weight. People learn rather easily not to bite their tongues painfully or to avoid pressure on a sprained ankle, but they are slower to learn not to smoke, overeat, or wear seatbelts. Thus, for certain pairs of needs and responses, because of a natural anatomical juxtaposition, the occurrence of the response automatically satisfies the need. For example, the connection between scratching a mosquito bite and the temporary reduction in itching is so intimate that no one has to be taught how to do it; similarly for eating and hunger, drinking and thirst, etc. These responses lead with high reliability to rapid satisfaction of specific needs. The promptness and reliability which characterize these innate learning linkages is not easily simulated in the ordinary pedagogical situation. To approximate the efficiency of these natural paradigms it is necessary to have a totally dedicated, errorless, omnipresent instructor, or to

Barry R. Dworkin

create within the student both a strong need or motivation to perform correctly and the critical ability to know immediately when he has done so. However, for the beginning music student the first goal is remote, and except for the occasional genius, the second impossible.

Motivation is necessary if reinforcement is to be effective. A reinforcer must be able to satisfy a contemporary need promptly and accurately. The structure of motivation is probably the most complex area of behavioral theory. Most of our basic knowledge of learning comes from the study of animals in the laboratory environment, and human behavior differs from animals most dramatically with regard to motivation; consequently our scientific understanding of behavior is most deficient in this regard. In some sense our best understanding of the issues of human motivation comes not from scientific experiments, but from the experience of clinical investigators such as Freud,[6] Adler,[7] Allport,[8] Rogers[9] and McClelland.[10]

Motivation is based upon need; while simple animals have a few needs which relate directly to survival and reproduction, the need structure of humans is much more complex. For most individuals in developed societies food, water, warmth, etc. are not really needs because they are more or less guaranteed to everyone, but the process of socialization develops other needs. Most people desire prestige, possessions, self-respect, independence, and aesthetic satisfaction, while some individuals have additional needs to explore, create and discover. We have learned by three different kinds of observations that these needs exist: we perceive them in ourselves, other people speak, write, paint, or sing about them, and, possibly most convincingly, we can see that under the appropriate circumstances behaviors which efficiently satisfy these needs will develop and persist. This last point is the most important for the successful application of learning theory to teaching: motivation must be present at the time that learning takes place.

In lower animals the kind of motivation present is usually closely related to the kind of learning that can be achieved for simple survival responses. However, for the complex and comparatively abstract behaviors involved in learning musical skills it is unlikely that humans have evolved particular response-motivation linkages. Motivation which is not directly related to accomplishing a specific behavior is referred to as extrinsic motivation and must be developed in musical and other kinds of training, but first the needs must be either identified or developed on an individual basis. Following that identification a symbol for the need and its satisfaction, sometimes called a secondary reinforcer, must also be developed.

Intrinsic motivation, on the other hand, has certain technical as well as "philosophical" advantages. If a student genuinely enjoys hearing perfect scales, then he has a need which can be directly satisfied by the behavior of practicing the scales and getting them correct. Such reinforcement is prompt, reliable and self-generated. Most of us believe that it is more desirable to be motivated by an appreciation of the result than by some ulterior goal. Industrial employers have begun to place greater emphasis on employees taking "pride" in the quality of their workmanship rather than looking only to the paycheck or day off, and we all talk about getting "satisfaction" from our jobs.

Sociologically this kind of emphasis on intrinsic motivation emerged dramatically in the early 1970s when it seemed as though there was an entire generation in America wandering around, looking for some occupation which would be intrinsically pleasing and effortless. Many hypotheses have been proffered to explain their behavior, ranging from the relatively new easy availability of illicit drugs, to a sense of dissatisfaction with the status quo and increased social commitment growing out of the political activism of the War years. While these were certainly important factors some more simple and less dramatic aspects of their early experience may have also influenced the expectations and attitudes of this generation. The "learning should be fun" idea which dominated educational dogma during the late 50s and early 60s represented a similar solipsistic orientation. This movement manifested itself in a range of forms from the modest introduction of colored ink and a few cartoons into social studies and math workbooks, to a comprehensive doctrine stating that "genuine" learning was not possible unless all of the student's satisfaction was derived directly from the sensory-motor experience of the task. While entire schools were established based upon these untested principles, many more students received the message in a significant but less concentrated form in traditional public and private educational institutions through teachers who were introduced to these appealing avant garde concepts as part of their training in educational theory.

Intrinsic motivation derived directly from the behavior being learned is certainly not inferior to extrinsic or socially conditioned motivation, in fact, it is probably always more effective. However, if the student does not happen to be motivated by specific intrinsic features of the learning situation, a reasonable alternative to undertaking the complex and long process of acculturation to those features, at least in the short run, is the introduction of extrinsic motivational devices.

PRACTICE AND SKILL TRAINING

To achieve rapid and robust learning of any skill, next in priority to motivation, is the scheduling of practice to achieve efficient utilization of time and development of good habits. In an automated teaching environment, practice and active instruction are indistinguishable. However, even the conventional learning situation can benefit from the introduction of specific learning principles and some limited technology.

Individual practice is certainly the most essential component to the development of musical skill, yet, it is almost always by necessity left to chance. Individual practice in conventional musical training is by definition unsupervised, and the student is left to develop his own procedures within the broad advisories set down by the teacher during the formal lessons.

Efficient time utilization is the first consideration: the duration of a practice session has no meaning without a sense of the density of activity in the session, and intense, extended activity is valueless without direction and feedback. These relative self-evident statements can, however, lead to incorrect conclusions without a proper appreciation of the sequential response dependence that they imply. Sophisticated, enlightened teachers will sometimes advise students not to practice if they do not feel self-motivated. This advice may be appropriate for advanced students or adults with well established discipline, but for the child or adolescent the message may be completely misunderstood. In any behavioral situation, stimuli, circumstances, and previous responses will determine the probability of subsequent responses. For example, the decision as to whether to watch a VCR movie or read a book will be strongly influenced by the relative accessibility of the movie cassette and book. Everyone who has been to college knows that the advantage of studying in the library is that there is nothing much else to do in a quiet, bare study room. Daydreaming, doodling, or counting the tiles in the ceiling are possibilities, but far less attractive than talking to a friend, watching television or playing cards. To carry things a step farther, a criterion of performance which takes into account quality of effort, rather than simply duration of the activity, will further reduce the probability of engaging in extraneous responses. For example, a daily sojourn in the library, which is defined in terms of the number of physics problems completed rather than a certain number of hours spent, will probably result in more efficient behavior.

Nevertheless, it is of utmost importance that the activity be approached carefully and thoughtfully: the physics problems must be done correctly, the scales must be played accurately, the concerto must be practiced by stopping to correct each error, etc. However, while this assertion of the importance of quality of practice is undeniable, it is equally necessary to recognize that behavioral shaping is a gradual and progressive process. The shortest path from the initial undesirable behavior to the final desirable behavior may not be direct, and may not always lead through an obvious series of increasingly more desirable states – often the route is circuitous and sometimes apparently antithetical to the goal. For example, if a novice picks up a tennis racquet and begins to return serves, he may be able to successfully intercept four or five out of ten, but if he continues to employ his intuitive approach to holding and swinging the racquet he will probably never, no matter how much he practices, become a good tennis player. Suppose that following his first try he decides to take up the game more seriously and begins lessons. In the first lesson he will probably be taught the "proper" stance and grip. Paradoxically, he will probably do worse in actual number of serves returned when he first begins using this orthodox swing: he will find that it "feels awkward" and requires more effort and concentration than his old autodidactic approach. However, if he persists he will eventually appreciate that this "awkward grip" was the most direct route to a better game. The concept of "form" in athletics is an implicit acknowledgement that there is a need for an intermediate basis for evaluating performance **prior** to the ultimate criterion of competitive success.

Because of the above considerations the decision about which response patterns should be shaped and in what order, should be based on an accurate and coherent analysis of the requirements for progression from novice to expert, rather than abstract philosophical or pedagogical concepts. In this vein, I would argue that a student cannot practice well until he is playing and holding the instrument, and cannot play at all until he has entered the practice room. This position in no way conflicts with valid ideas concerning the importance of quality in contrast to quantity of practice effort. In fact, by critically monitoring performance and providing the student with a continuous accurate and objective assessment of variations in technical accuracy, a behavioral approach to teaching musical technique supports a commitment to insuring that practice time is efficiently utilized. Being in the practice room, touching and manipulating the instrument, playing the specified exercises without inordinate procrastination, are all necessary responses in the sequence which leads to effective and efficient practice. How to insure that this type of structured regime will eventually lead to self-motivated independent musicianship is another much more complicated problem, but it is almost certain that students who do not learn how to begin practicing will never become self-actualized musicians. What methods can help shape these initial but necessary elements of the practice sequence?

In the conventional learning situation the teacher has limited information with which to assess the density of practice activity of a given student. Progress and the student's report of session duration are the only data available. While some students may delight in practicing, one could argue that for most people working hard enough to achieve progress is not usually fun, at least in the beginning. Once some suitable place and schedule for practice are agreed upon, procrastination becomes the next problem. How is the teacher able to know whether or not the student is actually playing his instrument for the required time? There is a simple, convenient, and inexpensive way to obtain this information: the student can tape record his practice session. Duration, density and quality are the goals in the development of a successful practice routine. What the clock is to duration, the tape recorder is to density. By simply requiring that the recorder run only during actual playing and agreeing upon an appropriate amount of completed tape the student can be effectively reinforced for amount of playing rather than length of time.

The use of a tape recorder to monitor practice density is an example of how simple technology can be used to improve the conventional teaching situation. However, future musical training can go far beyond this type of simple device and create a new type of teacher-student interaction with the use of advanced computer-aided instruction.

AUTOMATED MUSICAL SKILL TRAINING

Until relatively recently the application of computer technology to music education has been hampered by a lack of necessary technology. Twenty years ago there were only a handful of digital music synthesizers in the world. The measurement of the behavior involved in the production of music on conventional acoustic instruments, and the evaluation of the music itself in real time, required elaborate and expensive electronic devices coupled to the fastest and most powerful state of the art computers. The production of electronic music using digital technology which was compatible with computers was similarly expensive and highly specialized. However, advances in microelectronic technology in the past ten years have reduced the cost of functionally equivalent computer equipment by at least two orders of magnitude. Simultaneously, with the economic incentive of a huge and profitable popular music industry as their market, several major electronics firms have begun to develop and produce a wide range of highly sophisticated low cost electronic musical instruments. These instruments now exceed the features and sound quality of the most sophisticated synthesizers of the previous decade.

The more advanced examples of the present crop of electronic keyboards, rhythm generators and sound modification devices include standardized interfaces for connection to specialized and general purpose microcomputers. Some of the specialized computers are marketed by the musical instrument manufacturers (e.g., Yamaha, Korg, Kawai) and contain built-in programs for automated control and synchronization of several electronic instruments, digital recording, mixing and modification of music generated on the instruments, and composition, editing and printing in standard musical notation of the scores.

Within the last two years general purpose microcomputers using some of the most advanced available microprocessors, with large memories and capable of high speed operation, have appeared in the general market at a cost of approximately one thousand dollars. Some of these machines incorporate standard (MIDI) electronic music interfaces as part of the base hardware configuration and almost all of the new personal computers have the standard interface available as an optional component at a modest additional cost. These general purpose microcomputers also have extensive and flexible high resolution graphics systems, which can be combined with inexpensive speech generation modules to provide detailed, explicit and intrinsically reinforcing informational feedback. Thus, with the components presently available, a complete hardware configuration consisting of a programmable keyboard and a compatible general purpose personal computer can be assembled for less than five thousand dollars. Furthermore, the system can be made to function without fabricating any additional special components.

In addition to appropriate hardware it is necessary to develop programs or software for musical training. At present the material available is limited in both scope and quality. Most music education software has been developed for hardware systems which have both inadequate computational power and insufficient musical quality to be genuinely useful, and in most cases the developers have not had sufficient background in either music training and theory, behavioral technology or both to achieve a product which can supplement and improve upon conventional training approaches. This situation is in sharp contrast to recent software for performance or editing, which runs on the most advanced equipment and has been designed with the benefit of input from a wide range of professional musicians.

Nevertheless, the development and increasing general availability of electronic instruments, digital sampling technology and low cost, high speed, large memory, graphics oriented personal computers will soon revolutionize musical training. These devices, when connected through the industry standard MIDI interface, are a ready substrate for sophisticated learning theory based musical training programs. These programs will allow a single teacher to direct and monitor the

Barry R. Dworkin

skill development of as many as twelve beginning students as though his or her individual attention were constantly focused on each one.

The MIDI interface allows two-way communication between a microcomputer and an electronic instrument. The computer can monitor the student's performance and either indicate that it is satisfactory or suggest corrections. The information can be presented to the student on either a standard color monitor, in natural language using an inexpensive voice synthesizer, or as music played directly on the student's electronic instrument.

For an example of how such a system would work: suppose a keyboard student is learning to play a C major scale with a simple crescendo. The computer would initiate the lesson by presenting the musical problem combined as a set of verbal instructions and a standard musical score. Assume that the student is young and just beginning to learn to read music. The program may start with a voice prompt such as:

"Today you are going to learn to play the C major scale. Please pay attention to the screen where you will see the notes of the scale."

The screen would then display the staff and notes. The program could then check to be sure that the student was paying attention by asking simple questions about the notation such as:

"Is this the treble or bass clef? If it is the treble clef, press high C; if it is the bass clef, press low C."

The student presses high A instead of C and the voice of the computer says:

"You correctly identified the clef as treble, but you pressed an A instead of a C. I will now sound the correct note and you try and find it on the keyboard."

(C is sounded on the keyboard through activation of the MIDI interface and the student finds it immediately)

"Good, you were probably not paying close attention before. You should know the notes very well by now – but let's just be sure. Press middle C."

"Good... now try high A and the A#... O.K. very good. Now we will continue with the C major scale. If you make an error the computer will signal you with this sound" (buzzing sound) "and you will not be able to continue the scale until you correct the note."

Since the MIDI interface can both monitor the student's behavior and control the keyboard all within hundredths of a second, the computer can respond instantaneously with a correction of an error, or a positive acknowledgement of correct performance. Because **efficient learning requires immediate reinforcement** this feature of speed and accuracy in evaluation and feedback, make the computer based trainer a superhuman supervisor of drill and routine practice, thus freeing the musician/educator's time for the more creative functions related to interpretation and aesthetic comprehension.

A well designed music training program would incorporate a continuous record of each individual student's past performance, thus, if the student in the above example had previously demonstrated mastery of the keyboard layout, the computer would have saved time and spared him the "humiliation" of determining if he could find high and low C. The MIDI computer controlled keyboard also provides some interesting and unique methods for explaining and demonstrating techniques which go beyond the usual repertoire of instruction, demonstration and emulation. The following example illustrates an innovative approach to learning simple dynamic modulation of the scale.

"You seem to have the C major scale down pretty well. Now we will add some dynamics. The mark which has been added to the notes on the screen is a crescendo. It means that each note should get a little louder than the last. Listen." (The keyboard plays the C major scale with a crescendo.)

"O.K. First, the computer will do the crescendo, while you play the motes."

The MIDI interface allows this kind of flexibility, i.e., the computer can control the dynamics, the student selects the pitch by pressing the appropriate keys.

"That was good. We will do it several more times. Do you hear how it is supposed to sound, an even progression of loudness? Before you try to play the C major crescendo yourself, I will let you practice increasing the pressure on the keys. While you press only the middle C with increasing pressure the computer will produce the correct notes." (MIDI interface selects the notes and assigns them to the middle C key while the loudness is controlled by the key pressure.) "That was O.K., but you increased the loudness too rapidly in the beginning. Do it again and try to make it more even."

"That was better. Now try playing the C major scale with the crescendo."

A number of other modes are possible to help the student match his crescendo to one which has been stored in the computer memory. For example, the student's performance can be closely interleaved with the computer's – the computer plays a note of the proper pitch and loudness, and the student matches the note. The degree of accuracy in matching which the computer requires, i.e., the criterion for correct performance, can be controlled in a progressive manner by an automated shaping algorithm. The shaping algorithm gradually advances the degree of precision required based upon a dynamic evaluation of the student's instantaneous skill level. At the beginning of the exercise the computer may require that the student have only very rough or approximate control over the dynamics, e.g., within 6 decibels, but as the student's skill level increases, the computer may require greater and greater precision. It is not necessary that the criterion be specified in terms of absolute loudness; a ratio of loudness between any given note or groups of notes would be easily implemented with a modern microcomputer. Similarly, more than one musical parameter can be shaped simultaneously. With the better velocity sensitive keyboards which are now available, the detailed characteristics of the key-strike can be analyzed and subjected to a progressive criterion.

My brief scenario of computer directed piano instruction is only intended to suggest the simplest possibilities for computer aided musical instruction. Effective programs must be designed under the direction of qualified musician/instructors who understand the aesthetic goals. Because of the recent technological revolution in microcomputer hardware and software, and electronic music production, the musician who designs and uses the computer aided instruction system will no need extensive knowledge of the technical aspects of the system.[11]

The real advantage of computer aided instruction is that the student is never without guided practice. Continuous moment to moment feedback is provided for each stage in the development and refinement of technical skills. The student is reinforced immediately for correct responses, and bad habits do not take root as they might tend to in unsupervised practice sessions. As illustrated in the above automated keyboard instruction session, each and every time the beginning student plays the keyboard he is being specifically directed toward the correct responses which will lead eventually to skill mastery, in this case, how to play a correct crescendo. In short, in automated training there is no differentiation between instruction and practicing; skill development takes place as a direct interaction between the student and his instrument and thus can proceed much more rapidly than in the usual one hour a week lesson.

An important limitation of the present technology is the analysis and shaping of the posture and movement required for the eventual development of good technique. While devices exist which can visually monitor arbitrary physical patterns of movement, they are presently at least an order of magnitude more expensive than the type of sound production based system which I have described above. The cost of automated movement training devices will probably become reasonable within five to ten years as they are more widely implemented for automated training of athletic skills and for the very important function of automated physical therapy for the disabled.

The system which I sketched was intentionally keyboard based, because the electronic keyboard is readily available and the interfacing of an acoustic instrument would be more difficult and ultimately limited. For example, a computer string-trainer could not produce sounds directly on the instrument, it would have to work through a synthesizer and be limited to monitoring the student's performance and demonstrating the desired sound pattern. While actual control of a string instrument is not impossible, it would be far more difficult than control of a keyboard.

The standard keyboard is not the only interface between the student and the computer which is easily implemented. A variety of special purpose entry devices could be developed for individuals with specific physical limitations. Because of the flexibility of computer based systems, input could be achieved with a wide range of manipulanda and this would open the possibility of professional musical careers to many individuals who lack the necessary dexterity because of special physical limitations. In the extreme, there are those individuals with relative severe handicaps, whose range of motion and strength or brain function are probably inadequate for real time musical performance even with extensive modification of the input manipulanda. Many of these individuals have substantial talent and the creation of music could be a powerful way for them to express their emotions and perceptions of the world. For these people automated music systems will provide the possibility of "low-bandwidth" input to musical computers with subsequent realization at normal tempo as recorded music. This goal is becoming more realistic because recorded music, as the motion picture, has become an increasingly important and respected artistic medium. Some musicians and listeners may feel that only the live performance can convey the full potential of the artist and composition, but many people obviously find listening to high quality recordings on excellent audio equipment, in the comfort of their homes, a highly rewarding experience. Some artists may prefer the excitement of live audiences, but others opt for the greater creative opportunities and better quality of sound offered by the studio production. Indeed, one of the greatest pianists, Glenn Gould, believed that recording was the ideal medium for music performance and he never performed publicly at the height of his career.

Musical artistry is a particularly appropriate profession for the handicapped because traditionally musicians have been evaluated for what they can do and not what they cannot do. Music has never codified a set of standard requirements for all members – even the ability to read musical notation is not essential for recognition as a musician. Nevertheless, musicians are acknowledged professionals. Musicians devote years to concentrated training and disciplined practice to achieve competence, and this investment of time and effort is in large part the basis of their professional status. Thus, the spirit of the music community is inherently open, tolerant, and positive. Musicians are valued for what they do – if you can make beautiful music, that is all that really counts. Automated musical training and electronic instruments will open this possibility to many.

GLOSSARY OF TERMS

Algorithm: a procedure for solving a problem in a finite number of steps that frequently involves repetition of an operation.

Criterion: a standard on which a judgement or decision may be based.

Digital: data in the form of numerical digits. A digital recording is made from magnetic tape on which sound waves have been represented as a code of zeros and ones.

Extrinsic motivation: responding in such a way as to achieve a secondary goal such as receiving money or praise for a job well done.

Hardware: the electronic and digital components of a computer system.

Innate: factors existing in or belonging to an organism from its inception.

Input: information (or data) fed into a data processing system such as a computer, an electronic keyboard, or a synthesizer.

Interface: the place at which independent systems, as in a computer and an electronic keyboard meet, and communicate with each other.

Intrinsic motivation: a need emanating from within the organism to achieve a certain goal.

Low bandwidth: a limited transmission rate capability. Extensive and complex information may be conveyed accurately in low bandwidth communications but the transmission time required will be quite long. For example, smoke signals or semaphore flags are very low bandwidth communications.

Microprocessor: a computer processor with memory contained on a miniature integrated circuit chip.

MIDI: the standard interface of the electronic music industry. A 32 kilobaud serial communications link which permits two way transmission of information and control signals among electronic instruments, synthesizers, sequencers, and general computers. For extensive technical details see *BYTE,* 11(6), 1986, or *Understanding MIDI* a special issue of *MUSICIAN* available from *MUSICIAN*, Box 701, Glouchester, MA 01930.

Motivation: something (as in need or desire) that causes a person to act.

Paradigm: an outstandingly clear and typical example or archetype.

Real time: the actual time, as in seconds, minutes, or hours, during which something takes place. A computer can change a variety of inputs and data, which have been previously entered or internally generated into real time events.

Reinforcement: a stimulus which strengthens the probability of a response that immediately preceded it.

Response: a pattern of behavior of sequence of activities that occur as a coherent unit. It can be simple such as an eyeblink, or a complex series of movements such as playing a scale.

Barry R. Dworkin

Shaping: the process of modifying behavior by rewarding changes that progressively tend toward a desired response.

Software: a set of programs, procedures, and related documentation associated with a computer system.

Synthesizer: a computerized electronic apparatus for the production and control of sound.

Voice synthesizer: a computerized device that simulates a human voice and is able to pronounce words in such a fashion that they can be understood by the human ear.

REFERENCES

1   Thorndike, E.L.: *The Fundamentals of Learning*. New York: Teachers College, 1932.
2   Trowbridge, M.H., Cason, H.: An experimental study of Thorndike's theory of learning. *J Gen Psych*, 1932, **7**, pp. 245-258.
3   Hilgard, E.R.: *Theories of Learning*. New York: Appleton-Century-Crofts, 1956
4   Reynolds, G.S.: *A Primer of Operant Conditioning*. Glenview, IL: Scott Foresman and Co., 1975.
5   Wooldridge, C.R., Russell, G.: Head position training with the cerebral palsied child: An application of biofeedback training. *Arch Med & Rehab*, 1976, **67**, pp. 407-414.
6   Freud, S.: *A General Introduction to Psychoanalysis*. New York: Liveright Publishing Co., 1924.
7   Adler, A.: *The Practice and Theory of Individual Psychology*. Paterson, NJ: Littlefield, Adams and Co., 1963.
8   Allport, G.W.: *Becoming: Basic Considerations for a Psychology of Personality*. New Haven: Yale University Press, 1955.
9   Rogers, C.R.: *Client Centered Therapy*. Boston: Houghton Mifflin Co., 1951.
10 McClelland, D.C.: *The Achieving Society*. New York: Haldsted Press, 1976.
11 Dean, C., Whitlock, Q.: *A Handbook of Computer Based Training*. New York: Nichols Publishing Co., 1983.

MOTOR CONTROL PROBLEMS IN MUSICIANS

Baghwan T. Shahani
D. Cros

INTRODUCTION

Awareness of the "Neurology of Music"

Although human practice of music is an ancient art, few scientific studies of the "neurology of music" are available. In recent years, there has been a revival of interest in medical problems experienced by musicians in relation to their art in the United States. This is partly due to the publicity received by motor control problems of two famous concert pianists, Leon Fleischer and Gary Graffman who were, at one time, two of the world's finest musicians. Both had malfunctioning right hands where the fourth and fifth fingers tended to curl in towards the palm whenever they tried to play the piano. Both these fine artists have done a great service to their fellow musicians by highlighting and publicizing their personal difficulties through the media. This has led to a better awareness of these problems both among physicians and among musicians, with subsequent development of special clinics of "music medicine" all around the country. In this chapter, we describe our experience of motor control problems with musicians in the past seven years.

Many musicians, including pianists, violinists, and a sitar player, were evaluated in our laboratory. Many of them were seen after the onset of their symptoms and following many medical consultations.

The clinical evaluation was conducted with and without the musical instrument. In addition to a subjective description of the complaints, we find it very useful to examine the patient while s/he is playing. Disorders such as tendinitis, arthritis or tenosynovitis, or noninflammatory tendon or joint disorders were often suspected following clinical examination and managed through referral to the appropriate specialists. The patients in whom peripheral nerve or motor control disorders were suspected were then subjected to a series of specialized investigations.

ELECTRODIAGNOSTIC EVALUATION

Nerve Conduction Studies

Nerve conduction studies (electroneurography) represent the first step in this evaluation. They consist of percutaneous stimulation of the fibers of a given peripheral nerve while recording the compound muscle action potential (CMAP) (motor conduction studies), the sensory nerve action potential (sensory conduction studies), or a mixed nerve action potential (mixed nerve conduction studies), the latter assessing the function of the fastest conducting fibers in the body responsible for information pertaining to proprioception. These nerve conduction studies were performed on distal and proximal segments of the nerves of the upper extremities, the median, ulnar and radial nerves. Particular attention was paid to evaluation of distal branches of these nerves, and we systematically studied sensory fibers to each of the five digits in the hand. Owing to the fairly wide range of normal values for amplitude and latencies to the nerve action potentials recorded, we always compared the results obtained in the affected limb with those in the contralateral extremity. It was thus possible to detect a significant asymmetry even though the abnormal potential(s) remained within the normal range in some cases. In addition to these motor, sensory and mixed nerve conduction studies, F response latencies and ranges were also systematically obtained from median, ulnar and radial innervated muscles and compared with the contralateral side. These responses are a useful adjunct to confirm mild impairment of function of motor fibers, e.g., incipient compression or entrapment, suspected by other means of investigation.

Electromyography

Conventional needle electromyography was usually performed in selected muscles. This is achieved by inserting a needle electrode into the muscle, which provides the means to pick up the electrical signals generated by the muscle fibers. The signals are filtered, amplified, and displayed on an oscilloscope screen and through a loud speaker. The muscles are studied at rest and during voluntary activity. At rest, electrical silence is normally present in muscle. Spontaneous activity consisting of fibrillations and positive sharp waves develops when some of the motor fibers supplying this muscle have degenerated, thus leaving a subpopulation of muscle fibers denervated. As the patient voluntarily contracts the muscle under investigation, discrete activity is seen on the oscilloscope screen. The discrete spikes correspond to motor unit potentials, each of which represents a quantum of force generated by the motor system. As voluntary contraction augments, the motor unit potentials become fused in an interference pattern, and single spikes are no longer recognizable. Reduction in the interference pattern upon maximum voluntary contraction is seen in neuropathies causing loss of motor units, due to focal demyelination (functional loss) or to axonal degeneration. In the latter case reinnervation of the denervated muscle fibers by neighboring motor units leads to characteristic changes in the morphology of individual motor unit potentials. The pattern of abnormalities seen with conduction studies and needle EMG results in accurate diagnosis of focal disease of peripheral nerves (compression or entrapment).

NEUROLOGICAL DISORDERS OF MUSICIANS

In musicians, entrapment or compression neuropathy, related to their professional work, was demonstrated in approximately one third of the patients. This lesion, even mild, resulted in lack of coordinated activity of the whole hand in and "flexion dystonia" of digits 4 and 5 in many cases. This was often seen in many pianists. Some of the patients had a carpal tunnel syndrome, a lesion reported to be observed among guitar players. Others had injury to a different peripheral nerve, or to a nerve root, or to the brachial plexus. In most cases, branches of the median, ulnar or radial nerves were affected. However, we have seen patients with involvement of a branch of a proximal nerve (axillary nerve) which resulted in incoordination of voluntary movements of the whole upper extremity.

In patients with no evidence of focal neuropathy, the movement disorder was analyzed by multiple, simultaneous recordings of EMG from several muscles of the extremity during appropriate tasks for different types of musicians. This is a useful approach to detect abnormally sustained activity in a given muscle which is going to perturb the harmony of voluntary movements in the upper extremity as a whole.

In some patients, the behavior of single motor units was studied. Motor units represent the quantal basis of voluntary activity that can be graded by the central nervous system. There are different types of motor units with different anatomic and physiologic properties. The tonic motor units are characterized by a low-amplitude, long duration twitch; they can fire for long periods of time (non-fatigable); their muscle fibers depend mostly on energy derived from aerobic metabolism and are rich in oxidative enzymes; and the cell body of the motor neuron is of small size with a relatively slow conducting axon. The phasic motor units, on the other hand, have a high amplitude, short duration twitch; are easily fatigable; their muscle fibers are rich in myophosphorylase and depend predominantly on the anaerobic glycolytic pathway for their energy supply; their motor neurons are of large size and the motor axons are fast conducting and of large diameter. This is of great functional significance because the wide range of physiologic and histochemical characteristics of motor units may suggest that different types of motor units in a given population are specialized for particular physiologic functions or particular patterns of voluntary activity. The functional activity of a given motor unit, however, is dependent not only on its physiological properties but also on the organization of the synaptic input on that particular motoneuron. There are a variety of inputs that include information originating in muscle receptors such as neuromuscular spindles and Golgi tendon organs, as well as from a number of cutaneous receptors. Some of these inputs are excitatory, producing excitatory post-synaptic potentials (EPSPs), and some are inhibitory, producing inhibitory post-synaptic potentials (IPSPs) or presynaptic inhibition. In addition to intricate circuitry at the segmental level in the spinal cord, there are a variety of control or reflex loops at different suprasegmental levels in the CNS that play a significant part in the modulation of motor activity before the final product comes out in the form of motor performance. Since musicians need to perform accurate and rapid movements of their upper extremities, it is relevant to consider in some detail the physiological mechanisms underlying the generation of force.

In 1962, Harrison and Mortenson[1] reported that human subjects could selectively activate any one of several motor units in a given muscle within the pick-up area of the EMG needle electrode, and maintain activity in that unit for some time. Subsequently, Basmajian[2] has claimed that when human subjects activate several motor units, they can easily learn in a short time to control activity of any single motor unit within the recording range of the electrode. From the physiological point of view, this is an interesting notion because if it is correct, one could, depending upon what particular motor performance one is asked to perform select any unit from a motoneuron pool for appropriate phasic or tonic activity. In other words, depending upon the type of motor performance (from the watchmaker to the Olympic high jumper), it should be possible to selectively activate phasic (fast twitch [type II]) vs. tonic (slow twitch) motor units which would be more appropriate to a given type of activity. This possibility, however, is in contrast to the widely held concept that higher centers in the CNS do not control the activity of each motoneuron on a separate basis.

Clinical electromyographers have noted for many years that during a graded voluntary contraction there is a specific pattern of recruitment of motor units. With minimal effort, one or two single motor unit potentials of low amplitude are recruited. As the voluntary effort increases, larger amplitude units can be seen on the oscilloscope screen. Although these observations were initially made on human subjects, it was Henneman et al.[3][4] who demonstrated that under a variety of experimental conditions, single motor neurons are activated sequentially in a fixed order determined by the size of their cell bodies. The smaller motoneurons have lower thresholds than the larger ones which require greater amounts of excitatory input to fire. All smaller cells must be activated when a certain larger cell is activated. In order to resolve the controversy as to whether the human nervous system can select out of the available motoneurons any single motor unit which could then be used according to the wishes and needs of the moment, Henneman, Shahani and Young[5] performed some studies on human subjects. The subjects were asked to activate single motor units in the extensor digitorum proprius muscle by dorsiflexing the index finger. After establishing the normal order of recruitment for two single motor units that could clearly be distinguished from each other, the subjects were instructed to either reverse the normal recruitment order or to silence the activity of unit one without the activity of unit two. These simple performances were considered crucial tests for the claims of selective control of single motor units. In every subject, it was possible to recruit a single motor unit with minimal tension with an initial frequency of discharge of 3-5 Hz, which increased to 10-15 Hz as tension increased. When the tension in this muscle was reduced, the frequency of discharge gradually decreased and finally ceased when the muscle was relaxed. With higher tension in this muscle, a second motor unit could be recruited in addition to the first one. The initial discharge frequency of the second unit was usually 2-3 Hz which increased to 10-15 Hz in a fashion similar to the one noted for the lower threshold unit. With a gradual reduction of tension in this muscle, the second higher threshold unit always derecruited before the first lower threshold unit (Figure 1).

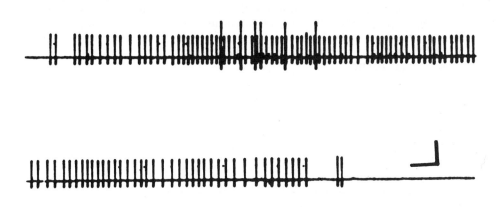

Figure 1: Consecutive segments of EMG recorded from Extensor Indicis Proprius muscle. The subject is dorsiflexing his index finger. The recording demonstrates recruitment of a first motor unit, whose firing frequency increases until a second motor unit is recruited. Then, as tension gradually decreases, derecruitment of these two motor units occurs.

Calibration 500 msec and 200 microvolts.

The pattern of recruitment so described appeared to be somewhat fixed and the subjects were unable to explain how this particular change was accomplished. When only the lowest threshold single motor unit was recruited it was possible, using audio-visual feedback, to recruit that unit at very slow frequencies of one every several seconds or to activate the unit in the forms of trains to 2-3 impulses at 10-15 Hz every few seconds. Therefore, it is possible to train single motor units or groups of motor units by audio-visual feedback, to be activated in ways different from what is required by the human motor system to perform usual activities. Henneman, Shahani and Young's results were therefore radically different from those of Basmajian.[2] It should be recognized that when EMG audio-visual feedback is available to given subjects, it is not possible to activate a higher threshold unit before lower threshold units. The usefulness of EMG audio-visual feedback is that it provides better control of recruitment and derecruitment of groups of motor units without changing the fixed order of recruitment.

Another study of interest in musicians who must control sustained activity in their muscles very precisely is the firing pattern of individual motor units. In any subject it is possible, with a little practice, to recruit a single motor unit with minimal tension. While monitoring the tension, the subject is instructed to keep it constant and the discharge of this single motor unit is recorded on tape. Later, it is then possible to analyze, through computer assisted techniques, the firing frequency in its relation to the force generated. In normal subjects, instantaneous frequency plots would show a fairly stable firing frequency as long as the force is maintained constant. Joint interval histograms (JIH) represent the analysis of adjacent interspike intervals and have proved to be a sensitive measure of motor dysfunction in disorders affecting the upper motoneuron. In normal subjects, statistical analysis of consecutive interspike intervals reveals a negative serial correlation[6][7] (Figure 2). This negative serial dependence of neighboring intervals indicates that intervals longer and shorter than the mean tend to alternate. The mechanisms responsible for such discharge by discharge variations in firing rates of each motor unit are not understood. In musicians with motor control problems, the joint interval histograms were always normal in individual muscles, yet the patients were still unable to produce coordinated movements necessary for playing their instruments. In order to produce the fine coordinated movements required by musicians, there is obviously a need for proper integration of signals not only from suprasegmental structures but also from reflex and sensory inputs at the segmental level. Any lesion producing the slightest abnormality of any of the inputs may result in the loss of finely coordinated movements essential for a particular skill.[8] Although the whole hand is affected, the abnormality seems to be most prominent in digits 4 and 5 which are the most vulnerable from the point of view of motor control.[8]

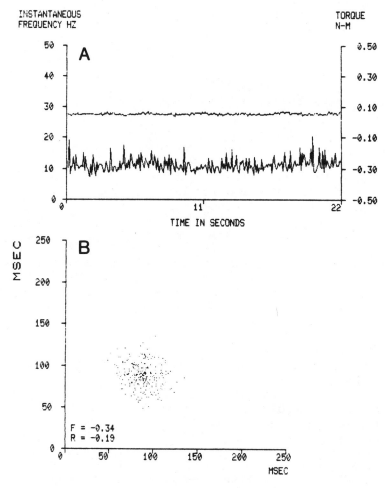

Figure 2:   Recording of single motor unit activity in the Biceps Brachii
muscle.
A.   Top represents the torque kept constant by the subject.
Bottom is the instantaneous firing frequency of the motor unit
under study showing fluctuations from 8-18 Hz.

B.   Joint interval histogram showing the negative serial
correlation typical of normal subjects (r = - 0.19).

B.T. Shahani and D. Cros

This firing pattern of recruitment of the motor units may be applied to train the motor control for musicians with or without disorders of the motor system.

The motor unit is actually the final common pathway of the motor control system. In order to produce movements by this functional unit, there is obviously need for proper integration of signals from suprasegmental structures, reflex activities, and sensory inputs at the segmental level. As stated above, any lesion producing the slightest abnormality of any of the inputs may result in the loss of finely coordinated movements essential for a particular skill. This is especially true for musicians. All of these abnormalities may benefit from the relearning of control and the learning of coordination through an organized rehabilitation program.

In many of these patients, early detection and treatment of an entrapment syndrome resulted in significant improvement of function. In others, in whom the process has lasted for a long period of time, it may have resulted in changes in the central motor programs. In those cases, there is a need for retraining with physiological techniques such as EMG audio-visual feedback in addition to treating the primary cause.

REFERENCES

1   Harrison, V.F., Mortenson, O.A.: Identification and voluntary control of single motor unit activity in the tibialis anterior muscle. *Anat Rec*, 1962, **144**, pp. 109-116.

2   Basmajian, J.V.: Control and training of individual motor units. *Science*, 1963, **141**, pp. 440-441.

3   Henneman, E., Somjen, G., Carpenter, D.: Functional significance of cell size in spinal motoneurons. *J Neurophysiol* , 1965, **28**, pp. 560-580.

4   Henneman, E., Somjen, G., Carpenter, D.: Excitability and inhibitability of motoneurons of different sizes. *J Neurophysiol*, 1965, **28**, pp. 599-620.

5   Ibid., pp. 73-78.

6   Andreassen, S., Rosenfalk, A.: Regulation of the firing pattern of single motor units. *J Neurol Neurosurg Psychiat*, 1980, **43**, pp. 897-906.

7   Shahani, B.T., Wierzbicka, M.M.: Electromyagraphic studies of motor control in humans. *Neuroligic Clinics*, 1985, **5**, pp. 541-558.

8   Shahani, B.T.: Tremor associated with peripheral neuropathy. In: *Movement Disorders*. L.J. Findley and R. Capildeo (Eds.): London, U.K.: Macmillan, 1984, pp. 389-398.

A NEW AGE OF MUSIC IN MEDICINE

Steven Halpern

The use of music as an adjunctive aid to "traditional" medicine has long been acknowledged. During the last decade, however, its scope has broadened enormously, and we are now at a point where a new generation of composers are composing music specifically for therapeutic effect.

The result marks a change in the sounds heard in hospitals, clinics and individual physicians' offices. In addition, patients can now take home "sound prescriptions" to assist them in regaining health.

This chapter does not purport to be a comprehensive overview of all the ways that music has been employed therapeutically over the years, as that task has already been adequately handled by many authors. Rather, this paper will address issues of a current nature and include contexts heretofore neglected in the literature. Furthermore, some of the larger ramifications of the nature of the healing environment, with special concern for the role of sound and music, will be discussed.

The Body as a Human Instrument

One of the overriding considerations that has influenced my work over the past fifteen years has been an understanding that the human body is very much like a fine musical instrument in many respects. Empirical studies have demonstrated that tones of different frequencies resonate in different areas of the body, i.e., low sounds resonate in the lower part of the torso, midrange sounds resonate in the chest area, and high-pitched tones resonate in the head.[1]

Although some of this is no doubt due to varying degrees of bone density, the fundamental principle is that "every atom, molecule, cell and gland in the body vibrates at a characteristic frequency." Even more importantly, due to the nature of the laws of physics, "every atom, molecule, cell and gland therefore also radiates and absorbs frequencies specific to it."[2] In effect, *each organ may have its own keynote frequency!*

When we consider that sound, and music in particular, is nothing if not pure frequency, we can accept that the vibrations built into a symphony, a New Age chamber music composition, or the buzzing of the fluorescent lights may easily resonate with the body that is impacted by that stimulus.

I would like to emphasize that research has demonstrated that one need not audibly "hear" music or sound in order to register an effect.[3] The entire body is sensitive to sound and responds on a frequency-specific basis that has nothing whatsoever to do with academic training, intellectual sophistication or music preference.

The other primary principle not ordinarily covered in publications on this subject relates to the fact that the body, when in a relaxed state, exhibits a striking phenomenon: the heart-aorta system becomes a resonant system – a tuned system – in which the length of the aorta forms one-half of a wavelength of this system.[4] This harmonious condition is highly efficient for the body in terms of energy expended, and provides a clue into what the "natural state" of the body is.

It is of particular interest to note that this system resonates at approximately 8 Hertz. Not coincidentally, this is the same frequency as the Schumann resonance of the earth itself. In effect, when a body is tuned in to this frequency, it is in tune with the dominant frequency to which all life forms on earth pulsate.

A New Age in Music Composition

During the past two decades, a new genre of music has blossomed into a significant trend in contemporary music. The umbrella classification of "NEW AGE MUSIC" is a broad category as currently used, but it was originally intended to focus specifically on therapeutic and transcendent purposes. For our purposes, we will ignore the Comtemporary Instrumental/pop/jazz/ subgenres, and speak about those composers and compositions who are working specifically with the intent to create music in which beauty, consonant harmonies, and a general purpose of uplifting the audience are the prime concerns. Many of these compositions expand upon or ignore Western European rules of composition, and reflect a sensitivity to world music and "inner music".

My own focus has been with a form of music that is particularly oriented toward facilitating the "relaxation response." We call it "The Anti-Frantic Alternative" to distinguish it from other subgroups of New Age music. In this art form, there is no recognizable melody, no insistent rhythmic pulse, and no recognizable harmonic progression.

These factors predispose the listener to experience an immediate and effortless relaxation state. The usual cues of "tension and resolution" in which the listener awaits the completion of a melodic phrase or the continuation of the rhythmic figure are eliminated. It has been found that it is precisely these factors that tend to get the listener stuck in what I call "the anticipation reflex."[5] In short, we have been culturally conditioned to respond to most music in a prescribed manner and it is precisely for this reason that such music cannot provide the optimum results when relaxation is the desired outcome.

This, of course, is not to demean the classics which have certainly earned their place in the pantheon of therapeutic resources. For many reasons, such as familiarity, previous memories, and analytical appreciation, traditional compositions work more on the emotional and psychological level rather than on the cellular or bio-resonant level.

It is precisely on these levels that such music can contribute most effectively in many cases. The point is, after all, not to say one format is better than another, any more than we would say that penicillin is better than tetracycline. They each have their own best applications and we should welcome the broadest range of resources, of music software, into our listening library as well as our medicine chest.

Having thus laid the theoretical bases, let us consider several ramifications.

Given the fact that the body responds to external sonic stimuli, is it not possible to project onto the body a supportive resonance or vibratory pattern to which the body could attune itself? If the body were already in harmony, wouldn't such supportive vibrations enhance that harmony? If the body were out of harmony, couldn't a corrective waveform help the body retune itself?[6]

Research from around the world suggests that this is indeed the case. Recent reports from the All-Union Research Institute in the Soviet Union say, "Some oscillation, when applied to the human body, will effect a micro-massage of tissues and cells which will effect a balance and improve blood circulation, metabolism and the pulsing of the nervous system and endocrine glands."[7]

A London hospital reports that certain wounds heal in two-thirds of normal time when bombarded with sound waves.[8]

Music of various kinds is now heard in many contexts in hospitals around the world. Direct contact with a number[9] of them attests to the efficacy of employing this nonaddictive, legal and renewable resource. Before we continue without theoretical groundwork, let us consider the reality that surgeons are now requesting music to be played during operations. (This in addition to many patients who request to bring music with them to help them relax during their operation.)*

Since 1975, when I began to bring my music to the public, I have received feedback from patients who have found it helpful in preop. and postop. recovery settings. Nurses find the stress reduction aspects helpful to their own sanity and efficiency.

In fact, a recent study at the Pomerado State Hospital in California[10] suggests that when patients have access to relaxation music ("Spectrum Suite" and "Comfort Zone" were two of the titles tested), the pain level of patients decreased, as was the amount of medication requested. One of the additional measures included monitoring the number of times patients rang the nurses' button for medication or attention. Again, the results were highly positive, and correlated with a proper choice of music affecting measurable results other than those typically considered in the literature.

It appears that such music speeds up the healing process and also can decrease the amount of anesthesia necessary since the patient will be more relaxed going into surgery. It should also be noted that, since so many diseases are traceable to high stress levels, a modality that reduced stress levels effortlessly and effectively might help prevent the onset of many afflictions in the first place.

Our space here is too short to reference the many pertinent texts in the fields of holistic health, but the reader is referred to the bibliography in my text, *Sound Health: The Music and Sounds that Make Us Whole*,[5] for specifics.

According to most authorities, a relaxed individual will respond more effectively to medication. In a relaxed state, all systems in the body appear to function more effectively. . . harmoniously, if you will.

It is for these reasons that music which facilitates a relaxation state is seen as being of importance in therapeutic contexts. Even at a low, background volume, the free-floating, breathlike nature of this music nurtures the natural body processes.

How the Music is Delivered

Traditionally, music was piped into patients' rooms over a general public address system. Typically, this was a voice-quality system, not designed for music reproduction. It also limited the individual's choice in terms of program content, volume and available listening times.

With the advent of portable, personal cassette players and stereo headphones, individuals can, in most cases, enjoy high-fidelity sound without disturbing their neighbors. Many hospitals are now renting these units to patients or suggesting to patients that they bring their own with them. Some hospitals are keeping a library of titles geared to this new awareness of the positive effect of relaxation music. Many will supplement this with selections from the classical literature.

---

* See "The anxiolytic effects of music" chapter by Ralph Spintge, page 82.

Steven Halpern

Interestingly, in at least one hospital I know of, the tapes are kept locked up right next to the narcotics! This does not imply a danger in their use, but rather that they are so popular with patients that it is important to prevent their unintentional removal from the premises. To this end, many hospital gift shops are carrying such tapes.

Clinical evidence, anecdotal reports, etc. have been available for years. Hard data and laboratory experimentation are somewhat beside the point, since we are working in the laboratory of life. However, the following will summarize some of the parameters that have affirmed the theoretical constructs mentioned earlier.

The phenomena of resonance and entrainment are related. Resonance is a natural vibratory reality occurring on atomic, cellular and molecular levels. Entrainment is an event that happens between two or more vibrating realities when they come into phase with each other. Such an in-phase system can resonate as an entirety. To put it another way, entrainment is the mutual phase-locking of two oscillators. (An oscillator is any object that pulses or vibrates in a regular, periodic manner.) Thus, living organisms are oscillators and entrainment is happening in our bodies at all levels.

If we look at our bodies as bioresonators, we are relaxed when our physical system is operating in resonance, i.e., when there is a high degree of biorhythmic entrainment going on among the oscillators within the organism.

The Music Research Foundation, set up by the Sugeon General's Office in 1947, defined some music as "relaxing/meditative/soothing."[11] However, in landmark studies conducted in 1973,[12] researchers discovered that that music did not produce nearly as deep and consistent a relaxation effect as original music composed by this author. This is not altogether surprising, in view of the fact that most traditional music was not consciously composed to be relaxing or healing.

Using parameters of this measurement including galvanic skin response, Kirlian photography and later electroacupuncture and kinesiology, it was discovered that what the listener might subjectively report as "a relaxed state" may not be corroborated by instrumentation.[1] This suggests that most people are not sufficiently aware of their own physiological states and brainwave patterns to make an adequate and accurate appraisal. In these studies, over 95% of the listeners exhibited a significant relaxation effect, as defined by accepted parameters with these indices.

Why This New Music Works Differently

As mentioned earlier, this "new music" does not stimulate the listener in familiar conditioned patterns. For this reason, the listener is no longer unconsciously coerced into responding in a prescribed fashion.

Because of the lack of central rhythmic stimulation, the body is allowed to establish its own most natural breath rate. This naturally tends to manifest the synchronous reflex discussed earlier, in which the whole body resonates at approximately 8 Hz. When the body is in resonance, it sets up a host of associated phenomena that are beneficial to the individual: the heartbeat becomes more regular, the breathing slows down and the mind activity slows down into alpha brainwave range. This is assisted by the free-form yet beautiful nature of the musical stimulus, which gives the listener something to focus on without being an external source of focus. The reader is encouraged to experience this music for him/herself to truly understand the significance of this modality.

In the final analysis, however, it may not be as important to say that it is the music itself that causes the relaxing, and thus, the precondition for healing, or that it simply assists the body to relax itself. We do know that the body wants to be balanced.[12] We know that the body is a self-rectifying organism, if we give it a chance. Such music allows the body the healing environment so it can mobilize inherent potentialities while minimizing distractions. Thus, it may be that music is basically amplifying the body's own healing and relaxing abilities. Even thus, music can be a powerful adjunct to the healing process. After all, the bottom line is the health and well-being of our patients and ourselves.

To provide an uplifting, relaxing and therapeutic environment can be as simple today as choosing the proper music and playing it on a cassette player.

In his book *The Psychology of Consciousness*, Dr. Robert Ornstein[13] states that "our medical endeavor is primarily directed towards the treatment of diseases, not toward individual responsibility for health. We attempt to control bodily problems from the outside with drugs rather than attempting to employ the individual's built-in capacity for self-regulation."

While a physician's focus is on curing a disease and helping to prevent future problems with it, a health specialist's focus is on helping us manifest our own highest well-being. Perhaps the new orientation may prove a viable addition to existing procedures, as we shift emphasis to doing things with patients in which they take a conscious role in their own healing and growth. Prescribing a proven therapeutic listening program for home or institutional follow-up would be one such innovation.

Many hospitals are now allowing and inviting music inside their walls. Throughout the United States and abroad, patients in pain can turn not only to medication but also to periods of soothing music and guided relaxation programs on a tape player. Doctors at Kaiser-Permanente in California often prescribe music tapes instead of pain killers and tranquillizers. At other facilities, relaxation music tapes and guided imagery, such as that pioneered by Dr. Helen Bonny, RMT, are being used before cardiac surgery, during chemotherapy, with chronic back pain and other acute injuries. Outpatients with stress-related illnesses such as high blood pressure, migraine headache, and ulcers are encouraged to do the same with music and relaxation training.

Having music available throughout the hospital, rather than just in the music therapy wards, or administered solely by music therapists, is a relatively new development. It is not intended that such developments eliminate trained therapists. Rather, since their time is limited, it makes the benefits available more widely and allows the music therapists to focus their attention on the most pressing situations. Notable among the institutions employing such music are Walter Reed Army Hospital, Washington, D.C.; Mt. Zion Hospital, South Carolina; A.R.E. Medical Center, Phoenix; Pomerado Hospital, San Diego; and Goldwater Memorial Hospital, New York City.

Music is being used to personalize the often sterile atmosphere of hospitals in many ways. It must be emphasized, however, that the use of heavy or loud rock music, or even much classical music, will not get the same results as using specifically composed relaxation music.

Properly composed music can thus facilitate both a generic relaxation effect on the mental and physical organism, as well as a balancing, tuning effect that assists the overall health and healing of the patient. It is hoped that this will encourage others to carry on and expand the work.

Steven Halpern

New Age Music and the Rehabilitation Patient: A Sound Suggestion

In summary, the use of relaxational music that goes beyond mere relaxational parameters to include the energetic balancing of electromagnetic fields, as measured by electroacupuncture, GSR and applied kinesiology, is perfectly suited to use with handicapped patients. If headphones are suitable, the quality of sound will be maximized, but even with low fidelity reproduction equipment, the raw material, the balancing and healing sounds, will mobilize, catalyze and generally support the body's intrinsic ability to heal itself, on the physiological, emotional and spiritual levels.

Clearly, such music is not a panacea, nor will it produce instantaneous miracles (though a number have been documented). It does represent, however, an additional arsenal in the armamentarium of health professionals, to engage the synergetic support of one of the most ancient of the "healing arts." The beauty of this music is that is does not interfere with any other modality of treatment; rather it is flexible and amenable to background or foreground use, with or without guided imagery.

Such music is said to be able to speak to that part of an individual that is eternal, and not bound up in the perceptions of handicappedness or abnormality. In its effortless ability to bring joy into an individual's life, we all have a treasure that needs to be mined.

REFERENCES

1   Halpern, S., Kientz, D.: Field effects of music on the electromagnetic energy body. Santa Rosa, Psychotronic Research Center, 1973.
2   Tiller, W.: On the nature of reality. Lecture at the University of California Extension, Santa Cruz, 1976.
3   Diamond, J.: *Your Body Doesn't Lie*. New York: Warner Books, 1980.
4   Bentov, I.: *Stalking with Wild Pendulum*. New York: Dutton, 1977.
5   Halpern, S., Savary, L.: *Sound Health: The Music and Sounds That Make Us Whole*. New York: Harper & Row, 1985.
6   Manners, P.: The future of cymatic therapy. *Technology Tomorrow*, June 1980. (Volume number and page number required)
7   Tompkins, P., Bird, C.: *The Secret Life of Plants*. New York: Harper & Row, 1972.
8   Lewis, M., Butler, R.: Aging and mental health. In: Tompkins, P., Bird, C.: *The Secret Life of Plants*. New York: Harper & Row, 1972. (A page number reference required)
9   Halpern, S.: Personal correspondence
10 Cooper C,: Unpublished report.
11 Gutheil (ed.): *Music and Your Emotions*. New York: Liveright Pub., 1952.
12 Halpern, S.: *Tuning the Human Instrument*. Belmont, CA: Spectrum Research Institute, 1978.
13 Ornstein, R.: *The Psychology of Consciousness*. New York, Penguin Books, 1975.

THE ANXIOLYTIC EFFECTS OF MUSIC

Ralph K.W. Spintge

THE EMOTIONAL SITUATION OF THE PATIENT

The Patient's Anxiety

At present, there is still no conclusive "Psychology of the Patient" dealing with the experiences of a medical client, that is the patient's view, in the areas of architectural sensitivity, adequacy of patient information, ergonomic design of technical equipment, interaction of personnel and patient, etc. However, we know that eating different food, a deficit of social contacts, a feeling of helplessness, different clothing, etc. do impair the emotional state of patients, thus reducing compliance and cooperation. At the same time, patients endure a certain amount of psychological and physiological distress whenever they are either waiting for medical treatment or experiencing the treatment itself, independent of the basic disease. This is true in clinical situations as well as with ambulatory patients treated in private practice and it always causes a significant amount of irritation to the whole human organism. The main stressors creating this irritation are anxiety and pain, which have strong mutual interactions. In this chapter, we will deal mainly with the patient's anxiety.

Contents of Patient's Anxiety

Our patients usually name three main reasons for their concern:

- the medical treatment itself;
- the necessary anesthesia;
- the impending hospital stay.

The fears of patients are listed in detail in Table 1.[1 2 3 4 5 6]

Incidence of Patient's Anxiety

There is a great variation in the incidence of a patient's anxiety in the literature, the range being between 40% and 86% for non-premedicated patients and between 26% and 92% for premedicated patients (Table 2).

Insufficient Coping Strategies

Many patients say that they cannot find any reason for feeling anxious, but when speaking with them one can, in some cases, help the patient to find the reason. Most of these patients are not ready to analyze their emotional state, and are captured by an emotional and intellectual regression,[7] which makes it impossible for them to rationalize their anxiety and to cope with it adequately. Sheffer and Greifenstein[8] described insufficient coping strategies, noting that only 38% of their patients tried to rationalize their fears; 62% did not admit to having any fears about themselves or anybody else. These "suppressors" in particular have a high incidence of perioperative complications.[9 10 11 12 13] In addition, 67% of the patients in this study showed a conversion of anxiety into senseless and aimless activities such as walking around, fumbling around, nail biting, etc. It was also found that preoperative sleep is disturbed in about 40% of all patients.

Pathophysiology of Patient's Anxiety

The pathophysiological implications of this emotional distress (i.e., strain) are of great importance. Anxiety is defined by an irritation of the whole organism and an activation of instinctive defense mechanisms, called "alarm reaction" by Cannon[14] and "stress reaction" by Selye.[15] Table 3 shows the respective pathophysiological reactions that were identified in many clinical studies. These psychovegetative reactions not only cause the patient more suffering,[16][17] but also make medical treatment more difficult and reduce resistance in the organism.[13][18] [19][20]

When the general immune response is reduced,[21][22][23] resistance to infectious diseases and the healing of wounds are impaired;[16][24][25][26][27][28][29][30][31][32][33] the basal metabolic rate increases and the incidence of heart attacks and of cardiac infarction rise.[33][34] The demand for analgesics, sedatives and anesthetics also increases.[20][35][36][37] The worst outcome of these irritations may be cardiovascular collapse and death.[38][39] Obviously, the emotional state of the patient is also responsible for the degree of postoperative pain sensations and, thus, it directly influences compliance and cooperation in rehabilitation. However, it is possible to reduce the demand for drugs and the duration of the hospital stay significantly through relatively simple psychological intervention including the use of anxiolytic music.[40][41][42][43][44][45][46]

NONVERBAL ACOUSTICAL MEANS TO REDUCE ANXIETY – ANXIO-LYTIC MUSIC

The psychophysical situation of the patient can best be described as "regression." This regression needs some kind of nonverbal communication that can, at least, establish an emotional connection between patient and physician. In addition to the anxiety provoking stimuli listed in Table 1, the patient also suffers from a lack of stimulation in his normal environment, being separated from his family, friends, job, colleagues, etc. A human being needs a certain level of stimulation from the normal life situation to live in psychic and somatic harmony. Music that is familiar to the patient can, in this sense, be a bridge to the normal life.

For the last twelve years, our research team has conducted several clinical, controlled and randomized studies in various medical specialties to determine the respective therapeutic values of anxiolytic music.

Method and Regime of Application

The term "anxiolytic music," as used in all these studies, is meant in a pragmatic and empirical sense. Music is anxiolytic if it has the proven psychological, social and physiological effects mentioned in Table 4. To achieve these effects, the following preconditions must be fulfilled:

a) Musical works should be selected according to duration, instrumentation, dynamics and interpretation. It is important that there are no extremes in rhythm, melody or dynamics and that instrumental rather than vocal music be chosen.

b) Patients should make their own selections.

c) The effects of individual pieces and combinations of pieces should be tested and verified in ongoing clinical studies so that new trends to taste and new technologies can also be considered.

d) Recordings should be of high quality, yet technically simple and reliable (laser-CD-disc preferable).

It is important that the patient, not the doctor or the nurse, choose the music. Pieces chosen by the patient should then be screened for a final selection of familiar melodies and simple rhythmic structures.

At present, this way of selecting the music is appropriate but it is still a relatively unspecific way. In cooperation with Manfred Clynes, we are now working on computer music programs which could enable us to compose and interpret music for specific medical applications. The preliminary results are very promising indeed, but a musical pharmacy is not yet a reality.[47]

Table 5 illustrates the choices made among approximately 56,000 patients, examined from 1977 to 1986 who were given five categories of music from which to choose. The five categories had been established by the patients themselves.

The procedure for using anxiolytic music in various medical specialties is quite similar. The following describes the procedure used in our department of anesthesiology at Sportkrankenhaus Hellersen and several other places.

The day before the operation, the patient receives a preoperative questionnaire asking about medical anamnesis as well as musical preferences. On the morning of the operation, the patient is wheeled into the preoperative waiting area and given earphones to listen to the music s/he has selected. Today we only use laser CD disc players to play the music since the quality of music reproduction is unmatched and highly appreciated by the patient. Furthermore, handling is very easy and wear on the disc is not a problem. In cases where general anesthesia is used, the earphones are worn until the patient is asleep. When local or regional anesthesia is given, the patient listens to music throughout the entire operation (Figure 1).

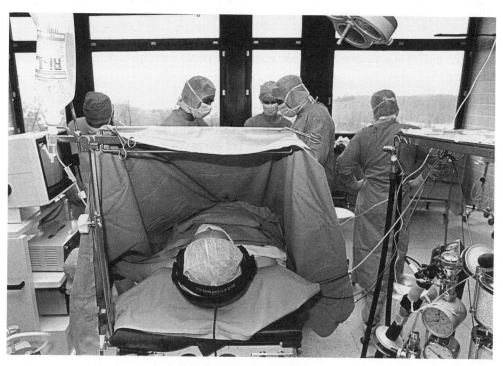

Ralph K.W. Spintge

As part of the postoperative procedure, the patient receives another questionnaire concerning subjective feelings about the operation, anesthesia, postoperative complaints and, of course, the music. The same regime for application and control of effect is easily adaptable to any treatment situation in any hospital or private practice.

Clinical Application in Different Medical Specialties

Our studies indicate that patients listening to anxiolytic music of their choice during medical procedures experience a significantly better psychological and physiological outcome of treatment than those who do not have anxiolytic music.[47 48] A variety of beneficial effects have been replicated in all our studies, demonstrating a significant reduction of stress response, especially in the cardiovascular and endocrinological systems.

Anesthesiology

Most experience in the area of anxiolytic and algolytic music has taken place in anesthesiology as an interdisciplinary medical subject.

Our research team conducted a series of clinical, controlled and randomized studies with about 8,000 patients in private practice, hospitals, university hospitals, dental clinics, etc. in Europe and Asia. Furthermore, we routinely monitor the effectiveness of our perioperative musical anxiolysis through pre- and postoperative standardized questionnaires. To date, we have collected data on more than 56,000 patients in this manner.

In all studies, perioperative anxiety occurred in about 17% of the music patients as opposed to findings in the literature which cited the minimum percentage as 26% for nonmusic patients (Table 2).

Emotional relaxation achieved by anxiolytic music is much better than that achieved by sedative drugs, both in our opinion and in the opinion of our patients. About 50% of the usual dosage of sedative and analgesic drugs can be saved[6] and the music is welcomed by 97% of the patients. Plasma levels of stress hormones such as cortisol, adrenocorticotrophic hormone ACTH, prolactin,[49 50] and ß-endorphin[49] are significantly lower in patients receiving music compared to patients without anxiolytic music.

In regional anesthesia as well, anxiolytic music is a very valuable means of reducing perioperative distress, a fact that has been confirmed by several other authors.[51 52 53 54] Undesired reactions of the cardiovascular system in particular can be avoided.

Being in an intensive care ward is one of the most extreme distress situations for a patient. Patients suffering from cardiac infarction experience marked emotional relaxation and distraction listening to anxiolytic music.[55] It is even possible to restore communication with coma patients suffering from heavy brain injuries.[56]

Pain Therapy

Music can be used for anxiolytic and algolytic purposes in the multimodality treatment of cancer pain with great success.[57] We use music in some chronic pain patients either as real music or as sinustones of different frequencies and intensities in the "music-bath."[58] Both applications have a beneficial therapeutic effect, especially in cases with increased muscle tonus. However, we still do not have enough data about the long-term effects to draw a definite conclusion.

Gynecology

In gynecology, emotional distress ranges from a common sense of shame to an extreme fear of cancer. Anxiolytic music can be used during gynecological operations carried out with regional anesthesia to reduce waiting time and distract from the environment.[59]

In private practice music can be used in the waiting area to create a more relaxed atmosphere and, at the same time, it can work as an acoustic curtain covering confidential talks.

During an abortion, where suction-curettage is used, music decreases the necessity for sedatives and anesthetics.[60]

Obstetrics

In another study we found that peripartal distress could be significantly reduced by anxiolytic music. Not only was music a better "help" than the respective husband (!), but at the same time there was a marked decrease in cardiovascular and endocrinological stress response. The circadian rhythms of ACTH, ß-endorphin, arterial blood pressure, and heart rate were measured prepartal, during labor and on the first postpartal day. All parameters showed a highly significant lower level in the music group compared with the control group[61] (see Figure 2). More than 80% of the women stated that music was a real help for them during labor and that it was much more of a help than their own husbands. Although the midwives were quite skeptical at the beginning of the study, afterwards they became very enthusiastic about the use of music. Their fine sensitivity to the psychophysical state of the women in labor made them realize the de-stressing effects of music in the delivery room.

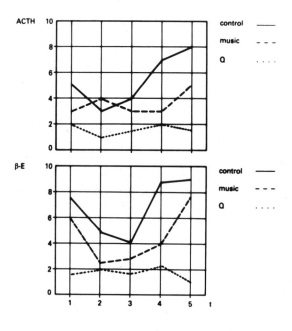

Figure 2

Ralph K.W. Spintge

In future studies we will look at the effect music has upon the unborn fetus and the newborn. It has been well established that there is acoustical reception before birth with consecutive reactions in the cardiopulmonary system of the fetus.[47]

Dentistry

In dentistry, more than in any other medical specialty, anxiety governs the relationship between patient and physician. Anxiety is not only of great distress to the patient, but it is also an additional burden on the dentist. Many patients only come to a dentist when their pain has become intractable. We know that most patients would like to listen to music during waiting time and during treatment.[62]

Audio-analgesia for reduction of pain during treatment has already been in use for about 80 years, especially in the United States and in Scandinavia.[63][64][65][66] In a controlled randomized study, we compared the psychological and physiological reactions of patients to dental treatment with and without music.[67] Before treatment, 88% of the patients in both groups admitted to some degree of anxiety. After treatment, 84% of the music patients stated that there was a marked decrease of anxiety, compared with 16% of the nonmusic patients. Cardiovascular and endocrinological parameters were measured before, during, immediately after and 15 minutes after treatment. While listening to music, heart rate, arterial blood pressure and ACTH levels showed a highly significant decrease in the music group compared with the control group (Figures 3, 4, 5). Human growth hormone, prolactin, cortisol and ß-endorphin levels showed a similar reaction in both groups, but the music values were always lower than control values.

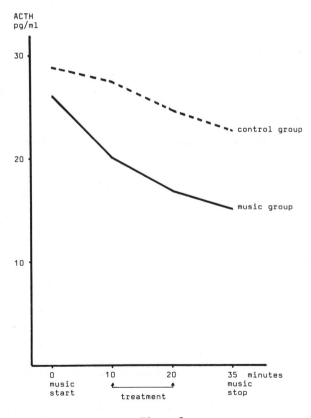

Figure 3

The Anxiolytic Effects of Music

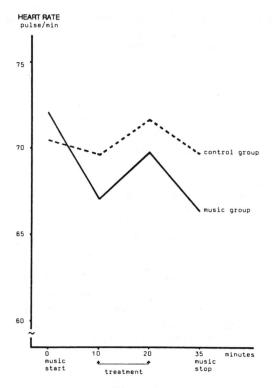

Figure 4

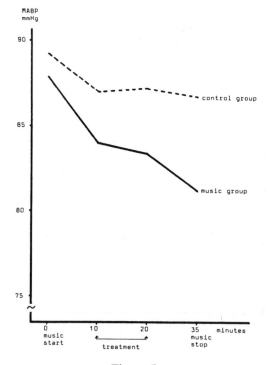

Figure 5

Ralph K.W. Spintge

Rheumatology

In the therapy of rheumatic disease, mobilization of the affected joints plays a decisive role. The patient's motivation and cooperation during the mobilization therapy depends mainly upon the degree of pain experienced during the respective physical training. Playing an instrument such as piano, violin, triangle or xylophone was shown to be a very effective way of mobilizing the affected joints without much pain.[68] [69]

Rehabilitation After Cardiac Infarction

Today rehabilitation after cardiac infarction includes some physical training in special coronary exercise group. A decisive factor in the success of this rehabilitative training is the decrease of the patient's many fears (e.g., death, job loss, etc.) in order to motivate the patient to cooperate. In many such training groups, special selections of anxiolytic music are successfully used for this purpose.[70]

Musicmedicine

In all medical specialties, in clinical medicine as well as ambulatory therapy in private practice, the patient suffers from a certain degree of anxiety independent of the basic disease. In this paper we describe the beginning of what we call "musicmedicine" as an adjuvant way to apply specific music with regard to certain indications and contraindications.

Music, as any other medical drug, should only be used for these purposes under the guidance of a physician and in consideration of the following criteria:

1. Ingredients (title, instrumentation, interpretation, arrangement, size of orchestra, etc.);
2. Dosage (duration of application, intensity, loudness/volume, etc.);
3. Indications (patient's choice, application to the situation [i.e., waiting/treatment], etc.);
4. Effects (sleep-inducing, relaxing, cheering-up, exciting);
5. Side effects/risks;
6. contraindications (exciting music in cardiac rehabilitation, sedative music in physical rehabilitation);
7. Ways of application (loudspeaker/earphones, stereo/mono, wire/wireless, analog/digital, etc.).

Thus far our data on the use of music in many medical specialties show that no undesirable side effects occur if music is used in accordance with these criteria. Rather, it seems that there may be no medical procedure and no waiting area where music, especially anxiolytic music, cannot be a valuable contribution to benefit the patient. In this sense we can indeed speak of the beginning of musicmedicine.

TABLE 1

Contents of Patient's Anxiety

1. The Hospital Stay

   - separated from family and friends
   - strange environment, unknown sounds, smell and food
   - lack of social/personal contacts
   - feeling sick
   - pain
   - concern about future (family, job, health)
   - something unknown is approaching
   - loss of personal responsibility
   - feeling of helplessness

2. The Medical Treatment

   - surgery as injury to body and soul
   - result of treatment (cosmetics, cancer, amputation)
   - sequela (sexual disability, being handicapped)
   - post-treatment time (more pain, injections, catheters)
   - precedent bad experience
   - bad stories told by others
   - news in the press about malpractice

3. The Anesthesia (local and general)

   - effectiveness(pain)
   - complications
   - injection
   - infusion
   - unknown technical equipment
   - feeling of helplessness
   - general anesthesia (fear of death, narcosis as pseudodeath, the mask, previous bad experience, news about risks, telling personal secrets)

Ralph K.W. Spintge

TABLE 2

Incidence of Patient's Anxiety Perioperatively (details, see ref. 47)

Percentage	No. of Patients	Premedication	Research Method
26.0	3464	thioridazine meprobamate	postop. questionnaire
76.5	149	?	questionnaire 5 years postop.
83.0	95	no	questionnaire first postop. day
92.0	100	?	questionnaire 1. - 10. postop. day
30.0	539	Papaveretum+scopolamin or pethidin+atropine	observed after premed.
40.0	124	-	questionnaire before premed.
62.0	143	-	dto
63.6	22	-	dto
86.0	122	-	dto
47.0	600	-	observed before premed.
79.0	43	-	dto
84.0	150	-	dto
33.0	353	?	preop. questionnaire
12.4	1910	2 mg flunitrazepam i.m. 1 hr preop.	questionnaire 24 hr postoperative
22.2	1910	20 mg triflupromazine 1 hr preop. i.m.	dto
19.7	1462	dto	dto
17.9	4002	dto + information book	dto
18.1	2074	dto + music	dto
17.0	1378	dto	dto

TABLE 3

Pathophysiology of Patient's Anxiety
(details and references, see ref. 47)

Reacting System	Reaction
Cardiovascular system	atrial and ventricula tachyarrhythmia ventricular and atrial fibrillation reduced coronary perfusion, heart attack rise of arterial blood pressure vertigo, headache
Respiratory system	hyperventilation increase of oxygen consumption dyspnea, asthma

Endocrine system and metabolism	increased plasma levels of:
	    catecholamines
	    thyroxine
	    steroides
	    glucose
	    free fatty acids, triglycerides,
	     cholesterin
	    prolactin
	    ß-endorphin
	    antidiuretic hormone ADH
	    human growth hormone HGH
	    renin

Motor system	general excitation tremor increased muscle tonus singultus, gastrospasm
Excretion	increased perspiration polyuria, pollakisuria
Reception and Perception	hyperaesthesia lowered pain threshold decreased pain tolerance
Response to stimuli	exaggerated pain reaction

Ralph K.W. Spintge

TABLE 4

Physiology of Anxiolytic Music
(details and references see ref. 47)

Reacting System	Reaction
Cardiovascular system	decreased heart rate decreased arterial blood pressure anti-arrhythmic effect
Respiratory system	decrease of ventilatory minute volume reduced oxygen consumption ventilatory rhythm synchronised

Endocrine system and metabolism	decreased plasma levels of:
	    catecholamines
	    adrenocorticotrophic hormone ACTH
	    cortisol
	    prolactin
	    ß-endorphine
	reduced basal metabolic rate
	sleep induction

Exocrine secretion and excretion	reduced perspiration decreased salivation
Reception and perception	raised pain threshold increased pain tolerance
Motor system	reduced restlessness decreased muscle tonus eased muscle cramps

TABLE 5

Anxiolytic Music — Patient's Preferences
(frequency of choice percentages among 56,000 patients)

Music category	Frequency of Choice %
Popular music (James Last style)	44
Actual pop hits	25
Classics (romantic and baroque period)	15
Military music	10
Soft popular music	6

REFERENCES

1   Emmerich, M.: *Wie erlebt und beurteilt der Patient die präoperative Phase vor einer Allgemein - bzw. Regional anaesthesie.* Dissertation, Medical Faculty, University of Mainz, 1981.
2   Emmerich, B.: *Intra- und postoperative Erfahrungen der Patienten mit Regional - oder Allgemeinanaesthesie.* Dissertation, Medical Faculty, University of Mainz, 1981.
3   Seide, B.: *Präoperatives und postoperatives Informationsniveau und Informationsbedürfnis.* Dissertation, Medical Faculty, University of Erlangen-Nürnberg, 1981.
4   Scheller, I.: *Präoperative Vorbereitung chirurgischer Patienten mit Hilfe von schriftlichem Informationsmaterial.* Dissertation, Medical Faculty, Univesity of Erlangen-Nürnberg, 1982.
5   Spintge, R., Droh, R.: Perioperatives Befinden mit anxiolytischer Musik und Rohypnol (Flunitrazepam) bei 1910 Spinalanaesthesien. In: Droh, R., Spintge, R.: *Angst, Schmerz and Musik in der Anaesthesie.* Grenzach: Editiones Roche, 1983, pp. 193-196.
6   Spintge, R.: *Psychologische und psycho-therapeutische Methoden zur Verminderung der präoperative Angst – ein Beitrag zur Beziehung zwischen Angst, Informationsbedürfnis und Musik.* Dissertation, Medical Faculty, University of Bonn, 1982.
7   Janis, I.L.: *Psychological Stress - Psychoanalytical and Behavioral Studies of Surgical Patients.* London, U.K.: Academic Press, 1974.
8   Sheffer, M.B., Greifenstein, F.E.: Emotional responses of patients to surgery and anesthesia. *Anesthesiology,* 1960, **21**, pp. 502-507.
9   Tolksdorf, W., Berlin, J., Rey, E.R.: Präoperatives psychisches Befinden und Risiko der Anaesthesie. In Droh, R., Spintge, R.: *Angst, Schmerz und Musik in der Anaesthesie.* Grenzach: Editiones Roche, 1983, pp. 61-67.

Ralph K.W. Spintge

10 Abraham, H.S.:, Gill, B.F.: Predictions of postoperative psychiatric complications. *New Eng J Med*, 1961, **265**, pp. 1123-1128.

11 Horatz, K., Schöntag, G.: Die Angst des Patienten vor Narkose und Operation. *Praktische Anaesthesie*, 1978, **13**, pp. 123-126.

12 Wiemers, K.: *Postoperative Frühkomplikationen*. Stuttgart: Thieme, 1969, p. 62.

13 Wilson, W.E.: Preoperative anxiety and anesthesia: Their relation. *Anesthesia Analgesia Current Research*, 1969, **48**(4), pp. 605-611.

14 Cannon W.B.: *Wut, Hunger, Angst und Schmerz*. München: Urban & Schwarzenberg, 1978.

15 Selye, H.: *Stress*. Reinbek: Rowholt, 1977.

16 Birbaumer, N.: Zum Problem der Psychosomatik. In: Birbaumer N. (ed.): *Psychophysiologie der Angst*. München: Urban & Schwarzenberg, 1977, pp. 296-332.

17 Bodley, P.O.: Preoperative anxiety: A qualitative analysis. *J Neurol Neurosurgery and Psychiatry*, 1974, **34**, 230-239.

18 Gedda, L., Rizzi, R.: Psychologische Verfassung des Individuums vor und nach dem Eingriff und der Anaesthesie. *Anesthetist*, 1962, **11**(12), pp. 378-385.

19 Williams, J.G.L., Jones, J.R.: Psychophysiological responses to anesthesia and operation. *JAMA*, 1968, **203**(6), pp. 415-417.

20 Collins, N.W., Moore, R.C.: The effect of a preanesthetic interview on the operative use of thiopental sodium. *Anesthesia Analgesia Current Research*, 1970, **49**(6), pp. 872-876.

21 Henry, J.P., Stephens-Larson, P.: Specific effects of stress on disease process. In: American Physiological Society (ed.): *Animal Stress*. New York: 1985, pp. 161-175.

22 Birkenbosch, F.: The role of catecholamines in the control of the secretion of pro-opiomelanocortin derived peptides from rat's pituitary gland and its implications in the response to stress. Ph Thesis University of Amsterdam, 1983.

23 Meehan, J.P.: Stress, vascular changes and the potential for behavioral modifications. *J of Southern California Medical Assoc*, 1983, pp. 18-46.

24 Larbig, W.: *Schmerz*. Stuttgart: Kohlhammer, 1982.

25 Gottschalk, L.A., Welch, W.D., Weiss, J.: Vulnerability and immune response. *Psychotherapy and Psychosomatics*, 1983, **39**, pp. 23-35.

26 Corvino, N.A., Dirks, J.F., Fish, R.J., Seidel, J.V.: Characteristics of depression of chronically ill medical patients. *Psychotherapy and Psychosomatics*, 1983, **39**, pp. 10-22.

27 Kiecolt-Glaser, J.: Exam stress and immunity. *Psychosomatic Medicine*, 1984, **46**, pp. 7-14.

28 Ader, R.: *Psychoneuroimmunology*. New York: Grune & Stratton, 1981.

29 Bradley, C.: Psychological factors affecting recovery from surgery. In: Watkin, J., Salo, M. (eds.): *Trauma, Stress and Immunity in Anesthesia and Surgery*. New York: Butterworth, 1982, pp. 315-361.

30 Carolis, C., *et al.*: Evidence of an inhibitory role of ß-endorphin and other opioids on human total T-rosette formation. *Experientia*, 1984, **40**, pp. 738-793.

31 Jennot, J.B., Locke, S.E.: Psychoimmunology. *Psychological Bulletin*, 1984, **95**, pp. 78-108.

32 Levi, L.: Stress: Nebenniere und Schilddrüse. In: Eiff, A.W.: (ed.): *Seelische und körperliche Störungen durch Stress*. Stuttgart: Fischer, 1976, pp. 47-64.

33 Eiff, A.W.: Die Diagnose des Stress. In: Eiff, A.W. (ed.): *Seelische und körperliche Störungen durch Stress*. Stuttgart: Fischer, 1976, pp. 194-217.

34 Eiff, A.W.: Zur Physiologie des emotionellen Stress. In: Eiff, A.W. (ed.): *Seelische und körperliche Störungen durch Stress*. Stuttgart: Fischer, 1976, pp. 18-46.

35 Raginsky, B.: Some psychosomatic aspects of general anesthesia. *Anesthesiology*, 1950, **11**, pp. 391-408.

36 Williams, J.G.L.: The psychological control of preoperative anxiety. *Psychophysiology*, 1975, **12**(1), pp. 50-54.

37 Jackson, K.: Psychologic preparation as a method reducing the emotional trauma of anesthesia in children. *Anesthesiology*, 1951, **12**, pp. 293-300.

38 Tolksdorf, W.: Das präoperative psychische Befinden. *Med Habil Schrift*, Universität Heidelberg, 1982.

39 Selbach, H.: Operationsgefährdung durch Psyche und Vegetativum. *Langenbecks Archiv Klinische Chirurgie*, 1965, **292**, pp. 70-78.

40 Felton, G., Huss, K., Payne, E.: Preoperative nursing intervention with patients for surgery: Outcome of three alternative approaches. *International J Nursing Studies*, 1973, **13**, pp. 83-96.

41 Lindemann C.A.: Nursing intervention with the presurgical patient – phase two. *Nursing Research*, 1971, **21**, pp. 196-209.

42 Lindemann, C.A., Stetzer, S.L.: Effects of preoperative visits by operating room nurses. *Nursing Research*, 1973, **22**, pp. 4-16.

43 Lindemann, C.A., Aermann, B.: Nursing intervention with the presurgical patient – the effects of structured and unstructured preoperative teaching. *Nursing Research*, 1971, **20**, pp. 319-331.

44 Healy, K.M.: Does preoperative instruction make a difference? *Am J Nursing*, 1968, **68**, pp. 62-67.

45 Egbert, L.D., Battit, G.E., Welch, C.E.: Reduction of postoperative pain by encouragement and instruction of patients. *New Eng J Medicine*, 1964, **270**, pp. 825-827.

46 Mumford, E., Schlesinger, H.J., Glass, G.V.: *Overtreated and Underserved*. New York: International University Press, 1982.

47 Spintge, R.: *Anthropological and Therapeutic Aspects of Music*. Stuttgart: Fischer, 1989.

48 Spintge, R., Droh, R. (eds.): *Music in Medicine*. Berlin-Heidelberg-New York: Springer, 1987.

49 Oyama, T., Sato, Y., Kudo, T., Spintge, R., Droh, R.: Effects of anxiolytic music on endocrine function in surgical patients. In: Droh, R., Spintge, R. (eds.): *Angst, Schmerz und Musik in der Anaesthesie*. Grenzach: Editiones Roche, 1983, pp. 147-152.

50 Kamin, A., Kamin, H.P., Spintge, R., Droh, R.: Endokrinologische Wirksamkeit anxiolytischer Musik und psychologischer Operationsverbereitung. In: Droh, R., Spintge, R. (eds.): *Angst, Schmerz und Musik in der Anaesthesie*. Grenzach: Editiones Roche, 1983, pp. 163-166.

51 Tanioka, F., Oyama, T., Takazawa, T., Kamata, S., Kudo, M.: Hormonal effect of anxiolytic music under epidural anesthesia. In: Droh, R., Spintge, R. (eds.): *Music in Medicine*. Grenzach: Editiones Roche, 1985, pp. 285-290.

52 Sehhati-Chafai, G., Kau, G.: Vergleichende Untersuchung über die anxiolytische Wirksamkeit von Valium und Musik bei Patienten während einer Operation in Regionalanaesthesie. In: Droh, R., Spintge, R. (eds.): *Music in Medicine*. Grenzach: Editiones Roche, 1985, pp. 231-236.

53 Sold, M., Schedel, R., Kühn, R.: Die Bedeutung von Persönlichkeitsmerkmalen inklusive Stressreagibilität und Stressbewältigung für das Erleben operativer Eingriffe in Regionalanaesthesie und die Rolle der Musik. In: Droh, R., Spintge, R. (eds.): *Music in Medicine*. Grenzach: Editiones Roche, 1985, pp. 257-270.

54 Kau, G.: *Vergleichende Untersuchung über die anxiolytische Wirksamkeit von Valium und Musik bei Patienten während einer Operation in Regionalanaesthesie*. Dissertation, Medical Faculty, University of Mainz, 1982.

55 Klapp, B.F., Neuhof, H.: Musikangebot an internistische Intensivpatienten. Manuscript received 1984.

Ralph K.W. Spintge

56 Meyer, C., Eckert, F.: Musik in der Therapie Schädel-Hirn-Verletzter. Paper read at the seminar "Music in Medicine", MEDICA-congress, Düsseldorf, 1984.

57 Foley, D.M.: The treatment of cancer pain. *New Eng J Med*, 1985, **313**, pp. 84-95.

58 Skille, O.: The music bath. In: Droh, R., Spintge, R. (eds.): *Angst, Schmerz und Musik in der Anaesthesie*. Grenzach: Editiones Roche, 1983, pp. 111-113.

59 McGlinn, J.A.: Music in the operating room. *Am J of Ob and Gyn*, 1930, **20**, p. 678.

60 Shapiro, A.G., Cohen, H.: Auxiliary pain relief during suction curettage. In: Droh, R., Spintge, R. (eds.): *Angst, Schmerz und Musik in der Anaesthesie*. Grenzach, Editiones Roche, 1983, pp. 89-93.

61 Halpaap, B.B., Spintge, R., Droh, R., Kummert, W., Kögel, W.: Anxiolytic music in obstetrics. In: Droh. R., Spintge, R. (eds.): *Music in Medicine*. Grenzach: Editiones Roche, 1985, pp. 145-154.

62 Ebenbeck, G., Raith, E., Schreiber S.B.: Die Angst des Zahnarztes vor der Angst des Patienten. Paper read at the 5th Congress of the German Society for Medical Psychology, München, 1984.

63 Ziemann, J.: *Die Musik in der medizinischen Theorie und Praxis des 19 Jahrhunderts*. Dissertation, Medical Faculty, University of Frankfurt, 1970.

64 Stern, R.: Musiktherapie in der zahnärztlichen Praxis. In: Droh, R., Spintge, R.(eds.): *Angst, Schmerz und Musik in der Anaesthesie*. Grenzach: Editiones Roche, 1983, pp. 167-172.

65 Stern, R.: Musiktherapie in der zahnärztlichen Praxis. In: Willms, H. (ed.): *Musik und Entspannung*. Stuttgart: Fischer, 1977, pp. 90-95.

66 Geirl, B.: Walkman in der zahnärztlichen Praxis. *Zahnärztliche Mitteilungen*, 1982, **6**, pp. 339-343.

67 Oyama, T., Sato, Y., Kudo, M., Spintge, R., Droh, R.: Endocrine effects of anxiolytic music in dental patients. In: Droh, R., Spintge, R. (eds.): *Angst, Schmerz und Musik in der Anaesthesie*. Grenzach: Editiones Roche, 1983, pp. 143-146.

68 Seeger, W.: Übungsbehandlung für Rheumakranke mit Musik. In: Droh, R., Spintge, R. (eds.): *Music in Medicine*, Grenzach: Editiones Roches, 1985, pp. 221-229.

69 Lippmann, H.I.: Mastering a musical instrument can be occupational therapy for arthritis. In: Volume of Abstracts 4th International Symposium of Music: Rehabilitation and Human Well-Being, New York, 1985, pp. 54-55.

70 Rothmaier, D.: Gymnastik nach Wunsch für Herzpatienten und Senioren. *Sport & Gesundheit*, 1985, **2**, pp. 11-15.

THE SHARP FOCUS

PHYSICAL REHABILITATION OF DISABLED MUSICIANS

Heinz I. Lippmann

Physical rehabilitation is the restoration to "health" of an individual who is handicapped, impaired or disabled from disease, injury or inborn (genetic or congenital) defect. Rehabilitation methodology is adapted to the patient's individual needs for functioning in his or her usual environment. Our society expects a "healthy" person to possess some basic attributes: s/he should be independent in communicating, in moving about, in eliminating in a socially acceptable manner, and should behave appropriately. The practicing physiatrist needs to know a patient's motivation and cognitive capacity; s/he must assess the patient's environmental resources and be familiar with therapeutic technology to supplement the biomedical knowledge acquired in medical school. Such information will come in good stead when a musician who is impaired or disabled as a result of disease or injury asks for help.

In my orbit, this is rarely the case. The majority of musicians whom I am called to see have developed problems related to instrument-player interaction. To help such an individual, medical experience alone is insufficient, it must be complemented with a capacity to listen to the language of music and with some know-how of the intricacies and peculiarities of musical instruments and the techniques used in playing them.

Interestingly, in a trendy burst of popularity, "music-medicine" (musicine?, practiced by musiphysicians?, studied by musicinologists?) is growing into a health care field of its own that differs from such medical specialties as neurology, orthopedics or sports medicine, but bears a soul-kinship to physiatry, in which an individual is assisted in regaining function rather than being treated for the elimination of a disease. The physician advocate of a basically healthy musician who has a problem with playing or performing will have to focus on both patient and instrument.

Physical and occupational therapy rank prominently among the therapeutic modalities in physiatry: physical therapy aims at restoring mobility; occupational therapy aims at healing through purposeful activity. Playing a musical instrument is in itself a powerful therapeutic modality that meets the scope and incentive of both physical and occupational therapy provided it is carried out in a physiologic manner.

Playing an instrument "physiologically" has been a traditional battleground among musicians. Music teachers, apart from their mission to convey an understanding of music to their students, have, since the time of Leonardo da Vinci[1] and Philip Emanuel Bach, been concerned with developing efficient methods of playing an instrument, basically to obtain maximal physical output with the least amount of energy. The fascinating history of the respective theories and practices will have to be told on another occasion.

A professional virtuoso on any instrument, to prevail in his or her career, must master technique in a physiological way. However, a capacity to analyze the essentials of a proficient technique in terms of human engineering is not given to everyone. Technique, whether generated by natural talent or acquired by hard work, cannot be transferred to the student through the written word, but must be supervised and corrected by the teacher at the instrument. Some – like my teacher Georg Bertram – have an intuitive notion of the physiologic intricacies of the human body and its upper extremities. But thus far, objective criteria for "physiologic" playing are missing, while adequate methodology for the solution of this problem, I believe, is available. Objective data for physiologic playing ought to be at the beck and call of music teachers in our lifetime. The theory of physiologic playing will be described later. It is supported by my experience with musicians in search of help. In many cases where disease or injury was not present, the musicians' difficulties could be attributed to their playing habits, and restoration of function could be achieved by applying the principles of this theory.

Music-medicine encompasses another area of concern that derives from our present culture: the strains and distresses that emerge from a new life-style, into which many musicians who play in orchestras, opera companies, sundry rock groups and entertainment assemblies are forced. They often travel under poor hygienic conditions, work strenuously without adequate sleep, nourishment or relaxation. This area of concern is little explored, and in this chapter only an approximate outline can be ventured. More research in this field is needed so that factual knowledge can spark some remedial effort which may well include legislative action.

In this fast developing field of music-medicine, specific concepts of prevention, diagnostics and management are about to develop. Prevention in this new field, apart from general health and hygienic measures, will have to include some knowledge about the human body and mind. Some facts about anatomy and physiology, in keeping with the principles of human engineering, should be part of the material taught children in elementary school, particularly to those interested in learning how to play an instrument. Many musicians I know have never heard of the need for warm up periods before any kind of physical exercise, and most are unfamiliar with even the simplest bases of human anatomy.

A diagnosis in this field can well be expressed in medical terms for those malfunctions that are due to disease or injury. Certainly, bursitis or carpal tunnel syndrome which has developed as a secondary problem is a diagnostic and therapeutic medical problem. But, in the majority of cases, medical diagnoses like "tendinitis," "overuse syndrome" or "tennis elbow" obscure rather than clarify the problem in terms that might serve as a guide for helping the musician in his/her difficulty.

In my experience, "tendinitis" has, for the past few years, become an umbrella that covers several unrelated conditions, including subacromial bursitis, sundry trigger points, hip joint contracture,[2] cervical rib and other outlet syndromes, inexpert playing techniques and, in one unusual case, a generalized muscle disease, to quote just a few unrelated conditions. Tendinitis, which is the laceration, partial rupture, calcification or inflammation of a tendon or its synovium in a noninjured individual, is seen rarely in my practice. Traumatic tendinitis in musicians usually involves the supraspinatus, the abductor or the extensor tendon of the thumb.

In my practice, "overuse" syndromes have included such distinct conditions as bad posture, reactive depression, anxiety states and tiredness from insufficient sleep or unphysiologic playing techniques. Again, this is an incomplete list. The small number of musicians I have seen with true overstress syndrome does not claim to be of statistical significance. Fry,[3] who has seen numerous overstressed musicians, probably has access to a different population of musicians.

Special problems may be added to playing difficulties by the oft-prescribed long abstention from playing. Not infrequently, careful "playing through" a mild pain, even if it causes anxiety, may be therapeutic. Weekly or monthly rest periods and the associated deconditioning may be devastating psychologically, physically and musically. The medical indications for complete rest in acute inflammatory disease, muscle or tendon rupture or other injuries do not contradict this statement. Such indications are more common in dancers or artists who violently stress their lower extremities, but are rare in uninjured instrument players.

"Tennis elbow," a frequent culprit, also may cover the sins of bad playing habits. Its classic form, epicondylitis that manifests with tenderness of the lateral elbow bone, is often associated with painful trigger points in the supinator muscle. This is usually caused by forceful supination with the elbow fully extended, a painful experience which is often forgotten but will come to light upon questioning. Such an injury can hardly occur during instrument playing since, in most instrument playing, the elbows are flexed. In epicondylitis with trigger points in the supinator, pain often radiates into the thumb adductor area. The complex anatomy around the human elbow is well described in the literature.[4] In pianists who inadvisedly play with their hands stretched out for long periods (such danger exists in Chopin's "Étude Op. 10 No. 1," for example), trigger points may develop in the long finger and wrist extensors, all of which undeservedly carry the label of tennis elbow. Neck problems, especially nerve root compression at C-7, may equally initiate elbow pain and trigger points. Entrapment of the radial nerve may occur near the elbow. In addition, an examination may reveal that the muscles around the elbow, other than the supinator, that are involved in moving the forearm, wrist and fingers, are ailing. All of this may go under the scrambled name of tennis elbow, a diagnostic hodge-podge that must be unscrambled to lead to successful treatment. Except for nerve root irritation or nerve entrapment, either of which warrants individual clinical decisions that are hard to predict, playing an instrument through the treatment period, with proper precautions that include warm up and cool down periods, yields better results than putting an ailing arm to rest for any length of time.

In order to lay a foundation for the rehabilitation of handicapped or disabled musicians, some pertinent facts will be discussed regarding:

1) the physiology of exercise;
2 the mental bases of making and learning music; and
3) some rules deemed useful for the playing of instruments.

SOME NOTES ABOUT THE CONTRIBUTION OF MUSCULAR ACTIVITY TO MUSIC MAKING

Obviously playing a musical instrument involves an exercise in the service of communication. The language of music, jointly with body language and olfactory signalling, are probably the oldest means of communication among living creatures, part of a 350 million year evolution of the species on earth from paleozoic creatures to modern human beings. Today, it is clearly possessed by fish, birds and mammals. For a musician, the spoken word encompasses only a small part of communicative power.

Nonmusicians interested in the mechanics of motion have likened the actual work at a musical instrument to an "athletic" exercise.[5] Musicians may find it difficult to accept this simplistic characterization since the muscular part of music making, though strenuous, complex and precise, is not, as in athletics, self-fulfilling. There are also fundamental physiologic differences. Of the four parameters of motion – strength, endurance, speed and coordination – the latter two are at the center of a musician's concern, training and practice; with endurance being optimal but not maximal; and strength, the hallmark of many types of athletic exercise, requiring adequate, but not maximal development.

The accomplishments in speed (of instantaneous contraction – relaxation) and ongoing coordination (of prime movers, antagonists, and stabilizers) of professional masters of instrument playing are indeed prodigious. Music can be played without fatigue for respectable lengths of time with great speed, and may approach the limits of physiologic capacity. For example, in playing Alexander Scriabin's "Étude Op. 8 No. 10" at proper speed, a pianist may depress the keyboard 11.1 times per second with the right hand and 7.9 times per second with the left for 22 seconds without let up. Or take Robert Schumann's "Toccata Op. 7": Vladimir Horowitz, in 2 performances, strikes the keyboard 22 times per second (13 times with the right hand and 9 times with the left) for 378 seconds for 279 seconds respectively; in one performance he repeats the first part, and in both performances, several years apart, his speed is precisely the same - while Joseph Lhevinne strikes 20 per second (12 with the right hand and 8 with the left for 313 seconds, and Simon Barere, who derived great pleasure from playing this piece faster than anyone else,[6] hits the keys 25 times per second (15 times with the right hand and 10 times with the left) for 252 seconds without tiring, leaving out a note or making a mistake.

Playing speed is naturally limited by muscular endurance. As in other work, if carried on for long periods without tiring, energy supply and consumption must be in balance. Few people reach optimum endurance without intense long practice. Skeletal muscles are composed of different kinds of fibers, some of which are adapted for aerobic, some for anaerobic work. Muscles that primarily provide strength differ functionally from those that are needed for speed. They often are classified by the time it takes them to contract ("twitch time"). We know of three physiologically distinct types:

1) Slow-twitch are red "type I" fibers which develop maximum tension after a relatively long period of 80 milliseconds (msec). They are resistant to fatigue, do not develop great force or tension and, by virtue of their enzymatic and biochemical properties, are prone to work aerobically. They possess an abundant blood supply.

2) Fast twitch are white "type IIb" fibers which develop high tension within 30 msec but fatigue fast. They are switched on when movements are intended to be fast or powerful, but they also depend on the position of the limb, and their response can be controlled by other messages, e.g., from the skin. They are, by virtue of their enzymatic and biochemical properties, prone to brief bouts of anaerobic exercise.

3) In animal experimentation, a second group of "fast twitch" white fibers have been identified, the "type IIa" fibers which probably exist in human muscle as well. They develop maximal tension at an intermediate 40 msec, develop less than the "type IIb," but more than the "type I" fibers.

In playing a musical instrument, all types of fiber participate, i.e., the fast move fibers need stabilizers for steady work and these must be simultaneously recruited. For each type of motion, the sequential incorporation of these fibers is fairly stereotyped.[7] In mild isometric work (muscle tightening without joint motion), type I fibers are recruited at a low frequency (5-10 Hz) and, with increasing tension, the recruitment rate gradually rises. At a frequency of 20-30 Hz the muscle goes into tetanic contraction which becomes smooth at about 60 Hz. These low twitch fibers are recruited for almost all kinds of motion, regardless whether it results from reflex or volitional activity. With motions that are intended to be fast of forceful, type IIb and type IIa fibers are also stimulated. The incorporation of different fibers not only depends on continuation and intensity of effort, but is influenced by feedback from the muscle itself (the muscle spindle). When the intensity of muscular effort is increased, type II fibers are preferentially activated.

Fatigue may be due to depletion of energy fuel which is somewhat different in type II from that in type I fibers. Fatigue, however, is more likely to set in when stimulation from the nervous system wanes (central fatigue).

While each motor neuron (governing a group of muscle fibers) stimulates contraction in an "all or none" fashion, the fine nuances of applied muscle force a musician needs for playing an instrument are miraculously provided for by a number of mechanisms. These include the number of motor units recruited, the relative participation of type I and type II fibers, the energy stored in the fibroelastic tissues which retard its release, and the percentage of measured force due to leverage (the distance of the muscle attachment from the joint and the angle at which the muscle pulls).

Heinz I. Lippmann

Generally, the time relation of agonist-antagonist action largely depends on the intended purpose of muscular effort. In a sudden (ballistic) motion, the agonist stays active for a relatively long time until the antagonist stops the motion in a planned ending. In forced motion (working full force from the beginning), both agonist and antagonist after a very short time continue to fire together, with the result that the antagonistically innervated fibers lengthen but store some energy which is released later on, a mechanism which is exploited effectively in some athletic activities, e.g., in sprinting. In controlled movements, more applicable to muscle work while learning a piece of music, the agonist and antagonist remain alternately active throughout the motion, thereby slowing it down. This hindrance usually smooths out with increasing musical technique.

Little is known about the mechanisms of controlled immediate relaxation, especially the time interval (latency) after a muscle contraction which, in proficient musician, is extremely short. Trained athletes are known to possess the capacity to relax their muscles faster than those who are untrained.[8] Relaxation is measured electromyographically by the time a volitionally working muscles relaxes to complete electric silence. The relaxation techniques that have been developed for a whole person, e.g., Alexander[9] or Yoga[10] may or may not bear a relation to the instant relaxation after a muscle contraction, the latency for which shortens as the playing technique advances.

Repetitive habitual concentrated exercise is unlikely to transform one type of muscle fiber into another. This would entail a turnover of the biochemical makeup, enzymatic composition, mitrochondrial concentration and finer structure of myofibrils, myosin and actin. However, experience with instrument playing indicates that sequential incorporation and relative fiber recruitment can be modified by practice. An example would be the incorporation of a stabilizer in fast wrist motion, e.g., during octave playing in pianists, which can be enhanced by training.

SOME NOTES ABOUT MUSIC MAKING AND LEARNING

Music making is a highly entangled, engram-guided, muscle-transmitted language, a complete analysis of which is not possible at this time due to its complexity. A performer uses mass motions comparable to those needed for walking, swimming or bicycling, activities which must be learned by trial and error before becoming engrammed as habitual units of motion. In contrast to these means of locomotion, which, in spite of ample provision for variants in posture and muscle coordination, have become semi-automatic after years of practice, each piece of music must be learned anew. Correct attention must be paid to rhythm, melody, harmony and overall timing to capture its meaning. A skillful performance, like that of other learned skills, can be achieved only after numerous repetitions in concentrated awareness. The acquisition of optimal skill in mechanical tasks by factory workers has been estimated to require 500,000 to 1,000,000 repetitions in actual performance or in concentrated thinking of the kinesthetic adaptation to the hand,[11] to which timing and a special kind of motivation are added as integral parts in music. It is possible, though conjectural, that a musician can acquire skill in performing a piece of music in a shorter amount of time. In fact, "talent" in absorbing music after a smaller number of repetitions may correlate with the time it takes to appropriate such complexity. To my knowledge, no scientific study has been made of this fundamental problem in music making.

A human being is endowed with 69 upper extremity muscles of the hand, forearm, wrist, arm and shoulder girdle on each side, each with additional prime movers of their own, represented by the motor units in each muscle. Each one of these prime movers may become agonist, antagonist or stabilizer during the complex motion of the upper extremity during playing. Each of these hundreds of prime movers on each side, guided by our central cerebral computer, contracts with precise timing and intensity and relaxes with precise timing, while the stabilizing muscles continually adjust the level of firm support.

Mathematical models of such complex activity would imply millions of permutations and thousands of combinations in alternative muscle coordinations. Such complexity can only be realized through pre-programmed mass motion, certainly not by volitional innervation of individual muscles which in fact would disrupt smooth performance. The human brain perceives motion rather than individual muscle work.[12]

Since all motor activity is basically derived from intrinsic reflexes, skill is acquired by volitional concentrated and attentive repetition of the integral parts of complex motions.[13] A complex motion therefore can become one unit of mass motion only by practice; this process of acquisition is far from being understood in all detail.

The motor "engram," which discharged in the performance as one unit, is hypothetically perceived as dynamic complex circuitry involving cortical,[14] subcortical[15] and cerebellar[16] synaptic pathways and neurons with feedback from other "engrams" and centers,[17] that has become habitual by the repetition of "paving a path" through the maze of millions of preformed neuronal and synaptic pathways. It can be invaded by other engrams which may use some of its pathways. This, of course, is only an empirical description and in need of verification.

The musical engram for performing not only includes rhythm, melody and harmony, but a time factor and kinesthetic muscle awareness as well. It is continually monitored, in some by the visual image of the written music, in others by the auditory system. It excludes supernumerary muscle participation.[18]

If the initial engram is precise, the performance will be precise. Hence the slow learning technique of new music which all experienced performers stress, well described by Gieseking-Leimer.[19] Inaccurate learning requires wasteful dishabituation preceding relearning, leading to delays in memorizing and mastering music.

SOME NOTES ON PLAYING MUSICAL INSTRUMENTS

Since it is virtually impossible to develop a mathematical model for alternative mechanisms of playing an instrument, one must rely on empirical data. Generally, a motion is optimally effective if it is carried out with minimal energy consumption. This truism does not help us in devising methods of assisting ailing musicians or teaching music students. In pianism, we have learned by observation that the force of gravity must be incorporated into the production of sound to achieve effective playing. This principle, with modifications, is applicable to other percussion instruments and to string players. It may play a role in wind players and brasses, in whom additionally, the resiliency of the respiratory and chest tissues, including the diaphragm, is utilized in the production of sound to spare muscle effort.

In pianism, the hand is brought into the most appropriate position by muscular action. Fortissimo playing is mediated by the fall of the full weight of the arm while soft playing is accomplished by the weight of only the forearm or parts of it and very soft playing by the weight of the hand or parts of it. The trunk serves as a stabilizer when the relaxed shoulder-arm unit produces a fortissimo sound, while the muscular apparatus giving strength to the fingers is fully recruited, so that the weight of the falling arm is transmitted to the keyboard without any of the finger joints caving in. In soft playing, the shoulder and arm muscles become the stabilizers, and the recruitment of the finger flexors is only partial, enough to sustain the lesser weight of forearm or hand. Thus, the innervation of the shoulder and hand muscles is reciprocal, and the continuous shifting of the stabilizers helps to control the fine dynamic touch.

Heinz I. Lippmann

Looseness of the shoulder girdle, except for the times when the shoulder is the stabilizer, during soft dynamics is essential. Such relaxation can be enhanced by slight abduction of the arm during playing, a posture which is well described by Joseph Lhevinne[20] as a feeling of "floating the arm", i.e., to have the limb in constant balance.

There are many means of maintaining this "freedom" at the level of the keyboard. The position of the hand and wrist has been debated in the past by many music teachers and educators. Both the flexed and the straightened out finger position will do, as long as the full weight of the arm is sustained during loud playing. Those artists who play with flat outstretched hands, i.e., S. Richter and V. Horowitz, have strong hands. The flexor apparatus of the fingers is threefold: The intrinsic muscles flex the fingers at the metacarpophalangeal joints (the knuckles), the sublime flexors bend the interphalangeal joints (midfinger joints) and the deep flexors bend the terminal phalangeal (endfinger) joints. They are located at the knuckles, three quarters up the flexor surface of the forearm near the elbow, in the same order. All of these must be strong to prevent the fingers from caving in during playing.

The reciprocal innervation of shoulder and finger muscles comes naturally to some "born" artists, but most must acquire this by practice. The strengthening of the wrist and finger muscles, like the maturation of musicality, follows a natural course which can be accelerated only to a certain degree. The artist who has played and practiced the piano from an early age on has a certain advantage. Many of the younger budding artists of today who exercise for many hours to prepare for the ubiquitous competitions without possessing the needed strength in their fingers run into malfunctions, presenting as muscle triggers in forearm flexors, or shoulder girdle problems and are diagnosed as tendinitis or overstress syndrome while the problem is inadequate physical preparation for a taxing self-imposed schedule. If in an enthusiastic, young ambitious artist such mistreatment is driven to an extreme, a whole musical career can go to pieces.

I saw a 24-year-old college student, a former drummer in his school orchestra, bent on studying percussion seriously. At age 22, however, he had decided to switch to pianism and conducting. Immediately he plunged into piano practice for five to six hours per day, hitting the piano as he hit his drums. He developed cramps in both arms. When I saw him eighteen months later, he had developed muscle problems galore, apart from a thoracic outlet syndrome. Even though he relearned writing and playing the piano, he had to give up his ambition to become a professional musician.

MANAGEMENT OF HEALTH PROBLEMS IN MUSICIANS, EXCLUDING MANIFEST DISEASE OR PRECEDING INJURY

Health problems that stem from instrument playing interaction are difficult to categorize in an orderly fashion. Every case has its unique features and stands on its own. Often symptoms develop because of pre-existing functional difficulties that, from a medical point of view, are within the range of normal. However, in this section, we cannot always be certain that a long-forgotten illness or long-healed injury may not be a factor in malfunction.

In the following section, the problems described will be in order of frequency, as they presented in my office.

Postural Changes

The position or posture in which a musician sits in relation to his/her instrument has a bearing on music making. In pianism the seat should be adjusted so that the elbow is at the level of the keyboard.[21] Too low a seat may interfere with the ongoing shift of the stabilizing part which, in dynamic playing, may be the trunk, the shoulder, the arm or the forearm. In such a case, the shoulder girdle would have to be raised and fixed, temporarily denying it freedom of motion. This commonly results in muscle trigger points (in order of frequency) in the levator scapulae, upper trapezius, supra and infraspinatus, rhomboids, latissimus dorsi, teres major and splenii capitis and colli and occasionally the sternocleidomastoids. Pain from these muscle problems may radiate into the arm and hand posteriorly as well as the shoulder and neck. Successful management not only requires adjustment of the seat height, but treatment of all muscle trigger points by the method of Travell and Simons.[22] Seats at the piano are rarely adjusted too high; the player feels uncomfortable.

Harpists, particularly students of the instrument, have usually been young women of small stature disproportionate to their large instruments. Since, in addition to their rather complex proper playing posture, their playing position is low it forces them to elevate the shoulder, keeping their hands in radial deviation. Cramps in the forearm and, if not attended to, in the shoulder and neck, or occasionally in the hand, lead to the suspicion of seat malpositioning. Again, in addition to correction of the seat and the player's vicinity to the instrument, all secondarily involved muscles must be treated separately. Independently, harpists often complain about low back pain caused by the heavy instruments they have to carry on tour from concert to car and vice versa.

Postural abnormalities far removed from the upper extremities can lead to playing problems. A gifted violin student was referred by his teacher for tendinitis of the right shoulder. His right arm tired after ten minutes of practice in a standing position. He presented with an exaggerated upper dorsal kyphosis related to an old left hip flexion contracture of long healed Legg-Perthes disease. After gaining a few degrees of hip extension through physical therapy, he was able to practice adequately without tiring in a more normal standing posture.

Musicians in orchestras who sit in a theater pit or on a crowded stage and play from the printed page occasionally find it difficult to gain a favorable angle of vision, resulting in tension headache or tightening of the arm or forearm muscles.

Abnormal postural attitudes are not always due to physical conditions. A female musician complained of increasing weakness of both hands, of two months duration (coffee cups were falling out of her hands, etc.) and a constant feeling of insecurity when handling her wind instrument. She had been healthy previously and had played without trouble in a large professional symphony orchestra for several years. Prior workups in two music-medicine groups had excluded physical disease. I agreed, after examining her, that neurologically, rheumatologically or myologically there was no abnormality. Her hands were in fact strong. While normally a wrist is held in extension when a fist is made, she assumed an unusual posture: after making a fist with the wrist in extension, immediately thereafter she volitionally brought the wrist to maximal flexion. This, of course, put the long flexor tendons in slack, preventing the development of strength in her hand grip. This was explained to her and immediately remedied. While discussing this most unusual and unphysiologic postural attitude with her, she volunteered that she had, for the past two months, been awakened in the morning with upper and lower extremities in flexion which she recognized as a "fetal position" and a manifestation of a deeper problem which several years earlier had brought her to a psychiatrist, to whom she was advised to return. She has not been followed up for a long time, but when last heard from, she no longer had the feeling of weakness.

A widely publicized case of malfunction relates, at least in part, to a postural problem, namely a wrist held in strong ulnar deviation which became a habit of one of the most gifted pianists. It started with neglect of the fourth and fifth fingers in octave playing for a long period, which became resistant to dishabituation, so that the right hand with nonparticipating (in fact flexed) fourth and fifth fingers had become useless to this artist as a professional performer. This case also reveals our as yet inadequate therapeutic methods for getting rid of a bad habit. Several music-medicine experts have failed to solve this artist's (I believe well diagnosed) problem, probably because attempts at therapy, by necessity, have been long-interval and short-term in comparison to the continuous and long term formation of a habit which must have entailed hundreds of thousands of the same repetitive postural errors, counted during playing and thinking, both effective in forming an engram. This has led to an almost reflex misposture defying dishabituation.

An experienced professional flutist, second chair in a large orchestra, asked for help when he felt unable to play fast sequences, trills, etc. with his left fourth and fifth fingers; this had developed over one year and caused great anxiety. Physical (including electric) examination revealed no upper or lower motor neuron abnormality; in fact his hand was strong and his finger control complete on a table. When he played his instrument for me, I noticed his left arm was held tightly to his body, a posture which he had invented some two years previously and which he had difficulty in abandoning. Most flutists I know or have observed play with a slightly abducted and flexed left arm. His problem was solved in a most trivial way: A small cushion under his left axilla forced the left arm into abduction and flexion and resolved his playing and anxiety problem.

Guitar players may develop problems from bad posture: A case of femoral vein thrombosis has been reported in a guitarist who pressed his instrument hard into his left groin.[23] Cases of mastitis from the pressure of the instrument to the chest have been reported.[24] [25]

A case of "cello scrotum" is worth mentioning[26] as well as another report which asserts that knowledgeable cellists would not develop pressure on the scrotum.[27]

A violin student referred by her teacher complained of pain in her left shoulder and upper back radiating down toward the midline between her shoulder blades. She played with her left shoulder elevated in a fixed position to hold the instrument between the chin and clavicle. Trigger points had developed in the upper and middle trapezius on the left, the left elevator scapulae and the rhomboids. She was a tall young woman with an unusually long (Modigliani-like) neck. An additional cushion under her chin rest and some training to keep the shoulder relaxed and down, helped. The trigger points were treated in the usual way. A previously suspected cervical radiculopathy and a thoracic outlet syndrome were both ruled out by examination.

Trouble From Instrument Contact

Contact with an instrument may produce skin reactions as most violinists know. In the area of contact, sundry cutaneous lesions described as acanthosis, hyperkeratosis, follicular plugging, epidermal cysts and lichenification,[28] can become symptomatic, i.e., painful or itching. Apart from the effects of pressure, an immune reaction to the wood or varnish on the instrument has been postulated as the cause. Some violinists, among them one world famous artist, retired by now, with whom I spoke recently, never developed a skin reaction, in spite of a popular concept that "fiddler's neck" is every violinists trademark. Occasionally the condition is relieved by changing the instrument's chin rest but dermatologic care is usually needed.

Flutists occasionally develop an eruption of the chin with pustules and papules or hyperpigmentation as a result of saliva dripping during playing. One such case has been described in which acne had been present earlier in life.[29] As a preventative measure, growing a beard below the lower lip was suggested, which was believed to function as a protective shield.[30] I hesitated to pass on such obviously macho-inspired advice to an itching flute player recently.

Interestingly, considering the history of string instrument playing, the early players of the viola da braccio, the predecessor of our violins and violas, must have sensed an inherent problem while holding their instrument on top of their left shoulder; later on, they pressed the instrument against their sternum while playing as paintings of the period indicate.[31]

Long sustained pressure against the skin results in thickening of the upper layer of the skin and finally in the formation of calluses. Tense individuals develop calluses more easily than those who are relaxed. Thickly callused fingertips may lose some of the sensitivity required for them to act as feedback receptors in string players and in guitarists. Many string instrument players file down thick calluses, while other more relaxed persons never have to do that. Students of the guitar, the lute, the piano or string instruments, particularly the violoncello or double bass, find out for themselves that callus growth can be controlled by less vigorous pressing against the strings or keyboard. Occasionally, though, callus problems cannot be solved to everyone's satisfaction. A few years back, a young female cello student, accompanied by her father, asked for help because of heavy calluses over all her fingertips which hurt and split. They had inadvisedly been removed surgically and had grown back rapidly. Her pain radiated into the left arm and shoulder, making playing impossible. I could not discover any abnormality, including nervous or musculoskeletal system. Two friends helped with my puzzlement, both professional cellists and music teachers, who assured me that this kind of difficulty usually was solved by the student her/himself. If not, "look for emotional trouble!" I was fully aware that many cellists, among them my two friends, may have calluses over the radial aspect of their left thumb, but their other fingers gave them no problem, even if the skin was somewhat thickened.

Armed with that insight, I asked the young woman, with her father removed from the room, what really bothered her when playing the cello. She burst out that she hated the instrument that her father, who was a frustrated cello player himself, insisted she learn to play. She confided that she loved skiing and painting, which was what I advised. Her father was not my friend when they left, but she gave up her cello and both calluses and pain vanished.

Tissue Laxity

Ehlers-Danlos syndrome is an inherited disorder which manifests with joint hypermobility, skin stretchability and tissue fragility. The condition is inherited as an autosomal dominant and occasionally as a recessive. Laxity of the joints without skin involvement, which may or may not be a "forme fruste" of Ehlers-Danlos syndrome, is common in otherwise normal people. It is recognized by the ease with which the terminal joint of the thumb, or other joints, including elbows or knees, can hyperextend. Such individuals are prone to injury in activities usually considered "safe." Instrument playing is no exception.

A professional pianist developed a severe cramp in her right hand after an unusually long and intense practice session. The next day the pain radiated into the arm and shoulder. She was advised not to touch the instrument and to hold the arm tightly in a sling. After a few days of this, the pain in her hand weakened but neck pain developed. Two months later, not playing during the whole period, she saw me, requesting help for her "tendinitis." An examination revealed some shoulder stiffness, but no other sign of rheumatic disease or neurological abnormality, except for atrophy of her right wrist and finger flexors, the cause for which had to be interpreted as deconditioning. Except for her shoulder joint, all her joints were lax and could be hyperextended, including her carpus, the bones of which could be painlessly slightly displaced, with the exception of the capitate bone, even light displacement of which against the navicular and lunate was extremely painful. In fact, it reproduced her original hand pain. She also had formed trigger points in the right finger extensors and in some of her shoulder muscles, pressure on which also produced pain into the elbow and hand. Treatment consisted of applying a wristlet and the immediate resumption of playing the instrument with precautions. She had to learn how to warm up and cool down, not to play against pain, even if that meant for her to interrupt her practice several times a day, and avoid playing music that forced her to stretch the hand more than an instant.

Trigger points were attacked in the usual fashion by a therapist. Her arm pain improved shortly after resumption of playing. She is a resolute and persevering woman and her ultimate prognosis is good, although deconditioning will delay her recovery by several weeks. Her wrist flexors have regained some tone and roundness.

A professional harpist who was left handed had been suffering for fifteen years with pain in her second, third and fourth fingers during and for a while after playing, in both hands. She usually disregarded the pain and kept playing against it. More recently, the right thumb had become more painful after practicing for only 30 minutes. All her joints tested, including upper extremity and shoulder joints, were mobile 20-30 degrees beyond normal, in all direction. The right radial styloid process was exquisitely tender, although she could not recall any injury that might have caused her De Quervain syndrome. She responded well to a cockup splint which she wore night and day, as long as she did not play her instrument. In commenting, I would like to note that I defer local injections of steroids or anesthetics in musicians for as long as possible. This woman continued to play with some pain, to which she had grown accustomed since it was bothersome but certainly not disabling. I learned from this and other similar cases that individuals with hyperextending articulations may have to put up with some nondisabling pain during and immediately after playing the harp and probably other instruments. This woman was quite relieved to know that the sharp wrist pain did not represent a progression of her condition.

Stretching a hand with lax ligaments can become traumatic. Such a case was reported[32] in a classical guitarist whose left wrist, after intense practicing, became swollen and inflamed. A diagnosis of traumatic synovitis was made and treated with one injection of triamcinolone; the pain subsided and the artist was able to resume normal practice sessions. All his finger joints were abnormally flexible and distensible. The author pointed out that the trend for hyperextensibility is not uncommon in the population.

Problems that may arise in musicians who have various forms of arthritis will be dealt with later on.

Problems Caused by Weak Hands

Caving in during loud playing on the piano is a rather common cause of dysfunction, mostly in students of the instrument and rarely, if at all, in experienced pianists who could not have pursued their careers without strong hand support. Caving in most commonly involves the fourth and fifth finger terminal, interphalangeal or matacarpophalangeal joints, singly or in any combination. Involvement of other fingers usually indicates some preceding pathology while both fourth and fifth fingers are often weak because of inadequate preparation in perfectly healthy individuals. As was mentioned previously, during playing the shoulder muscles and the hand and wrist flexors are reciprocally innervated, a function that is natural to only few musicians, while most others have to learn it through practice. When the shoulder is kept loose, the wrist and hand, i.e., each finger that transmits the force of the full falling arm, must sustain a considerable force, if only for an instant, preceding instant relaxation. Any joint caving in at that moment strains the respective flexor muscle. This results in pain and stiffness, which radiates up if untreated, and is responsible for a gradually increasing disability, usually termed "tendinitis" or "overuse" syndrome. The leading symptom is most often cramps or stiffness; strengthening of the wrist and hand is the therapeutic answer, even though various modalities of heat, deep or superficial, may temporarily reduce pain. Therapy must include advice about practicing habits which often are in need of complete revision and which require good communication between player and musiphysician.

As to the modes of practicing, while travelling through Switzerland in a train compartment, I remember sitting opposite one of the greatest virtuosi of all time, Moriz Rosenthal, who continued, without let up, practicing on a mock keyboard while reading a newspaper or conversing with me. I was a teenager at the time and was greatly impressed. In the meantime, I learned that mechanical practice of an instrument is of scarce or no value. Experienced teachers assert[33] that meaningful instrumental practice mandates concentrated awareness of finger position and motion, of the musical contents and timing, in order to appropriate the whole as an engrammatic program that can be reproduced at will, to make practice productive and worthwhile. Even experienced artists would find it difficult to sustain this kind of practice for longer than three to four hours at a time, which should be the limit of uninterrupted practice for most musicians. If this includes the learning of new music, which it does for most artists, four hours pass fast. If pain, cramps or feelings of weakness manifest, practicing must be interrupted until such symptoms subside, usually in a matter of minutes, and then practice may be continued. Rules of this kind should be suggested to students; it would be presumptive to advise experienced artists who have developed their own best methods, but occasionally such suggestions are part of a prescription for rehabilitation.

When caving in of finger joints is observed, each joint is tested for flexor strength since there exist about thirty possible combinations of involvement in each hand. When this diagnosis is established, the corresponding muscles, in their anatomical order, are explored by palpation and often, though not always, found to be the site of bunched up fibers. Restorative management consists of strengthening the weak muscles by progressive resistive exercises and treating the muscle trigger points. If fingers other than the fourth or fifth are involved, musculoskeletal disorders are likely to be found which require treatment or further diagnostic work. Progressive resistive exercises are carried out according to the principles of DeLorme: only the flexor of the joint under treatment is allowed to contract against a resistance of 80% capacity, alternating contraction and relaxation. I use five seconds on, five seconds off, twenty times, once or twice a day. A modified blood pressure cuff can be used to estimate maximum capacity, but the musician is soon taught how to proceed by him/herself. The exercise protocol also provides for increasing resistance with increasing strength. If the student follows the directives, an increase in strength is observed after four to six weeks, or earlier in some cases. Supervision is usually recommended as a safeguard against the nonparticipation of unneeded muscles, especially the shoulder girdle muscles. This form of isolated exercise is but a shortcut to the normal strengthening that is spontaneous in the course of serious practicing. Such exercises are useful for those students who embark on playing in competitions or early recitals before having acquired enough strength through natural development. They are, however, useful for restoring function after pain and stiffness have brought them to the physician.

FUNCTIONAL PLAYING PROBLEMS, WITH OR WITHOUT ORGANIC CAUSES

Again, a systemic presentation of functional playing difficulties is impossible, as each case is unique and stands on its own.

A violinist of international fame developed a serious functional problem after many years of successful concertizing, losing control over his bow arm the instant the tip of the bow was to touch the instrument. This occurred at irregular intervals, and not necessarily only when he was tired or after long playing sessions. He developed a fear that such instantaneous insecurity might repeat itself during a concert.

Actually, the moment the bow makes contact with the violin, especially in soft playing, complex coordination and very precise control are required. The scapula is fixed from above, behind and in front, and the shoulder is steadied while the narrow motion is effected by the pro- and supinators, the flexors and extensors of the elbow and the flexors of the wrist and fingers, a motion in which almost all upper extremity muscles play a part, as agonists, antagonists or stabilizers, requiring steady pressure, arm weight and timing.

The artist, on examination, did not have any weakness or neurological abnormality; he well understood that fear was a factor. I suspected that his symptom might have developed as a result of some experience when he was extremely tired. I understand that his uncertainty has become quite rare now.

A similar problem arose in a violist, an excellent artist and chamber musician. In him, however, there was an organic abnormality, i.e., a calcific subacromial bursitis that was painful on shoulder motion and which interfered with the accustomed smooth motion needed to touch his instrument with the bow, playing softly. His anxiety level increased and aggravated his functional difficulty. Spraying of the shoulder, followed immediately by active exercise with small weights, reduced the pain on shoulder motion. In commenting, I refrained from injecting the bursa which is common therapy in nonmusicians, and was spared the need to do so, because the patient improved and did not have to give up concertizing.

Another professional violist, a member of a large professional orchestra, after years of playing, noticed a weakness in his left shoulder which prevented him from holding his instrument in a playing position for more than a few minutes. He had developed a rotator cuff rupture in the left shoulder, lesser in the right, which was evidenced by an arthrogram CT scan. His long biceps tendon was not located in the normal groove, perhaps having been displaced or ruptured. Nothing short of surgical treatment could have re-established normal conditions, but he insisted on temporary stop-gap measures. A support made from T-foam firm cushion was constructed which rested on his left thigh when he played and held his arm up with the instrument, without interfering with his freedom of arm motion in a horizontal plane. This enabled him to continue playing, but he ultimately will have to undergo surgical repair.

The case of a cellist is reported[34] whose left fourth and fifth fingers became numb and paralyzed after a few minutes of playing. He had a habitual spontaneous dislocation of the ulnar nerve when he bent his arm. The nerve then snapped from its groove to the front of the medial epicondyle. Ulnar nerve conduction velocity across the elbow with the elbow in extension was 67 m/sec; with the elbow bent and the nerve dislocated it dropped to 57 m/sec. The condition was bilateral, but on playing the cello, was dislocated only on the left side due to the angle in which the two arms are engaged during playing. The author transposed the nerve anteriorly to the medial epicondyle on both sides, allowing the patient to play his instrument without discomfort. Dislocation of the ulnar nerve due to local injury or to elbow fracture can lead to serious problems in a musician. Early in his career, after an automobile accident, a young violinist, now of international renown, had the terrifying experience of feeling his left fourth and fifth fingers growing paralyzed in the midst of a recital in a large concert hall, forcing him to stop playing. Translocation of the nerve probably saved his brilliant career.[35]

A pianist and piano teacher, after a blunt trauma to the left medial epicondyle, developed an ulnar entrapment, the symptoms of which initially improved after transposition of the nerve anteriorly. Thereafter, some adhesions formed which constricted the nerve and new symptoms set in after another minor compression she suffered at home. Reoperation by another hand surgeon revealed that the median nerve as well was bound to the fasciae of the flexor carpi ulnaris and the pronator teres, all of which resulted in a long drawn out problem of rehabilitation requiring a careful and gradual process of relearning on a path avoiding the dangers of deconditioning and of overstress, keeping with the pace of natural healing. A proper choice of music played during this recovery period is part of the therapeutic process, and should be decided upon after consultation with the physician.

Long forgotten trauma to individual joints in the hand, due to vibration from baseball bats or golf clubs or to forces that longitudinally hit an outstretched finger, may turn out to be troublesome to musicians. A typical example is that of a twenty-five-year-old piano student who, after questioning, finally remembered that six years previously, during a tennis game, she experienced a sharp pain in her left third metacarpophalangeal joint which lasted for two weeks. She is left handed. Four weeks prior to her present visit, while practicing hard for a recital, the same site in her hand started to hurt. The hand was stiff when she woke up in the morning, but straightened out after she got dressed. Except for the fact that both parents were adult onset diabetics, her medical history was noncontributory.

All her finger, wrist and upper extremity joints were hyperextensible but painless and non-tender, with the exception of the third left MCP joint which was slightly warmer, swollen and had some effusion; its synovium was slightly thickened. All blood and chemical tests were normal, and no evidence of systemic metabolic or rheumatic disease could be obtained. Roentgenfilms showed no gross abnormality, and there was no need to have a bone scan, in view of the clinical findings. We had to assume that the previous injury had caused some local structural damage, a weakness which was unlikely to be totally reversible by commonly used intraarticular therapy or joint replacement. A more carefully planned practice schedule and a night splint enabled this young lady to practice adequately and give her recital and, we hope, many more. In other similar cases, although one may have to resort to anti-inflammatory drugs and intraarticular injections, proper practice schedules ought to be part of the therapy.

The situation is different when, in the not uncommon case of a musician who shows a tendency for a collagen disorder or predisposition for rheumatic disease, a similar history is obtained.

A musician who has rheumatoid arthritis seems to be more susceptible than normal to suffer structural damage from mechanical injury in individual joints of the hand. It is remarkable that such individuals do not tend to develop ulnar deviation, since during playing the piano, finger posture is straight while in daily life activities a posture in ulnar deviation prevails. Playing of the instrument should be encouraged with the usual precautions, viz. warming up and cooling down and a planned schedule for practicing, stopping as soon as pains or cramps are felt. Playing under these constrictions is therapeutic.

A special contingency arises in musicians who have or tend to have psoriasis. Their mono-articular affliction usually is quite painful; in fact, if a musician presents with complaints of pain that seem to exceed that which inspection and examination of the joint justify, psoriasis should be suspected. In these individuals, minor trauma suffices to involve other joints, with disappearance of the symptoms at the original site.

Naturally, the indications for treatment, by pharmacologic or physiatric means, follow the rules established by rheumatologists. Again, practice at the instrument should be planned in conjunction with the other modalities of treatment, taking into account the patient's strength, endurance and fatigability. I find that most activities to which a professional musician is exposed can be continued, unless the disease is advanced or in an active stage. I assume that such individuals would have had to give up music as a profession, so that I would have no opportunity to see them. I also assume that travelling from recital to recital would be incompatible with an existing collagen active disorder or a rheumatic disease.

Musicians who blow to produce sound, the wind and brass players (vocalists are not discussed in this chapter), may develop problems. Saxophonists are reported to increase their intra abdominal pressure to abnormally high levels.[36] The case of a young trumpet playing musician is reported whose neck enlarged painfully and massively when he played.[37] As a youth I waited impatiently for the few bars before the second theme in the last movement of Brahms' *Symphony No. 2*, just to observe our orchestra's first clarinetist's cheeks and neck blow up, similar to Dizzy Gillespie's when he blows his glorious trumpet. In all these cases, as with those reported earlier in players of percussion instruments, guitars, or harps, laxness of tissue probably is present which may or may not be a variant of Ehlers-Danlos syndrome as some observers rightly suspect.[38]

Double reed players (oboists, bassoonists, English hornists) need to develop high pressure in their oral cavity, oropharynx or hypopharynx.[39] Some players develop a temporary weakness of their velum palatinum which then opens the nasopharynx, permitting the pressured air to escape through the nose ("losing the seal") producing no sound. This certainly temporarily disables a professional oboist, and no medical treatment exists which could control such an ordeal. I have treated a professional oboist, who after a long career playing his instrument, developed headaches and attacks of dizziness which seemed to be related to his playing. At rest, his hemodynamics were normal, including the condition of his carotid and vertebral arteries, as seen by non-invasive tests; his vestibular apparatus was normal as were both central and peripheral nervous systems. Since I never had the opportunity to examine him during or immediately after his playing, I had to assume that a form of cerebral ischemia or a pressure-induced form of abnormal cerebral circulation was responsible for these attacks. A beta blocker appeared to help, but the condition was never fully under control. However, he did not have to give up his playing.

HEARING PROBLEMS IN MUSICIANS

In spite of rising interest in chamber music that soothes the ear of the music lover, noise pollution is generated by various forms of music making, as in the case of large orchestras. Our young generation loves electronically amplified music, rock and pop which produce respectable clusters of decibellage. Although the fear expressed by a British physician in 1974 that widespread deafness would result from such noises if superimposed on declining hearing in old age[40] might have been exaggerated, some serious defects have been documented.[41] [42] [43]

Anybody who has ever played in a modern symphony orchestra knows that in the midst of a loud passage it becomes well nigh impossible to discern the music that comes out of one's own instrument. This is a chronic problem for those musicians who play in orchestra pits or flat stages on which opera orchestras or travelling groups often have to play. In many such instances, players now are being protected by noise insulating shells mounted to their chair. The first harpist of one of our great symphony orchestras told me that placing his seat in the orchestra has become a difficult problem; his traditional place near the tympani impairs his hearing and his auditory self-control. Other examples are the four French horn players who sit in front of the trumpets and trombones. The first French horn blows into the left ear of the second, who blows into the left ear of the third who blows into the left ear of the fourth who sits near the tympani which block the hearing in his right ear. Do those and other anecdotal reports measure up to indicating a long-term threat to the hearing of these musicians?

Evaluating the hearing of musicians is a complicated undertaking. It includes the study of functional and structural alterations in the middle and inner ear, sharpness of tone distinction and cognitive response, and the understanding of the musical structure and instrumentation. Such an evaluation also has to take into account other musically unrelated sources of hearing impairment such as old age and sundry industrial noises that fill the air in cities. Relatively noise-free populations, in contrast to our own society, like the Mabaans in central Sudan, are reported to possess near normal hearing into ripe old age.[44] Aging individuals in Western[45] and Oriental[40] societies gradually lose hearing with advancing age, as measured by an increase in their hearing threshold. Such loss of hearing is permanent and must be distinguished from common temporary tiring of hearing, measured by a reversible temporary increase of hearing threshold, after exposure to loud music for awhile.[46] The permanent hearing defects of aging individuals in our society are particularly pronounced at frequencies of 4 and 6 KHz.[42]

Careful studies have been conducted with the Minnesota[47] and various other orchestras, mostly by Scandinavian authors.[48] Altogether about 500 musicians have been examined in the course of these studies. Poorer hearing was found to correlate with a greater number of hours per week and minutes per session during which the musicians played.[49] Brass musicians had the greatest hearing loss, especially in the upper registers, indicating nerve damage. Yet, these studies were not statistically significant on an acceptable level, probably because the number of musicians studied was not large enough. Another study showed that violinists, flutists and, unexplainedly, double bass players, had unilateral hearing losses, probably because of the placement of their instrument nearer to one ear.[50] Those reports that tried to evaluate the impact of seating arrangements in orchestras on the hearing of musicians came to no conclusion; no evidence of damage relating to the place in the orchestra was obtained in any of these studies.

The question of permanent hearing losses due to music making in orchestra musicians, therefore, remains as yet unanswered. Statistically significant conclusions will require more data.

Hearing loss in pop musicians and rock and roll groups were found mainly for frequencies for 2 through 8 KHz.[51] A similar impairment had been found earlier in randomly examined children in public schools.[52] In general, people exposed to loud sound will develop similar hearing losses.[53] Structural damage to the fine haircells in the inner ear caused by high-pitched loud noises in blacksmiths has been demonstrated almost 100 years ago![54]

In spite of the paucity of statistically conclusive data concerning hearing losses in musicians, many well documented individual cases of such hearing loss cannot be dismissed. In some countries, Workmen's Compensation laws have been taking such reports into account.[55] It would also be prudent for musicians playing in large orchestras or in rock groups to use ear plugs or other protective devices while playing. No physiological mechanism can be protective against inner ear damage from loud noise or music, even though a process of mental, intentional or subconscious suppression of incoming noxious auditory stimuli in well motivated musicians[56] may afford some protection, as yet inadequately evaluated in context. There seems to be no protection in our society against the inexorable decline of hearing in aging individuals since noise pollution in one way or another is a way of life in our culture.

REHABILITATION IN SEVERELY DISABLED MUSICIANS (2 CASE REPORTS)

If an artist is strongly motivated, disciplined and persevering, he or she can overcome impairments, handicaps or disabilities that at first glance seem to indicate a hopeless situation.

A violinist of outstanding accomplishment and solid fame fell, with both hands outstretched, downhill on stony ground. In addition to cuts and bruises, he crushed the head of his left radius (comminuted fracture) and his left triquetrum (a wrist bone at the ulnar edge). When I saw him, the plaster cast had just been removed two months after his radial head had been surgically removed. His shoulder, elbow, wrist and finger range of motion of the left side were all extremely restricted. Pronation and supination were possible for three degrees each; shoulder motion was restricted in all directions to about one quarter of normal motion. The elbow was stiff in the position it had been in the cast, i.e., at 150 degrees, and could be flexed five degrees more with pain but could not be extended. Fortunately, the radial nerve was intact. The left forearm was shortened because of the removal of the radial head. Prospects for restoration of normal function were dim indeed, since wrist mobility, supination and elbow and shoulder range of motion must be near normal to play the violin.

A full-time program of physical therapy, every day for at least five to six hours, was arranged with warm up periods for exercises and preparatory applications of deep and superficial heat. Most exercises were of the active-passive type. Check-ups were frequent. Cooperation between therapist and artist was intense and continued for six months, after which time the elbow could be extended with only ten degrees to spare; supination had returned to normal values; wrist extensor support was slightly lower than normal. Wrist ulnar and radial deviation returned to normal within one year and wrist flexion remained shy a few degrees. The artist was able to continue and expand his successful career as a recitalist of international fame.

In commenting, this artist who had enjoyed excellent orthopedic care immediately after his accident, was immensely well disciplined and persevering, overcoming pain and moments of despair, and had a positive approach all through the difficult six months of therapy. He was instructed to continue playing his instrument during this whole period, with certain precautions, which helped his morale and prevented deconditioning as much as possible. He thoroughly understood the physiologic needs of a violinist, namely the capacity to flex the wrist, supinate, bend the elbow and provide free motion to the shoulder, in addition to some radial and ulnar deviation of the wrist. Without a close mutual understanding with the therapist, a reservoir of will power and a hopeful attitude, this result would not have been obtained. This artist emerged from his ordeal intact and rehabilitated.

An orchestra conductor, well know internationally for his numerous recordings of classical music, arrived in our hospital with a dense right hemiplegia and aphasia which was global at first, since he did not speak or understand. For two months, he "looked through" anybody who tried to speak to him, to communicate with body language, with music or with sounds. One day, after two months, when one of our residents walked by his wheelchair whistling a melody, he was seen to look up smiling. We followed this cue and systematically approached him whistling or singing a theme from his symphonic repertoire which we presumed he must have known well. One day he responded, clearly indicating his interest and capacity to finish the theme. After establishing contact through music, a musician speech therapist took over. The patient, after a few weeks, started reading music and scores that were brought to him; yet, he could not speak. By the beginning of the fourth month after the stroke, he started to hum melodies and made some grunts, with his facial expression indicating his mood. A few weeks later he started to say a few words. He continued speech therapy after his discharge, at which time he was able to say a few words correctly. More of his speech returned later, and he resumed his position as the conductor of a professional symphony orchestra without ever being able to move his right arm which he kept in his pocket, or to speak normally and freely. He managed to go through rehearsals and recitals, conducting with his left arm, and make himself understood to his fellow musicians. He also resumed conducting classical music for records on well known labels.

In commenting, we will never know how much this patient's motivation helped in restoring his capacity to conduct music, after a clearly hopeless situation. Recovery after as dense a stroke as this is a most unusual event in a nonmusician. Physical exercise is a way of life in an orchestra conductor. Perhaps recovery of function is enhanced in individuals who have been habitually active physically and musically all their lives.

HEALTH PROBLEMS DUE TO CHANGES IN LIFE-STYLE IN CONTEMPORARY MUSICIANS

In Western culture, and perhaps for much longer in the history of the human race, sports and the arts have served well to ease the strains and distresses of life. With the unprecedented aging of our society in the 20th century and with technology revolutionizing our communication systems, the traditional balancing role of the arts and sports is fading. In organized sports, today's strategies for being a leader with popular appeal, for attracting star performers and for accumulating capital is superceding traditional individual striving for healthy exercise and playful combat. In the arts, competition for public recognition and monetary reward of real or symbolic value inspire many budding artists and launch early careers, often distorting time scales for natural maturation.

Music continues to help some of us music lovers to relax in the midst of the information explosion and political tension. The professional musician works hard for a performance and renders a public service like that of the professional athlete who, however, is more generously rewarded. Professional music making today carries various health hazards. This is especially true for the musician who works in groups or in orchestras and not infrequently is forced to perform under unhealthy environmental conditions. The resulting strains and actual physical ailments ought to elicit some public concern, and have in fact led to legislative action in another society.[52]

Life is strenuous and hectic for the musician who travels with his symphony orchestra, opera company, jazz, pop or rock group. Tours are usually well organized for the great orchestral institutions travelling with ninety or more musician-artists who, by proficiency and experience, are among the leading musicians of our time. Such tours entail frequent daily performances, often preceded by rehearsal with little time to relax or to freshen up. Few free days are planned. One of our leading symphony orchestras recently travelled for thirty one days, covering two continents outside the USA and crossing country lines thirteen times. They cancelled two concerts which would have brought them into an additional country, only because of terrorist activities in that country, which added two free days to their six planned free days. They played in black tie in sweltering heat in the southern European and Middle Eastern summer, in the absence of air conditioning.

Still, compared to the unforeseen hardships and health hazards that smaller, less well endowed groups have to go through, such prominent orchestras are well cared for. A number of anecdotal reports I received from members of jazz, pop or rock groups indicate that nightly automobile trips from place to place in lieu of a night's sleep in a hotel are not unusual, that eating habits on travels like these often become irregular and unhealthy, and that facilities for rest and freshening up before a rehearsal, and for concentration before a concert, are often difficult to obtain. This area of music making by small meandering music groups is little explored or verified for any conclusion as to its significance as a public health problem. The impression that the number of such groups is quite large will have to be supported by facts.

Anyhow, at this time, groups of musicians performing classical, popular, jazz or rock and roll music continue, like the roaming troubadours of the Middle Ages, to criss-cross the land. Around 2500 BC, the Egyptian medical papyri of Kahum described music as the "physic of the soul." Confucius pronounced music to be an integral part of harmonious living and Plato, in the *Republic*, stated that music is necessary for health of mind and body. If music continues to be the elixir of our lives, we must see that the artists who keep us enriched with this gift of God remain among us in good health.

Heinz I. Lippmann

IN CONCLUSION

Dysfunctions in musicians that develop as a result of music making have contributed to creating a new field in health care: "Music-medicine" which not only requires experience in medical diagnostics and therapeutics but competence in playing and understanding musical instruments. Every case of a musician in trouble on this basis shows unique features that hardly lend themselves to generalization. Such dysfunctions are not infrequently due to bad playing habits. Another kind of trouble may be generated by changes in life-style that many contemporary musicians are forced to accept in the pursuit of their profession.

Hodge-podge diagnostic terms such as "tendinitis", "overuse syndrome" or "tennis elbow" rarely fit the needs of such cases and do not help in restoring such musicians back to function; this is true for the majority of musicians who ask me for help. Problems that are caused by a preceding injury or by disease are less common in my experience as such patients are more likely to be cared for by their primary health professional.

The care for musicians who run into playing troubles because of injury or disease is not dealt with in any detail in this brief chapter, nor are the dysfunctions in vocalists with whom I have had little experience.

REFERENCES AND SUGGESTED READING

1   Winternitz, E.: *Leonardo da Vinci as a Musician*. New Haven/London: Yale University Press, 1982, pp. 1-241.
2   Lippmann, H.I.: The strains of music. *Am Ensemble*, 1983, **6**(4), pp. 17 -25.
3   Fry, H.J.H.: The physical injury (overuse) due to music making. *MEH Bull*, 1985, **1**(2), pp. 22-49.
4   Travell, J.G., Simons, D.G.: *Myofascial Pain and Dysfunction. The Trigger Point Manual*. Baltimore/London: Williams & Wilkins, 1983, p. 513.
5   Release from Massachusetts General Hospital, 1983.
6   Simon Barere: Personal communication.
7   Shephard, R.J.: *Physiology and Biochemistry of Exercise*. New York: Praeger Publishers, 1982, p. 119.
8   Basmajian, J.V.: *Muscles Alive, Their Functions Revealed by Electromyography*, 2nd Edition. Baltimore: Williams and Wilkins, 1967, pp. 1-421.
9   Jacobson, E.: *Progressive Relaxation*. University of Chicago Press, 1938.
10 Mookerjee, S., Chahal, K.S., Giri, C.: Impact of yogic exercises on the Indian field hockey team. In: *Exercise Physiology*, F. Landry., W.A.R. Orban, (eds.). Miami Symposia Specialists, 1978, pp. 389-396.
11 Crossman, E.R.F.W.: A theory of the acquisition of speed skill. *Ergonomics*, 1959, **2**, pp. 153-166.
12 Granit, R.: *The Purposive Brain*. Cambridge, MA: MIT Press Publishers, 1977, pp. 157-175.
13 Kottke, F.J.: From reflex to skill: The training of coordination. *Arch Phys Med Rehab*, 1980, **61**, pp. 551-561.
14 Changeux, J-P.: *Neuronal Man, The Biology of Mind*. New York: Pantheon Book Publishers, 1985, p.46.
15 Kottke, F.J., Halpern, D., Easton, J.K.M., Ozel, A.T., Burrel, C.A.: Training of coordination. *Arch Phys Med Rehab*, 1978, **59**, pp. 567-572.
16 Eccles, J.C.: A re-evaluation of cerebellar function in man. In: *Human Reflexes Pathophysiology of Motor Systems Methodology of Human Reflexes*, J.E. Desmedt (ed.),

Vol. 3 of: *New Developments in Electromyography and Clinical Neurophysiology*. Basel: S. Karger, 1973, pp. 208-224.

17 Paillard, J.: The patterning of skilled movements. In: *Handbook of Physiology-Neurophysiology III*, 1976, pp. 1679-1707.

18 Granit R.: *The Purposive Brain*. Cambridge, MA: MIT Press Publishers, 1977.

19 Gieseking, W., Leimar, K.: *Piano Technique*. New York: Dover Publishing, 1972, pp. 1-48.

20 Lhevinne, J.: *Basic Principles in Pianoforte Playing*. New York: Dover Publishing, 1972, pp. 1-48.

21 Philipp, L.H.: *Piano Technique, Tone, Touch, Phrasing and Dynamics*. New York: Dover Publishing, 1982, pp. 1-89.

22 Travell, J.G.:, Simons, D.G.: *Myofascial Pain and Dysfunction. The Trigger Point Manual*. Baltimore/London: Williams & Wilkins, 1983, p.165-660.

23 Semple, R., Gillingham, J.: Letter to the Editor. *Brit Med J*, June 1, 1974, **I**.

24 Curtis, P.: Guitar nipple. Letter to the Editor. *Brit Med J*, April 27 1974, **I**.

25 Thomas, J.M.: Musical bumps. Letter to the Editor. *Brit Med J*, June 1 1974, **I**.

26 Murphy, J.M.: Cello scrotum. Letter to the Editor. *Brit Med J*, May 11 1974, **I**.

27 Scheuer, P.: Cello scrotum. Letter to the Editor. *Brit Med J*, June 1 1974, **I**.

28 Peachey, R.D.G., Matthews, C.N.A.: Fiddler's Neck. *Brit J Dermat*, 1978, **98**, pp. 669-674.

29 Dahl, M.G.C.: Flautist's chin, a companion to fiddler's neck. Letter to the Editor. *Brit Med J*, October 7 1978, **II**.

30 Gardner, M.D.: Flautist's chin. Letter to the Editor. *Brit Med J*, November 4 1978, **II**.

31 Winternitz, E.: *Musical Instruments and Their Symbolism in Western Art*. New Haven/London: Yale University Press, 1979, pp. 1-153.

32 Bird, H.A., Wright, V.: Traumatic synovitis in a classical guitarist: A study of joint laxity. *Ann Rheum Dis*, 1981, **40**, pp. 161-163.

33 Hofman, J.: *Piano Playing*. New York: Dover Publishing, 1976, Piano questions, p. 48.

34 Grevstenm, N. *et al.*: Recurrent ulnar nerve dislocation at the elbow. *Acta Ortho Scand*, 1978, **49**, pp. 151-153.

35 Meyer, Dr. L.: Personal communication.

36 Shea, M.J.: Saxophonists divertoculosis. Letter to the Editor. *Brit Med J*, May 9 1979, **I**.

37 Levine, H.L.: Medical news, *JAMA*, 1984, **252**(8), p. 988.

38 Males, J.L.: Musicians and their conditions: Pros and cons. Letter to the Editor. *JAMA*, 1985, **253**(12), p. 1723.

39 Smith, R., and Levine, H.L.: Hypopharyngeal dilatation in musicians. *Med Prob Perf Art*, 1985, **1.1**, pp. 20-21.

40 Swan, M.S.: Disco deafness. Letter to the Editor. *Brit Med J*, November 30 1974, **II**.

41 Mori, T.: Effects of record music on hearing loss among young workers in a shipyard. *Int Arch Occup Environ Health*, 1985, **56**, pp. 91-97.

42 Axelsson A., Lindgren F.: Hearing in pop musicians. *Acta Otolaryngol*, 1978, **85**, pp. 225-231.

43 Zober, A.: Noise as an important stress factor in occupational and other environments. *Zbl Bakt Hyg I*, **B179**, pp. 1-31.

44 Rosen, S. *et al.*: Presbycusis study of a relatively noise free population in the Sudan. *Ann Otol Rhinol Laryncol*, 1962, **71**, pp. 727-743.

45 Nodar, R.N.: The effects of aging and loud music on hearing. *Clev Clin Quart*, 1986, **53**(1), pp. 49-52.

46 International Labor Office. *Encyclopedia of Occupational Health and Safety, 3rd Edition*. Geneva: ILO Publ., 1983, pp. 593-596.

47 Johnson, D.W., *et al.*: Extended high frequency hearing sensitivity, a normative threshold study in musicians. *Ann Otol Rhinol Laryngol*, 1986, **95**, pp. 196-202.
48 Karlsson, K., *et al.*: The hearing of symphony orchestra musicians. *Scan Audiol*, 1983, **12**, pp. 257-264.
49 Johnson, D.W., *et al.*: Effects of instrument type and orchestra position on hearing sensitivity for 0.25 to 20 kHz in the orchestral musician. *Scan Audiol*, 1985, **14**, pp. 215-221.
50 Westmore, G.A., Eversden, I.D.: Noise induced hearing loss in orchestral musicians. *Arch Otolaryngol*, 1981, **107**, pp. 761-764.
51 Axelsson, A., Lindgren, F.: Does pop music cause hearing damage? *Audiol*, 1977, **16**, pp. 432-437.
52 Lipscomb, D.M.: High intensity sounds in the recreational environment: Hazard to young ears. *Clin Pediatr*, 1969, **8**, pp. 63-68.
53 Chüden, H.: Hörschaeden durch Lärm. *Dtsh Med Wchschr*, 1984, **109**(38), pp. 1429-1432.
54 Haberman, J.: Über die Schwerhörigkeit der Kesselschmiede. *Arch Ohrenkeilkunde*, 1890, **30**, p. 1.
55 Loock, F., Lorenz, M.: Über die berufsspezifische Arbeitsunfähigkeit, die Berufskrankheiten sowie die Rehabilitationsmassnahmen bei Künstlern der Theater und Orchester der DDR. *Z Ges Hyg*, 1978, **24**, pp. 177-179.
56 Hibler, A., Wallner, K.: Ist Musikempfindung messbar? *Laryng Rhinol*, 1981, **60**, pp. 284-28.

MUSIC MAKING FOR THE DISABLED PERSON

The Risks and the Prevention of Overuse Injury

Hunter J.H. Fry

INTRODUCTION

It is now generally accepted that music making can involve significant risks to the physical health of the player,[1] [2] [3] and that in the case of the professional musician, this may cause loss of career. Since many disabled persons are able to find expression in the field of performing arts, particularly music, how does the risk balance up with the benefit? The disabled person may have less physical reserve and be more impaired by disablement of, say, the upper limb, than the non-disabled person who is better able to bear the risk.

Are there guidelines which will enable the disabled person to make positive, informed decisions to enjoy making yet keep out of trouble? Much is now understood about the overuse process and while there is more to learn, prevention of overuse literally is control of use. On this principle, overuse is theoretically preventable.

There is one very common condition about which this chapter is mostly concerned. It is totally separate from a number of distinct clinical states, causing upper limb pain, which are generally easily recognized and form a standard part of medical practice. Examples of such clinical conditions are the nerve entrapment syndromes, true tenosynovitis, degenerative or rheumatoid arthritis, degenerative disease of the spine. All of these states may interfere with music making and in turn be worsened by the act of music making itself. To give some examples, tenosynovitis is an inflammatory or quasi-inflammatory condition of tendon sheaths which may cause jamming of the tendon in the sheath. Trigger finger, trigger thumb or deQuervain's tenosynovitis which involves the dual tendon sheath of the thumb extensors at the wrist, rheumatoid tenosynovitis may affect flexor or extensor tendons causing not only jamming of the tendons in their sheaths, but actual tendon ruptures which would be extremely serious for any instrumental musician. Carpal tunnel syndrome is probably the best known nerve entrapment syndrome and is verifiable and usually treated surgically. Thoracic outlet syndrome is a more contentious peripheral nerve affection where the nerves are said to be subject to pressure or tension as they come out of the thoracic outlet over the first rib or in some cases, an abnormal cervical rib. These and similar known conditions may be aggravated by music making and may themselves interfere with music making, though essentially they are not purely music related conditions. Patients may develop such conditions without much hand-use intense activity at all and there are unquestionably genetic and environmental influences operating which cannot always be identified. The conditions referred to above come from diverse pathological processes and their appearance on the scene in music is largely fortuitous. When occurring in the musician, however, the most important thing to remember is that they may be imitated by a much more common condition, that of overuse injury syndrome. Since true tenosynovitis and nerve entrapment syndromes may be treated surgically, there is the ever present potential for misdiagnosis and failed surgery. There is also the possibility, however, that overuse injury syndrome will co-exist with these other conditions.

WHAT IS OVERUSE INJURY SYNDROME?

It is a primary condition of pain and loss of function in the working structures, mainly the muscles but also joint ligaments, brought about by excessive or unaccustomed use. The condition may occasionally be painless, and present as loss of coordination. This is termed 'focal dystoma' or 'cramp.'[4] Use or activity which is excessive for one individual may not necessarily be excessive for another, hence, a considerable amount of individual variation and susceptibility is one of the special dangers of this condition. An individual's threshold for overuse injury syndrome cannot therefore be predicted in advance.

The muscular condition is related in the present context to the muscular effort expended in music making and occurs when the use of these structures causes them to be taken beyond their upper biological tolerance so that some form of damaging change results. All tissues have such upper limits, therefore it is perfectly logical to propose that all instrumental musicians must have their 'damage point' if they practice long enough and intensively enough. The disabled person (and indeed those without handicaps) must aim to keep well clear of this damage point even though it cannot be precisely defined in any one individual until or unless the disorder occurs.

HISTORICAL PERSPECTIVE

Overuse syndrome in musicians was described well over a century ago.[5] This group was recognized as the second most frequently affected after writers. When telegraphers' cramp was reported in 1975, musicians were displaced into third in order of occurrence. However, many other hand-use intense occupations were listed. For instance, Riggs 1892[6] listed 22 occupations apart from writers and musicians and Gowers[7] (1888) mentioned 13, Morris J. Lewis[8] (1886) listed 26, saying "writers, telegraph operators and musicians are those who by far are the most frequently affected, the others being almost curiosities." The disorder was most frequently called *musicians cramp* and the term was sanctioned by common usage though many questioned the appropriateness of the word 'cramp.' The other commonly used term was *occupational neurosis*. The word neurosis meant a neurological disorder and not a psychiatric condition. Other terms used for the disorder included *overuse, professional impotence, over-fatigue,* and *exhaustion neurosis.* There was general agreement amongst the writers that the condition was brought about by excessive muscular activity but it was debated as to whether this was a primary condition of muscular overuse or whether it was basically a central nervous system disorder expressing itself in muscular failure such as in progressive muscular atrophy.

The historical review of literature between 1830 and 1910 describing this condition in musicians included 21 text books and 54 articles in medical journals.[5] Thirty-five of these papers describe, discuss or mention the condition in musicians, most commonly in pianists and violinists. The disorder was investigated by the methods of the day and in the debate which involved two different theories, one *central* and the other *peripheral.* Perhaps the most important evidence was that some of the small muscles of the hand when stimulated directly by electric current, showed decreased irritability, less shortening and did less work. Since the nervous system was bypassed in these experiments the implication was obvious, i.e., that is was a *primary condition of muscles* (peripheral) rather than a *central* nervous system lesion.

Muscle biopsy evidence, however, was not destined to confirm this until the following century.[9] The clinical features of muscular overuse were described not only in the upper limb, but also in the lower limb seen in dancers and treadlers, the latter working with foot powered sewing machines for long hours. The clinical features of overuse were described with remarkable clarity including the prodromal symptoms, the spread of pain from one muscle group to another and from one limb to the opposite side. The involvement of other uses of the hand was clearly described. There was universal agreement amongst these writers that the only treatment which had any effect was many months of rest and that rest had to be so total that pain was not produced at all or aggravated by any use of the hands.

Then, as now, surgical operations were found to be ineffective, other remedies occasionally giving rise to claims of improvement. Drug treatment was a failure. The only established reported cures were on a total rest program. The clinical detail and perception of these writers of one century ago was quite astonishing. For reasons which now appear obscure, these terms, occupational cramp and occupational neurosis and others, died out in the early part of the 20th century and were replaced by the terms tenosynovitis or tendonitis/tendinitis. Whereas the writers of 100 years ago list tenosynovitis as being a condition from which overuse had to be *distinguished*, the term now came to be used interchangeably with overuse, much to everyone's confusion.

Further changes of name occurred since 1960 and these terms include *cumulative trauma syndrome, cervical-brachial disorder, regional pain syndrome, repetitive strain injury* and others. These terms are rather vague and have come to mean pain in the upper extremity for many conditions including some which mimic muscular overuse and require surgical treatment. Terminology has therefore caused a special problem in this condition because of the frequent and unnecessary change of names as well as the misnomer "tenosynovitis."

THE MODERN PERSPECTIVE

There was adequate evidence from modern studies[10][11][12][13][14] that overuse syndrome is very common in musicians. In the writer's studies the prevalence in music schools[3] was at least 9.3% and probably nearer 20%. In the symphony orchestra,[2] the incidence of occupational pain was well over 50%. A five interval grading of severity (Table 1) using empiric criteria, when applied to the symphony orchestras, still left a 40% prevalence when grade 1 was excluded. The high prevalence of overuse in the symphony orchestra was established by the time the players were aged around 30 years, i.e., less than ten years after leaving music school. At the other end of the scale the condition may occur in high school children, one of the most common being due to loading an 830 gram clarinet onto the small right thumb.[15] Other instruments, particularly piano and violin, may cause overuse in school children.

While the prospects for a disabled person deliberating upon these figures may be somewhat daunting, this should be seen in context since overuse should be preventable by control of use. The most important tool in the prevention of this malady is the basic information necessary to recognize it and take appropriate action to avoid injury.

Tissue Overuse

Overuse is a condition of the tissues caused by exceeding their biological tolerance with use. All tissues, indeed all materials, have these tolerances beyond which they cannot be taken without some kind of degradation. In the case of biological tissues, their ordinary function occurs within certain well-defined tolerances within which a period of use is followed by a period of recovery which is complete. When major overuse has occurred, the tissues show some structural change, usually accompanied by pain and loss of function in the overused structures. In early or minor cases of overuse, structural change is minimal and even before this there are often clear warnings which are all to often ignored. Observance of sensible habits of use are vital to the disabled person and no apology is made for the following digressions.

The Skin

This is adapted to withstand frictional loads and sheering stresses and even blunt injury so long as it is not too major. Sensible precautions will avoid injury, minor or major.

The Eye

The eye is an extension of the central nervous system, highly specialized. It receives and to a degree, processes, visual information. Both the quality and intensity of light, however, must be controlled to keep the eye in the normal operating condition for excesses may cause damage so that the organ is unable to resume a baseline state. Sensible precaution precludes, for instance, the direct observance of an eclipse of the sun.

The Ear

Sound induced hearing loss is produced by excessive levels of sound which damage the structures which translate the sound vibrations into electrical impulses in the internal ear. The internal ear is situated within the temporal bone of the skull which is normally well protected. Orchestral musicians are becoming more concerned with the high level of sound in their work.

However, a much more common danger is the excessively high level of amplified sound used at rock concerts and even in the home when damaging levels can be achieved simply by turning a knob. Younger people usually have a better psychological tolerance to these excessively high sound levels than older people so that self damage is easier to achieve. Acute discomfort and actual damage do not, unfortunately, always match up because tissue damage may be quite 'silent' and occur without discomfort whereas intolerable discomfort may not necessarily result in damage. However, those avoiding high sound levels because of discomfort are probably displaying good survival behavior.

Bone

The bones of the skull and spinal column give protection to the very soft nervous center of the human body. The skull contributes form and the spinal column some shape and rigidity. The limb bones contribute form and rigidity so that pressure and forces may be applied and resisted, the movement occurring at the joints between bones. In everyday life bony structures are used well within their tolerances but if very high forces are applied, as may occur for instance in the ballet dancer or the gymnast, tiny cracks called stress fractures or overuse fractures may appear in the bone. Pain is nature's warning signal and, unless it is heeded, the area of weakness may suffer more substantial injury with further use. One might regard any broken bone brought about by violence as an example of acute overuse in that forces are applied to the bone which are beyond its limit to tolerate. The stress fractures mentioned above, however, are much closer to the subject under consideration. Musicians do not generally use the degree of force necessary to affect bones in this way, though joint ligaments may become involved. (See below.)

Joint Ligaments

Ligaments are sensitive to pain from direct injury, particularly excessive stretching forces. Within bounds, however, ligaments normally function quite painlessly, tolerating stretching forces within their tolerance. These ligaments are strong fibrous cords which join one bone to another across a joint allowing that joint to move. They have to be very tough to allow the forces to be transmitted across the joint as well as permitting movement. They are thus very specialized tissues whose continued normal functioning depends upon the forces applied to the ligaments being moderated both in magnitude and time.

A 'sprained ankle' is probably the most familiar example of acute overuse in a ligament. Here an excessive tensile force is applied to the ligament in excess of its tolerance and this causes damage and persisting pain. Such acute situations will usually resolve acutely and, with the appropriate degree of rest, the ligament should become pain free in about three weeks.

Chronic ligamentous strain is probably better known in the lower limb than in the upper limb. In the case of the ankle it is often treated with a supporting brace to spare the tensile stresses on the overused ligaments. In the upper limb, however, and in overuse syndrome in particular, certain ligaments may become chronically painful. Pain can be reproduced if the ligament is either pressed on or stretched, thus demonstrating tenderness in these structures. The demonstration of such tenderness is a partly subjective physical sign which can be demonstrated to others. Ligamentous structures about the wrist, particularly on the radial side, may become chronically painful in overuse syndrome and such tenderness may be demonstrated on examination. The ligaments at the very base of the thumb where it joins the wrist are subjected to loading on a very long lever and are also commonly affected. Sometimes the ligaments of the first two joints of the fingers and even the end joint may become similarly affected, as may occur occasionally in the ligaments of the elbow joint. Where the ring of muscle around the shoulder joint fuses with the ring of ligament about the joint, this compound structure is highly vulnerable to overuse and quite often the muscle tissue itself is involved, giving rise to a compound lesion of joint capsule, tendon and muscles, sometimes called rotator cuff tendinitis but probably better called rotator cuff overuse. When the whole of the arm is loaded onto the shoulder joint and on such a short lever, the rotator cuff musculature has to work very hard, hence its particular susceptibility to overuse.

Muscular Overuse

The preceding examples of tissue damage by exceeding permitted tolerances largely conform with common experience, but it is often not realized that muscles can damage themselves extensively by their own contractions. Acute muscle tears may occur when the only force operating is the contraction of the muscle itself. Sometimes such damage may be gravity-assisted. Muscle activity, however, which is well below maximum force, may be clearly responsible for self injury if continued long enough. This was clearly realized by the 19th century writers, though at the time muscle biopsy evidence was not available to prove it.

In 1937, painful forearm muscles involved in overuse were biopsied by Nelson Howard[16] at Stanford University and microscopic damage in the muscles was shown, whereas the tendons and their sheaths were shown to be perfectly normal, thus giving lie to the misnomer 'tenosynovitis' for this condition. These findings were confirmed by Thompson, et al.[14] in 1951 in Britain and, although the clinical presentation of the patients was a little different, the damage in the structures which were doing all the work left no doubt as to the correctness of the views of these investigators.

The painful hands in wrists in musicians' overuse was often thought to be due to tenosynovitis, but clinical evidence[17] was presented in 1986 showing that it was not the tendon sheaths but the intrinsic muscles and certain joint ligaments which were tender and which were clearly causing the pain. Clinical findings have now been investigated by the muscle biopsy.[9] The forearm muscles are also frequently affected as may be the 'elbow ends' of these muscle groups as they arise from the epicondyles of the humerus. When these origins become painful and tender they may be called 'tennis elbow' or 'golf elbow.' The term 'epicondylitis' should not be used as it is not the epicondyle which suffers any change. The triceps muscle at the back of the arm which straightens the elbow is frequently involved, as are, at times, the biceps and brachialis on the front of the upper arm which bend the elbow. The large deltoid muscle covering the shoulder may become overused but much less commonly than the rotator cuff complex referred to earlier. The muscles of the shoulder girdle as they attach to the spine and chest are quite frequently affected and the trapezius muscle is probably the most often affected. This muscle can be felt in the angle between the neck and the shoulder and often goes into unwanted prolonged contraction, raising the shoulder if the pianist become too tense.

Hunter J.H. Fry

The longitudinal muscles of the spine right from the base of the skull down may become painful and tender but in spinal pain there are other pain sensitive structures also involved. Muscular overuse however is a significant factor in the causation of spinal pain in this context, particularly in younger people where degenerative diseases cannot be playing a part.

There are many parallel examples of muscular overuse syndromes:

1. The 'iron pumpers' may suffer muscular damage from prolonged, excessive body building exercises and this may take many months to resolve. This is well known to sports medicine practitioners but there are no muscle biopsy studies.

2. Dancers and sewing machine operators may suffer muscular overuse in the lower limbs. The writers of one century ago recorded the condition in both of these groups, the sewing machine operators' condition was called 'treadlers cramp,' for they powered their sewing machines by sheer leg work. This condition is not common now but still does exist as some of these nonelectric sewing machines are still used.

3. Marathon runners. While the runners of shorter distances do not appear to suffer obvious overuse, all marathon runners at the end of their run have CK enzymes in their blood indicating cellular damage. Muscle biopsy studies have indicated extensive damage to muscular fibers from marathon running and these are repaired by muscle regeneration which has also been documented by biopsy studies.[18]

4. The muscle fibers which survive after an attack of poliomyelitis in childhood are trained to 'over-perform.' It is this training in many instances which allows the affected individuals to take off their knee braces or to get out of a respirator. If they become too active in later life they suffer overuse, for these muscles fibers are much closer to the threshold of overuse because of their chronic over performance. Biopsy studies have been carried out in this condition.[19] Recovery after poliomyelitis or spinal injury when respiratory muscles have been affected might contra-indicate resumption of high pressure wind instruments.

KEY FACTORS LEADING TO OVERUSE

There are three main factors in the genesis of overuse. They are the factor of intensity multiplied by the time of use, the musician's technique itself and the individual variation in susceptibility. The writers of one hundred years ago were well aware of these three factors, particularly the first and third.[4] Of these three factors involved in overuse, this would appear to be, by far, the most important and is totally within the control of the musician. While some overuse injuries may occur quite acutely after inordinately long playing or practice sessions, most derive from constant, chronic, long, hard use of the limb with music practice. Students at music school most commonly notice the condition when the practice load is raised prior to an examination, recital or a competition. Practicing a new or difficult piece, exercises in technique and studying with a new teacher may be associated with its first appearance. One of the most obvious examples is seen in the music camp prior to which a clarinettist might practice up to an hour and a half a day, the 830 gram clarinet being loaded totally onto the right thumb. At music camp this playing and practice time may be quadrupled and students report with painful thumbs and wrists one after the other. Theoretical considerations would indicate that if these young students practised hard enough for a long enough time, they would all suffer the injury. Those students using the clarinet with a post support so that the instrument itself becomes weightless, do not seem to suffer these injuries. (Figure 1) The orchestral players who earn their living by performing music may play exceedingly long hours if one adds up the orchestral rehearsals, performances, recording sessions, teaching, chamber music and solo work. The overuse process appears to arise on a more extended time scale than that of the student and many of these musicians are asking too much of their bodies. It is essential that the disabled person pursue a clear and definite policy about the wonderful art form of music so as to avoid this needless risk of overdoing it.

Figure 1: Eleven-year-old children can play wind instruments most safely when weightless. Loading 600-830 grams on the right thumb for long periods is undesirable, detracts from technique and limits legitimate practice time.

Technique

The music technique is of great importance. The music teacher will teach the student the most energy efficient, well managed, coordinated technique of which he is capable. In addition to actual movement of fingers and wrists, etc., a great deal of muscle power goes to stabilizing the remaining joints and it is here that a great deal of muscle power may be wasted. If the joints are inadequately stabilized (too relaxed), the executant muscles have to work harder, but most commonly the joints are over-stabilized with excessive tension. This means that the muscles responsible for striking the keys, etc. have more resistance to overcome, more force has to be used and it also means that the joint will not respond as quickly, for there is greater resistance to overcome. The ideal level of muscular use, while varying from one individual to another, is the skilled province of the music teacher. The avoidance of awkward or extreme positions is likewise generally taught, for the closer a joint is towards an extreme position in its range, the more force is needed to keep the ligamentous structures on the stretch and the further it has to move in some other direction for a following maneuvre.

Most books written on piano technique tend to emphasize differences rather than similarities and the basic principles of muscle and joint function are unfortunately often ignored in these dedicated deliberations. Excellent results are obtained with a variety of different methods so long as the basic principles are observed and this factor of music technique is at least partly under the control of the musician, but the more skilled help that can be obtained, the better the musician's changes of keeping out of trouble from overuse. Dorothy Taubman's concern and dedication in this area are well known and respected.

Individual Susceptibility

Why is it that some musicians get this condition and others do not? One hundred years ago it was realized that some individuals were much more vulnerable to overuse than others; to quote Warrington Hayward[20] "what will over-fatigue one pupil will not necessarily over-fatigue another." Again Dr. George Vivian Poore[21] stated, describing the same condition in writers. ". . . in many cases of writers' cramp no overuse of the muscles has taken place and in such cases. . . the muscles are so deficient in staying power (notwithstanding their ability to contract forcibly for a short time) that they become useless or nearly so when called upon for prolonged, steady contraction."[5]

The situation has not changed in a century. One sees the blatant examples of students who are practicing far to much, who have a tense technique and who are practicing works above their level, yet they appear to escape the scourge that may strike down the better student who practices with a more relaxed technique.

If one deliberates upon competitive physical endeavor, it is obvious in questions of endurance that some are better endowed than others. Some individuals are simply more fatiguable than others and with every individual being a genetic 'one-off' it would be surprising if the tissue damage point were exactly the same in every person. It was known to the 19th century writers, as it is acknowledged today, that emotional and psychological pressure can aggravate many physical conditions and it is likely that it could be some sort of pre-disposing factor here.[5] Even allowing for matters of general health and all other known factors, some non-scientific hunch indicates that there could well be a 'X factor,' probably environmental in origin, which can influence susceptibility. Whether this be biologically active substances we ingest which preserve food, kill lower forms of life, or alter the ecology, would be sheer speculation. Figures are not available to compare incidence from one country to another. The condition is certainly common in Australia, North America and the United Kingdom.

Psychogenic Factors

There is no evidence that overuse syndrome is directly caused by psychological or psychiatric factors. The 'mad and bad' psychiatric salad ocasionally proposed to explain many or most instances of overuse, is unsupported either by theory or data, and is basically offensive.[1] To satisfy the criteria of conversion hysteria when a psychological factor is converted into a physical one, it must be shown that there are no physical explanations for the physical symptoms (criteria 1) and that the psychological dynamic responsible for the conversion is clearly demonstrable to mainstream psychiatry (criteria 2). Conversion hysteria is said to be uncommon to rare in the community at large.[22] Psychological symptoms, however, do occur in all patients and their obvious interpretation is that they are secondary to a disabling condition which is both painful and threatening. Indeed such symptoms are expected. The great Greek physician Hippocrates wrote many aphorisms. His aphorism, book 2, number 6 reads as follows: "Persons who have a painful affection in any part of the body and are in a great measure insensible of the pain, are disordered in intellect."[23] Paraphrasing this in the present context, this aphorism might be re-written: "Musicians who have painful overuse and have no psychological symptoms are probably mad!"

THE MUSICIANS' MUSCLE USE

Muscle is a tissue which converts chemical into mechanical energy so that the muscle shortens against resistance and will move joints. In a resting state, the muscle is provided with full energy which begins to be drained as soon as muscle use occurs. Like the lead-acid battery, the muscle appears to be more comfortable when it is nearer to full charge.

Muscle has the capacity to suffer oxygen and chemical debt and tolerates a certain buildup of metabolic products, some of which are capable of causing pain. In a rest period these products are quickly removed. During vigorous muscle use, energy use cannot be restored from the oxygen and glucose, etc. in the blood as fast as it is being used. Rest periods therefore are essential for full restitution. The musician is involved in three types of muscle use. The first is the action of the postural muscles which hold the player in the playing position. The second is static loading or holding up of the instrument, such as a clarinet, French horn or a violin. The third type of use is composed of the skilled movements involved with music making which represent some of the most highly learned motor functions known to man. In many instances the same muscle groups and joints involved in holding up the instrument are also involved either directly or indirectly with the skilled keywork, fingering, etc. on which the technique depends. The static loading involved in holding up the instrument is therefore directly counter-productive and impedes or competes with the technique.

Support of the clarinet on a post, the violin on a violin support,[24] putting the bassoon on a spike on the floor, are sensible measures to minimize the competitive nature of these two types of muscle use. The disabled person particularly must seek to eliminate this type of non-productive and often risky continued muscular activity. Heavy instruments should not be held up for long periods time, i.e., segments should not be too long and rest periods periods should not be just for a few seconds or a minute or two, but at least 5 minutes to rest the muscles and joint ligaments. The concentration span may not exceed 30 minutes anyway, and it is common experience that after a short period of rest the muscles are more responsive. There is, therefore, everything to gain and nothing to lose by the more disciplined practice habit of 25 minute segments at most, followed by a 5 minute break.

Clinical Presentation

It is of the utmost importance to be aware of prodromal symptoms, that is to say the minor, apparently unimportant symptoms which may herald overuse. These were also well known to the 19th century writers and consist of odd feelings in the upper arm, perhaps a feeling of tightness, heaviness, odd pins and needles, sensations which are quite often inarticulate yet all the more convincing after the observer has seen many examples.

The causal activity must be stopped when this occurs if one wishes to avoid damage. Pain, however, is the dominating symptom though it does not occur in all patients. The pain may be sharp or dull but it is more often of a dull type and often not at all well localized. When it first occurs it may not even be obvious that it is aggravated by the causal activity. Sometimes the pain may come well after the causal activity has ceased and it is not uncommon for the musician to be awakened at night by the first appearance of the pain, resulting from a very heavy day of practice. Post activity pain is very common. It is unfortunate that the cause and effect relationship is sometimes not clear enough to signal the danger warning in sufficiently strong terms so that the musician stops playing, which is what should happen. The other main symptom is loss of function and, in the worst examples, this usually involves weakness, loss of agility and speed and loss of control (loss of accuracy). This loss of function may be a transitory or a stable feature. If music playing and practice is continued, the condition will tend to become worse. In the early stages of the condition the muscles are more irritable (this was noticed in the 19th century), the technique becomes more tense and the musician may continue practicing to overcome what might appear to him to be a technical fault or shortcoming. This may well have the effect of causing conversion to a higher grade of injury.

Depression in the established cases may be quite pronounced and not entirely explained by the fact that the patient has a disabling and threatening condition. This is also considered under treatment. The affected musician may notice rather odd reactions to hot and cold and in fact may develop spontaneous skin sensations related to disturbances of hot and cold. All of these symptoms may in some instances be worsened by changes in weather and by emotional factors. Psychological symptoms have already been referred to but these were grossly exaggerated in instances where the musician had been told that there was nothing really wrong with them, that it was 'all in the mind' or that they were doing things the wrong way. The loss of self esteem in these individuals was often as disabling as the original condition.

Physical signs consist mainly of demonstration of tenderness in the muscles and joint ligaments which have been overused. There is usually no objective spasm in the muscles, swelling is usually minor, more obvious to the patient than the examiner, although there are exceptions to this. In the case of the painless overuse (distonia) with loss of coordination, loss of independent control may be demonstrable on a 'five finger exercise.' The performance, however, must be examined to appreciate the full blown condition.

Changes in skin sensation can sometimes be demonstrated, particularly over involved muscle groups. It is important to appreciate the difference between a symptom and a sign. A symptom is something the patients feels, i.e., pain or nausea or headache but this cannot be demonstrated to a third party. A physical sign is something that can be seen, measured or demonstrated. A swelling, a deformity from a broken bone or a red and swollen area are good examples. Tenderness is something which can be demonstrated and it is different from pain. Pain is purely the symptom. It may not be well localized to a particular structure, but one may show that pressure on a particular structure reliably reproduces pain and the appropriate body reaction to it. Demonstration of this sort of physical sign should be reproducible, i.e., another doctor can produce the same result on examination and the nonverbal communication of body language of the patient registers the pain just as effectively as the patient's own verbal response. The demonstration of tenderness of structures is a most important physical sign in clinical surgery. Experience and clinical skills are required. It is helpful for instance in diagnosis in the following examples: a swollen joint may be tender or nontender, a suspect tooth may be tender or non-tender to percussion. In a patient complaining of abdominal pain, the presence of localized tenderness in the lower right hand side of the abdomen, may be virtually diagnostic of appendicitis and be the key factor in the decision to submit the patient to operation. A particular type of abdominal tenderness termed 'rebound' tenderness has a special importance because it indicates peritonitis, which is a serious complication of a number of intra-abdominal conditions and the sign is elicited after gentle pressure by removing the hand quite quickly. It hurts the patient more when the hand is removed than when it is pressed onto the abdomen.

So it is that in overuse injury syndrome it is possible to demonstrate tenderness in the overused muscles and joint ligaments in a satisfactory and reproducible way. Pain may be complained of in the hand, wrist, forearm, elbow, upper arm, shoulder and shoulder girdle, neck and the rest of the spine. In more severe examples of overuse it is possible to demonstrate tender muscles, muscle origins or ligaments in the area where the pain is complained of. With painful hands, for instance, the condition in the past has often been called tenosynovitis or tendinitis, but it is the small muscles in the hand which are tender.

As mentioned earlier it is important not to confuse the specific clinical entities with overuse syndrome as described here. In the physical examination of these patients, demonstration of tenderness may be followed by aggravation of the pain for some hours and this should always be explained to the patient. Examination of such a patient, however, using resisted muscle actions, may distress the patient little at the time, but this may be followed by pain for some days and a worsening of the condition. If the patient is on a total pain avoidance program, such examinations may be highly counter-productive and cause them to lose ground in their recovery. Wherever possible, it is better to examine both hands or arms simultaneously.

When only one arm or hand is involved, display of the difference in the two sides adds credibility to the physical signs. When both sides are involved and they are both examined at the same time, the patient does not have a single focus of attention so that the non-verbal registration of pain is all the more convincing, particularly if a difference happens to exist between the two involved sides.

It is probably not possible to demonstrate the loss of response and control of the muscles by examination unless one requests the musician to play the instrument. While the general rule is to validate all symptoms and points in the history of the condition, there are usually so many independent observations of failure of performance, that this can sometimes be left out. It is undesirable to test the strength of the grip with a dynomometer, as this may not only cause prolonged distress, but may be counter-productive to treatment as previously indicated.

Further Investigations

Apart from the common surgical conditions mentioned at the beginning of this chapter, overuse syndrome must be distinguished from many other disorders including rheumatoid disease, osteo-arthritis, spinal disorders and others mentioned previously.

If psychological factors appear to predominate, it is appropriate to examine the patient's personality prior to the onset of the present trouble, as this may be important in treatment of the patient as a whole. A multi-disciplinary approach may be needed with many such patients.

Grading of Severity

An arbitrary grading system has been found useful in overuse syndrome. While this can never be scientifically precise, some workable scale of severity is better than none at all, as it directly affects prognosis and treatment. The following five interval grading system has been found workable and useful:

TABLE 1

Grade 1: Pain in one site on playing the instrument, no other uses of the hand affected by pain which stops when music making stops.

Grade 2: Pain in multiple sites on playing the instrument, no other uses of the hand affected by pain which stops when music making stops.

Grade 3: Pain persists away from instrument and involves some other uses of the hand apart from music making. There may be some muscle failure as expressed by weakness, loss of response, loss of control. Tenderness in working structures demonstrable to examination.

Grade 4: All uses of hand and arm cause pain which is usually present for most of the time, even at rest. Weakness, loss of response and loss of control, frequent marked physical signs of tenderness in muscular and ligamentous structures. Hand use continues as pain is tolerated.

Grade 5: As for Grade 4, but so severe that the capacity for ordinary hand use is lost as pain is too severe, i.e., may appear after writing one to two lines, to a degree that the patient cannot continue.

When deciding between a high Grade 3 and a low Grade 4, other factors may need to be taken into consideration such as length of symptoms, severity of physical signs.

TREATMENT

Many musicians and those of other occupations unfortunate enough to contract overuse syndrome, will have prodromal or warning symptoms before the condition becomes established. Any unfamiliar or strange feelings in the limb should be taken seriously and the treatment is to cease playing *immediately*. Playing should not be resumed until these sensations are entirely gone and, when resuming, it should be done gradually, commencing with just a few minutes of very easy practice, perhaps three times a day and gradually working up. If there is any recurrence of the prodromal symptoms, and particularly should there be any pain, playing should cease immediately and preparation should take place for what is clearly going to be a longer period of rest.

Mild degrees of the condition, particularly Grades 1 and 2, should be treated by rationalization of practice habits, review of repertoire, review of technique. A preliminary reduction in practice hours may be desirable and above all the static loading of the weight of the instrument should be reduced as much as possible. Modes such as Alexander, Feldenkrais, Yoga and others are useful for body awareness and body control. Sporting and gymnastic activity should be encouraged to develop the maximum range of motion to support that spine which has maximum strength and endurance. This is a healthy counter-balance for the hours a musician spends in a relatively cramped position with a limited range of motion of the spine and limbs.

Even some Grade 3 overuse patients will respond to these measures. Any exercise or work that causes pain should be abandoned. The risk is simply too great and the outcome uncertain should it continue.

For the more serious examples of the condition, the only treatment which has any beneficial effect is rest. The rest must be total so that all acts causing pain are avoided. This is styled "Total Avoidance of all Pain-Inducing Activities" (T.A.P.I.A.). A century ago the only established cures were provided by this treatment which was applied for many months. For details of the many writers of the 19th century describing this total rest program, the reader is referred to The Historical Review,[4] mentioned earlier. Its application in the modern context differs little from these original descriptions. The principle is simple. Anything causing or aggravating the pain is forbidden. Not only is the musician forbidden to play the instrument, but also housework, writing, driving an automobile, gardening, food preparation and indeed anything else which appears to cause pain. The practical day to day management is one of finding a way around carrying something out which normally requires the use of the hand and will cause pain.

In the more advanced cases the teeth should be cleaned by an electric toothbrush held in both hands, hair grooming should be carried out by somebody else or with a blow dryer on a stand. Meals may have to be cut up and a light plastic spoon or fork used. Lever faucets are fitted so that these are turned on and off with the elbows. Doors are left open so that the knobs don't have to be turned. They should not ride a bus as they have to use the hands to hang on or stabilize themselves. Similarly the train is undesirable. Instead they must be driven in a car for transport and they should not open the car door themselves. Students should use tape recorders with a foot switch and seek permission to carry out examination by scribe. The musicians must be psychologically prepared for the restrictive lifestyle and boredom of the months ahead and all measures should be taken to find constructive outlets for intellectual and even physical activities. Instrumentalists should have voice lessons, paramusical subjects should be encouraged, sometimes travel is possible but generally speaking a full year away from the performance course will be required.[25] Impatience and frustration are the greatest enemies of recovery.

In the first three weeks or so of the rest program, the pains become worse, sharper in quality and arise from new areas. Physical signs may transiently increase. Depression, which is a feature of this condition, may become worse for a short time. When this phase is passed the condition will wax and wane, even when the rest program is punctiliously observed. Medical monitoring in the early stages should be performed weekly to avoid premature abandonment of the radial rest program.

During the recovery phase, progress is marked by the good days and not by the bad days. They will almost inevitably alternate and, after a time, the bad days become less bad. The first totally pain-free day is a big landmark. As recovery proceeds it is very tempting to do more with the hands. This temptation must be vigorously resisted, for recovery can be postponed almost indefinitely into the future by yielding to what would, in other circumstances, be quite a reasonable desire. At many times during the recovery phase, the condition appears to be static and morale sinks. Support with the appropriate encouragement from the attending physician is vital for the patient's family, friends and institution. The primary goal then is to become pain free, and not until this stage has been reached should the long, slow process of rehabilitation be commenced.

Rehabilitation means restoration of performance on good terms. Tissue regeneration can not be hurried by any known medication or influences. There are many things, however, which will delay these processes and this must always be borne in mind. At the end of the rest program whether it be 5 months, 9 months or 18 months, the muscles are capable of training and do not undergo any obvious irreversible change. During the rest program, the joints and the muscles are continually put through a normal range of motion, but any contraction of the muscles against resistance or loading of the joint ligaments has been avoided as far as it is possible to do so. Now with rehabilitation, they will respond to ever-increasing work and re-develop their strength and endurance. This, however, must be commenced very, very slowly, and I usually start the musician on one minute of low, easy practise twice a day. This sounds like hardly more than a gesture, yet even this may produce transient discomfort to begin with. This is raised to one minute three times a day and finally the one minute segments are increased by one minute per segment every few days, of easy slow practice. Once ten minute segments are reached without problem, the speed and the intensity may be slowly elevated. Ultimately as twenty minute segments are possible, more is being done. Twenty-five minute segments should be the final maximum and, to begin with, may be hourly, so there is in fact a thirtyfive minute rest between segments. Perhaps when full recovery finally takes place, quarter hour breaks are largely hypothetical and somewhat average, for each person will be a little different.

In the 12 months following the beginning of rehabilitation, the musician will notice the hands and arms feeling progressively more and more comfortable, and the feeling of normality and strength during the rehabilitation phase. Impatience and frustration are again the great enemies, for the musician naturally wants to return to performance at the earliest possible moment, and inevitably will go too fast at this stage if left to his own devices. While practice is slowly increasing, the musician should not give way to the temptation to use the hands too much in other directions. This must be strictly controlled, all forceful movements avoided, always carrying any light cases, etc. by shoulder strap, not taking the lids off jars or turning taps, etc. With the self-discipline learned during the total pain avoidance program, it is usually possible to tolerate the slow rehabilitation, because improvement is clearly occurring in the music making capacity. Try to avoid psychological stress as far as possible and attempt to develop a philosophical approach to

Hunter J.H. Fry

those areas of stress which apparently canot be controlled. Have realistic expectations and, above all, if there is even the slightest cause for concern, report it early while there is still time.

PREVENTION

Overuse syndrome as described here is theoretically preventable, even allowing for the individual susceptibility to the condition, which varies greatly from one individual to another. Most often adequate warnings are given, by strange sensations in the arms and hands, and this should be regarded the same way as one would regard the sword of Damocles.* Ignoring these warnings is committing an act of utter folly, fraught with risk, even if there is an important competition next week.

Accept the guidelines for disciplined practice habits which will be more productive anyway. The musician may not feel like stopping at a twenty-five minute 'by the clock' measured interval of time. However, it is better to be safe than indulgent. A five minute break totally away from the instrument is required, this being an arbitrary figure, but reasonable guideline. Go for a walk, have a cup of coffee, do some exercises (not involving the upper limb too much), or watch television, so long as it is a complete break from the activity of music making. Set some sensible and practical upper limits of practice and playing. Any musician involved in 14 hours of playing or practice per day is running a high risk of overuse and will be fortunate to escape physical consequences from this amount of playing.

In those afflicted musicians where there has not been any warning, the pain may follow a heavy session of music making by an apparently symptom-free interval to that the damage is done before the symptoms are felt. Unless all of these observations and conclusions about music related injury are totally incorrect, every musician has the potential to become injured through music making if the intensity and time of playing are sufficiently elevated. The disabled person has less reserve so particularly must 'play it safe'.

---

* Damocles was seated at a feast with a sword suspended over him supported by a single hair. This was to teach him of the ever present risk in matters Damocles appeared to take for granted.

REFERENCES

1   Fry, H.J.H.: Overuse syndrome in the upper limb in musicians. *Med J of Australia,* **144**(4), pp. 182-185.
2   Fry, H.J.H.: Incidence of overuse injury syndrome in the Symphony Orchestra. *Med Problems of Perf Artists*, March 1986, **1**(1), pp. 36-38.
3   Fry, H.J.H.: The prevalence of overuse [injury] syndrome in Australian music schools. *Brit J Indus Med* (in press).
4   Fry, H.J.H., Hallett, M.: Focal distonia (occupational cramp) masquerading as nerve entrapment or hysteria. *Plast and Reconstr Surg*, 1986, **82**, pp. 908-910.
5   Fry, H.J.H.: Overuse [injury] syndrome in musicians - 100 years ago, an historical review. *Med J of Aust.* Submitted for publication.
6   Riggs, C.E.: In: *A System of Practical Therapeutics.* Hobart Hare, (ed.), W. Chrystie, (assist.). Philadelphia: Lea Bros, & Co., 1892, **111**, pp. 419-427.

7   Gowers, W.R.: In: *Diseases of the Nervous System*. London, U.K.: J. & A. Churchill, 1888, **11**, pp. 656-676.

8   Lewis, M.J.: In: *A System of Practical Medicine*. William Pepper (ed.) Louis Starr (assist.). London, U.K.: Sampson, Low, Marston, Searle & Rivington, 1886, **V**, pp. 504-543.

9   Dennett, Y., Fry, H.J.H.: Overuse syndrome: A muscle biopsy study. *The Lancet*, 1988, **1**, pp. 905-908.

10 Hochberg, F.H., Leffert, R.D., Heller, B.D., Merriman: Hand difficulties among musicians. *JAMA*, April 1983, **249**(14), p. 1896.

11 Fry, H.J.H.: Occupational maladies of musicians: Their cause and prevention. *International J Music Education*, November 1984, **2**, pp. 63-66.

12 Owen, E.: R.S.I. Overuse injury syndrome in musicians. *J Occupational Health and Safety*, Australia and New Zealand, **1**(2), pp. 135-139.

13 Lederman, R., Calabrese, L.: Overuse syndromes in musicians. *Medical Problems of Performing Artists*, March 1986, **1**(1), pp. 196-200.

14 Thompson, A.R., Plewes, L.W., Shaw, E.G.: Peridendinitis crepitans and simple tenosynovitis: A clinical study of 544 cases in industry. *Brit J Indus Med*, 1951, **8**, pp. 150-160.

15 Fry, H.J.H., Ross, P., Rutherford, M.: Music related overuse in secondary schoold. *Med Problems Perf Artists*, 1988, **3**, pp. 133-135.

16 Howard, N.J.: Peritendinitis crepitans. *J of Bone and Joint Surgery*, April 1937 **2**(19), pp. 447-459.

17 Fry, H.J.H.: Physical signs in the hand and wrist in the overuse [injury] syndrome. *Aust and NZ J Surgery*, January 1986, **56**(1), pp. 47-49.

18 Hikada, R.S., Staron, R.S., Hagerman, F.C. et al: Muscle fiber necrosis associated with human marathon runners. *J Neuro Science*, 1983, **59**, pp. 185-203.

19 Dalakas, M., et al: Muscular symptoms in patients with old poliomyelitis: Clinical, cirological and immunological studies. In: *Late Effects of Poliomyelitis*. Halstead, L.S., Weichers, D.O. (eds.). Miami, FL: Symposia Foundation. 1985, pp. 73-89.

20 Haward, Warrington: Note on pianists cramp. *Brit Med J*, March 1887, **1**(1369), p. 672.

21 Poore, G.V.: In: *A System of Practical Medicine*. R. Quain (ed). Part 11. Longmans Green & Co., 1885, pp. 1792-1794.

22 Ostwald, Professor P.M.: Personal communication, 1985.

23 *The Genuine Works of Hippocrates* - Aphorisms 3 & **6** translated from the Greek by Francis Adams, LL.D. Vol. 1. London. *The Classics of Medicine* library, Division of Gryphon Editions Ltd. P.O. Box 76108, Birmingham, Alabama.

24 Fry, H.J.H.: Overuse syndrome in musicians: Prevention and management. *The Lancet*. Review (in press).

25 Fry, H.J.H.: Overuse injury in the music school. *MEJ*, May 1986, **72**(9), pp. 46-49.

COMATOSE AND HEAD-INJURED PATIENTS: APPLICATIONS FOR MUSIC IN TREATMENT

Mary Elinor Boyle

ABSTRACT

This review examines data-based research in music related to the comatose and/or head-injured patient. The inclusion of music as auditory stimulation for these patients is commonplace in acute care and rehabilitation settings. However, there is a paucity of published research with this population. This review draws parallels between the use of music with other handicapped populations for similar behavioral skills or deficits and its potential application with the traumatic brain-injured patient.

INTRODUCTION

Coma, "one of the most enigmatic and least predictable conditions in clinical medicine,"[1] describes a transition from consciousness to either death, the *vegetative state*,[2] or recovery. Traumatic brain injury strikes an estimated 400,000 persons in the United States each year.[3] Death confronts approximately 100,000 of these persons, while 3% of the survivors remain in the *persistent vegetative state*.[4] Due to the tremendous technological advances in medical care, over 1,000,000 patients in the United States have survived traumatic brain injury during the 10 years, 1975-84.[3] Their disabilities range within mild,[5] moderate,[6] and severe categories varying by degree and deficit. Of immediate concern to families and care-givers is the "quality of life" of these survivors. Ethical considerations concerning the "quality of life" and its costs have been the controversial topic of two Presidential Commissions.[7] [8]

The recency and urgency created by rising medical costs as well as technological advances is seen in the formation of the National Head Injury Foundation (NHIF) in 1980 by the mother of a head-injured patient. The NHIF promotes public awareness of the problems faced by both patients and families and encourages the development of rehabilitation programming and support groups for those facing the crises related to head injury.

Music has typically been perceived as an art relating to the "quality of life" for all. Yet when one includes music in the care and treatment of the handicapped in the 80s, it is necessary to account for its inclusion in treatment programs as "treatment." This is especially true given the cost factors related to rehabilitation for the head-injured.[9] [10]

Here is presented a rationale for the inclusion of music in therapy as "treatment" for the head-injured client founded upon data-based research with normal and handicapped persons. There is a paucity of published research incorporating music as treatment for the comatose[11] or head-injured.[12] [13] [14] There are several studies regarding musical abilities of patients following head trauma or neurosurgery.[12] [15] The lack of data-based music therapy treatment techniques specifically for the head-injured is not surprising given the recency of the increased survival rates of patients following coma.[9] The situation is further complicated by the inapplicability of traditional group research designs for treatment analyses, i.e., diffuse head injury cannot be averaged across clients. Single subject research designs are occurring more frequently in behavioral medicine.[16] For assessment and treatment decisions, these designs[17] offer new avenues for research. Despite this minimal data basis, families are counseled to treat the patient as if he could hear even while in acute coma.[18] Radios are frequently turned on as auditory stimulation for patients. (Patients who recover may recall conversations among other persons at their bedside.)

COMA

In 1978 the New York Academy of Sciences sponsored an international symposium on brain death, states of consciousness and coma to examine questions of diagnosis and treatment of coma and brain death. No one definition of coma was promulgated as a result. However, a widely accepted definition is that of Posner, [19] "those states in which cognitive functions are diminished and the patient is unresponsive to all outside stimuli."

Gradations within coma from deep to light and noncognitive states, including the persistent vegetative states and the apallic syndrome, are posited by Plum and Posner.[20] Clear cut agreements among medical personnel (i.e., neurosurgeons, general surgeons, and nurses) on overall levels of coma are difficult to obtain.[21] To facilitate the development of reliable observational measures, neurosurgical centers in Scotland, The Netherlands, and the United States have collaborated on developing a data bank to evaluate severe head-injured persons in coma and to adopt procedures (The Glasgow Coma Scale) to predict outcomes from severe head injury.[22] The Glasgow Coma Scale, as well as the Munich Coma Scale developed by Brinkman, et al.[23] are behavioral scales rating simple observed behaviors, such as eye blinking, reflex responses, and pain responses.

Although some authors regard the vegetative state as a form of coma, the more common interpretation allows for a more conservative estimate of coma as a sleep-like state where the patient is unarousable to external stimuli.[19] Levy, et al.[24] state "the common denominator of the vegetative state is the appearance of wakefulness without any external evidence of communication or complex behavior."

As coma and the vegetative state may be transient,[19 25] several assessment scales have been developed to examine disability/ability levels.[26 27] Rappaport, et al.[27] make the point that it is easier to identify disability or impairment level than "wellness" level. Their observation may be carried another step in terms of the difficulties encountered documenting treatment effectiveness as it relates to wellness.

Rimel, et al.[5] correlated the Glasgow Coma Scale scores in the 13-15 range (GCS range: 3-15[22]) with disability caused by minor head injury. Deficits were demonstrated in terms of attention, concentration, memory and judgments despite normal neurological examination. Rimel, et al.[6] also correlated Glasgow Coma Scale scores of 9-12 with moderate head injury. Deficits observed within the best recovery range (only 38% of this class) included headaches, memory difficulties, and problems with daily living skills. Parallels within the music therapy literature can be drawn between these problems and varied treatments.

CONTINGENT MUSIC

Numerous studies have documented the effects of music consequences as potent reinforcers for behavior changes with handicapped and normal populations.[28 29] Madsen, et al.[29] cited over 200 studies and Greer[28] cites 109 studies. Music has frequently been used with mentally retarded populations for behaviors as diverse as the arithmetic performance of educable mentally retarded persons[30 31] and imitative behaviors of severely retarded adults.[32 33] Music has also been shown to function as a reinforcer with normal subjects altering response such as vocal pitch acuity,[34] prereading behaviors[35] and arithmetic responses.[36]

Hefferline's[37] work in covert conditioning of escape and avoidance behaviors suggests potential applications of music within an operant paradigm to the awakening comatose patient. To consider conditioning effects, Hefferline chose a behavior so minute as to be indiscriminable and thereby not mediated by verbal behavior. He then examined it across four conditions. The first condition consisted of noncontingent music with a contingent 60 cycle hum played through earphones for the subject. The subject was told "to listen to the music and otherwise to do nothing" (p. 127). Each time the subject's correct thumb muscle twitched the 60 cycle hum was interrupted for 15 sec. Cumulative 15 sec. delays were possible with increases in thumb twitching. The second condition consisted of contingent noise with music as in the first condition, however, the verbal directions were "that a specific response, so small as to be invisible" (p. 127) controlled the application of noise. The third condition entailed solely the verbal directions to twitch a small left thumb muscle. The fourth condition consisted of a verbal direction and visual feedback on a left thumb muscle. Hefferline found that verbal directions with visual feedback produced the quickest rate of learning. However, he also found that subjects in the two noise contingency conditions, both of which were unaware of left thumb twitches, produced them to avoid the application of noise over music. The only group which did not learn to twitch the correct left thumb muscle was the group given verbal directions only.

The work of Epstein, et al.[38] follows the tradition of Hefferline. In examining tension headache, they calibrated low electromyographic recordings of the frontalis muscle to trigger music feedback. This treatment resulted in consistently low electromyographic recordings.

Concurrent with Hefferline's[37] covert conditioning work is the overt conditioning work of Barrett.[39] She reduced multiple tic emmission of an adult male from a range of 64 to 115 tics per minute to a range of 15 to 30 tics per minute. Following in the tradition of her work is that of Ball, et al.[40] and Wolfe[41] with head positioning behaviors of cerebral palsied children. Neilson and McCaughy[42] trained the self-regulation of spasm and spasticity with an on-line display of feedback and activation of preferred music.

Of particular interest is the work of Selinske (Note 1) in which she investigated lateral eye movements and toe movement of a 70-year-old comatose male. An ABA, withdrawal design[17] was used to examine the contingent use of a treatment package of 15 sec of Irish music, i.e., "Stack of Barley," experimenter praise and experimenter pats on the shoulder on eye and toe movements. As a family member was often in attendance, spontaneous familial verbalizations regarding experimenter directions and praise occurred. The patient awakened from coma, i.e., opened his eyes, 11 days after onset of coma during a treatment session. Prior to awakening, the patient tapped his toes rhythmically to the music. No reliability was reported. Due to use of a quasi-experimental design and the high probability of spontaneous remission of the coma within two to four weeks of onset,[20] no definitive conclusions concerning the treatment package can be drawn. Despite methodological difficulties, the Selinske study confronts researchers with questions concerning the definition of coma, mechanisms of operant conditioning and the nature of the human organism.

Boyle and Greer[11] examined operant responses of three patients. One patient was in the persistent vegetative state 38 months prior to initiation of the experiment; the other patients were in the vegetative state for 6 months and 10 months following acute coma. The third patient died one week following termination of the treatment condition due to an extremely labile hypertensive condition. Systematic responses were noted under conditions of 15 seconds of preferred music for three motor behaviors to two of three behaviors of each of the other two patients.

NONCONTINGENT AUDITORY STIMULATION

Related to Selinske's work (Note 1) with acute coma victims is the work of Pollack and Goldstein.[43] They employed gentle tactile and auditory stimulation by family members to prevent continuing elevations of intracranial pressure in Reye's syndrome with seven comatose patients. In the absence of family members, taped conversations of family members were used. The tapes were played on cassette tape recorders placed at the heads of the patients' beds. This stimulation consistently reduced intracranial pressure from a range of 15 to 19 mm Hg to 10 mm Hg.

This treatment procedure parallels the work of Dorow and Horton[44] with severely/profoundly retarded crib confined females. Dorow and Horton examined the effects of proximity of a sound source (cassette tape recorder) to severely/profoundly retarded crib confined females. They found that placement of the sound source 5 inches from the patient's head increased movement activity over the placement of the sound source at the foot of the patient's bed.

OPERANT CONDITIONING WITH THE PROFOUNDLY RETARDED

The profoundly retarded constitute a population which share certain characteristics with the awakening comatose patient. The first case of operant conditioning of a profoundly retarded male[45] was in fact entitled, "Operant Conditioning of a Vegetative Human Organism." In commenting on the difficulty of determining reinforcing stimuli for "vegetative patients" (profoundly retarded), Rice and McDaniel[46] reported the preference of a "vegetative patient" for only one specific music selection. They also reported that moderate food deprivation did not seem to alter a subject's performance when food was used as a reinforcer, bringing into question whether even food functioned as a reinforcer under moderate deprivation for some patients. Rice, et al.[47] reported on another "vegetative" patient's unique tantrum response to classical music.

Literature on the reinforcement properties of music with the profoundly retarded confirms the initial findings of Rice and McDaniel[46] that for some subjects music does function as a reinforcer, while for others it does not.[48 49 50 51 52] However, Dorow[32 33] demonstrated that for those subjects with whom music does not function as a reinforcer, music can be paired with food to acquire reinforcing properties.

Whereas with the profoundly mentally retarded, it may be necessary to condition music as a secondary reinforcer through pairing with food, as primary reinforcer,[32 33] the awakening comatose patient may have previously experienced music as a reinforcer prior to the injury or illness which resulted in coma.[11] The question becomes whether music will function as a reinforcer following coma and its concomitants for individual patients.

BIOFEEDBACK

Some contributors to the biofeedback literature are undecided as to whether biofeedback belongs entirely to the operant paradigm. Miller[53] defines biofeedback as "feedback provided by a device that provides prompt measurement of a biological function." (p. 421) However, Shapiro[54] defines biofeedback "in terms of the applications of operant conditioning methods in the control of visceral, somatomotor, or central nervous systems." (p. 421) The controversy is only important to awakening comatose patients in that they are incapable of utilizing biological feedback information in the sense of Miller's definition. Shapiro's definition does not exclude the effectiveness of specific applications of music to bring selected behaviors of the patient under operant control.

Typical uses for nonmusical auditory biofeedback strategies include modifying foot dragging behaviors of cerebral palsied males,[55] genu recurvatum with head-injured patients,[56] lateral weight shifting in ambulation training of the physically impaired,[57] and skin potential of normal subjects.[58] Brudny, et al.[59] employed electromyographic monitoring coupled with contingent auditory feedback to train voluntary movements of hemiparetics.

Brudny, et al.[60] realized dramatic results with several patients suffering from disorders of the central nervous system by employing an operant treatment package. The treatment package consisted of visual and auditory electromyographic displays of information, a shaping procedure with a changing criterion design and the fading of the electromyographic display. The disorders treated included torticollis, dystonia, and hemiparetic-spastic disorders, which had been treated for up to 25 years with minimal or no improvement. They found that, "Apparently, a significant number of patients with disrupted internal feedback loops can incorporate the learned movement pattern by using those components of (the) neuromuscular system that are still functionally available" (p. 925).

The type of feedback used in these and similar studies is not discriminable by the awakening comatose patient. Music might however function as a desirable reinforcer in a manner similar to that demonstrated by Hefferline.[37] While Hefferline conditioned normal subjects to perform an act of which they were not "conscious," Boyle and Greer[11] investigated whether it is possible for a person considered lacking in "conscious behaviors" to perform behaviors considered as conscious acts, i.e., compliance with verbal directions.

A comment of Shapiro's[54] regarding the properties of biofeedback mechanisms is relevant to the consideration of music as a biofeedback device. ". . . A biofeedback stimulus-reinforcer need not be simply an informational stimulus. . . Incentive and other properties associated with the biofeedback signal are also critical. . . " (p. 455).

THE LEVELS OF COGNITIVE FUNCTIONING SCALE

To this point we have examined general considerations of contingent music, noncontingent auditory stimulation, operant conditioning and biofeedback, related to coma and traumatic brain injury. This section will draw parallels in terms of behavioral skills and deficits outlined by the Rancho Los Amigos Levels of Cognitive Functioning Scale[61] and treatment programs with other populations. Because of the quality of the behaviors in many cases the primary parallels will be drawn between treatment for the developmentally disabled.

The Levels of Cognitive Functioning Scale[61] delineates eight levels of patient behaviors in the weeks and months immediately following injury. They are:

I   No response,
II   Generalized response,
III   Localized response,
IV   Confused, agitated,
V   Confused, inappropriate, non-agitated,
VI   Confused appropriate,
VII Automatic appropriate,
VIII Purposeful, appropriate.

These levels are used frequently in rehabilitation programming considerations for the head-injured.

At the first and second levels of the Scale, "I. No response: Unresponsive to any stimulus," and, "II. Generalized Response: Limited, inconsistent, nonpurposeful responses, often to pain only", assessment is key to the inclusion to music in treatment. The inherent difficulty in assessment at these levels relates to the necessity of a client initiated response rather than a therapist initiated response. Plum and Posner[20] state, "Behaviorally, one can estimate another person's self-aware consciousness only by his response to the examiner's verbal commands or gestures" (p. 32). Most assessment tools are inapplicable due to the severity of the disability, e.g., many patients do not orient to light or sound sources.[62 63 64] The Glasgow Coma Scale[22] and the Munich Coma Scale[23] test overt respondent behaviors of the comatose patient to certain external stimuli. Measurement procedures with the brain-injured are at present primarily dependent upon visual observation which has several weaknesses.[65] Most procedures for the severely-profoundly retarded[66 67] require greater physical and cognitive abilities than are evident with the brain-injured physically involved client.

Despite the difficulties in assessing what type of treatment might be appropriate for this population, certain clients have received legislative mandates that services must be delivered, i.e., those patients under the age of 21 (P.L. 94:**142**, Sec. 612[3]). At present the effectiveness of certain "treatment" procedures is unknown due to lack of client initiated responses. The author is presently testing an Operant Sensory Awareness Assessment Instrument (OSAAI) with patients in the vegetative state (Note 2). The OSAAI is an instrument which allows the patient to activate the sensory stimulus, i.e., a videotape recorder, tape recorder, fragrance atomizer, light and/or fan, by triggering a switch (adapted to the physical needs of the client). The instrument can be set for varied reinforcement times from 1 to 20 sec. An Esterline Angus Graph Recorder records patient responses. Assessment of client interaction with the environment is possible by examining data in terms of the event itself, the frequency of the triggering responses for a given sensory modality, and the delay between triggering responses, as well as the sensory modalities within which the client responds optimally or negligibly. Similar assessment instruments have been devised for the profoundly retarded using only one or two modalities.[68 69] This procedure differs in the use of an alternating treatments design with criterion referencing.[17] Hopefully this simple device requiring a client initiated response rather than a therapist initiated one will allow for assessment of client sensory awareness and the development of data-based treatment procedures in terms of sensory input. In the acute states of coma and in the vegetative state, researchers have not typically examined operant behaviors. This may affect the perception of the category, "No response."[61]

The third level of the Cognitive Function Scale is: "Localized Response: Purposeful responses, may follow simple commands; may focus on presented object."[61] In this area, there are many parallels that can be drawn for data-based techniques.[70 71 72] Johnson and Zinner[73] examined stimulus fading and schedule learning on subject's ability to discriminate colors and increase on task behaviors. Underhill and Harris[72] increased imitative behaviors with music as a contingent reinforcer with behaviorally disturbed retarded children.

Level Four describes patients in terms of "Confused, Agitated: Heightened state of activity; confusion, disorientation; aggressive behavior; unable to do self care; unaware of present events; agitation appears related to internal confusion;" while Level Five describes patients in terms of "Confused, Inappropriate, Non-Agitated: Appears alert, responds to commands; distractable; does not concentrate on task; agitated responses to external stimuli; verbally inappropriate; does not learn new information."[61] Several researchers[72 74 75] address the difficulty encountered by professionals working with the profoundly multiply handicapped attempting to determine reinforcing properties of sensory stimuli. Wacker, *et al.*[75] tested a procedure involving microswitches to evaluate reinforcer preferences. As they state, "Once a stimulus is thought to be reinforcing, the student is then exposed to the stimulus intermittently throughout the school day in a contingent fashion. As a result, the student may be provided with aversive rather than

Mary Elinor Boyle

reinforcing stimuli" (p. 173). The avoidance of aversive stimuli could agitate the already confused patient.

Aggressive behaviors are severe problems with any population; a total treatment plan is obviously necessary. Two examples of such plans incorporate the use of contingent music. Davis, et al.[76] found the contingent removal of music and a verbal "No" to be effective in reducing the ruminating and out-of-seat behaviors of a profoundly retarded male. Reid,e t al.[77] reinforced appropriate social behaviors to a nonverbal, hyperactive 8-year-old male in several settings with a remotely controlled tape recorder.

Level Six addresses behaviors such as: "Confused, Appropriate: Good directed behavior, needs cueing; can relearn old skills as Activities of Daily Living (ADL); serious memory problems awareness of self and others."[61] The use of music as a cue for patients with frontal lobe damage is presently being investigated by Wharen and associates in Pittsburgh (Note 3). Tape recordings related to ADL skills are given to patients. Simple songs outline the steps to be taken in performing a given skill. Patients are trained to activate the tape recorder and to use the tapes as cues. The program has been highly successful to date. Music has often been used as a cue with other populations as well. Many of us learned the alphabet with the help of Jiminy Cricket and "The Alphabet Song." Music has been used as a prompt for communications skills,[78 79 80 81] money skills,[82] and hand washing.[83] The small group music session can be an excellent occasion for training appropriate social skills.[84]

Level Seven, "Automatic Appropriate: Robot-like appropriate behavior, minimal confusion, shallow recall; poor insight into condition; initiates tasks but needs structure; poor judgment, problem solving and planning skills"[61] focuses on the patient's extensive disabilities. For the music therapist, it may be appropriate to focus on the development of a leisure time skill. Depending upon the patient's motor ability a variety of experiences/instruments may be appropriate, e.g., playing a stereo, harmonica, dulcimer, guitar, portachord, omnichord, electric keyboard or piano. Behavioral contracts with task analyses can be developed and negotiated in terms of literature and skills covered allowing a client a certain independence.

Level Eight describes patients in terms of: "Purposeful Appropriate: Alert, oriented; recalls and integrates past events, learns new activities and can continue without supervision; independent in home and living skills; capable of driving; defects in stress tolerance, judgment, abstract reasoning persist; many function at reduced levels in society."[61] At this level, it is important for the client to have developed appropriate leisure skills so that he/she can enjoy life. Music may provide an appropriate outlet for the patient at this time.

DISCUSSION

The importance of continued research in music with the brain-injured relates to ethical, "quality of life," and behavioral research issues. At this time, most research with this population relates to outcome diagnosis or predicted outcome rather than treatment. This is an initial societal coping measure made necessary by rapid technological advances in medicine. We are confronted in certain cases with persons who are being maintained with no knowledge of whether appropriate treatment procedures could alleviate their pain or provide pleasure. It is encumbent upon a society that maintains these patients to provide some basic investigations concerning care, if that in the end is only contingent sensory stimulation. It is possible that for some this may constitute "treatment." In the words of Melin, et al.,[62] "Due to an increasing interest in the interdependencies between neural function and behavior, it is now clear that not only can physiological changes affect behavior, but also behavioral operations can bring about nontrivial changes in physiology" (p. 269). Although the focus of this review of literature has been data-based techniques involving music, music cannot be isolated from a total rehabilitation program due to the nature of traumatic brain injury. Music can be an integral part of treatment programming ranging from contingent auditory stimulation to the development of the new lifetime leisure skills for the traumatic brain-injured patient.

NOTES

1. Selinske, J.E.: The effect of Irish music on unconscous patients following a cerebral vascular accident. Unpublished manuscript, 1979. (Available from author, Neward, New Jersey.)

2. Boyle, M.E.: Validation of an operant sensory awareness assessment procedure with profoundly mentally impaired patients. Experiment in progress.

3. Wharen, R.E., Nagle, A.: The use of music as a cueing device with patients with frontal lobe injury. Research in progress. (For information, please contact Dr. Robert E. Wharen at Harmarville Rehabilitation Center, Pittsburgh, PA.)

REFERENCES

1 De la Torre, J.C., Trimble, J.L., Beard, R.T., Hanlon, K., Surgeon, J.W.: Somatosensory evoked potentials for the prognosis of coma in humans. *Exp Neurol*, 1978, **60**, pp. 304-317.
2 Jennett, B., Plum, F.: Persistent vegetative state after brain damage: A syndrome in search of a name. *The Lancet*, 1972, **1**, pp. 734-737.
3 National Head Injury Foundation: The silent epidemic. Framingham, MA, 1984.
4 National Head Injury Foundation: Coma: Its treatment and consequences. Framingham, MA.
5 Rimel, R.W., Giordani, B., Barth, J.T., Boll, T.J., Jane, J.A.: Disability caused by minor head injury. *Neurosurgery*, 1981, **9**, pp. 221-228.
6 Rimel, R.W., Giordani, B., Barth, J.T., Jane, J.A.: Moderate head injury: completing the clinical spectrum of brain trauma. *Neurosurgery*, 1982, **11**, pp. 344-351.
7 President's Commission for the Study of Ethical Problems in Medicine and Biomedical and Behavioral Research (1981). *Defining Death: A Report on the Medical, Legal and Ethical Issues in the Determination of Death.* U.S. Government Printing Office, Washington, DC.
8 President's Commission for the Study of Ethical Problems in Medicine and Biomedical and Behavioral Research (1983). *Deciding to Forego Life-sustaining Treatment.* U.S. Government Printing Office, Washington DC.
9 Levy, D.E.: Ethical consideration in the care of unconscious patients. In: Pfaff D.W. (ed.) *Ethical Questions Related to Brain and Behavior.* New York: Springer-Verlag, 1983, pp. 57-72.
10 Alexander, M.P.: Neurobehavioral consequences of closed head injury. *Neurology and Neurosurgery Update Series*, 1984, **5**, pp. 2-8.
11 Boyle, M.E., Greer, R.D.: Operant procedures and the comatose patient. *J Appl Behav Anal*, 1983, **16**, pp. 3-12.
12 Gouvier, W.D., Richards, J.S., Blanton, P.D., Janert, K., Rosen L.A., Drabman, R.S.: Behavior modification in physical therapy. *Arch Phys Med Rehab*, 1985, **66**, pp. 113-116.
13 Gates, A., Bradshaw, J.L.: The role of the cerebral hemispheres in music. *Brain and Language*, 1977, **4**, pp. 402-431.
14 Jacome, D.E.: Aphasia with elation, hypermusia, musicophilia and compulsive whistling. *J Neurol Neurosurg Psychiatry*, 1984, **47**, pp. 308-310.

15 Albert, M.L., Sparks, R.W., Helm, N.A.: Melodic intonation therapy for aphasia. *Arch Neurol*, 1973, **29**, pp. 130-131.

16 Melamed, B.G., Siegel, L.J.: *Behavioral Medicine: Practical Applicaion in Health Care.* New York: Springer Publishing Company, 1980.

17 Barlow, D.H., Hersen, M.: *Single Case Experimental Designs.* New York: Pergamon Press, 1984.

18 Hutchison, R., Hutchison, T.: *Head Injury: A Booklet for Families.* Houston, TX: Texas Head Injury Foundation, 1983.

19 Posner, J.B.: Coma and other states of consciousness: The differential diagnosis of brain death. *Ann NY Acad Sci*, 1978, **315**, pp. 215-227.

20 Plum, F., Posner, J.B.: *The Diagnosis of Stupor and Coma.* Philadelphia: F.A. David Co., 1980.

21 Teasdale, G., Knill-Jones, R., Van Der Sande, J.: Observer variability in assessing impaired consciousness and coma. *J Neurol Neurosurg Psychiatry*, 1978, **41**, pp. 603-610.

22 Teasdale, G., Murray, G., Parker, L., Jennett, B.: Adding up the Glasgow coma score. *Acta Neurochir*, 1979, supp 28, pp. 13-16.

23 Brinkmann, R., von Cramon, D., Schulz, H.: The Munich coma scale (MCS). *J Neurol Neurosurg Psychiatry*, 1967, **39**, pp. 788-793.

24 Levy, D.E., Knill-Jones, R.P., Plum, F.: The vegetative state and its prognosis following nontraumatic coma. *Ann NY Acad. Sci*, 1978, **315**, pp. 293-306.

25 Arts, W.F.M., van Dongen, H.R., van Hof - van Duin, J., Lammens, E.: Unexpected improvement after prolonged posttraumatic vegetative state. *J Neurol Neurosurg Psychiatry*, 1985, **48**, pp. 1300-1303.

26 Eson, M.E., Yen, J.K., Bourke, R.S.: Assessment of recovery from serious head injury. *J Neurol Neurosurg Psychiatry*, 1978, **41**, pp. 1036-1042.

27 Rappaport, M., Hall, K.M., Hopkins, K., Belleza, T., Cope, D.N.: Disability rating scale for severe head trauma: coma to community. *Arch Phys Med Rehabil*, 1982, **63**, pp. 118-123.

28 Greer, R.D.: An operant approach to motivation and affect: Ten years of research in music learning. In: *Documentary Report of the National Symposium on the Applications of Psychology to the Teaching and Learning of Music.* Washington, DC: MENC Press, 1981.

29 Madsen, C.K., Greer, R.D., Madsen, C.H. (eds.): *Research in Music Behavior: Modifying Music Behavior in the Classroom.* New York: Teachers College Press, 1975.

30 Dorow, L.G.: Televised music lessons as educational reinforcement for correct mathematical responses with the educable mentally retarded. *J Music Therapy*, 1976, **13**, pp. 77-86.

31 Miller, D.M.: Effects of selected music listening contingencies on arithmetic performance and music preference of educable mentally retarded children. *Am J Ment Deficiency*, 1977, **81**, pp. 371-378.

32 Dorow, L.G.: Conditioning music and approval as new reinforcers for imitative behavior with the severely retarded. *J Music Therapy*, 1975, **12**, pp. 33-39.

33 Dorow, L.G.: Generalization effects of newly conditioned reinforcers. *Ed Train Ment Retarded*, 1980, **15**, pp. 8-14.

34 Greer, R.D., Randall, A., Timberlake, C.: The discriminate use of music listening as a contingency for improvement in vocal pitch acuity and attending behavior. *Council for Research in Music Education Bulletin*, 1971, **26**, pp. 10-18.

35 Steele, A.L.: Contingent socio-music listening periods in a preschool setting. *J Music Therapy*, 1971, **8**, 131-139.

36 Madsen, C.K., Forsythe, J.L.: Effect of contingent music listening in increases of mathematical responses. *J Res Music Education*, 1973, **21**, 176-181.

37 Hefferline, R.F.: Learning theory and clinical psychology – An eventual symbiosis? In: A.J. Bachrach (ed.), *Experimental Foundations of Clinical Psychology.* New York: Basic Books, 1962.

38 Epstein, L.H., Hersen, M., Hempfill, D.: Music feedback in the treatment of tension headache: An experimental case study. *Behav Ther Exp Psychiatry*, 1974, **290**, pp. 646-649.

39 Barrett, B.: Reduction in rate of multiple tics by free operant conditioning methods. *J Nerv Ment Dis*, 1962, **135**, pp. 187-195.

40 Ball, T.S., McCrady, R.E., Hart, A.D.: Automated reinforcement of head posture in two cerebral palsied retarded children. *Percept Mot Skills*, 1975, **40**, pp. 619-622.

41 Wolfe, D.E.: The effect of automated interrupted music on head posturing of cerebral palsied individuals. *J Music Therapy*, 1980, **17**, pp. 184-206.

42 Neilson, P.D., McCaughey, J.: Self-regulation of spasm and spasticity in cerebral palsy. *J Neurol Neurosurg Psychiatry*, 1982, **45**, pp. 320-330.

43 Pollack, L.D., Goldstein, G.W.: Lowering of intracranial pressure in Reye's Syndrome by sensory stimulation. *N Engl J Med*, 1980, **304**, p. 732.

44 Dorow, L.G., Horton, J.J.: Effect of the proximity of auditory stimuli and sung and spoken stimuli on activity levels of severely/profoundly mentally retarded females. *J Music Therapy*, 1982, **19**, pp. 114-124.

45 Fuller, P.R.: Operant conditioning of a vegetative human organism. *Am J Psychol*, 1949, **62**, pp. 587-590.

46 Rice, H.K. McDaniel, M.W.: Operant behavior in vegetative patients. *Psychol Record*, 1966, **16**, pp. 279-281.

47 Rice, H.K., McDaniel, M.W., Stallings, V.D., Gatz, M.J.: Operant behavior in vegetative patients II. *Psychol Record*, 1967, **17**, pp. 449-460.

48 Haskett, J., Hollar, W.D.: Sensory reinforcement and contingency awareness of profoundly retarded children. *Am J Ment Deficiency*, 1978, **83**, pp. 60-68.

49 Jorgenson, H.: Effect of contingent preferred music in reducing two stereotyped behaviors of a profoundly retarded child. *J Music Therapy*, 1971, **8**, pp. 139-145.

50 Metzler, R.K.: The use of music as a reinforcer to increase imitative behavior in severely and profoundly retarded female residents. *J Music Therapy*, 1974, **11**, pp. 97-110.

51 Remington, R.E., Foxen, R., Hogg, J.: Auditory reinforcement in profoundly retarded multiply handicapped children. *Am J Ment Deficiency*, 1977, **82**, pp. 299-304.

52 Wolpow, R. I.: The independent effects of contingent social and academic approval upon the music on-task and performance behaviors of profoundly retarded adults. *J Music Therapy*, 1976, **13**, pp. 29-38.

53 Miller, N.E.: Biofeedback and visceral learning. In: J. Stoyva, J. Kamiya, T.X., Barber, N.E. Miller, D. Shapiro (eds.) *Biofeedback and Self Control 1977/1978.* New York: Aldine Publishing Co., 1979.

54 Shapiro, D.: A monograph on biofeedback and psychophysiology. In: J. Stoyva, J. Kamiya, T.X., Barber, N.E.Miller, D. Shapiro (eds.) *Biofeedback and Self Control 1977/1978.* New York: Aldine Publishing Co., 1979.

55 Spearing, D.L., Poppen, R.: The use of feedback in the eduction of foot dragging in a cerebral palsied client. *J Nerv Ment Disease*, 1974, **159**, pp. 148-151.

56 Hogue, R.E., McCandless, S.: Genu Recurvatum: Auditory biofeedback treatment for adult patients with stroke or head injuries. *Arch Phys Med Rehabil*, 1983, **64**, pp. 368-370.

57 Wannstedt, G., Craik, R.L.: Clinical evaluation of a sensory feedback device: The limb load monitor. *Bulletin Prosthetics Res*, 1978, **29-30**, pp. 8-49.

58 Shapiro, D., Crider, A.B., Tursky, B.: Differentiation of an autonomic response through operant reinforcement. *Psychonomic Sci*, 1964, **1**, pp. 147-148.

59 Brudny, J., Korein, J., Grynbaum, B.B., Belandres, P.V., Gianutsos, J.G.: Helping hemipatetics to help themselves: Sensory feedback therapy. *JAM*, 1979, **241**, 814-818.

60 Brudny, J., Korein, J., Levidow, L., Grynbaum, B.B., Lieberman, A., Friedmann, L.W.: sensory feedback therapy as a modality of treatmnet in central nervous system disorders of voluntary movement. *Neurology*, 1974, **24**, pp. 925-932.

61 Hagen, C., Malkmus, D., Durham, P.: The levels of cognitive functioning scale. Downey, CA, Professional Staff Association, Rancho Los Amigos Hospital, Inc., 1979.

62 Melin, L., Sjoden, P., James, J.E.: Neurological impairments. In: M. Hersen, V.B. Van Hasselt, J.J. Matson (eds.), *Behavior Therapy for the Developmentally and Physically Disabled*. New York: Acadmic Press, 1983.

63 Schuler, A.L., Goetz, L.: The assessment of severe language disabilities: Communicative and cognitive considerations. *Anal Intervention Dev Disabil*, 1981, **1**, pp. 333-346.

64 Whitman, T.L., Scibak. J.W., Reid, D.H.: *Behavior Modification with the Severely and Profoundly Retarded: Research and Application*. New York: Academic Press, 1983.

65 Bates, D., Caronna J.J., Cartlidge, N.E.F., Knill-Jones, R.P., Levy, D.E., Shaw, D.A., Plum, F.: A prospective study of nontraumatic coma: Methods and results in 310 patients. *Ann Neurol*, 1977, **2**, pp. 211-220.

66 Etzel, B.C., Bickel, W.K., Stella, M.E., LeBlanc, J.M.: The assessment of problem solving skills of atypical children. *Anal Interventional Dev Disabil*, 1982, **2**, pp. 187-206.

67 Goetz, L., Baldwin, M., Gee, K., Sailer, W.: Classroom based sensory assessment procedures for severely handicapped students: Case studies of a stimulus transfer paradigm. *Anal Intervention Dev Disabil*, 1982, **2**, pp. 171-186.

68 Bricker, D.D., Bricker, W.A.: A programmed approach to operant audiometry for low-functioning children. *J Speech Hearing Disord*, **34**, pp. 312-320.

69 Friedlander, B.Z., McCarthy, J.J., Soforenko, A.Z.: Automated psychological evaluation with severely retarded institutionalized infants. *Am J Ment Deficiency*, 1967, **71**, pp. 909-919.

70 Dorow, L.G.: Monograph: *Music Therapy with the Mentally Retarded: Data-Based Techniques from 1970-1980*. Washington, DC: National Association for Music Therapy, Inc., 1981.

71 Underhill, K., Harris, M.: The effect of contingent music on establishing imitation in behaviorally disturbed retarded children. *J Music Therapy*, 1974, **11**, pp. 156-166.

72 Ferrari, M., Harris, S.: The limits and motivation potential of sensory stimuli as reinforcers for autistic children. *J Appl Behav Anal*, 1981, **14**, pp. 339-344.

73 Johnson, J.M., Zinner, C.C.: Stimulus fading and schedule learning in generalizing and maintaining behaviors. *J Music Therapy*, 1974, **11**, pp. 84-96.

74 Fehr, M., Wacher, D., Trezise, J., Lennon, R., Meyerson, L.: Visual, auditory, and vibratory stimulation as reinforcers for profoundly retarded children. *Rehab Psych*, 1979, **26**, pp. 209-210.

75 Wacker, D.P., Berg, W.K., Wiggins, B., Muldoon, M., Cavanaugh, J.: Evaluation of reinforcer preferences for profoundly handicapped students. *J Appl Behav Anal*, 1985, **18**, pp. 173-178.

76 Davis, W.B., Wieseler, N.A., Hanzel, T.E.: Reduction of rumination and out-of-seat behavior and generalization of treatment effects using a non-intrusive method. *J Music Therapy*, 1983, **20**, pp. 115-131.

77 Reid, D.H., Hill, B.K., Rawers, R.J., Montegar, C.A.: The use of contingent music in teaching social skills to a nonverbal, hyperactive boy. *J Music Therapy*, 1975, **12**, pp. 2-18.

78 Alley, J.M.: The effect of music on acquisition and recognition of sign language. Paper presented at the National Symposium for Research on Music Behavior, New York City, 1980.

79 Deutsch, M., Parks, A.L.: The use of contingent music to increase appropriate conversational speech. *Ment Retard*, 1978, **16**, pp. 33-36.

80 Harding, G., Ballard, K.D.: The effectiveness of music as a stimulus and as a contingent reward in promoting the spontaneous speech of three physically handicapped preschoolers. *J Music Therapy*, 1982, **19**, pp. 86-101.

81 Seybold, C.: The value and use of music activitites in the treatment of speech delayed children. *J Music Therapy*, 1971, **8**, pp. 102-110.

82 Hanser, S.B.: Music as a cue for learning money skills. Paper presented at the National Convention of the National Association for Music Therapy, Philadelphia, 1975.

83 Kramer, S.A.: The effects of music as a cue in maintaining handwashing in preshool children. *J Music Therapy*, 1978, **15**, pp. 136-144.

84 Cassity, M.D.: Social development of TMR's involved in performing and nonperforming groups. *J Music Therapy*, 1978, **15**, pp. 100-105.

ASSISTIVE LISTENING DEVICES:
ACCOMMODATING OUR SENIOR ADULTS IN THE CLASSROOM

Niccola A. Bojanowski

The Peabody Institute of the Johns Hopkins University houses a conservatory of music and a preparatory school. The Prep concentrates its teaching efforts on spreading culture throughout the community. Our main focus has been the musical education of children but recently we expanded our music course offerings to include noncredit curriculum for adults and added a program for older adults called Elderhostel, a national network of educational opportunities now in every state and province in North America. The participants in this program are at least 60 years old and have retired or will soon be retiring from mostly professional careers. They register via a network controlled in Boston and travel from all parts of the country to week long programs held at participating campuses. Their interest in music is demonstrated by their choice of The Peabody course offerings over hundreds of other available schools. As we developed our syllabi, the faculty concentrated not only on the broader overview of a chosen area of study but on the presentation of the nuances we knew these people would expect. Listening exercises were crucial. Phrases, innuendos, dynamic variation, theme variations, etc. were to be discussed and demonstrated throughout the discussions of topics such as Mozart's operas, American composers or the works of Verdi. One of the classes planned involved learning to play the recorder in small groups. Participants would necessarily also learn to read music notation and we planned to encourage those who could, to join recorder groups in their communities as a means of further socialization.

Our first class offerings were presented to groups of approximately 40 participants. The curriculum was well received and generated a great deal of enthusiasm. As we suspected, a lifetime of learning has altered this student body profile considerably. Keen interests and a wealth of experience generated exuberant question and answer sessions. Most of the participants were absorbed in the material, concentrating well and participating with vigor, but we worried about those who were not. There were only a few people each session, but since the curriculum was their choice, we expected everyone to be involved.

The evaluations following the sessions gave us some indication that concentration or attention span was possibly an issue. The faculty were also aware that some individuals tended to nod off or seem to be distracted, especially if they were sitting toward the back of the room. Also we were aware that those individuals not particularly involved in the classroom discussions were also not good class attendees, missing a session here or there. In searching for an answer, one of the explanations offered was that they could not hear as well from the back of the room, and possibly they could not hear as well in any case.

Upon investigation, we discovered that over one third of all adults over 60 years of age can expect some hearing loss. In their homes, they are accustomed to turning up the TV just a bit and sitting close to the person they must hear. They can be unaware of the noises they no longer hear well. Psychologically, though, this can lead to a withdrawal from vital social areas that contribute to continued good mental health such as communication with others, church and social occasions and educational experiences, just to name a few. Also, if one hears only 85% of a conversation, one often misses a vital word or nuance and could misunderstand the entire meaning of the conversation leading to all sorts of complicated secondary problems.

We decided that this could be a problem in our classroom. Since our student body statistically had a better than 30% chance of unknown hearing loss, and that hearing sound was vital to our presentation, we needed to investigate further.

Concurrently, we were visited by Mr. William Paschell, a member of the Consumer's Organization for the Hearing Impaired (COHI). Mr. Paschell is profoundly hearing impaired and wanted to attend Elderhostel programs throughout the country including the program offered at The Peabody. His options however, were dramatically reduced to the programs offered at Gallaudet University for the Deaf in Washington, D.C. as their classrooms were equipped with resident audio loop systems and staff interpreters to assist hearing impaired participants. Gallaudet had previously only offered programs designed to inform persons with hearing losses about their options. Mr. Paschell wanted to mainstream and he wanted to help provide that same opportunity for others with hearing losses. We set up a joint meeting with representatives from Gallaudet, Miss Gina Oliva, a graduate student researching assistance devices, Miss Maureen Durkin, Special Projects Director, Mr. Paschell and our Peabody Staff, to discuss the issues involved.

It became apparent that very little was being done to alert and assist older adults with hearing losses and until the loss became extremely disabling, the individual tried to "work around it." Personality adjustments, social withdrawal and breakdowns in communication within partnerships and families were common. Too often, much needed hearing aids were sought only after major changes had already occurred.

It was generally felt that our program at The Peabody, was a good place to begin an awareness of the importance of hearing since we deal with listening skills in our classrooms. Our course material and classroom discussions center around the ability to hear and understand the meaning of sound. We felt that we could legitimately encourage good listening skills, and those individuals unable to hear properly could be encouraged to use assistive devices readily available.

Gallaudet University has had little experience with teaching persons with mild hearing losses. Most of their students have had little or no hearing since birth. Sign language is used extensively throughout their campus. Other colleges expect the individual to be aware of and prepared to adjust to their disability. Normal hearing students, during primary and secondary school years, have their hearing tested regularly and usually, if a loss is not found in the early years, they are not concerned during their young and middle age life.

Older adults, as a group, are more likely to have hearing difficulties and, since Elderhostel is for older adults, we felt an obligation to provide adequate facilities in which to present our program as well as a moral commitment to this ever growing segment of our population.

We were committed to two resolves. Could we adequately assist the profoundly hearing impaired to participate in an educational program such as Elderhostel and could we identify and assist those persons with mild hearing losses to be aware of their loss and to utilize equipment made available to them? It was agreed that a combination of listening assistive devices would be utilized at both The Peabody and the Gallaudet Elderhostel Programs. *Self Help for Hard of Hearing People* and *The National Association for Hearing and Speech Action* both provided mailing lists for us to publicize our programs to profoundly hearing impaired individuals who would not normally attend Elderhostel programs. The programs were also open to normal registration without reference to the fact that they were especially equipped to allow for a normal flow of participants. The Gallaudet program drew 34 participants of whom 26 had hearing losses. The Peabody Program drew 49 for week #1 and 35 for week #2. Of these, 13 and 14 people respectively, or 36% turned out to have some degree of hearing loss, supporting data from various sources.

Three audio assistive devices were used at Gallaudet and The Peabody programs in varying classrooms during the three weeks of classes. They were:

System One – The induction loop or "audio loop" which is a pre-wired loop that is placed around the classroom. A microphone and amplifier are connected from the source of the sound (the instructor) to the loop; the sound is transmitted to hearing aid users who have "telecoil" switches in their hearing aids. Receivers are also available for people not wearing aids.

System Two – The Infrared system which involves a microphone at the sound source relaying sound to an infrared light transmitter which in turn sends the sound to receivers worn by listeners with or without hearing aids through an infrared beam of light. The receiver for non-aid wearers resembles a stethoscope with a small control box. The receiver for the aid wearers clips onto clothing with a loop around the neck. Both units are completely portable and lightweight.

System Three – The FM system, the only wireless system, allowing full freedom of movement for the instructor and the students. The teacher wears a lavalier lapel mike connected to a small transmitter in a cigarette pack size case that can be put in a pocket. The receivers are the same size and can be used with walkman type ear plugs or earphones. The FM system works like an internal radio station, sending and receiving on any one of the 32 pre-set radio channels.

When the participants arrived, we conducted an orientation session explaining the project and asking for their cooperation. Some participants did admit to hearing difficulties. A few already wore hearing aids. All of the discussion was conducted by a leader using the assistive device microphone *and* a normal house amplification system. After passing out the earphones and receivers to all the participants, they were encouraged to try them on and listen to the speaker. They could judge for themselves if they had been hearing her all right or if they had been straining to hear. Those who were straining were immediately relieved to be able to hear more clearly. Those who had no problem in the first place, didn't have the same sense of relief. In any case, we signed out the receivers for the week and asked the participants to use them in class, returning them to us with their comments.

System One, used primarily at Gallaudet University is most beneficial to hearing aid wearers as it allows them to simply switch their aids to the "T" switch and use them like a radio receiver.

System Two is more assessible to a mixed group because the transmitting signal is a light beam which can be picked up by a receiver placed directly in the ear or to a receiver which assists an aid. It is also possible to install the system permanently in a classroom, concert hall or movie house for permanent use.

System Three, however, is the system we all preferred. The FM portable units actually allowed the greatest flexibility for the faculty, not only in their movements around the room, but on field trips, during demonstrations from others, while performing on instruments or listening to recordings. The faculty had only to wear the mike and forget it or place it near a speaker or on a stage for greater amplification. The participants could wear their wireless headsets or earphones and move around freely adjusting the volume as needed. The entire set of 20 receivers and the microphone transmitter could be carried in a small briefcase from room to room and everything ran on rechargeable batteries.

Observations by the faculty in regard to attention span and concentration were positive. There was a marked improvement in class attendance and involvement. The participants seemed to be paying more attention, asking more questions, volunteering more ideas. On a more personal level, participants who had not known they had a hearing loss were suddenly aware and became as excited as someone getting their first pair of glasses.

"By far the most significant observation made at the accessible Elderhostel programs held at the Peabody Institute was that participants will try the audio assistive devices and benefit from them, whether or not they previously, or even at the present time, acknowledge a personal loss of hearing. This is very inspiring because traditionally one of the biggest problems with hearing loss has been denial; it appears that the nature of the devices and the educational Elderhostel setting are conducive to personal acknowledgement of a need for assistance. At the very least, there is an acknowledgement that the devices are 'nice to have around.' "[1]

Participant's comments on final evaluation sheets were encouraging. Comments indicated to us that we had managed to get our message across.

Examples:

1. Learned several interesting items that I will investigate when I get home.

2. The assistive device . . . has been a great help to me and I hope to help others when I return home.

3. . . . we will pass on the information to friends who need help.

4. It was a revelation to me. . . I will go home and start over to find the proper hearing device.

5. This is my fifth Elderhostel. Others were worthwhile but this one I could hear better.

6. Other colleges pay too little attention to the problems of the hearing impaired.

7. I have enjoyed each program I attended but this one filled a real need in addition to being enjoyable.

In subsequent projects, Maryland Elderhostel, in cooperation with Gallaudet University has utilized the FM equipment in nine other college and university programs throughout the state. A variety of academic programs has been presented and, in every case, the faculty and coordinators have praised the use of the equipment, commenting mostly on the increased ability to achieve maximum communication and effective presentations in the classroom and on field trips.

The audio devices, while providing valuable assistance for participants with mild to moderate hearing losses, did not substantially improve conditions for those profoundly impaired. However, because of the consciousness raising effects of the presence of the equipment, the faculty and other participants seemed to be more aware of speaking slower and more directly to each other, allowing those profoundly impaired an opportunity to use lip reading skills already developed.

According to the American Association for Retired Persons, our older population – persons 65 years or older – numbered 28.5 million in 1985, representing 12% of the United States population. Between 1970 and 1985, their median level of education increased from 8.7 years to 11.7 years and the percentage who had completed high school rose from 28% to 48%. The older population is getting older, too. In 1985, the 65-74 age group (17.0 million) was nearly eight times larger than in 1900, but the 75-84 group (8.8 million) was eleven times larger and the 85+ group (2.7 million) was twenty-two times larger. In 1985, persons reaching age 65 had an average life expectancy of an additional 16.8 years.

Niccola A. Bojanowski

This large segment of our population will grow and will want to continue to have productive lives. Those who wish to continue their education will join the ranks of millions of adults now reaping the intellectual benefits of the extended classroom. The U.S. Department of Health and Human Services ranks hearing impairment *third* among the most frequently occurring chronic condition affecting the older adults (arthritis 53%, hypertension 42%, hearing impairments 40%, heart disease 34%). It is critical, therefore to provide listening devices for those who need them, just as we provide small chairs for elementary children or large computer screens for our new technology. Our social structure is changing, so must our services to the community.

****

The Peabody Institute, Maryland Elderhostel and Gallaudet University were jointly funded in the project by a Presidential Award grant provided by Gallaudet University.

For more information, the following sources are available;

American Association of Retired Persons, 1909, K Street, M.W. Washington, DC 20049

Consumer Organization for the Hearing Impaired (COHI), P.O. Box 8188, Silver Spring, MD 20907

Gallaudet University, 800 Florida Avenue, N.E. Washington, DC 20002

National Association for Hearing and Speech action, 10801 Rockville Pike, Rockville, MD 20852

SEHAS, Inc., suite 307, 300 W. Wievca Road, Atlanta, Georgia. 30342

Sound Associates, Inc., 424 West 45th Street, New York, NY 10036

Self Help for Hard of Hearing People, 7800 Wisconsin Avenue, Bethesda, MD 20814.

REFERENCES

1   Oliva, G.: *A Field Test of Aural and Visual Communication*, Gallaudet University.

MUSICAL INVOLVEMENT OF VISUALLY IMPAIRED INDIVIDUALS: PHYSIOLOGICAL, PSYCHOLOGICAL AND SOCIAL IMPORTANCE

Dr. Fred Kersten

PRELUDE

This chapter is designed to consider the physiological, psychological, and social importance of musical interaction with visually impaired individuals. In addition, descriptive background information that is related and of a definitional nature is also included.

Music for the visually impaired has been an important area of concern for many years. As the association between visually impaired and music developed, many preconceived "myths" about aptitude and ability were developed and propagated. Many of these ideas such as "the visually impaired have innate aptitude for music because of their affliction," have no basis in fact and are being dispelled. We are now more interested in the use of music for total individual improvement than as a vocational avenue for performers as was the philosophy of the early 1900s; hence the emphasis at that time on aptitude.

> Psychological problems of blindness are more in the minds of
> others rather than in the blind themselves.[1]

For those working, or contemplating working with music as an improvement medium for these individuals, this statement might be expanded to include both physiological and social aspects of interaction as well. Music specialists may not have considered the power and influence music can have as an improvement factor in all aspects of each visually impaired individual's life style. Comprehension of visual acuity classifications or disability causality may also be at a minimal level. It is hoped that the information contained on the next few pages will provide some fulfillment of these needs.

DEFINITIONS

The music specialist, whether clinician or teacher, will be involved with various levels of acuity when working with the visually impaired. Terms, such as blind and partially sighted, are often used interchangeably; yet each connotes a certain level of acuity which may allow a completely different approach to interaction with music stimuli.

For purposes of continuity, the term visually impaired is used within the title and throughout this chapter. As utilized herein, the term refers to any individual who because of a loss in the acuity of sight cannot use regular musical materials (standard sheet music or music texts) and must resort to other forms of material for learning. Since this is a generic definition, various subheadings follow:

The Blind

The term "blind" refers to those persons who must learn to live aided by senses other than sight. They may be totally without vision, they may have light or object perception; they may be able to read large print to a limited extent. This general group is made up of two distinct classes based entirely on the time of the loss of sight. Baker[2] defines as follows:

A) The congenitally blind: those who were born blind.
B) The adventitiously blind: those who have lost their sight through illness or accident.

The vision of a person who is blind is 20/200 or less, according to the Snellen Symbol E chart. The term 20/200 is not a fraction denoting 10 percent vision, but rather that an object ordinarily seen by the normal eye at a distance of 200 feet can be seen only when it is as close as twenty feet. Furthermore, this vision at twenty feet is possible only in the better eye after the maximum correction by glasses has been achieved.

The Partially Sighted

Elam[3] defines partially sighted in the following manner:

The "partially sighted" are those persons whose visual acuity is between 20/70 and 20/200 in the better eye after all medical and optical help has been provided.

Educationally Limited Blind

Children who have some residual vision that might by utilized are sometimes considered under an educational definition of blindness. This means that while they still can see to some degree, they will profit at a higher level by using braille or other methods. Abel[4] illustrates:

... a child whose visual loss indicates that he can and should function in this total educational program chiefly through the use of the braille system, audio aids, and special equipment necessary for him to pursue his education effectively without the use of his residual vision.

Legal Definition of Blindness

Because of the need for legal guidelines for such societal functions as issuing drivers licenses, a legal definition of blindness has been developed. This definition as indicated by Abel[4] follows:

Central visual acuity of 20/200 or less in the better eye, with correcting glasses, or central vision acuity of more than 20/200 if there is a field defect in which the peripheral field has contracted to such an extent that the widest diameter of visual field subtends an angular distance no greater than 10 degrees.

State Education Definition (Sight-saving)

A guideline used in some states to set up specific classes (sight-saving) for the visually impaired. An example of standards set forth by a state department of education may be found in Ohio. Such standards are defined by Hissong.[5]

1. Children having visual acuity between 20/70 and 20/200 in the better eye, or who cannot read print smaller than 19-point.

2. Children who have three or more diopters of progressive myopia, especially where there are indications of a pathological condition.

3. Children with visual acuity between 20/50 and 20/200 having congenital cataracts, secondary cataracts, malformation or fundus lesions, corneal opacities, and inactive keratitis.

4. Any child who, in the opinion of the examiner, would benefit by placement in a sight-saving class.

Note: Children having less than 20/200 vision in the better eye should be considered for possible placement in braille classes or in schools for the blind, unless they are able to read print in 14-point type.

Those working with visually impaired should obtain a professional assessment of specific aspects of visual acuity of each person. An individualized program may then be developed that can employ various audio, tactile and large print music materials which can be procured from specific services or can be designed to the needs of the person involved.

CAUSALITY

Knowledge of causality is important as those who have become visually impaired later in life (adventitiously) have had some knowledge of the sighted world and an individualized program can be developed based on this prior experience. It should be emphasized that not all visually impaired individuals have sight loss dating to birth. (Presently, a serious cause of sight destruction includes accidents in which car batteries explode when they are started through the use of jumper cables.) Understanding the specificity of cause can also aid in communicating with each handicapped individual in a more effective manner.

Delimiting traditional factors such as myopia, hypermetropia (nearsightedness, farsightedness) puncture and abrasive wounds, the following included as causes of visual disability:

Albinism – An inherited condition that results in a lack of pigment (melanin) in the body. The eye is extremely sensitive to light and defective vision may include myopia and astigmatism.

Cataracts – A gradual clouding of the lens in relation to aging or a lack of developing transparency in children (congenital). Both can result in severe loss of sight but are successfully treated by surgery.

Conjunctivitis – An inflammation of the mucous membrane covering the front of the eye and inner eyelid. (Sometimes called pink eye.) Responds well to antibiotics; however it is highly contagious.

Detached Retina – Separation, thinning, or blocking of the attachment between the retina and choroid. This can be the result of physical accident or disease. Surgical procedures in many cases may be used to alleviate blindness if employed soon after the condition is diagnosed.

Fred Kersten

Diabetes (mellitus) – A lack of insulin secreted by the pancreas which results in excess sugar in the body. Resulting chemical changes in the eyes can increase vision problems. It is thought that cataracts and/or eye hemorrhages are possibly related to diabetes in some cases.

Glaucoma – a progressive and usually painless disease caused by increased pressure in the eye. Early diagnosis, especially during middle age, and release of pressure through medication can prevent severe sight loss.

Nystagmus – "Rapid involuntary movements of the eyes that may be from side to side."[6] Can be congenital or associated with brain and neurological damage and diseases such as multiple sclerosis.

Retrolental Fibroplasia – a scarring condition of the retina that causes blindness. Sometimes known as "Blue Baby" disease, the causal agent is excessive use of oxygen with premature babies after birth.

Rubella (German Measles) – A contagious disease spread by direct contact. Important because women contracting the disease during the first three months of pregnancy may conceive children with visual defects.[7]

Trachoma – A contagious disease caused by a filterable virus that forms hard granules on the conjunctiva. It is highly painful and first evidenced by inflammation. Treatment: extensive hygiene and antibiotics. At one time trachoma was the most common cause of blindness and still occurs in countries where standards of health and sanitation are low.[8]

MUSICAL INVOLVEMENT

Physiological Importance

Movement

Kappy[9] provides specific answers to the importance of physical response to music in an article "Rhythm in the lives of the blind." She states:

> Rhythm also helps to overcome two great handicaps of blindness: First, limitation of experience due chiefly to difficulties of moving in space and second, dependence on others due to these difficulties. Rhythmic movement is a definite and desirable end in itself for everyone but is vital for the blind. There is no question but that the enriching of experience through greater freedom of movement means enrichment of the intellectual life.

Stimulation

Music can provide a basis for psychomotor stimulation that may not be available from other sources. Goodenough and Goodenough[10] state:

The lack of visual stimulation tends to delay the motor development. By using music as an incentive it is possible to develop the necessary use of large and small muscles. For example, the early reaching motions which come so naturally with the sighted infant must by stimulated by some other means with the totally blind.

The answer to this problem could be a musical toy given to the child by the parents.

Many authors support the utilization of eurhythmics and other psychomotor activities to get the visually impaired up and moving about. Kappes[11] indicates that as a special subject taught in the Cleveland public schools in braille and sight-saving classes: "... we would use music as a means to stimulate, regulate and control physical activity..."

Baker[12] provides a more detailed summary indicating that progressive homes and schools include these activities within the education framework:

> As a means of physiomotor stimulation, music offers to the blind ever fascinating physical action of a kind that ignores the inability to move about freely when away from home. Such activity in places with which they are familiar may include, besides singing and the playing of instruments, dancing and dramatic action. In the more progressive homes and schools these activities have been given a definite place in educational and recreational plans. In working with dancing and dramatic groups the music leader must see to it that physical tensions are released and clumsiness and poor coordination lessened, and the acting, dancing, singing, and instrumental playing must provide the participant with an individual emotional and artistic goal.

A progressive home or school in 1955 was one which included music as physiological improvement for those with visual handicaps. If so, we have definitely continued this progressivism to the present day.

Relaxation

One of the most vexing problems that all visually impaired individuals live with is the physical problem of relaxing. Music is considered important as a means of relaxing tensions. Richardson[13] details this value in the following words:

> Lastly, I would like to mention a certain therapeutic value in music for the blind. Blind people live under tension not known to the sighted. Much locomotion is avoided. Inactivity leads to tension, which leads to the blindisms, such as the rocking motion of many children. Intense concentration is needed to execute simple tasks. Music often stimulated other activities and leads to an outpouring of emotions which alleviates many problems of those with visual handicaps.

The music program objectives stated for the Wisconsin school reflect this therapeutic aspect. Hoppe[14] indicates that one of the major aims is "to provide times of relaxation and refreshment throughout the school day and to add variety to a long day of other school activities."

The AAIB state their support of this important principle indicating the following objective: "To use music as a means of mental relaxation for the student in residential schools."[15] Musical means for the relaxation of tension may take many forms. Both psychological and physiological problems are involved. Sedative music (music of a relaxing nature) provides one answer to this complex situation.

Mannerisms (Blindisms)

Much has been written about mannerisms common to visually impaired persons. The development of these mannerisms, initially is based psychologically on anger. Sighted children can find objects to use as targets for this frustration. The blind child cannot locate targets visually and does not dissipate the anger. This lack of release causes a psychosomatic effect known as the mannerism. Knight[16] indicates:

> By the time a blind child is three years old, coping with frustration by noninstrumental gross motor discharge may be firmly established. As he grows older and becomes more socialized, the ferocity of his coping behavior will become tempered and restrained, the behavior itself often becomes restricted to what society labels a mannerism, such as a rapid bobbing or head-rolling when he encounters frustration.

Music instruments such as xylophones and hand drums are important for young children because frustrations can be vented in a physiological socially acceptable way. Older visually impaired individuals can also be provided opportunities for coping with frustration through music. These individuals can use physiological music activities to ease anxieties and improve their control over mannerisms.

Awkward Movement

A statement on the use of music to help awkward movement appears in a pamphlet by Richardson, "Music as an aid to social adjustment in elementary schools."[13] She indicates:

> Physical coordination results in a better adjusted blind child. If we can teach them control, etc., we will be reducing the number of blindisms that are often the problem of these children. Music can be utilized along these lines. We find many young blind children who have difficulty in controlling their movements. This results in an awkward carriage which in turn draws attention to their handicap.

It should be noted that both physiological and social importance are described, as these aspects complement each other and eventually affect the psychological perception of personal self-esteem.

Rhythmic Exercises

Korhonen[17] indicated her view on rhythmic imitative and dramatic exercises and their contribution to the elimination of physical mannerisms of visually impaired. She states: "Rhythm can inspire dramatization of animals, instruments, people, and other imitative response. Good rhythm exercise helps the child develop graceful and coordinated physical movements." This philosophy is echoed throughout the programs for the visually impaired.

Eurhythmics

Programs that emphasize eurhythmics are based on the philosophy that this musical approach will help correct blindisms and should be included for this reason. As this approach usually is used as a basis to experience and perceive music through movement the inclusion of eurhythmics for the visually impaired is quite important. Hough[18] explains:

> As originally planned by Jacques-Dalcroze, eurhythmics was elaborated into a practically indendent branch of music study, but as used at the New York Institute it is entirely an accessory in the elementary study of music. However, it has also proved itself to be a great help to the blind in developing muscular coordination, physical poise and grace, in overcoming tenseness and fear, and in developing concentration.

The applicability of eurhythmics to the instruction of the visually impaired can take many forms. Circle formation, and similar exercises aid in developing awareness of group movement. Exercises in which change in tempo can be felt through clapping are at times easier for the visually impaired student than the sighted!

Educational Rhythmics

The original eurhythmics includes primarily standardized rhythmic movements. Modifications of eurhythmics and other created movement activities are presently utilized by therapists. Josepha in Gaston's *Music in Therapy*[19] explains:

> Both Gilliland (1955, p. 587) and Baldwin (1955, p. 599) have described the values that eurhythmics, or movement to rhythm, can have for blind children. Gilliland believed this activity gives them physical security and helps them develop grace of carriage and feelings of independence. Sighted children can derive similar values from participation in eurhythmics, but they can also attain them through the use of vision. According to Baldwin, free eurhythmics affords the blind a satisfying release that enables them to move about the bodily freedom of sighted children.

> Arje and Berryman (1966) report that educational rhythmics – a technique involving coordination of movement, music, and words – has definite therapeutic values for the blind child. While witnessing a demonstration of this approach – Arje and Berryman observed that blind children who were begin exposed to this therapy tended to reach with increased freedom and poise and with a more pronounced sense of direction. Educational rhythmics, as a method of practical application of coordinated movement in conjunction with music, was organized by Robins and Robins (1965) primarily for use with mentally handicapped children.

Thus through various rhythmic activities, poise, freedom, physical security, and sense of direction can result from the use of movement activities to music. Aspects of enjoyment and socialization with sighted individuals are additional advantages of the process.

Psychological Importance

The value of music as a psychological outlet for the visually impaired is a recurring theme throughout the literature on utilizing music with this disability. Whether the response be overt or covert, emotional response is important. Heim[20] explains the emotional needs of the visually impaired in the following way:

> The emotional need is as great for the blind as for the sighted. The very nature of his handicap produces a type of loneliness which can be fully understood only by those who do not see. Throughout the history of mankind music has spoken for him and to him in ways which no other art could. It has emotional value not only for the performer and composer but for the listener as well. One need not be a highly trained musician to benefit emotionally from music.

If music is important to all people, how much more so to the visually impaired! Depression can be alleviated, persons who feel sorry for themselves, or cannot accept their disability can find some outlet in musical achievement. Self-pity, frustration, and antagonism can be reduced, leading to an inner-emotional peace. Goodenough and Goodenough[10] indicate that music is extremely important in the adjustment to complex psychological stresses. The person who is withdrawn can be stimulated. Emotional stress due to lack of visual stimulation can be eased. Listening to sedative music can calm the person and lessen feelings of mental stress. The nonthreatening world of music provides a means for experiencing the various emotions without fear of failure. A statement from Juliette Alvin in *Music for the Handicapped*[21] is cited to show the role music plays in improving the emotional life of visually impaired individuals.

> Music may represent to him a nonthreatening world with which he can communicate, where he may know no failure, where he can integrate and identify himself. ...Music may be the only way he can realize himself.

A statement by Korhonen[17] indicates the importance of music in terms of emotional considerations in another way:

> The peculiar universal power of music as an expression of human experience – the total expression of the common yet profound human emotions – is completely within the ken of blindness.

Korhonen's statement considers two directions: (1) the understanding aspect of human emotion that cannot be observed and (2) the possibilities of expression of human emotions.

Final psychological importance can be supported by Richardson and Haldiman. Richardson[13] states: "The greatest potential for the largest number of students lies in music's unifying effects and its power as an emotional outlet." This philosophy is in concurrence with the study conducted by Haldiman.[22] He found that 73% of those surveyed considered "to furnish emotional outlet" as very important. Similarly, 28% considered this objective desirable with only 29% indicating it as "of minor importance."

Psychological importance of music for the visually impaired is an importance aspect in the development of music therapy programs. Releasing emotional stress and resolving human loneliness are two of the major goals to be attained. Music can play an important part in such attainment and should be considered in any formation of psychological goals for the visually impaired.

Social Importance

Socialization

The report of the AAIB convention in 1952[23] shows eight general objectives for music in the education of visually impaired. Of these eight, four are concerned with social aspects of life. These objectives are:

1. To develop personality of the whole child so that he might lead a normal life in his community

2. To give each child group work in order that he will learn cooperation through participation

3. To furnish the child with opportunities which will give him an appreciation of others' performances

4. To provide opportunities for the retarded child to express himself and to thereby become a fitted member of environment

Similarly the Haldiman study of music programs at residential schools[22] found a corresponding support for social goals. Out of eleven objectives considered pertinent to teaching visually impaired, five relate to social development as indicated in Table 1.

TABLE 1

Objective	Very Important	Desirable	Of Minor Importance
1. To adjust socially	90%	10%	1%
2. For cultural development	75%	28%	0%
3. To develop a sense of belonging through group participation	73%	28%	2%
4. To develop an understanding of different races through music	21%	60%	5%
5. To promote cooperation and good sportsmanship	69%	29%	5%

Three of the seven aims of the music program at the Wisconsin school were developed around social considerations. As cited by Hoppe[14] these include:

1. To build up music organizations within the school which will promote a general love for music, [really aesthetic] a social activity through group playing and singing

2. To help prepare students to use music as a part of their cultural lives away from school

3. To enable the music students, upon leaving the school, to use music as a means to become a useful member of the community and enhance the social life

Skougaard[24] provides additional reasons for including music in visually impaired programs:

Provides social experiences of community life such as:

a) Good fellowship

b) Celebration of civic and religious holidays

c) Common enjoyment of beauty

d) Acceptance of contributions from fellow beings

e) Satisfaction of a successful common endeavor

The statements previously cited bring a most important consideration under examination. Social interaction is vastly important through musical involvement of the visually impaired. Social goals are considered of overriding importance to those of musical development and performance quality for the *majority* of individuals experiencing music. This is not to say that for some, artistic quality performance should not be considered. However, the latter aspects are presently considered of secondary value by many working with visually impaired individuals.

Social Equivalence of Sighted and Visually Impaired

Individuals who are visually impaired find themselves at a disadvantage with the sighted. Including music in the training of visually impaired can provide a common avenue for communication between these individuals as equals. Heim[20] indicates the importance of music in providing interaction opportunities for visually impaired by citing a case study as an example.

> The blind person with some musical training can make a real contribution to his community through club and church activities. He may also find that it is a great asset at parties. The author recalls the case of a seventeen-year-old boy who had spent several discouraging years attempting to attend the public schools. When he first enrolled at a residential school for the blind, he was very withdrawn – almost anti-social. He was encouraged to take voice lessons. Gradually his voice began to develop. Near the end of his first year he gave a creditable performance in a school recital. Up to this time the attitude of the other students toward him had been rather negative. He had remained quite withdrawn. This performance proved to himself and to others that he, too, could achieve success. While he has never become a prominent individual, he has become a much happier and better adjusted member of society. As if often true, this case combines an instance of not only the social but also the emotional values of music to the blind.

Mahan[25] cites a case study similar to that of Heim. It illustrates the possibility of visually impaired functioning as equals with sighted in the real world.

What is the use of my studying music? I shall never earn a penny playing or singing. To this I can only say, that in my opinion music is the greatest social asset which a blind person can possess. One of our graduates is quite a successful business man. He plays the piano well and has a splendid, well-trained voice. He sings in one of the churches in his city, is a member of the Lions Club, and sings with the men's glee club of his town. One of our most successful blind teachers gives a brief opinion of what music means socially to a person without sight: "Had it not been for the musical knowledge obtained both at Talladega and Overbrook, I should not be known even in my own neighborhood; but as it is, I am recognized and respected by the best of people."

Goodenough and Goodenough[10] give their reasons for music as a way of sharing aural experiences with the sighted. Interestingly, the performance aspect on the part of the visually impaired individual who has been previously mentioned is not stressed, but listening as a social activity is:

Listening to music in a group helps to develop a sense of belonging and sharing activities with other individuals. Since this activity does not require sight, the opportunity for a visually impaired individual to participate with sighted groups is most beneficial. In preparing experiences for the blind student, teachers and parents should make an effort to include him in groups attending public concerts, which will give him the opportunity to interact with sighted persons.

Instrumental music is an important aspect in social communication with sighted peers. It shares in the philosophical considerations already mentioned. As an example, Richardson[13] indicates: "Skill in playing in instrument acts as a bridge for further communication with peers. Pride in a certain accomplishment will give a person the added confidence needed when in contact with sighted peers." "Sharing experiences in music" must be an important topic included within the music philosophy of teachers of instrumental music working with visually impaired. The musical instrument provides not only musical and personal interactions with the sighted but a third experience that is in many respects physical but can also be considered psychological. That consideration is ownership. By the very possession of a saxophone or trumpet, the visually impaired person gains a more equal place along side the sighted individual who holds an equivalent instrument.

Social Equivalence Through Technology

While it is not the purpose of this chapter to examine Audio/Visual/Tactile technology in detail, the prognosis for musical involvement of visually impaired individuals alongside the sighted through this medium is bright. Roberts[26] discussing the Kurzweil Reading Machine indicates that with its development the device is capable of providing visually impaired readers with new opportunities for the exploration of information sources. Utilizing an optical scanner, the machine will translate written material to an aural mode via speech synthesis. Therefore, music texts, records jackets, and concert programs can be immediately available for perusal, without transcription to braille or employing services of a reader, thus elevating the visually impaired person to the level of sighted colleagues.

Many individual use the Optacon (OPtical to TActile-CONverter) to read music. This device allows visually impaired persons to "touch" the printed musical score without conversion to braille. If a sighted teacher indicates interpretation marks on the page these can be readily

Fred Kersten

understood by the visually impaired musician, something that cannot be accomplished with hard-copy braille.

New computer programs allow printing of compositions initially played on MIDI equipped keyboard instruments. Materials received from Passport Designs, Inc., (1986) illustrates the variety of tasks that can be accomplished utilizing Apple computers. The Passport Polywriter[TM] program will allow transcription, transposition, and notation of up to 16 voices as only a few of its features. Imagine the esteem isually impaired persons will receive as they compose compositions at the keyboard and then have sighted counterparts play them back! What a marvelous feeling of belonging for the visually impaired composer when a piece is transcribed to full orchestral score format and read by a large group. Time in processing and expense of copying parts are eliminated. Many visually impaired individuals are fine keyboard players and also quality composers in their own right; their compositions can now be heard without complication and many times *elimination* because of symbolization semantic problems.

Goodrich[27] indicates the availability of computer programs and monitors, allowing magnification of normally small print connotation. Those who read large print can use numerous musical instruction programs available in specific areas such as theory. Many of these programs are being used in public schools and the visually impaired child who is "mainstreamed" can have immediate access to such material AND social equivalency with sighted peers. It is also possible to connect speech synthesis devices such as PC Vert[TM] (produced by Telesensory Systems Inc.) to the computer therefore obtaining a high quality voice rendition of the programs utilized.

Hooker[28] indicates the advantages of the Thiel Embosser (a high-speed braille printer) that improves opportunities for those using embossed braille. She states:

> Used in conjunction with a computer, the Thiel Embosser (pronounced "teal") revolutionizes the printing of Braille. Transcribers no longer have to sit for hours punching out the characters by hand, wasting a page every time they make a single mistake. The system works like a word processor, allowing both sighted and visually impaired users to edit their work before printing. It produces a page in about ten seconds. This works out to about 130 characters per second. The Cranmer "Perky" embosser, by contrast, prints about ten characters in the same length of time.

New technology also allows combining of braille keyboards *and* those of the computer. Through this hardware, typed braille may be converted into traditional print and vice-versa, allowing sighted and visually impaired to share written communications instantly.

Coda

Musical involvement, disability limitations, and causality aspects of visually impaired individuals have been fragmented and examined separately in this chapter. The intent has not been to dehumanize these individuals, or the causes and disabilities thereby resulting. Of first and foremost importance, visually impaired are human beings and individual personalities.

The music specialist working with visually impaired individuals must look to the humanistic aspect initially and throughout. Communications are the continuity thread to which the information presented here may be applied. It should be noted that the three "importance aspects" complement each other and should be thought of as interrelated value in terms of a balanced program of improvement through musical involvement. In this way the value of the visually impaired individual as a holistic human being will be preserved.

REFERENCES

1   Freedman, S. Psychosocial evaluation. In: S.J. Spungin (ed.): *Precollege Programs for Blind and Visually Handicapped Students.* New York: American Foundation for the Blind, 1975, p. 10.

2   Baker, H.J.: *Introduction to Exceptional Children.* New York: The Macmillan Co., 1955, p. 22

3   Elam, M.D.: *Methods Employed in Teaching Music to Blind Children at the Virginia State School, Hamton.* Unpublished master's thesis, Virginia State College, 1958, p. 7.

4   Abel, L.: The education of blind children. In: W.M. Cruickshank (ed.): *Education of Exceptional Children and Youth.* Englewood Cliffs,NJ: Prentice Hall, Inc., 1959, p. 296.

5   Hissong, C.: The education of visually handicapped children in the public schools of Ohio. *Research Bull,* 1951, p. 29.

6   Martin, E.A. (ed.): Laurence Urdang Associates, Ltd. *Urdang Dictionary of Current Medical Terms.* New York: John Wiley and Sons, 1981, p. 284.

7   Fishbein, M. (ed). *The New Illustrated Medical and Health Encyclopedia* (18 vols). New York: H.S. Stuttman Co., Inc. Publishers, 1970, **9**, p. 1174.

8   Ibid., p. 2304.

9   Kappy, M.: Rhythm in the lives of the blind. *American Association of Instructors of the Blind,* 1934, **25**, pp. 112-113.

10 Goodenough, F., Goodenough, D.: The importance of music in the life of a visually handicapped child. *Education of the Visually Handicapped,* March 1970, pp. 27-30.

11 Kappes, M.: Music though hearing and feeling. *Outlook for the Blind,* 1925, **19**, pp. 41-45.

12 Baker, H.J.: *Introduction to Exceptional Children.* New York: The Macmillan Co., 1955, pp. 109-110.

13 Richardson, P.: *Music as an Aid to Social Adjustment of the Blind in Elementary Schools.* Unpublished term paper, University of Wisconsin, 1963, pp. 7-11.

14 Hoppe, R.: *General Outline of the Music Program at the Wisconsin School for Visually Handicapped.* Verona: Wisconsin School for the Visually Handicapped, 1958, p. 1.

15 Haldiman, G.: *Music Education for the Braille Student in Residential Schools.* Unpublished master's thesis, Northwestern University, 1953, p. 60.

16 Knight, J.J.: Mannerisms in the congenitally blind child. *New Outlook for the Blind,* 1972, **66**, pp. 296-302.

17 Korhonen, G.V.: Music as an educational value for the blind. *New Outlook for the Blind,* 1956, **50**, pp. 91-95.

18 Hough, B.W.: Music education of the blind. In: M.E. Frampton (ed.): *Education of the Blind.* New York: World Blind Co., 1940, p. 63.

19 Gaston, E.T. (ed.): *Music in Therapy.* New York: The Macmillan Co., 1968, p. 111.

20 Heim, K.E.: *Musical Aptitude of Senior High Students in Residential Schools for the Blind as Measured by the Wing Standardized Tests of Musical Intelligence.* Unpublished master's thesis, Univesity of Kansas, 1942, pp. 13-14.

21 Alvin, J.: *Music for the Handicapped Child.* London, U.K.: Oxford University Press, 1966, p. 32.

22 Haldiman, G.: *Music Education for the Braille Student in Residential Schools.* Unpublished master's thesis, Northwestern University, 1953, p. 89.

23 American Association of Instructors for the Blind: *Proceedings of the Forty-first Convention.* Louisville, KY: Author, 1952, pp. 94-95.

24 Skougaard, F.N.: *Music: An Important Factor in Institutions for the Handicapped.* Unpublished research paper, Harvard University, 1938, p. 5.

25 Mahan, L.: The importance of music in schools for the blind. *International Journal for the Education of the Blind,* 1961, **1**, pp. 24-26.

26 Roberts, M.L.: Welcoming disabled readers to a new world of information. *Texas Libraries,* 1985, 46, pp. 54-59.

27 Goodrich, G.L.: Applications of microcomputers by visually impaired persons. *J of Visual Impairment and Blindness,* November 1984, **78**, pp. 408-414.

28 Hooker, F. Computerized braille: The Boulder story. *Vilson Library Bull,* April 1985, **59**, pp. 527-530.

SUPPLEMENTAL BIBLIOGRAPHY

Arje, Frances, B., Berryman, Doris L.: New help for the severely retarded and emotional disturbed child. *J Rehab,* 1966, **32**, pp. 14-15.

Baldwin, Lillian: Music and the blind child. In: P. Dykema and Hannah M. Cundiff (eds.): *School Music Handbook.* Boston, MA: C.C. Birchand, 1955, pp. 598-606.

Editor. *The Optacon Print Reading System.* Telesensory Systems, Inc. Mountain View, CA, 1986. Brochure R17613C.

Editor. *Polywriter Music Printing Series.* Passport Designs, Inc. (Promotional Literature), Half Moon Bay, CA, 1986.

Friel, J.P. (ed.): *Dorland's Illustrated Medical Dictionary.* Philadelphia: W.B. Saunders Company, 1974.

Gilliland, Ester, G.: Functional music for the exceptional child in the special schools of Chicago. In: P. Dykema and Hannah M. Cundiff (eds.): *School Music Handbook.* Boston, MA: C.C. Birchand, 1955, pp. 585-591.

Hathaway, W.: (Revised by Foote, Hryan, Gibbons). *Education and Health of the Partially Seeing Child.* New York: Columbia University Press, 1969.

A NEUROANATOMICAL MODEL FOR THE USE OF MUSIC IN THE REMEDIATION OF APHASIC DISORDERS

Dale B. Taylor

ABSTRACT

The complexity of the human brain affords the distinctly human behavior of speech. Damage to certain left hemisphere cortical regions leads to aphasia, a disturbance of language usage. The brain normally uses language symbols for speaking, reading, writing, and listening. Comprehension of speech entering through the auditory tract requires use of Wernicke's area. Damage to Wernicke's or Broca's area results in impaired speaking ability. The visual cortex, angular gyrus, and Wernicke's area are needed for reading, along with Broca's area for reading aloud or writing.

Research has shown the left hemisphere to be dominant for verbal and analytic behaviors, while the right hemisphere is more active for nonverbal, holistic functions such as most musical skills. Because singing ability is retained following left hemisphere damage and because the brain functions as a whole with the corpus callosum providing interhemispheric holological information processing capability, specific musical techniques can be identified for rehabilitative work with patients having specific forms of aphasic cortical damage.

INTRODUCTION

The complexity, diversity and yet unrealized range of human behavior has stimulated the creative genius of scientists, artists, and philosophers for centuries. Although nearly every thesis has been met with an antithesis, there is general agreement that it is the human brain that affords such an extremely wide range of potential behaviors as man adapts to the vastly different environmental conditions to be found on this earth. Among the various behaviors of which humans are capable, the one that has been referred to as "that single most distinct capability of humans"[1] is Speech. Because the auditory system must function to its fullest extent of acoustical perception and interpretation in the processing of human speech, it has been hypothesized that musical behavior evolved as a mechanism for training the cortical areas specialized for speech perception in sophisticated sound pattern recognition for development of the acoustic sense necessary for language acquisition.[1] It appears then that if any individual possessing human biological characteristics is to realize full human potential, he must learn to participate in the making of music.[2]

For those individuals whose specialized cortical tissue is damaged so as to render them incapable of exhibiting the full range of normal language behaviors, a model of treatment is offered which utilizes the genetically endowed mechanism of music to stimulate undamaged cranial structures to generate specific forms of language symbol manipulation. This model rests on the already recognized ability shown by the brain for one portion to take over the function of another if the original portion is damaged or ceases to function.[2]

First, terms describing impairment in language behavior will be identified, and will be followed by a review of the neurological structures normally required for language usage in four primary communication modes. Next will be a description of certain forms of aphasia resulting from damage to specific cortical structures. Research will be reviewed describing differences in hemispheric functioning during specific musical behaviors.

168

DEFINITION OF APHASIA

Persons with language disorders have varying degrees of difficulty in understanding or in producing language symbols. When there is a serious language disorder resulting from injury to the brain, it is referred to as *Aphasia*.[3] The illness may take the form of *receptive aphasia*, in which there is loss of the ability to understand spoken or written language, or *expressive aphasia*, which involves the inability to speak or to produce written language.

Aphasic patients show a wide variety of manifestations of the illness. Continuing investigation and exchange of observations is increasing the ability of medical personnel to predict the location of the cranial lesions resulting in aphasic disorders.

Related to expressive aphasia is a clinical syndrome known as *Apraxia*, which has been defined as a disorder of learned movement.[4] A patient whose apraxia results in disorders of speaking or writing behavior is referred to as 'apraxic.' While there is no impairment in muscle function, sensory input, comprehension or attention, the apraxic individual does not voluntarily and consciously execute learned movement. The phenomenon will be exemplified in later sections.

CRANIAL LANGUAGE CENTERS

Human beings use language symbols to accomplish four primary modes of communication. The two expressive modes are speaking and writing. The receptive modes are reading and aural comprehension of spoken language, the latter to be referred to herein as 'listening.' Although the processing, manipulation, and use of language symbols includes other behaviors such as learning, remembering, sequencing, recalling, and specialized skills such as typing and sign language, the primary behaviors involved in normal reception and expression of language are speaking, reading, writing and listening. To accomplish these behaviors, the brain utilizes one or more of four specialized cranial areas. A review of these neurological centers and their connecting pathways yields the following summary of the structures, their language functions, and forms of aphasia which correspond to damage in each area.

Listening

When the sound of a spoken word is heard in the auditory cortex, it is the result of a long and complex journey of sound energy which began as mechanical energy in the vibration of air molecules whose traveling waves move toward the listener. As this motion reaches the outer ear, the external auditory meatus channels air pressure waves to the tympanum, which vibrates according to the frequency and intensity of the waves. Attached to the inside of the tympanum is the malleus which passes the vibration on to the incus and stapes. From the oval window which is attached to the stapes, the inner ear fluids receive vibrations which cause the basilar membrane of the cochlea to move. The hair cells of the Organ of Corti along the basilar membrane respond by sending electrochemical signals into the central nervous system via the auditory nerve. These signals move in turn to the spiral ganglion, ventral and dorsal cochlear nuclei, the ipsilateral and contralateral superior olives, the reticular formation, the lateral lemniscus, the inferior colliculus, the medial geniculate body, and finally to the auditory cortex[5] where the psychological sensation of sound is experienced.

It should be noted that the pathway as far as is described above is identical for perception of speech, music and all other sounds. It is after this point that sounds identified as words are forwarded primarily to Wernicke's area for processing auditory word forms. As shown in Figure 1, this specialized area lies immediately adjacent to the primary auditory area.[4]

A Neuroanatomical Model for the Use of Music in the Remediation of Aphasic Disorders   169

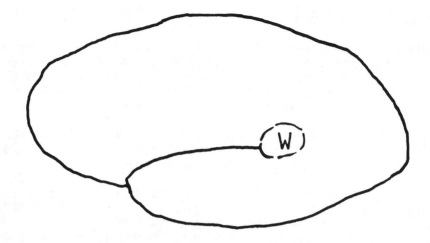

Figure 1: W. *Wernicke's Area*

A lesion in Wernicke's area causes an aphasic loss of speech comprehension.[4] Although these patients hear nonverbal sounds and music correctly, they do not understand spoken language and they speak without using the proper words to communicate content of intended messages.

Speaking

When an individual wishes to speak a word, this decision is passed on from cortical association areas to Wernicke's area where the auditory pattern is formed. From here it is transmitted via a nerve bundle known as the arcuate fasciculus to Broca's area located immediately adjacent to the left premotor region,[4] the area of the brain that controls the muscles of speech. This area is found in the left hemisphere in approximately 97 percent of all cases. Here the articulatory configuration is aroused for use by the left precentral motor area and, via the corpus callosum, the right motor area shares in the coordination of facial and other muscles for correct word formation.

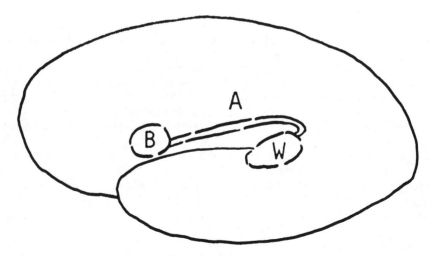

Figure 2: W. *Wernicke's Area*, A. *Arcuate Fascilus*, B. *Broca's Area*

Dale B. Taylor

Left hemisphere damage in Broca's area leads to a disorder of spoken language. A large lesion may affect the adjacent precentral motor area in addition to Broca's area, and may result in a disorder of both spoken and written expression.[6]

A lesion may damage the arcuate fasciculus which would disconnect Wernicke's area from Broca's area while not injuring either area. In such cases, speech is preserved along with listening comprehension. However, the repetition of spoken language is seriously impaired due to the inability of words received in Wernicke's area from the auditory cortex to be passed successfully to Broca's area. This disorder is termed 'conduction aphasia.'[6]

Reading

When a word is to be read, the output from the primary visual cortex is sent to the left angular gyrus located immediately posterior to Wernicke's area. There the visual stimulus is converted for use by Wernicke's area which produces the auditory form. The word is then relayed to cortical association areas for speech comprehension. If the word is to be read aloud, the auditory pattern is also sent via the arcuate fasciculus to Broca's area for use as described above.[6]

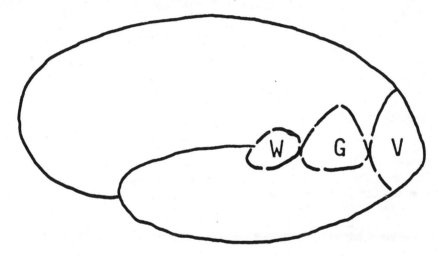

Figure 3: W. *Wernicke's Area*, G. *Angular Gyrus*, V. *Visual Cortex*

It should be noted that because of retinal image reversal and the anatomy of optical nerve pathways, visual information from the right visual field goes primarily to the left visual cortex, and left visual field stimuli are received in the right visual cortex. Language information from the right visual cortex becomes accessible to speech centers in the left hemisphere after being transmitted through a portion of the corpus callosum known as the splenium. Destruction of the splenium prevents such transfer to the left angular gyrus for conversion to the auditory form as a prerequisite to comprehension.[6]

A lesion in the left angular gyrus would separate the visual and auditory language areas. Written words would be perceived as visual patterns without auditory correlates or specific meanings to be comprehended.

Writing

In order to write a word, it is first conceptualized in cortical association areas and is then formulated through auditory recall in Wernicke's area. Next the angular gyrus transmits the auditory form to the visual association cortex where the written form is recalled. The visual information reaches Broca's area by a route which may involve a return through the angular gyrus, Wernicke's area, and the arcuate fasciculus, or may use neuronal pathways available through cortical association areas. In Broca's area, instructions for coordination of digital musculature are determined and are passed on to the adjacent motor cortex for control of writing movements through efferent pathways in the central nervous system.

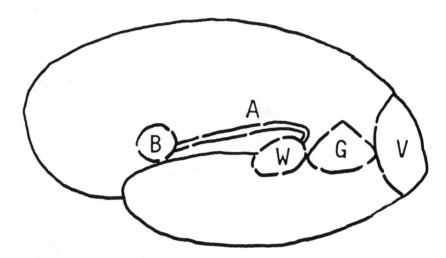

Figure 4: W. *Wernicke's Area*, A. *Arcuate Fascilus*, B. *Broca's Area*, G. *Angular Gyrus*, V. *Visual Cortex*

A lesion in the angular gyrus results in a condition known as alexia with agraphia, loss of the ability to read and write. An attempt to write a word would be frustrated by the inability of the auditory form to reach the visual association cortex. Without visual recall, Broca's area has no cues for instructing the motor cortex in creating a graphic pattern of the word. Patients with lesions in the left angular gyrus also cannot spell or recognize a spelled word.[6] Damage to Wernicke's area also leads to a disorder in the use of expressive written language.

Patients with damage to the splenium portion of the corpus callosum can copy written words correctly, although they cannot comprehend written words.[6] Patients whose corpus callosum has been surgically transected as a therapeutic measure cannot verbally describe an object, written word, or event localized in the left visual field.[7]

In discussing neurological structures for language behaviors, the left hemisphere has received primary consideration due to repeated findings of specialized centers on that side of the brain. Comparisons of right and left hemispheres have revealed certain asymmetries. For example, the upper surface of the temporal lobe which lies within the Sylvian Fissure includes an extension of Wernicke's area known as the 'planum temporale.' The left planum has been found to be one-third longer than the right planum in 65 percent of cases, equal in 24 percent, and larger on the right side in 11 percent. Because infant brains also show planum asymmetry, it has been suggested that such asymmetries are genetically determined.[6] Roederer also suggests that a relatively large right-side planum temporale indicates a greater inborn capacity for nonverbal sound processing, and that it could be a measure of inborn musical ability.[7]

Significant anatomical variations between hemispheres have also been found in other portions of the auditory cortex. While certain areas of the superior temporal gyrus are generally

Dale B. Taylor

larger in the left hemisphere, the polar area of the superior temporal region[5] is generally larger in the right hemisphere. Damage to this right temporal area often results in amusia, a condition characterized by loss of musical abilities.

HEMISPHERIC DOMINANCE IN MUSIC

In order to use music to help the aphasic person regain lost abilities, the separate processing functions of the right and left hemispheres must be understood. Differences in the processing of musical experience by the two brain hemispheres have been studied using EEG measurement of brain waves during musical tasks, single hemisphere anesthetization to isolate functions, dichotic listening tests to determine auditory processing, and examination of brain damaged patients with abnormal hemispheric functions. In a 1985 presentation at a conference in New York City, Arthur Harvey summarized research by various investigators who used these techniques. Among their findings were results showing that musical pitch, melody and musical imagery seem to be processed in the right hemisphere. Musical information and rhythm have been shown to be perceived temporally and processed principally in the left hemisphere. Trained and educated musicians, however, have been found to use the left hemisphere for most musical processing or to distribute equally between hemispheres.

In the following discussion it will be important to note the contralateral relationship between each ear and each hemisphere. Approximately 60 percent of the fibers in the auditory tract cross to the hemisphere opposite the ear of origin. Although information from both ears is received on both sides, each hemisphere is more sensitive to impulses arriving from the contralateral ear and will suppress signals from the ipsilateral ear if necessary.[5] For example, Kimura completed studies in which a right-ear advantage was found for speech recognition, and left-ear advantage for melody test performance.[8] Such findings support data showing that analytic and language functions are handled on the left side in about 97 percent of subjects, while more holistic, synthetic relationships are perceived on the right side. Tests on patients with right hemisphere lesions reveal impairment in visual pattern recognition, a necessary skill for reading music, and auditory pattern recognition which is necessary for timbre and tonal memory. This appears to indicate that the principal mechanisms for musical perception are located primarily in the temporal lobe of the right hemisphere.[7]

Other investigations summarized by Hodges[5] show left hemisphere superiority for identifying changes in frequency of less than 30 cents. The right hemisphere demonstrates greater accuracy in discriminating changes in intensity of sound, in perception of musical chords, and in melodic perception. The right hemisphere is also dominant in singing. Removal or anesthetization of the right hemisphere results in loss or severe impairment of singing ability. The left ear is superior when melodies are hummed, indicating processing of nonverbal vocal sounds in the right hemisphere.

Although some studies indicate left hemisphere dominance for perception of rhythm, other research seems to show the opposite. Legato transients are processed more effectively in the left hemisphere with attack transients in the right hemisphere. Some research on musicians indicates right ear-left hemisphere dominance for melody recognition and melody fragment indentification, while other research has found no difference. It has been suggested that differences in hemispheric dominance in processing auditory stimuli are due not only to the type of verbal-nonverbal or analytic-holistic stimuli being processed, but are also affected by the task required of subjects. After reviewing over 200 studies of hemispheric specialization in music perception, Gates and Bradshaw[9] concluded that the left hemisphere is dominant in sequential and analytical aspects of music and the right hemisphere may be more active in formulating a musical gestalt.

A Neuroanatomical Model for the Use of Music in the Remediation of Aphasic Disorders   173

Dramatic results have been obtained by injecting the anesthetic sodium amytal into the carotid artery on one side or the other side of the neck to depress activity in half the brain while the subject was singing.[2] All sense of the melody was lost in midtune upon anesthetization of the right hemisphere while the lyrics were retained. Depression of the left hemisphere caused loss of the lyrics but not the melody. Left hemisphere depression using sodium amobarbital results in loss of both language facility and singing, although singing is regained more quickly than speech.[5]

MUSIC AND APHASIA: A TREATMENT MODEL

Because of the inherent organic involvement of damaged brain tissue in all forms of aphasia, the prospects for successful therapy for language disorders may appear relatively small. However, the remarkable plasticity of the central nervous system has shown that many aphasic disorders can be totally overcome or helped to some degree. Even in early investigations, some aphasic patients developed symptoms that were much milder than would be expected from the nature of the cortical damage. Other patients recovered completely from lesions that normally would lead to permanent aphasia. Still others showed aphasic disorders to a lesser degree over time.[6]

Scientists have searched extensively for explanations of how the brain accomplishes independent recovery of speech function. It has been suggested that because children tend to make better recovery than adults with like damage, the right hemisphere has the capacity during childhood to take over language behavior processing. For example, adult patients who have experienced surgical removal of left hemisphere speech centers during childhood often do not exhibit severe language disorders. This may be due to long years of using the right hemisphere for language functions following surgical treatment for epilepsy. Other patients with Broca's aphasia who may be able to produce one or two poorly articulated words often are able to sing a melody with words rapidly, correctly and expressively. The large number of cases of aphasic patients who can sing and participate in a normal fashion in a variety of musical activities suggests that adequate language processing capabilities still exist in the brain even after the normal speech centers are incapacitated.

From one viewpoint, singing may be looked upon as a form of sustained speech. Both singing and speech involve production of pitch and pitch changes, rhythm, dynamics, tempo, tone production, breath control, sentence structure, phrasing, expressive use of tone quality, and cortical control of oral articulators to form words. The difference may be that speech requires short-term sequencing mainly involving short-term memory. Musical expressions, however, generally exceed short-term storage time and memory capacity and are processed as holistic, long-term patterns in time. The brain seems to recognize music as holistic auditory sequences whose temporal progression bears an intrinsic gestalt value.[7]

In the following discussion of a neurological model for using music in treating aphasia, the "split" brain concept of hemispheric dominance is superseded by a unitary brain function paradigm based on recent renewed investigations of the importance of the corpus callosum, and supported by findings indicating holological processing of information within the brain.

The role of the corpus callosum in facilitating shared responsibility by both cerebral hemispheres has been identified largely through analysis of syndromes resulting from damage to this tract of nerve fibers. These disorders are referred to as 'human callosal syndromes'. In the normal, healthy brain, the 200 million fibers of the corpus callosum provide interhemispheric communication at the rate of four billion impulses per second.[2] Because information can be transferred immediately with learning or exchanged later upon demand, the hemispheres function to represent the environment in a global integrated fashion within the brain rather than operating as separate processors. For example, consider the instrumentalist whose printed sheet music designates use of the *left* hand to play a given note. When the auditory form of the word 'left' passes through Wernicke's area, it must somehow reach the right motor cortex in order to deliver a command to the left hand. This information may go from Wernicke's area to the left premotor region, then via the corpus callosum to the right premotor region, and finally to the right precentral motor cortex in the precentral gyrus which controls the left limbs. Another route suggested by Geschwind[4] goes from Wernicke's area directly through a more posterior section of the corpus callosum to a corresponding area in the right hemisphere and from there to the right premotor and precentral motor regions.

Noteworthy in the above description is the absence of Broca's area in the circuit. This is due to the fact that the word did not need to be written or spoken, but did indicate a nonlanguage motor response. For patients with Broca's aphasia, use of the right hemisphere to facilitate recovery of motor functions may begin through reading instrumental music. This skill requires translation of visual symbols into motor activity. Because the right hemisphere is dominant for both auditory and visual pattern discrimination, it would be useful to follow instrumental score reading with reading vocal melodies by humming.

Singing familiar melodies utilizes association areas surrounding the primary auditory zone that are concerned with retention of aural memories.[5] For patients with conduction aphasia, the singing of familiar melodies makes use of motor patterning previously stored within long-term musical memory and which can then be sent directly to the motor cortex for efferent signals through the pyramidal tract of the central nervous system.[7] If the lesion occurs in the left angular gyrus, recovery of the ability to relate visual, auditory and verbal information may be facilitated through simultaneous presentation of the printed score and the singing of a previously memorized song. The score may stimulate recall in the visual association area while the auditory form would come from temporal association regions in both hemispheres.

Use of the auditory and visual pattern recognition functions of the right hemisphere may allow the learning of new songs when they are presented orally to an aphasic patient whose aural interpretation and visual reception mechanisms are intact. This hemisphere could interpret auditory stimuli in terms of holistic gestalts and accomplish motor planning by associating these auditory forms with sequential visual pattern recognition of the mouth movements of the presenter. This type of learning should be possible with damage to any of the primary speech areas in the left hemisphere. Even with a callosal lesion or when the corpus callosum has been sectioned, information from the right hemisphere may be shared with the left via the anterior commissure, another bundle of nerve fibers connecting the hemispheres. It may also be possible for the right hemisphere to take over language comprehension and motor planning.[4]

The involvement of Wernicke's area in each of the four primary modes of speech communication indicates the importance of formation and comprehension of auditory forms in language usage. Right hemisphere dominance for melodic and harmonic perception suggests that guided music listening experiences may assist recovery in individuals whose comprehension of spoken language is impaired by damage to Wernicke's area. Active listening tasks would not only facilitate right hemisphere usage in perception of auditory forms, but also could enhance comprehension by stimulating awareness of emotional meanings afforded by reactions of the hypothalamus and limbic system, as well as symbolic meanings by association of music stimuli with ideas and concepts previously learned and stored in long-term memory areas of the association cortex. If responses could not be verbalized orally or in writing due to damage to Wernicke's area, they could be expressed in graphic art, creative movement, or musical expression including singing.[7]

For the musical activities cited above, the right hemisphere is fully intact. Although its comprehension of language may be defective or absent, it can still be expected to respond correctly to nonverbal stimuli. In those cases where overt response to right hemisphere stimulation is inadequate or incomplete, the use of visual or tactile aids such as pictures or objects may improve response patterns. It has been suggested that the right hemisphere may retain motor learning that is released upon presentation of more than the normal amount of information.[4] Aphasia patients have been helped toward recovery through melodic patterns of speech that also utilize visual and kinesthetic cues in order to facilitate use of both cerebral hemispheres in language behaviors.[3]

An unusual case was reported by Geschwind[6] in which a woman experienced accidental carbon monoxide poisoning which isolated the speech areas but left them intact. She did not use speech spontaneously and did not show ability to comprehend words. She could, however, repeat sentences that were spoken to her, complete poems from memory after hearing only the first few words, and learn new songs by repeated listening, which she could subsequently sing from memory without errors in words or melody. This case shows the ability of right and left hemispheres to share in the auditory and motor processing of verbal behavior both upon initial learning and in recall performance.

Another case involved a stroke patient who suffered apraxia of speech, aphasia, right hemiplegia, and right hemianopsia. When singing was introduced as therapy, the patient not only could sing songs, but could identify objects in song if the naming task was presented in a melody. Using singing as a regular communication mode, the patient was able to improve to a level that verbal melodies were no longer necessary for expressive speech. She also improved her language performance in all modalities tested by the Porch Index of Communicative Ability.[10]

Recent advances in brain function research have generated new theories to help explain the types of therapeutic gains described or proposed above. It has been discovered that during learning, wide-spread electrical changes occur in the brain. These changes accompany memory formation and are not localized to any single hemisphere or region.[2] To account for this phenomenon, Pribram[11] has proposed a holographic model of brain functioning. According to this theory, sensory input is encoded in such a way that all parts of the stimulus image can be sent to all parts of the brain simultaneously for manipulation or response to the stimulus as needed. Enormous numbers of bits of information could be dispersed and released to memory storage as the stimulus field changes from moment to moment. Whole stimulus fields could be recalled for display within the brain just from presentation or recall of a meaningful fraction of the image.

Distribution throughout the brain of vast amounts of coded information serves to protect it from loss due to brain damage as in aphasia or through normal attrition of brain cells. Distribution through hololagic representation allows retention and retrieval of all parts of an image if partial damage occurrs to the original stimulus or to cranial areas in which the image is stored. These conclusions are based on observations of holograms that can be produced by laser projections of images into three dimensional space.

In human sensory perception, images such as melodies or chords may be received in specialized locations along the sensing mechanism – the basilar membrane in this case – but their final representation in the cortex assumes no such localized representation. The activity from each point on the basilar membrane is projected onto a large collection of neurons. Only a partial reenactment of the original stimulus is necessary to recall the full display of stimulus activity. Electrode stimulation of specific points in association areas of the brain results in reported generation of complex images.[1] Such findings provide strong support for a holological interpretation of brain function. Use of language information that can be learned or recalled from memory in the right hemisphere should provide an effective tool for helping the whole brain regain speech functions that may be lost due to left hemisphere damage.

THERAPEUTIC CONSIDERATIONS WITH MUSIC FOR APHASIA

In applying musical procedures in the treatment of aphasic clients, some specific recommendations should be considered. These suggestions are based on literature appearing during the past two decades describing therapeutic applications of music with aphasic patients.[3][12][13]

a) Music therapy for the aphasic patient must be tailored to each individual in order to maximize its effectiveness in treating the specific speech and language disorders of that person.

b) Tempos must be considerably slower than normal to increase the time available for perceiving and forming syllables. In a study by Laughlin, *et al.*,[14] Melodic Intonation Therapy[15] was used with five male patients who had suffered cardio-vascular accidents, two of whom exhibited global aphasia, two presented mixed aphasia, and one was found to have Broca's aphasia. The investigation was based on prior investigations showing that aphasic patients with left hemisphere damage and auditory processing disorders benefitted from expanded duration of both verbal and nonverbal acoustic stimuli. Performance of subjects was compared under conditions of 1.5 and 2.0 second syllable durations. All subjects exhibited the highest number of correct phrase productions with the 2.0 second syllable duration, next highest with 1.5 second syllables, and the lowest number with nonintoned regular speech. These findings support use of slower tempos as well as slowed conversational speech in music therapy work with aphasic patients.

c) Singing activities should include songs having very few words with frequent repetition of fairly regular rhythmic patterns, e.g. "Frère Jacques," "Row, Row, Row, Your Boat."

d) Present each song as many times as is necessary to allow patients to correct errors.

e) Use large song cards or large type song sheets with only one song per card or page. Point to words as they are sung in order to assist in visual pattern discrimination and sequencing.

f) Work separately for improvement in those components of vocal production that are common to singing and speaking. These include tempo, rhythm, pitch control, loudness, tone quality, breath control, articulation, comprehension, sight-reading and songwriting. Success in each of these areas can generate motivation to use all available brain functions to achieve greater success in language functioning.

g) Treatment objectives should include social, emotional and nonlanguage motor skills in addition to specific communication behaviors.

h) A melodic setting of words should be used that enhances normal speech accents and inflections. This adds expressive value and stimulates participation with greater verbal consciousness.

REFERENCES

1   Roederer, J.G.: Neurophysiological processes relevant to the perception of music – an introduction. In: Spintge, R., Droh, R. (eds.): *Music in Medicine*. Basel, West Germany: Roche Publishers, 1985, pp. 61-88.

2   Hodges, D.A.: Neurophysiology and musical behavior. In: Hodges, D.A. (ed.): *Handbook of Music Psychology*. Lawrence, KS: NAMT, 1980, pp. 195-223.

3   Miller, S. G.: *Music Therapy for Handicapped Children*. Washington, D.C.: NAMT, 1982.

4   Geschwind, N.: The apraxias: Neural mechanisms of disorders of learned movement. *Am Sci*, 1975, **63**, pp. 188-195.

5   Hodges, D.A.: Human hearing. In: Hodges, D.A. (ed.): *Handbook of Music Psychology*. Lawrence, KA: NAMT, 1980, pp. 43-62.

6   Geschwind, N.: Language and the brain. *Sci Am*, 1972, **226**, pp. 76-83.

7   Roederer, J.G.: *Introduction to the Physics and Psychophysics of Music*. New York: Springer-Verlag, 1975.

8   Kimura, D.: The asymmetry of the human brain. *Sci Am*, 1973, **228**, pp. 70-78.

9   Gates, A., Bradshaw, J.L.: The role of the cerebral hemispheres in music. *Brain Lang*, 1977, **4**, pp. 403-431.

10 Keith, R.L., Aronson, A.E.: Singing as therapy for apraxia of speech and aphasia: Report of a case. *Brain Lang*, 1975, **2**, pp. 483-488.

11 Pribram, K.H.: *Languages of the Brain*. Englewood Cliffs, NJ: Prentice-Hall, 1971.

12 Klinger, H., Peter, D.: Techniques in group singing for aphasics. In: Schneider, E.H. (ed.): *Music Therapy 1962*. Lawrence, KA, NAMT, 1963, pp. 108-112.

13 Goodglass, H.: Musical capacity after brain injury. In: Schneider, E.H. (ed.): *Music Therapy 1962*. Lawrence, KA, NAMT, 1963, pp. 101-107.

14 Laughlin, S.A., Naeser, M.A., Gordon, W.P.: Effects of three syllable durations using the melodic intonation therapy technique. *J Speech Hear Res*, 1979, **22**, pp. 311-320.

15 Sparks, R.W., Holland, A.: Method: Melodic intonation therapy for aphasia. *J Speech Hear Disord*, 1976, **61**, pp. 287-297.

MANAGEMENT OF THE PROFESSIONAL VOICE PATIENT

Pi-Tang Lin
Wilbur J. Gould

Vocal communication is a vital part of any therapeutic process. At this time we will limit our discussion to the area of the more serious users of vocal communication: the so-called professional. Our definition of professional is that individual whose vocation depends upon the use of the voice. (Table 1). This, of course, includes the singer of both classical and popular music of any type. This definition also holds true for the therapist in music work and the client who is using the vocal tool. The professional includes the actor, lawyer, teacher, minister, doctor or therapist, as well as the salesperson and waiter/waitress. Since their needs are similar, they are grouped together, even though the preparation utilized by each different group varies considerably. The person who depends upon his/her voice for singing or stage work is usually far better trained than those individuals who spend all of their effort in developing their craft but very little in the actual skills that they will need so badly as a debater or speech maker, as in the case of a politician. This, unfortunately, causes them many problems that are the result of such poor training. It is for this reason that we stress training throughout our discussion.

There is no question that the knowledge of one's instrument is vital. There is no question that correct utilization of the instrument is vital and there is also no question that this leads one to a more successful career. Success depends upon the ability to handle different situations and the ability to utilize the voice to its maximum degree.

Let us first define the method of production or the action of the vocal tract. The instrument for the voice or voice organ is a tract system which can be called the vocal tract.[1][2] The vocal tract consists mainly of the lungs, larynx and mouth (Fig. 1).

The first portion of this tract, the lower vocal tract, supplies air and energy and includes the thoracic cage. Further discussion about this section of the vocal tracts can be found under the chapter on respiration in an ordinary medical textbook. The study of its function is called the pulmonary function test. Since we are talking about phonation, it can be termed a phonating function test. A few basic measurements of pulmonary function need to be mentioned.[3]

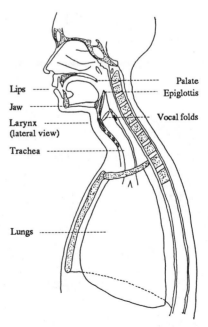

Figure 1. The Entire Vocal Tract

1) Tidal volume (TV) is the amount of air that enters and leaves the lungs at each natural, unforced respiratory effort;
2) Inspiratory capacity (IC) is the amount of air that can be exhaled from the end of tidal expiration;
3) Expiratory reserve volume (ERV) is the amount of air that can be exhaled by the most powerful expiratory effort after the tidal air has been allowed to escape quietly;
(4) Vital capacity (VC) is the amount of air that can be exhaled by the most vigorous possible effort after the deepest possible inspiration;
5) Functional residual capacity (FRC) is the amount of air in the lungs at the end of an unforced expiration;
6) Residual volume (RV) is the amount of air remaining in the lungs after the strongest possible expiration;
7) Total lung capacity (TLC) is the sum of the vital capacity and the residual air (Fig. 2).

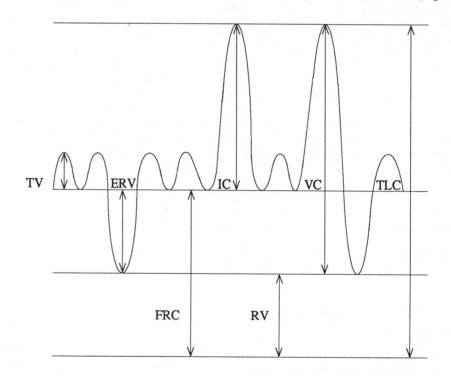

Figure 2. Lung Volumes obtained from pulmonary function test

The three most commonly used functions are vital capacity, residual volume and total lung capacity. When the vocal folds are taken into consideration, two additional measurements are performed:

1) Maximum phonating time is the longest time that the patient is able to phonate the vowel "ah" at a comfortable pitch and intensity;
2) Phonating flow rate is the ratio of vital capacity to maximum phonating time (Table II).

Pi-Tang Lin, Wilbur J. Gould

The second portion of the tract refers to the vocal cords or vocal folds of the larynx since the vocal folds vibrate the air flow and generate sound (Fig. 3).

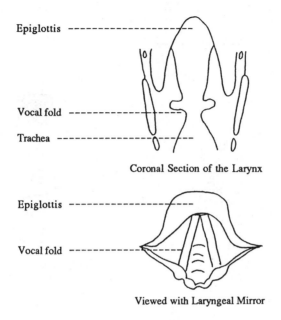

Epiglottis

Vocal fold

Trachea

Coronal Section of the Larynx

Epiglottis

Vocal fold

Viewed with Laryngeal Mirror

Figure 3. The Larynx

The third portion of the vocal tract, the upper vocal tract (Fig. 4), includes the supraglottic larynx and the rest of the aero-digestive tract. It resonates different wave frequencies by changing its shape and length. For instance, the length from the vocal folds to the lips is about 17.5 cm in length which will resonate a wave of 500 Hz.[1] Constriction at the base of the tongue will resonate a sound wave of 1500 Hz. Constriction of the body of the tongue will resonate a sound wave of 3500 Hz (Fig. 5). The position of the palate, pharyngeal wall and teeth all produce changes of the wave form to create a particular quality and character of the voice.

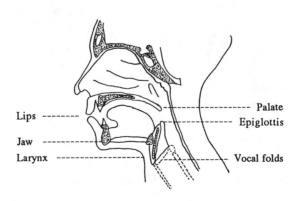

Lips

Jaw

Larynx

Palate

Epiglottis

Vocal folds

Figure 4. The upper vocal tract

Management of the Professional Voice Patient   181

Wave with wavelength 4x that of the upper vocal tract

1.

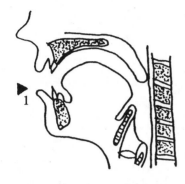

5A. opening of lips and jaw

Wave with wavelength 4/3x that of the upper vocal tract

1.   2.

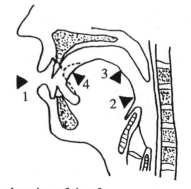

5B. constriction at base of tongue

Wave with wavelength 4/5x that of the upper vocal tract

1.   3.
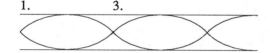

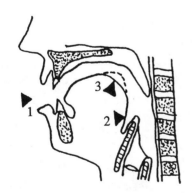

5C. constriction at body of tongue

Wave with wavelength 4/7x that of the upper vocal tract

1.   4.   3.   2.
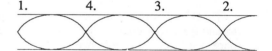

5D. elevation of tip of tongue

Figure 4. Waves with greater loudness due to resonance

At the beginning of sound, the vocal folds approximate tightly, the thoracic cage changes shape, then intrathoracic and subglottic pressure increases. As subglottic pressure increases to 27 cm H_2O,[1 4 5] the vocal folds separate, air escapes between them and creates rapid air flow. This flow will then produce negative pressure, pull both vocal folds toward each other and shut off the air flow so that a rhythmic, pulsating air flow is generated – that is – sound. The internal intercostal, external intercostal and abdomen rectus muscles are the three main groups of muscles that maintain the subglottic pressure constant at 27 cm H_2O in spite of the continuous loss of air through the glottis from the lungs. It is not surprising to discover that the nerves supplying these muscles are as delicate as those of the hand muscles, since the difficulty involved in voice production is comparable to that of producing hand movements.[6]

In evaluating a person with vocal problems, one should examine these three parts of the vocal tract. A thorough history and physical examination will often give clues to any condition that may interfere with the respiratory function, such as history of thoracic operation, asthma, emphysema, etc. Chest X-rays and a pulmonary function test are often needed to disclose the underlying problem. A laryngeal examination includes the traditional ear, nose and throat examination combined with modern, advanced techniques such as the use of a flexible fiberoptic scope in conjunction with simultaneous videotape recording and display of the findings.[8] Analysis of the vocal function, usually performed at a vocal dynamic laboratory, includes maximum phonating time, phonating flow rate and spectrogram.[7] For example, a vocal fold nodule will give a short phonating time and a large flow rate since there is excessive air leakage, although the vocal fold nodule is sometimes a coincidental innocent finding. Hemorrhage of the vocal folds can be seen in females during menstruation.

The examination of the upper vocal tract is easier, as the traditional ear, nose and throat examination and sinus X-rays are usually sufficient. A hearing test is an important part of the examination because phonatory control depends upon good auditory feedback.

When the apparatus has problems, we must consider the whole structure. Since the entire body is involved in vocal production, any defect along the physical structure or in the central control of the structure is reflected in vocal alteration as well. The first thing to consider is the energy source. The respiratory apparatus must be working efficiently for optimal vocal production. In many instances, the effort to phonate properly is impeded by improper physiologic control which can be altered by training.[8] For this reason, about eight years ago, we began studying a series of students at a vocal conservatory over their years of training. There was considerable objectively measured improvement of the inspiratory amount of air as well as the ability to expire air more effectively determined by the reserve of air that was left after expiring completely (Tables III and IV). This means that the subject was able to handle a greater amount of air exchange after training than prior to training (Fig. 6, Tables III and IV). We can also apply this in teaching the patient who does not breathe in the most effective way to increase lower chest expansion. The lack of awareness about expressing air in a most complete manner results in inefficient air exchange with a smaller capacity of usable air or energy for vocal production. Training and careful supervision are required to perform the function effectively. Of course, illnesses such as asthma and emphysema must be considered in such a patient in order to determine the cause of vocal efficiency based upon poor pulmonary reserve. When there is an acute infection it not only affects the nasal area which, by creating congestion, interferes with resonance, but also may cause swelling of the vocal folds and interfere with pulmonary action when bronchitis occurs.

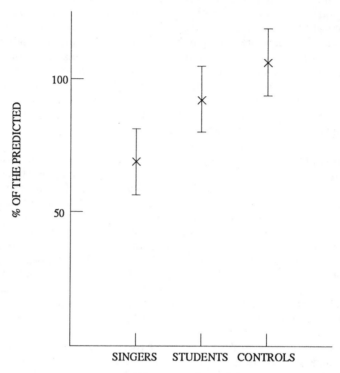

Figure 6. Ratio of RV to TLC. The ordinate is percent of predicted value. The cross is the mean of each group. The bar is one standard deviation of each group.

Therapy is dependent upon the individual's need.[9][10] It may require antibiotics if it is of bacterial origin; or decongestants which would be used when swelling is noted due to allergy or infection. Similarly, the acute swelling phase might be severe enough to require vocal rest if the vocal folds themselves are inflamed and have mucosal inflammatory changes. In rare cases, corticosteroids may be used when there is persistent swelling of the vocal folds more frequently due to either abuse or allergy. One must be very careful not to use corticosteroids routinely, as is so often the case with the professional singer. There are also multiple precautions that one must take when using medication which, at times, are dependent upon vocational needs. For instance, a singer should not perform if it will injure the inflamed vocal cord. Even if reduction of swelling can be created by the use of local sprays, such as the adrenalin-like products or occasionally by inspiration of a nasal decongestant spray such as Afrin or Neosynephrine[9][10], any possible inflammation could cause harm to a singer. A drying agent that will thicken mucus should not be used as it would create an obvious problem for a singer in handling the thickened mucus. Local cortisone sprays should not be used without adequate reason or without taking precautions such as using a tube extendor to lessen the particle size and washing the mouth after each usage. Fungal or oral contamination that will increase hoarseness can result if these precautions are not taken. Nasal decongestants such as Afrin or Neosynephrine should not be used habitually. Although the use of a beta blocker can decrease anxiety and stage fright, it can seriously endanger an allergic patient, especially if asthma is present, and can impair the fire and quality needed for optimal performance. There is no replacement for proper training which will allow better usage despite tension and its ensuing difficulties.

Pi-Tang Lin, Wilbur J. Gould

Irritants such as cigarettes or marijuana should not be used if one wants to use the voice effectively. If one is at a high altitude, especially when there is low humidity, there must be sufficient fluid replacement. A performance or overuse of the voice should not take place until acclimatization is sufficient.

Voice rest can be used judiciously for several days if there is an acute inflammatory problem or if there is a hemorrhage of the vocal cord. However, voice rest is not a panacea and, if improper usage is the cause for the vocal problem, voice rest is only a temporary expedient and the problem will still exist. Since it is extremely difficult for a patient to maintain complete voice rest, psychological problems can result as well. Therefore, there is no substitute for proper instruction (Table V).

The fact that trained singers have the ability to utilize air in the lungs more thoroughly and are able to control airflow in the vocal tract has important implications. The training of a singer is the training of the neuromuscular system with an emphasis on vocal tract performance. Since the vocal tract is actually the respiratory tract, it is reasonable to expect improvement in respiratory function with the techniques used in training singers.

TABLE I

LIST OF THE PROFESSIONAL VOICE USERS

SINGER OF CLASSICAL AND POPULAR MUSIC

ACTOR

LAWYER

TEACHER

SALESPERSON

STOCKBROKER

DOCTOR AND THERAPIST

MINISTER

TELEPHONE OPERATOR

POLITICIAN

TV AND RADIO ANNOUNCER

WAITER

TABLE II

PULMONARY AND PHONATING FUNCTIONS

MEASUREMENT	ABBREVIATIONS	AVERAGE VALUE
TIDAL VOLUME	TV	0.50 L
INSPIRATORY CAPACITY	IC	3.79 L
EXPIRATORY RESERVE VOLUME	ERV	0.98 L
VITAL CAPACITY	VC	4.78 L
FUNCTIONAL RESIDUAL CAPACITY	FRC	2.18 L
RESIDUAL VOLUME	RV	1.19 L
TOTAL LUNG CAPACITY	TLC	5.97 L
MAXIMAL PHONATING TIME	MPT	15~62 sec male
		14~40 sec female
PHONATING FLOW RATE	PFR	46-222 ml/sec male
		43-193 ml/sec female

TABLE III

THE VITAL LUNG CAPACITY, RESIDUAL VOLUME AND TOTAL LUNG CAPACITY. THE VALUES ARE EXPRESSED AS PERCENTAGE OF THE PREDICTED VALUES)

	VITAL CAPACITY			RESIDUAL VOLUME			TOTAL LUNG CAPACITY		
	mean	SD	range	mean	SD	range	mean	SD	range
Professional Singers	122.5	21.9	104-179	72.5	15.8	51-98	107.7	12.7	93-136
Students in Singing	106.6	8.4	92-122	90.6	5.5	66-108	101.6	5.5	91-11
Controls	99.3	9.4	83.121	100.7	14.4	65-130	98.2	8.5	84-117

TABLE IV

THE RATIO OF THE RESIDUAL VOLUME TO THE TOTAL LUNG CAPACITY

	OBSERVED VALUES, %			PERCENT OF PREDICATED VALUES		
	mean	SD	range	mean	SD	range
Professional Singers	20.9	5.0	12-33	69.7	13.7	37-92
Students in Singing	23.9	4.3	18-32	92.3	12.9	66-113
Controls	27.7	3.4	18.33	105.6	14.4	75-130

The ratio of RV to TLC. The ordinate is percent of the predicated value. The cross is the mean of each group. The bar is one stand-are deviation of each group.

TABLE V

MAIN CRITERIA IN MANAGEMENT OF VOICE PROBLEM

TRAINING IN CONTROLLING AIR EXCHANGE EFFICIENTLY

TREATMENT OF MEDICAL DISEASES IN VOCAL TRACT

STEROID IS RARELY USED AND COULD BE HARMFUL

DO NOT USE DRYING AGENT

AWARENESS OF HUMIDITY AND IRRITANTS IN THE ENVIRONMENT

VOICE REST IS NOT A PANACEA

CAUTION IN USING PROPRANOLOL (INDERAL) FOR STAGE FRIGHT

CAUTION IN USING NASAL SPRAY

REFERENCES

1   Sundberg, J.: The acoustics of the singing voice. *Scientific America,* March 1977, **236**(3), pp. 82-91
2   Schultz-Coulon, H.J.: The neuromuscular phonatory control system and vocal function. *Acta Otolaryngol*, 1978, **86,** pp. 142-153.
3   Lambertsen, C.J.: Physical and mechanical aspect of respiratory in V.B. In: *Medical Physiology* 13th Ed. Mountcastle (ed.). C.V. Mosby & Co., 1974, pp. 1361-1371.
4   Kitzing, P., Lofqvist, A.: Subglottal and oral air pressure during phonation-preliminary investigation using a miniature transducer system. *Medical and Biological Engineering*, September 1975, pp. 644-648.
5   Draper, M.H., Ladefoged, P., Whitteridge, D.: Expiratory pressures and air flow during speech. *British Medical Journal*, June 1960, pp. 1837-1843.
6   Campbell, E.J.M.: Phonatory and the respiratory bellows the respiratory muscles. *Annals New York Academy of Sciences*, 1968, **155**, pp. 135-139.
7   Gould, W.J.: Quantitative assessment of voice function in microlaryngology. *Folia Phoniat,* 1975, **27**, pp. 190-200.
8   Gould, W.J., Okamura, H.: Respiratory training of the singer. *Folia Phoniat,* 1974, **26**, pp. 275-286.
9   Gould, W.J.: Voice problems in singers. In: *Current Therapy in Otolaryngology - Head and Neck Surgery 1984-1985,* Gates, G.A. (ed.). Philadelphia: B. Decker, Inc., 1985, pp. 394-400.
10 Punt, N.A.: Laryngology applied to singers and actors. *Journal of Laryngology and Otology,* 1983, Supplement 6, pp. 1-24.

MUSIC AND RESPIRATION

François Haas
Horacio Pineda
Kenneth Axen

It would be hard to imagine two more naturally related areas than respiration and music. They converge quite obviously in vocal training and wind instrument playing, the basis of which is profound development of the capacity for breath control. Less obvious are the subtle, but measurable and predictable, effects of rhythm and tempo on the listener's respiratory pattern. They are studied in the context of "entrainment," whereby respiratory pattern is "captured" by the music, so to speak, and subtly transformed to resemble its tempo.

The use of music, then, would appear to be a natural in respiratory therapy at all ages, but for developing the respiratory muscles and breath control, and for treating conditions in which the natural respiratory rhythm is chaotic. Studying singing or a wind instrument would seem particularly ideal as respiratory therapy for children. They understandably find it very difficult to envision the long term benefits from the repeated practice of boring breathing exercises. Music is an enjoyable end in itself, which also happens to have several important side effects: substantially improved respiratory function, acquisition of a skill, and consequently improved self-esteem.

The surprise is that music has received very little positive attention. In a careful search of the historical and current literature, the association between pulmonary function and singing and/or wind instrument playing has largely been a negative one. Even as recently as 1948, these activities have been regarded as causing respiratory damage rather than helping to repair it. One exception is a 1982 Japanese publication describing the use of singing in controlling asthma attacks.

This chapter, then, rather than discussing the specific values of music in pulmonary rehabilitation, attempts to set the stage for the systematic study that is needed to use music effectively in this context. The section of "Mechanics of Respiration and Phonation" describes the respiratory demands of wind instrument playing and singing, and how the inspiratory and expiratory muscles function to meet them. "The Use of Wind Instrument Playing and Singing in Treating Pulmonary Diseases" is extremely brief because there is little to report. "Music's Effect on Respiration" discusses the progress of work on entrainment, and what it has helped us learn about the neural control of respiratory pattern.

Now it is up to those of us who hope to extend the horizons of current concepts in pulmonary rehabilitation to write the rest of this chapter. It is our job to design and carry out the research that will document the value of music as a therapeutic modality, and provide the guidelines for its most effective use.

PART I: MECHANICS OF RESPIRATION AND PHONATION

Respiratory Physiology and Control

The respiratory system's life-sustaining function is the concurrent replenishment of oxygen in the blood while removing excess CO_2. It must be done over a 20-fold range of metabolic demands, yet accomplished with minimal energy expenditure. This is achieved through a complex integration of systems: pulmonary, cardiovascular, neural, muscular, skeletal and blood. The final step in this process is gas exchange, which occurs in the lungs and tissues via the passive process of diffusion. The lungs meet the body's widely varying demands for rapid diffusion by providing a large membrane (50-100 m^2) and short diffusing distance (average thickness 0.5μm), a consequence of 23 dichotomous divisions of the bronchial tree. Each branch divides into two, each of those becomes two, etc. The bronchial tree's many branches eventually terminate in 300,000,000 alveoli, the lungs' functional units.

In addition to its primary chemostatic regulatory function, the breathing apparatus and its motor control systems also serve nonhomeostatic needs in posture and movement. The respiratory system is also involved in many behavioral and emotional reactions. The different neural pathways regulating the metabolic and nonmetabolic systems have been reviewed by Plum[1] and by Mitchell and Herger.[2] The metabolic respiratory pathways are located in the reticular formation of the lower pons and medulla. Behavioral respiratory pathways are located mainly in the somatomotor and limbic forebrain structures. These nonchemostatic demands, the existence of which depends largely on the state of wakefulness, are added drives to ventilation beyond immediate metabolic needs.[3]

In the awake state, therefore, breathing is regulated by the complex interaction of the respective mechanisms subserving chemical and nonchemical demands on the respiratory system. The specific nature of this interaction at any given time is governed by the relative strengths of the priorities currently in effect for each behavioral system dependent on the respiratory apparatus.[4][5][6] The balance between metabolic and nonmetabolic needs is such that behavioral pathways can temporarily interrupt metabolic pathways to gain control of the respiratory muscles.

Respiratory Muscles

At rest, about 6 liters of air – the product of tidal volume and respiratory rate – ventilate the lung each minute. This ventilation depends upon the ability of the respiratory muscles to overcome those mechanical properties of the respiratory system opposing their contraction. The diaphragm (Fig. 1a), a large dome-shaped sheet of muscle separating the thoracic and abdominal cavities, is the most important inspiratory muscle. It accounts for two-thirds of the tidal volume during quiet breathing. Contraction of the diaphragm enlarges the thoracic cavity by pushing the abdominal contents downward and outward to increase vertical diameter, and elevating the margins of the ribs to increase transverse diameter.

INSPIRATORY MUSCLES

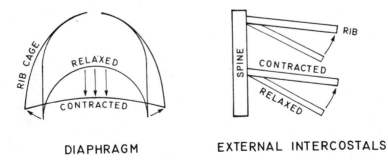

DIAPHRAGM   EXTERNAL INTERCOSTALS

Figure 1a

The external intercostal muscles (Fig. 1a) are inspiratory muscles connecting adjacent ribs. The fibres of these muscles are oriented so that their contraction pulls the ribs up and out, increasing the thorax's anterior-posterior and lateral diameters. Additional inspiratory muscles are the scalenes (which elevate the first two ribs) and the sternocleidomastoids (which raise the sternum).

During quiet breathing, only the inspiratory muscles come into play. The elastic tissues of the respiratory system – which are stretched during inspiration – passively accomplish expiration by recoiling to their equilibrium position. It is only during periods of increased ventilation or conditions of severe airway obstruction that contraction of expiratory muscles occurs.

EXPIRATORY MUSCLES

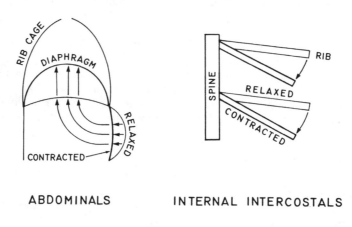

ABDOMINALS   INTERNAL INTERCOSTALS

Figure 1b

The most important expiratory muscles are those of the anterior abdominal wall (Fig. 1b). They depress the lower ribs and, more importantly, increase intraabdominal pressure to force the diaphragm upward. Since these muscles are necessary for generating high expiratory pressures and airflows, they also contract vigorously during coughing, straining and vomiting.

Contracting the internal intercostal muscles (Fig. 1b) – opposite to the external intercostals – moves the ribs down and in to reduce the volume of the thorax. It also stiffens the intercostal spaces, preventing them from bulging out during straining.

Mechanical Characteristics of the Respiratory System

"Elasticity" – the inverse of compliance – is that property of matter enabling it to resume its original shape after being deformed by an external force. Both the lungs and chest wall are elastic structures. If they were removed from the confines of the thoracic cage, the lungs would recoil to a much smaller volume while the chest wall would spring outward to a larger volume. But because the lungs and chest wall are a tightly coupled system, each continuously pulls against the other. The system stops moving at the point where the inward pull of the lungs and the inward pull of the chest wall are equal. This occurs at the end of a normal expiration, and is termed the resting end-expiratory volume. During inspiration, therefore, the inspiratory muscles

        Francois Haas, Horacio Pineda, Kenneth Axen

must work against the lungs' elastic recoil, which increases as the lungs continue to expand. Once inspiration stops, this elastic recoil returns the lungs to their resting end-expiratory volume.

"Resistance" determines the relationship between alveolar pressure (defined in the next paragraph) and airflow. Airway resistance (plus a small contribution due to the visceolastic properties, i.e., tissue resistance, of the respiratory apparatus) accounts for the total resistance of the respiratory system. Airway resistance depends on the diameter and length of the airways, the viscosity of the gas being breathed, and the amount of energy dissipated in turbulent airflow. Since halving the diameter of the airways theoretically increases resistance 16-fold, airway caliber is the primary determinant of airway resistance.

The changing relationships between pressure at three points in the respiratory system – mouth pressure, pleural pressure, and alveolar pressure – determine the parameters of the respiratory cycle. The outer surface of the lungs and the inner surface of the thoracic cage are covered with pleural membranes which slide easily over each other. This permits the lungs passively to follow the movement of the chest wall. The pressure between these two membranes is termed "pleural pressure." The relationship of pressure in the alveoli, termed "alveolar pressure", to mouth pressure is the driving force that causes air to flow in and out of the lungs. At any point during the respiratory cycle, airflow is determined by alveolar pressure and airway resistance. The alveolar-pleural pressure gradient combines with lung compliance to determine lung volume.

RESPIRATORY PRESSURES

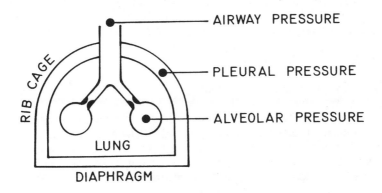

Figure 2

Respiratory muscle contraction alters both pleural and alveolar pressures (Fig. 2), creating the pressure gradients which either expand or collapse the lungs. Prior to the onset of inspiration, alveolar pressure is atmospheric. Pleural pressure is subatmospheric, reflecting the balance of the opposing recoil forces of the lung and chest wall. Inspiratory muscle contraction lowers both pleural and alveolar pressures, creating the pressure gradients necessary for inspiration to occur (Fig. 3). Inspiration – during which alveolar pressure continues to fall, then starts to rise – continues as long as alveolar pressure remains subatmospheric. Once lung recoil pressure – about 30 cm H_2O – matches the pleural pressure imposed by the inspiratory muscles and alveolar pressure becomes atmospheric, inspiratory airflow ceases. The inspiratory muscles relax.

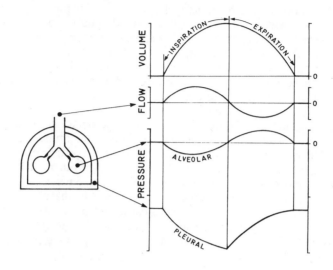

Figure 3

As a result of the lungs' unopposed elastic recoil, pleural pressure becomes less negative and alveolar pressure becomes positive. This altered gradient reverses the direction of airflow, and the respiratory system recoils passively to its end-expiratory position. If the expiratory muscles are brought into play, their contraction causes pleural pressure as well to become positive during expiration.

Phonation and the Respiratory System

Phonation, the production of vocal sounds, requires close coordination between the structures that form sounds and the respiratory muscles, which provide the power that generates them. Coordinated movement of the vocal cords and the suprapharyngeal vocal tract determine pitch, loudness, and sound quality. Action of the respiratory muscles provides the subglottic pressure, and consequent glottic airflow, needed to realize the actions of the vocal apparatus.

To produce a tone of constant loudness and pitch, subglottic pressure during phonation must remain constant. The rate that air leaves the glottis is, at any given instant, determined by the area of the glottal opening and the pressure difference across it. Because lung volume decreases during phonation, thereby reducing elastic recoil of the lung and chest wall, it becomes the task of the respiratory muscles to maintain a constant subglottic pressure.

Respiratory Adaptation During Wind Instrument Playing

Wind instrument playing is unique among the nongas exchange activities served by the human respiratory system. It is the most strenuous while also requiring extremely delicate skills. Wind instruments are played by driving a regulated flow of air (expiration), at a certain head of pressure, through a modified organ pipe equipped with a prime-mover – lips (brass instruments),

Francois Haas, Horacio Pineda, Kenneth Axen

single reed (clarinet, saxophone), double reed (oboe, English horn, bassoon) – which initiates vibrations of the air column in the instrument.

Arend Bouhuys[7] studied pulmonary function at rest and during instruments use in 42 professional wind players. The instruments include brass, single and double reeds. Although breathing pattern is qualitatively similar in all instruments – rapid, deep inspirations followed by prolonged expirations through the instrument – the mechanics differ. Depending on the instrument, the portion of the vital capacity used ranges from a fraction to nearly the entire volume. The higher an instrument's airflow resistance, the higher the mouth pressure required. Mouth pressure, which also increases with both pitch and loudness, ranges from about 4 to 215 cm H_2O. This pressure range rises from the lowest note on the oboe to the highest note on the French horn. Because high airflow resistance generates low airflow rates, the expiratory airflow range, from less than 0.05 to over 1.6 liters/sec, tends to reverse the instrumental order. Despite any mechanical differences, though, there were no gross changes in blood gases of pH after one-half hour of playing.

The wind player must acquire a high degree of control over his breathing. This becomes dramatically evident in the oboe player's highly unusual inspiratory technique. Because the oboe requires relatively low expiratory airflow rates (150 ml/sec as compared to 600 ml/sec for the flute), the oboist can play continuously for several minutes. See Fig. 4, in which a note requiring a mouth pressure of about 40 cm H_2O is sustained for about two minutes. During this period, the oboist's mouth pressure never drops below 35 cm H_2O/mmHg and there is only slight variation in sound level. Inspiration and expiration show a regular pattern throughout this sustained period. The interpretation is that the player inspires through his nose while closing off the oral cavity with his tongue and soft palate. During inspiration, the note is sustained by the pressure in the closed-off oral cavity. After inspiring in this way, the oboist expires in the regular fashion. the slight irregularities in the pressure record all occur at the time of inspiration, presumably from the act of closing off the oral cavity. Skilled performance, therefore, requires a high degree of control over the respiratory muscles, muscles of the mouth and neck, and muscles of the fingers which regulate the keys.

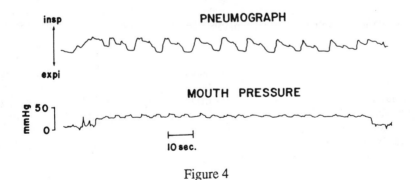

Figure 4

After a maximal inspiration, the pressure generated by lung recoil is about 30 cm H_2O.[8] When a low note is played on many wind instruments, mouth pressure must be kept below 30 cm H_2O regardless of inspiratory volume. Roos[9] understands this to happen by activating the inspiratory muscles to counteract the passive expiratory forces generated by high lung volumes. Maintaining mouth pressure constant at a level below the lungs' recoil pressure while lung volume is decreasing, therefore, requires continuous conscious adjustment of inspiratory muscle activity. Conversely, whenever the needed mouth pressure exceeds the prevailing lung volume's recoil pressure, the expiratory muscles must be activated.

Draper *et al.*[10] confirmed that during loud speech at a subglottic pressure of about 3 cm H_2O, initially the external (inspiratory) intercostal muscles are activated. This activity stops once lung volume has decreased to the point where recoil pressure equals the required subglottic pressure. Internal (expiratory) intercostal muscle activity occurs at lung volumes below this point.

Thus, the wind instrumentalist is limited by the mechanical characteristics of the lungs and thorax. With instruments, such as the French horn or trumpet, requiring high mouth pressures, the length of time that a high note can be sustained decreases as the required pressure nears maximum expiratory pressure. With instruments such as the piccolo or bass tuba, requiring high flow rates with only moderate mouth pressures, nearly the full vital capacity can be used. Vital capacity then appears to limit the time a note can be sustained. In yet another configuration, the length of time during which an oboist can sustain a note is not limited by pressure, volume or airflow needs, but by his breath holding time.

Some brass players experience dizziness and fainting spells. The mouth pressure and airflow data suggest two reasons. A high intrathoracic pressure, if sustained long enough, may induce hypotension and decreased cerebral blood flow in a manner similar to the effects of a Valsalva maneuver. Occurrence of this mechanism while playing an instrument requiring high mouth pressures has been demonstrated by direct blood pressure recordings.[11] In addition, instrumentalists who play long passages of low notes on an instrument such as the tuba, requiring little pressure but high flow rates, are likely to hyperventilate during these periods.

Respiratory Adaptation During Singing

Johannes Müller[12] working in the 19th century with experimental larynges preparations, showed that both loudness and pitch increase during phonation when subglottic pressure is raised. Thus, to sing a tone louder while maintaining the same pitch, subglottic pressure must increase while vocal cord tension decreases. Since this early work, we have come to learn that singing is a complex biomechanical process involving coordination of respiratory muscles with laryngeal, velopharyngeal-nasal and oral musculature. Knowledge of this complexity without a concomitant understanding of all the factors involved has given rise to a wealth of techniques that purport to utilize and develop these muscles. But despite the vast lore of "breathing techniques" referred to by music teachers, there have been few systematic studies to provide objective physiological data for them.

Like wind instrument players[7], trained singers of classical music use a breathing pattern of rapid, deep inspirations and prolonged expirations. A large portion – 80% – of the vital capacity is used, especially when singing loudly.[13] Initiating singing from high volumes offers two advantages. One is that the recoil pressure from the lungs is highest at high lung volumes, therefore providing the relatively high driving pressure required for loud singing. It also ensures a lung volume reserve whenever needed for the extended musical phrases characteristic of classical music.

Maintaining pitch and loudness during expiration means that subglottic pressure must be kept constant over a wide range of decreasing lung volumes. This requires finely graded muscular effort in which both inspiratory and expiratory muscles participate. During phonation at high lung volumes, inspiratory muscles keep pleural pressure below recoil pressure, i.e., below the natural end-expiratory position (FRC). If a note or phrase must be sustained beyond the FRC, the expiratory muscles keep pleural pressure greater than recoil pressure to maintain subglottic pressure. (As will be seen below, current experimental evidence indicates that expiratory muscles may well participate at higher lung volumes as well.)

Francois Haas, Horacio Pineda, Kenneth Axen

Bouhuys et al.[13] suggest that the function of the inspiratory muscles in reducing pleural pressure during phonation may correspond to what has been referred to in the vocal literature variously as *Atemstutze*, *Appoggio*, or "breath support". *Atemstutze*, for example, is defined as the support with which the inspiratory musculature opposes the chest's collapse.[14] Singers and singing teachers visualize several degrees of support, distinguishing between tones sung "without support," "with chest support," and with "diaphragmatic support." If, in fact, "breath support" does correspond to this critical ability to maintain pleural pressure below recoil pressure, then singers have no choice but to use some inspiratory muscle activity at all times, or pitch and loudness will not be maintained. The lore of technique aside, there are no unsupported tones.

Reducing pleural pressure during expiration can occur by contracting either the diaphragm or the intercostal muscles. There has been much discussion on the role of the diaphragm in regulating subglottal pressure during singing.[13 15 16] Most studies have concluded that diaphragmatic activity is restricted to a short period at the start of phonation. Of the variety of techniques used in these studies, only two directly reflect diaphragmatic activity. EMG recordings measure the muscle's electrical activity. EMG recordings measure the muscle's electrical activity. Transdiaphragmatic pressure readings indicate pressure above and below the diaphragm. Since diaphragmatic activity alters intrathoracic and abdominal pressures, an absence of transdiaphragmatic pressure reflects a lack of diaphragmatic activity.[17]

Using intraesophageal electrodes to measure the diaphragm's EMG activity during an utterance following a maximal inspiration, Draper[10] demonstrated a rapid decrease to zero during the first 3 seconds. Transdiaphragmatic pressure measurements in singers made by Bouhuys et al.[13], and magnetometer measurements of the anterior-posterior diameter of the rib cage and abdomen by Watson and Hixon [15], are consistent with an early inactivation of the diaphragm. Both studies conclude that the diaphragm only reinflates the lungs, while the inspiratory intercostals are the expiratory recoil during a sung phrase. (It should be remembered, however, that Watson and Hixon's [15] use of ribcage diameter did not directly measure diaphragm activity. In addition, Bouhuys et al.[13] specifically simplifies the vocal behavior they studied. They remind the reader that "Clearly our measurements relate to phenomena which, although necessities for sound production, are infinitely coarse in comparison to the modalities of expression of which the human voice is capable.")

Not everyone agrees, though, that the diaphragm is uninvolved in active vocal production. In the most current and comprehensive study to date, Leanderson et al.[16] studied singers during a variety of demanding vocal tasks – all involving rapid phonatory changes – that frequently occur during actual singing performance. In addition, they combined transdiaphragmatic pressure measurements and inductive plethysmography to gauge the relative contributions of the rib cage and abdomen. These researchers found substantial diaphragmatic activity during each vocal task studied while it was performed above resting end-expiratory position. During the first part of a phrase involving rapid phonatory changes, the diaphragm appears to act synergistically with the external intercostals both in counteracting the lungs' strong elastic expiratory recoil forces and in establishing rapid and precise decreases in subglottal pressure. (This latter function might be aided as well by the internal intercostals, as we discuss below.)

This use of the diaphragm in precision work contradicts Bouhuys et al.,[13] who argue that singers prefer not to use the diaphragm because both the intercostals and abdominal muscles have must more highly developed proprioceptive feedback control systems.[18 19] This characterizes the diaphragm as too clumsy for rapid, accurate control of subglottal pressure. But evidence drawn from the physiological arena supports Leanderson. The diaphragm can be driven by intercostal-to-phrenic reflexes which join intercostal proprioceptors to the phrenic motoneuron pool.[16 20 21] This could give the diaphragm the fine tuned capacity needed for balancing out the expiratory forces during a phrase's longer segments.[22]

There is persuasive logic for co-activation of the diaphragm with both sets of intercostals, as co-contraction of antagonists is common in the motor control system where speed and precision are required.[23] Respiratory muscles working on all sides of the thoracic cage certainly provide greater speed and precision in executing pressure changes. This draws a far more complex picture of respiratory muscle involvement during lung volumes above FRC, with both inspiratory and expiratory muscles carefully controlling the necessary pressures.

Leanderson *et al.*[16] also showed that, in some singers, co-activation of the diaphragm affects voice quality insofar as it affects vocal cord adduction,[24 25] which in turn affects voice timbre. At one extreme, high adduction activity and subglottal pressures create "pressed phonation." (This, for example, is associated with reduced amplitude of the fundamental [a singer's lowest tone]). At the other extreme, "breath phonation," subglottal pressure is low because the vocal cords are so weakly compressed medially that they cannot close the glottis. "Flow phonation" falls between these two extremes. Diaphragmatic co-activation presumably alters the mode of phonation fro "pressed" to flow". Leanderson *et al.* also obtained evidence that diaphragm co-activation is associated with reflexive stabilization of the larynx position. This is shown in reduced variability of a vowel's characteristic formant frequencies (the resonance bands that determine a vowels' phonetic quality.)

Pulmonary Function in Wind Instrument Players and Singers

Exercising the respiratory muscles in normal subjects, high pressure exercise (static contractions) increases muscle strength but not endurance, while low pressure exercise (deep fast breathing) increases endurance but not strength.[26] Impeding muscle shortening increases both strength and endurance.[27 28] Thus, the concept that isometric and high-load isotonic exercises selectively build endurance, appears relevant to respiratory muscles as well as to limb skeletal muscles in the healthy individual.[29]

For singers and wind instrumentalists, an unusually well-functioning respiratory system combined with effective training in voluntary breath control is assumed to be a prerequisite for proficient performance. It has been hypothesized that exceptional pulmonary function characterizes these musicians possibly through self-selection, or through appropriate training, or via the operation of both factors. Relevant studies, however, are equivocal. Some authors [7 30 31] do find better pulmonary function in wind players and singers, while others [32 33 34 35] find no difference in pulmonary function between these musicians and controls.

Differences, though, may have been obscured through comparing a variety of musicians over the different studies. Different wind instruments do not make equivalent demands on the respiratory system, so the apparently equivocal effects on pulmonary function may actually reflect the differential effects of different instruments played by musicians in the various studies. A more informative way of understanding the data, for example, might have been to group musicians according to the demands of their instrument. Brass players, for instance, must meet the demands of high pleural pressures, while required volumes are low. Reed players and singers, on the other hand, need high volumes, although pressure requirements are modest.

PART II: THE USE OF WIND INSTRUMENT PLAYING AND SINGING IN TREATING PULMONARY DISEASES

Among the claims put forth by the Renaissance composer William Byrd in *Reasons to purswade every one to learne to sing* was the following: "The exercise of singing is delightful to

Francois Haas, Horacio Pineda, Kenneth Axen

Nature & good to preserve the health of Man. It doth strengthen all the parts of the brest, & doth open the pipes. . . " Unfortunately, this good advice was never heeded because of the belief then that singers and wind instrumentalists suffered from chest diseases.

Thus Ramazzini, author of the 1713 tract *De Morbis Artificum*[36] stated that". . . flutists and those who play the pipes; all in short who play wind instruments with cheeks puffed out from the violent exertion of the breath necessary for blowing trumpets and flutes; they incur. . . ruptures of the vessels of the chest and sudden discharges of blood from the mouth." And Thomas Beddoes reported at the end of that century that "playing on wind instruments is known to injure the lung."[37] Even as late as 1948, we encounter such statements as: "wind players are sometimes afflicted with a disagreeable (sic) disease which occasionally compels the abandonment of the profession. It is known as emphysema. . . . "[38]

These unfounded statements have prevented a possibly useful therapeutic tool from being explored. The one exception has been informal attempts earlier in this century – in Europe and somewhat in the United States – to have asthmatic children play the recorder or harmonica (personal communication). It is interesting to note, however, two relevant developments over the last ten years. One is that training the respiratory muscles has become a focus of experimental investigation. The other is the development of a large number devices designed to train the respiratory system by making demands comparable either to singing (encouraging large volumes) or wind instrument playing (breathing against a resistance). One wonders if sticking to a long term training program, which is especially difficult for children, might be far less of a problem if actual musical training – with its independent challenges and gradual sense of mastery – replaces boring plastic devices.

Recently Tateno and Suzuki[39] developed a new method of diaphragmatic respiratory training, involving whistling and singing which they term "Asthma Music." Although we could not find literature assessing this treatment's efficacy, we remain impressed by the authors philosophy.

> Persistent asthma attacks tend to make us feel gloomy. We then desire to withdraw within ourselves. This would be an unfavorable reaction and delay the cure of the asthma. To enjoy singing on such an occasion would open the door to the heart, kindle hope and invite sunshine into every corner. The experience of relieving an asthmatic attack without the use of drugs provides courage and confidence to fight against asthma. The mood of dependence on drugs and physicians will be transformed to a positive attitude in confronting this disease. . . . The enjoyment of singing a song will enable you to feel light at heart and overcome troubles that burden your mind. Singing songs is in itself nothing but breathing.

PART III: MUSIC'S EFFECTS ON RESPIRATION

History

The earliest recorded "scientific" observation on the physiological effects of music is attributed to the French musician A.E.M. Gretry (1741-1813). Gretry described this experiment in his *Essais sur la musique*.[40] "I placed three fingers of my right hand on the artery of my left arm, or on any other artery in my whole body, and sang myself an air, the tempo of which was in accordance with the action of my pulse: some little time afterward, I sang with great ardor an air in a different tempo, when I distinctly felt my pulse quickening or slackening its action to accommodate itself by degrees to the tempo of the new air."

The first systematic experiments were carried out by J. Dogiel in the latter part of the 19th century.[41] In both dogs and man, he demonstrated that auditory stimuli increase heart rate and cause variable changes in circulation. He noted as an aside that, in some cases, respiratory changes accompanied the cardiovascular changes. Then in 1895, P. Mentz[42] published his experiments on the influence of auditory stimulation on respiration. He found that the influence of music depended on the listener's attitude. If the listener were passive, pulse and respiration slowed; with an attentive listener, these two functions accelerated.

Binet and Courtier[43] working at the turn of the century, investigated the influence on specific musical content on respiration in a single subject. They found respiratory rate to increase, with the degree dependent on the kind of music. Rate increased by 3.8 breaths per minute with march music, and only 2.6 breaths per minute with sad music.

Guibaud performed a similar experiment on a number of subjects,[44] and discovered the existence of reliable individual differences in respiratory response. Although different subjects responded differently to the same music, within the same individual the effects of a given stimulus were constant. Despite the overall variation in response, Guibaud did find that respiration generally became more regular with calm melodies and more irregular when rhythm or intensity were altered. He also observed that the rhythm of respiration tends to follow the music's rhythm, "especially when the latter grows slower."

Gamble,[45] studying the effects of music on respiration, concluded at the turn on the century that listening to music – whether loud or soft, in a major or minor key – tends to make breathing more rapid and shallow but does not markedly affect the regularity of respiration. At about the same time, Vaschide and Lahy's critical review of the existing literature[46] concluded that musical rhythm works by suggestion to produce a mechanical action in respiration. Twenty years later, their view had not changed. In Diserens' words:"...In general, respiratory rhythm follows that of the music, increasing or decreasing with the latter, without going beyond the limits of extreme variations."[47]

In the 1930's, Miles and Tilly[48] measured respiratory change during music-listening in a group of subjects during two states: when hypnotized, and again when conscious. The hypnotic state eliminated distracting stimuli. There were no significant qualitative differences in respiratory response between the two states of consciousness. The major finding – observed in those subjects with a strong interest in music – held tempo to be primarily responsible for respiratory changes.

A problem with early investigations was the lack of statistical analysis. Then, in the 1950s, Ellis and Brighouse[49] performed a carefully controlled experiment employing statistical methods. Thirty-six subjects listened to three musical selections: 1) Hall's "Blue Interval," 2) Debussy's "Prelude to the Afternoon of a Faun," and 3) Liszt's "Hungarian Rhapsody No. 2." Figure 5 summarizes their results, i.e., that respiration increased with all three selections, with the degree of increase associated with the tempo of each selection.

Francois Haas, Horacio Pineda, Kenneth Axen

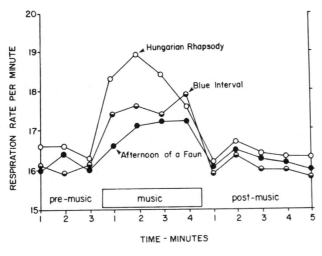

Figure 5

Current Research

Most recently, Haas, *et al.*[50] studied the influence of external rhythm on respiratory rhythm in twenty subjects, from experienced musicians to musically untrained people. (Figure 6 illustrates the equipment used in this project.) Although respiratory pattern can be influenced by use of a mouthpiece,[51] any such effects were assumed to be constant for the duration of the experiment. In addition, we assessed gross metabolic changes and chemical respiratory drive by measuring heart rate and end-tidal PCO_2, respectively.

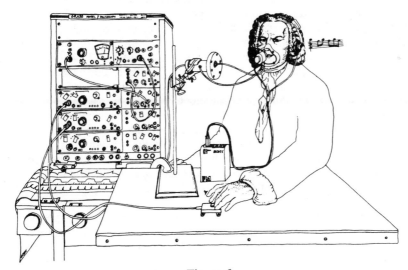

Figure 6

After a 15 minute familiarization period, subjects spent 5 minutes listening to a metronome set at 60 beats/min. They had to use one finger to tap out the metronome beat on a microphone amplifier, with the output recorded on a polygraph. Through this simultaneous use of the subject's information-processing capacity as a distraction to prevent attention to his breathing, this method did not appreciably alter the metabolic component of the respiratory system.

Subjects were then randomly presented with four musical excerpts and one 5 minute silent control period. The four selections, reflecting the need for varying levels of tempi and rhythmic complexity, were: 1) start of the second movement of Beethoven's *Seventh Symphony* (2/4 time, allegretto); 2) Albinoni's *Adagio* (3/4 time, largo); 3) Earl "Fatha" Hines' "Boogie Woogie on St. Louis Blues" (4/4 time, presto); and Thiago de Mello's "Summer Heat" (6/8 time, allegretto). To determine any underlying relationship between musical beat and breathing pattern, we calculated integer-ratio (to indicate when the respiratory cycle is a multiple of the beat frequency) and phase coupling (to indicate inspiration or expiration starting preferentially at a certain point within the measure).

Throughout, heart rate and end-tidal PCO_2 did not change appreciably. Although the effects of music-listening on the magnitude of the respiratory parameters was relatively small, there was a significant increase in respiratory frequency combined with a proportional drop in tidal volume. This change occurred with all musical selections and in most subjects. In addition, some form of unconsciously occurring coordination between music and respiratory pattern was found in a majority of subjects. These various forms were: 1) a uniformly significant increase in the regularity of breathing; 2) a small but significant correlation between music tempo and respiratory rate in half of the subjects; 3) integer-ratios and phase coupling in nearly half the subjects.

We concluded that listening to music influences respiration in two ways. The first, which is in general agreement with the majority of previous work, is a general increase in respiratory frequency regardless of the specific type of music. This acceleration probably reflects a heightened arousal level during listening. A similar increase in respiratory frequency observed with anticipation of exercise,[52] during anger and anxiety,[53] and during enhanced attention,[54] has been attributed to possible cortical inhibition of the limbic system.[55]

The second response, unconscious coordination between stimulus and respiration (termed "entrainment"), appears related to the intrinsic rhythm of the stimulus. Our data indicate that the combination of rhythmic auditory cues in entrainment of respiration and other motor activity is supported by several observations. There is significantly more entrainment between respiration and limb movement when a metronome is used to pace exercise.[56][57] No entrainment occurs in the absence of audible pacing.[57][58] Variation in EMG activity during a repeated motor task decreases significantly when the task is accompanied by an even auditory rhythm, but increases significantly with an uneven rhythmic accompaniment.[59]

Respiratory entrainment can be described as the driving of the central respiratory pattern oscillatory system by a second oscillatory system (e.g., the music rhythm). If the two frequencies are similar, coupling will tend to lock them both into the frequency of the driving oscillator. Relative entrainment – as demonstrated with music – occurs when the driving oscillator is unable to constrain a precise phase relationship.

Theoretically, entrainment can result either from feedback from peripherally located proprioceptors[60] producing a ventilatory stimulus secondary to mechanical excitation during motion,[61] or from feedforward during movement through cortical or subcortical irradiation to respiratory muscles.[62][63][64] Irrespective of the exact nature of the entrainment mechanism, the signal-to-noise ratio of the pacemaker signal (i.e., the music rhythm) must be high enough to interact with the metabolically driven central respiratory pattern generator (CPG). This can be achieved either by decreasing random input into the CPG or by increasing the signal strength (i.e., making the rhythm more obvious).

This information improves our ability to understand the nature of the center responsible for respiratory rhythm. We envision the CPG as an autonomous oscillator system whose frequency is primarily determined by metabloic drive. Small variations in frequency are determined by inherent timing errors of the neural elements making up the oscillator,[65] and are relatively small when it is running free. A relatively free-running state is observed in slow-wave sleep – during which breathing is regulated solely by the metabolic respiratory control system – that is characterized by stable respiration.[66] Any larger variation in frequency is assumed to result from the introduction of noise into the CPG.

During undirected arousal of higher centers – a state in which the individual is not concentrating on a task, e.g., wakefulness or rapid eye movement (REM) sleep – not only does respiratory frequency increase due to changed metabolic demands, but inputs from these higher centers introduce noise into the CPG that increases variation in respiratory frequency. Indices of variability in REM sleep compared to non-REM sleep, for example, increase from 55-410%.[67] As suggested by the reduced coefficient of variation during music-listening (from 23% to about 12%), directed arousal reduces noise input and the CPG approaches the free-running state.

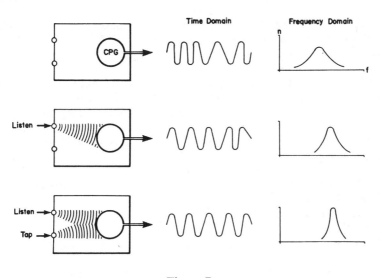

Figure 7

Figure 7 illustrates our conceptual model of rhythmic entrainment. In the upper panel, the CPG oscillatory system is impinged on by noise from the higher centers, resulting in a relatively large frequency variation. When the CPG is exposed to a musical rhythm with oscillators of four to eight times the resting breathing frequency, interaction of the two oscillators produces relative entrainment. The higher frequency of the musical rhythm has a magnet effect[68] on the slower respiratory oscillator, pulling it to a higher respiratory frequency (middle panel). When the external oscillator is combined with a second oscillator of the same frequency, the net signal to the CPG increases and entrainment is reinforced (bottom panel).

In conclusion, because both breathing and finger tapping followed the auditory stimulus, these data favor the feedforward hypothesis of entrainment. To the extent, though, that the finger tap closes a feedback loop, feedback can reinforce the basic entraining signal.

Additionally, these observations have direct bearing on two methodological aspects of respiratory timing studies. The first is that entrainment studies involving exercise should carefully consider the possible contributions for auditory cues. The second is that music is often used during respiratory experiments on the assumption that it is a neutral stimulus and therefore does not interfere with "natural" breathing. The present data show this not to be the case.

What is the importance of such control pathways in normal respiration? Metabolic factors are undoubtedly the dominant control variable driving the CPG, and during normal respiration in healthy individuals the effects of external cues such as music are probably negligible. But what about individuals who respond abnormally to increasing metabolic drive, and patients with an abnormal CPG? The therapeutic potential of this latter pathway in driving the respiratory system in such cases has not yet been adequately evaluated. Systematic study is obviously called for.

REFERENCES

1   Plum, F.: Neurological integration of behavioral and metabolic control of breathing. In: *Breathing: Hearing Breuer Centenary Symposium*, Porter, R. (ed). London, UK.: Churchill, 1970, pp. 159-175.

2   Mitchell, R.A., Berger, A.J.: Neural regulation of breathing. In: *Regulation of Breathing*, Hornbein, T.F., (ed.). New York: Dekker, 1981, **17**, pp. 541-620. (Lung. Biol. Health Dis. Ser.)

3   Euler, C. von.: On the central pattern generator for the basic breathing rhythmicity. *J Appl Physiol: Respirat Environ Exercise Physiol*, 1983, **55**, pp. 1647-1659.

4   Asmussen, E.: Regulation of Respiration "the black box". *Acta Physiol Scand*, 1977, **99**, pp. 85-90.

5   Parmeggiani, P.L.: Integrative aspects of hypothalamic influences on respiratory brain stem mechanisms during wakefulness and sleep. In: *Central Nervous Control Mechanisms in Breathing*, Euler C. von, Lagercrantz, H. (eds.). Oxford, UK.: Pergamon, 1979, **32**, pp. 53-69.

6   Purves, M.J.: What do we breathe for? In: *Central Nervous Control Mechanisms in Breathing*, Euler C. von, Lagercrantz, H. (eds.). Oxford, UK.: Pergamon, 1979, **32**, pp. 7-69.

7   Bouhuys, A.: Lung volumes and breathing patterns in wind instrument players. *J Appl Physiol*, 1964, **19**, pp. 967-975, 8.

8   Rahn, H., Otis A.B., Chadwick, L.E., Fenn, W.O.: The pressure-volume diagram of the thorax and lungs. *Am J Physiol*, 1946, **146**, pp. 161-178.

9   Roos, J.: The physiology of playing the flute. *Arch Neerl Phonetique Exp*, 1936, **12**, pp. 1-26.

10 Draper, M.H., Ladefoged, P., Whitteridge, D.: Respiratory muscles in speech. *J Speech Hearing Res*, 1959, **2**, pp. 16-27.

11 Faulkner, M., Sharpey-Schafer, E.P.: Circulatory effects of trumpet playing. *Brit Med J*, 1959, **1**, pp. 685-686.

12 Müller, J.: Von der Stimmme und Sprache. *Handb d Physiol des Mensches*. Coblenz: Holscher, J., 1937, Vol. 2, Book 4, 3rd part, pp. 133-245.

13 Bouhuys, A., Proctor, D.F., Mead, J.: Kinetic aspects of singing. *J Appl Physiol*, 1987, **21**, pp. 483-496.

14 Winckel, F.: Electroakutiche Untersuchungen und der menschlichin Stimme. *Folia Phonat*, 1952, **4**, pp. 93-113.

15 Watson, P.J., Hixon, T.J.: Respiratory kinematics in classical (opera) singers. *J Speech Hearing Res*, 1985, **28**, pp. 104-122.

16 Leanderson, R., Sundberg, J., Euler C. von.: Role of diaphragmatic activity during singing: A study in transdiaphragmatic pressures. *J Appl Physiol*, 1987, **62**, pp. 259-270.

17 Newson-Davis, J., Goldman, M. Loh, J., Casson. M.: Diaphragm function and alveolar hypoventilation. *Q J Med New Ser*, 1970, **XLV 177**, pp. 87-100.

18 Lansing, R.W., Meyerink, L.: Load compensating responses of human abdominal muscles. *J Physiol Lond*, 1981, **320**, pp. 253-268.

19 Corda, M., Euler, C. von, Lennerstrand, G.: Proprioceptive innervation of the diaphragm. *J Physiol Lond*, 1965, **178**, pp. 161-169.

20 Decoma, E.E., Euler C. von.: Excitability of phrenic motoneurones to afferent input from power intercostal nerves in the spinal cat. *Acta Physiol Scand*, 1969, **75**, pp. 580-591.

21 Remmers, J.E.: Extra-segmental reflexes derived from intercostal afferents: phrenic and laryngeal responses. *J Physiol Lond*, 1973, **233**, pp. 45-62.

22 Euler, C. von.: Some aspects of speech breathing physiology. In: *Speech Motor Control*, Grillner, S. (ed.). Oxford, UK.: Pergamon, 1982, pp. 93-103.

23 Euler, C. von.: Brain-stem mechanisms for generation and control of the breathing pattern. *Handbook of Physiology. The Respiratory Stytem.* Bethesda, MD: Am. Physiol. Soc., 1985, Sect. 3, vol. II.

24 Gaufin, J., Sundberg, J.: Data on the glottal voice source behavior in vowel production. *Speech Transmission Lab Q Prog Status, Rep.* 1980, **2-3**, pp. 61-70.

25 Rothenburg, M.: The glottal, volume velocity waveform during loose and tight voiced glottal adjustment. In: *Proceedings of the Seventh International Congress of Phonetic Sciences in Montreal.* The Hague: Mouton, 1972, pp. 380-388.

26 Lieth, D.E., Bradley, M.: Ventilatory muscle strength and endurance training. *J Appl Physiol*, 1973, **41**, pp. 508-516.

27 Gross, E., Riley, E., Grassino, A., Ladd, J., Machlem, P.T.: Influence of resistive training on respiratory muscle strength and endurance in quadriplegia. *Am Rev Resp Dis*, 1978, **117**, p. 343.

28 Haas, F., Haas, A.: Effect of inspiratory muscles training in healthy subjects. *Fed Proc*, 1981, **40**, p. 540.

29 Faulkner, J.A.: New perspectives in training for maximum performance. *JAMA*, 1968, **205**, pp. 117-122.

30 Stauffer, D.W.: Physical performance, selection and training in wind instrument players. *Ann NY Acad Sci*, 1968-69, **155**, pp. 284-289.

31 Gould, W.J., Odamura H.: Static lung volumes in singers. *Ann Otol, Rhino, Laryngol*, 1973, **82**, pp. 89-95.

32 Schorr-Lesnick, B., Tierstein, A.S., Brown, L.K., Miller, A.: Pulmonary function in singers and wind instruments players. *Chest*, 1985, **88**, pp. 201-205.

33 Heller, S.S., Hicks, W.B., Root, W.S.: Lung volumes of singers. *J Appl Physiol*, 1968, **15**, pp. 40-42.

34 Navratil, M., Rejsek, K.: Lung function in wind instrument players and glassblowers. *Ann NY Acad Sci.*, 1968-69, **155**, pp. 276-283.

35 Borgia, J.F., Horvath, S.M., Dunn, F.R., Von Phul, P.V., Nizet, P.M.: Some physiological observations on French horn musicians. *J Occup Med*, 1975, **17**, pp. 696-701.

36 Ramazzini, B. *De morbis artificum*, latin text of 1713, W.C. Wright (trans.), Chicago: pp. 329-385

37 Beddoes, T.: *Essay on the Causes, Early signs and Prevention of Pulmonary Consumption for the use of Parents and Preceptors.* 1799.

38 Whittaker A.H.: Occupational diseases of musicians. In: *Music and Medicine*, Schullian D.M., Schoen, M. (eds). New York: Henry Schuman, 1948, pp. 218-243.

39 Tateno, K., Suzuki, I.: Asthma music. *Brit J Music Ther*, 1982, **13**, pp. 2-13.

40 Chomet, H.: *The Influence of Music on Health and Life* (L.A. Flin, trans.). New York: Putnam, 1875.

41 Dogiel, J.: Über den einfluss der Music auf den Blutfreislauf. *Arch f Physiol*, 1880, pp. 416-428.

42 Mentz P.: Die Wirkung adustischer Sunnesreize auf Puls und Athmung. *Philos Stud*, 1985, **11**, pp. 16-124, 371-393, 563-602.

43 Binet, A., Courtier J.: L'influence de la vie emotionelle sur le coeur, la respiration, et la circulation capilliare. *Année Psychol*, 1896, **3**, pp. 65-126.

44 Guibaud, M.: Contribution à l'étude experimentale de l'influence de la musique sur la circulation et la respiration. *Année Physiol*, 1898, **5**, pp. 645-649.

45 Gamble, E.A.McC.: Attention and thoracic breathing. *Am J of Psycho*, 1905, **16**, pp. 270-280.

46 Vaschide, N., Lahy, J.M.: Les coefficients respiratoire et circulatoire de la musique. *Riv Musicale Ital*, 1902, **9**.

47 Diserens, C.M.: Reaction to musical stimuli. *Psychol Bull* , 1920, **20**, pp. 173-199.

48 Miles, J.R., Tilly, C.R.: Some physiological reactions to music. *Guy's Hosp Gaz*, 1935, **49**, pp. 319-322.

49 Ellis, D.S.J., Brighouse, G.: Effects of music on respiration and heart-rate. *Am J Psych*, 1952, **65**, pp. 39-47.

50 Haas, F., Distenfeld, S. Axen, K.: Effect of perceived musical rhythm on respiratory. *J Appl Physiol*, 1986, **61**, pp. 1185-1191.

51 Gilbert, R.J., Auchincloss, J.H. Jr., Brodsky, J., Boden, W.: Changes in tidal volume, frequency, and ventilation induced by their measurements. *J Appl Physiol*, 1972, **33**, pp. 253-254.

52 Miles, J.N.: Hyperpnea of effort. *J Physiol Lond*, 1945, **104**, p. 15.

53 Dudley, D.L., Martin, C.J., Holmes, T.H.: Psychophysiologic studies of pulmonary ventilation. *Psychosom Med*, 1964, **26**, pp. 645-660.

54 Foster, E., Gamble, E.A.McC.: The effect of music on thoracic breathing. *Am J Psychol*, 1906, **17**, pp. 406-414.

55 Planche, D.: Effects de la stimulation du cortex cerebral sur l'activité du nerf phrenique. *J Physiol, Paris*, 1972, **64**, pp. 31-56.

56 Bechbache, R.R., Duffin, J.: The entrainment of breathing frequency by exercise rhythm. *J Physiol Lond*, 1977, **272**, pp. 553-361.

57 Yonge, R., Peterson, E.S.: Entrainment of breathing in rhythmic exercise. In: *Modelling and Control of Breathing*, Whipp, B.J., Wiberg, D.M. (eds.). New York: Elsevier, 1983, pp. 197-203.

58 Kay, J.D.S., Peterson, E.S., Vejby-Christensen, H.: Breathing in man during steady exercise on the bicycle at two pedalling frequencies and during treadmill walking. *J Physiol Lond*, 1975, **251**, pp. 645-656.

59 Safranek, M.G., Koshland, G.F., Raymond, G.: Effect of auditory rhythm on muscle activity. *Phys Ther*, 1982, **62**, pp. 161-168.

60 Dejours, P., Mithoefer, J.C., Labrousse, Y.: Influence of local chemical changes on ventilatory stimulus from the legs during exercise. *J Appl Physiol*, 1957, **10**, pp. 372-375.

61 Comroe, J.H. Jr., Schmidt, C.: Reflexes from the limbs as a factor in the hyperpnea of muscular exercise. *Am J Physiol*, 1983, **138**, pp. 536-547.

62 DiMarco, A.F., Euler C. von, Romaniuk, R., Yamaoto, Y.: Changes in respiratory activity associated with locomotion. *Fed Proc*, 1981, **40**, p. 379.

63 Eldridge, F., Millhorn, D., Waldrop, T.: Exercise hyperpnea and locomotion: parallel activation from the hypothalamus. *Science*, 1981, **211**, pp. 844-846.

64 Krogh, A., Linhard, J.: Regulation of respiration and circulation during the initial stages of muscular work. *J Physiol Lond*, 1913, **47**, p. 112.

65 Gibbon, J., Church R.M., Meck, W.H.: Scalar timing in memory. *Ann NY Acad Sci*, 1984, **423**, pp. 52-77.

66 Phillipson, E.A.: Control of breathing during sleep. *Am Rev Resp Dis*, 1978, **118**, pp. 909-939.

67 Mitchell, R.A., Berger A.J.: Neural regulation of breathing. In: *Regulation of Breathing*, Hornbein, T.F. (ed.). New York: Dekker, 1981, Vol. 17, pp. 541-620. (Lung Biol. Health Dis Ser.)

68 Soberger, A.: *Biological Rhythm Research*. New York: Elsevier, 1965.

PIANO MUSIC FOR ONE HAND

Shirley Harris

Think of a pianist playing the pianoforte! The most common image that comes to mind is of someone seated at the instrument playing with two hands, ten fingers running up and down the keyboard. Although this is the usual situation, many people do play the piano with less than ten fingers, the use of only one hand or with other physical handicaps. To accommodate these performers, there is a vast repertoire of music written for one hand alone.

One hand piano music is not new, the the first piece having been written by Carl Philipp Emanuel Bach (1714-1788). Although the little clavier piece in A major can be played with either hand, it was probably written for the left hand as the composer was left handed.

In the question column of a piano magazine, *Fidelio Club,* dated 1905,[1] a teacher who wished to develop the left hand requested pieces of music solely in that area. The answer printed in the magazine read, "There are studies written, but I do not think they are beneficial. If you want to strengthen your left hand, you should pick out studies that are principally written for it." The Clementi and Chopin studies were recommended. This still seems to be the prevailing attitude as the rich repertoire for one hand alone has largely been ignored, the common belief being that this music consists of little ditties and melodies played with one hand.

Today, teachers and therapists need to be aware of the techniques and the music available for one hand alone, with its value to both the handicapped player and to the two hand performer. Physical handicaps, loss of an arm or fingers, or muscular problems may necessitate a one hand repertoire for life. A temporary handicap (e.g., fractures, sprains or other injury to the shoulder, arm or finger) can have a beneficial side effect in strengthening keyboard skills in the unharmed limb through the one hand repertoire.

In the *Musical Quarterly,* July 1935, Leopold Godowsky states that aside from the dearth of appropriate repertoire, he was inspired to write only left hand music because "as a result of the majority of people being right-handed, almost to the exclusion of the left hand, the right hand is constantly in a state of tension, while the left hand, owing to its freedom from cramped muscles, is in a better condition for the cultivation of the desired relaxation essential to a superior pianistic equipment."[2] He offers the pianist transcriptions of the Chopin Études for the left hand as well as a number of other pieces.

Like Godowsky, Raymond Lewenthal, in the preface to his collection of Piano Music for One Hand, offers the collection of music to two handed performers as well. He states, "Most people do not have two perfectly good hands. Their left hands are often underdeveloped. One of the surest ways to develop left hand technique is by playing pieces written for it alone, because they allow complete scrutiny of the left hand".[3] John Thompson,[4] Eric Steiner[5] and John Schaum[6] all offer their music for the injured student as well as for the elementary performer to develop technical prowess.

Since the majority of people are right handed, and this is often the hand which is injured when accidents occur, much music has been written so that the left hand can continue playing while the right hand heals. Although very few pieces have been written for the right hand alone, my own collection contains pieces by Australian composers Colin Brumby, Ross Edwards, David Gallasch, Miriam Hyde and Jeff Leask.[7]

Performing with one hand alone does not mean that the performer is going to miss out on the experiences of a two handed person, since a wide range of music is available. Concertos with orchestral accompaniment have been written by Bax, Britten, Demuth, Prokofiev, Ravel and Strauss. Janacek wrote a "Capriccio" for left hand piano and wind quartet, while Scriabin gave us a "Nocturne" and "Prelude." In the area of studies, works have been written by Bartok, Berens, Blumenfeld, Czerny and Moskowski. Count Zichy contributed with Opera. Alkan's Opus 76 has been described by Larry Sitzky as one of the most punishing pieces ever written for piano.[8]

Duets are another source of music for one hand since one part can be played with one hand alone. Music is now being written for one and two pianos played with three and five hands. Music that has been written for two hands can often be played with one. In addition, repertoire for violin, cello and woodwind instruments can be played on the piano with one hand, amounting to a considerable volume of music.

Since becoming interested in piano music for one hand alone, I have found over 900 albums or pieces of music, not all of which have been published.

Apart from my own list, which appears to be the most complete and current, five sources of recommended music for one hand are:

1. Reference sheet MP7, printed by the Disabled Living Foundation;[9]
2. *They Can Make Music*, Philip Bailey;[10]
3. The Rich Repertoire for One Hand by Raymond Lewenthal;[11]
4. *Bibliography of Piano Music for the Left Hand Alone*, Tracy Strain;.[12]
5. *Piano Music for the Left Hand Alone*, Theodor Edel.[13]

These lists contain references that are for left hand dominating as well as left hand alone, such as Czerny's Opus 399 and Opus 718. Some music requires alteration to note positions, or the omission of notes before the pieces can be used; however the quality and range of music available precludes the necessity for altering or adapting pieces. The handicapped person must reach up for standards, they should not be lowered for him/her.

TECHNIQUE OF PLAYING ONE HAND REPERTOIRE

Seating at the instrument is an important consideration in playing with one hand, as it is necessary to shift the piano seat to the right or left of center to give the widest possible use of the keyboard to the playing hand. The student should not sit on a cushion, which makes balance difficult, but if necessary sit forward on the seat, or on a large book. The use of a footstool with young children is highly recommended. Posture and hand positions are prime concerns of all ages, whether or not a handicap exists.

Technique is a matter to be considered by the teacher or therapist. Gross motor movements should always precede fine motor movements, with technique pared down to simple concepts relating to control and coordination at the keyboard.

Techniques, such as crossing over the thumb, passing the thumb under the fingers, and leaps, are required at an earlier stage and require preparation. The area of motor coordination is well covered in the book *New Pathways to Piano Technique: A Study of the Relationship Between Mind and Body* by Luigi Bonpensiere.[14]

Although music written for one hand can be played with the other, it is easier to play with the left as the strong fingers then have the upper notes of the melody and chords. Good fingering enables the use of fingers of greatest weight or strength on the most important notes of stress in the musical phrase. It is also advisable to practice parts separately as one would in playing with two hands. The two handed performer can benefit from playing some one hand repertoire with either hand.

Fingering is an important consideration in the building of good technique as well as consistency, which is essential to good fingering. Similar passages such as repetitions and sequences should, if possible, be played in the same manner, although exceptions do apply. It is necessary to have a good understanding of the fingering of a piece of music. The fingering marked, or that used by the performer before alterations, should be carefully perused as a number of fingerings are often suitable and it is necessary to decide which one is best suited to the hand of that performer. Having some knowledge of early keyboard fingering, which relies mainly on the middle three fingers of each hand, can be of great help in determining articulation.

Good fingering will enable the player to encompass as many successive notes in advance as possible to avoid frequent thumb shifts. One of the principles of good fingering is the avoidance of unnecessary hand movement; therefore the scale and chord fingering should be looked at first. In passages founded on broken chords, a good plan is to begin by practicing the chord in their block form, as they will show clearly where the most natural hand shifts occur. There are many awkward passages where it is difficult to determine which fingering is best to use and, at times, unorthodox fingering is required to maintain a *legato* touch.

The separate articulation of the fingers is one of the first difficulties to overcome. Playing at slow tempo must not affect the velocity of the finger movement and, even at slow tempo, the finger action must be fast. Speed and agility must be acquired first and power gradually added. Training young and weak fingers to produce power for tone places a burden on the muscles and tendons of the wrist, hand and fingers.

Force should never be used, nor should strain be put upon the joints when practicing. Should the hand begin to feel heavy, let it rest. Fatigue, tension and muscle cramp can result in injury to tissues unless care is taken and suitable rest periods given. Should one continue practice, injury to the hand may result. It must always be remembered that with one hand, tasks cannot be shared, so one hand does all the work.

The use of the damper pedal is very important and, if physical capabilities allow, is taught in much earlier lessons. Godowsky states that "the pedal becomes so important in its function that is almost replaces the other hand."[2] Frequent use of the sustaining pedal is required to assist in bridging awkward gaps and in maintaining *legato* touch.

Of great assistance to the performer is the middle, or sostenuto, pedal which enables any particular note or notes to be sustained without all of the strings vibrating sympathetically. Should the instrument have a sostenuto pedal, much can be gained from exploring its use.

In selecting music for the performer, care must be taken to select music suited to the hand, as often the music contains wide reaches. Consideration must also be given to the personality and mental ability of the performer.

CONDITIONS WHERE ONE HAND CAN BE OF BENEFIT

Paralysis of a limb or one side of the body, impairment of speech, vision, thought, memory or perception can result from conditions such as stroke or cerebral palsy, depending on the damage caused to the brain cells. Recovery following stroke is variable but teaching music skills will aid the return to physical independence and can increase development despite the physical restriction.

Cerebral palsy is classified according to the involvement of the limbs. As each hemisphere of the brain controls functions and movement on the opposiste side of the body, damage to the right side of the brain results in disability on the left side and vice versa. In my experience working with hemiplegics who have two limbs on the same side affected, when there is no associated mental handicap, lessons can be conducted in the usual manner but should progress according to the mental capabilities of the student.

Congenital malformation of the limbs may be a reason that lessons in music are sought. In some cases, due to an accident, the use of a limb may be lost. An understanding of physiology and anatomy, along with a knowledge of the physics of movement, can be of benefit in teaching.

Dr. Sidney Licht recommends the piano as it offers excellent opportunities for flexion of the fingers and thumb extension, abduction of the wrist as well as flexion and abduction of the shoulders and exercise of the neck and back.[15] A number of students with spina bifida have limited or no use of their legs and therefore require special assistance to be able to use the pedal.

Sufferers of the two common types of arthritis, osteoarthritis and rheumatoid arthritis, can be assisted by using the skills that pianoforte playing afford. In cases involving osteoarthritis, good muscle tone, mobility and activity can be achieved.

After the initial phase in rheumatoid arthritis has passed, tuition in pianoforte can be of assistance in relieving joint stiffness and strengthening muscles. Carpal tunnel syndrome is commonly associated with rheumatoid arthritis, thus eliminating playing with one hand for a time and allowing techniques for one hand to be employed.

Many people who can benefit from piano playing have more than one handicap, including learning difficulties and emotional and social problems, and it is of great benefit to have some knowledge of these problems. The rehabilitation process can be assisted by sympathetic support and an empathetic awareness of how the patients perceives his/her difficulties in addition to an understanding of teaching techniques and repertoire for one hand piano music that is available for the patient who can already play the piano, or tuition in the instrument for one who has not played before. When a number of problems occur as a result of brain damage or other injury, the support of a professional group working as a team can be of great benefit.

Parents of handicapped children want them to succeed not only in schoolwork, but allow their children to be involved in extracurricular activities such as piano lessons, swimming and tennis so that they can "conquer" a new field rather than enjoying or achieving. They often move on to another field before the necessary skills are really developed. Motives and needs really must be considered in selecting piano tuition for the handicapped student.

SOME PERFORMERS OF ONE HAND MUSIC

Brahms (1833-1879) transcribed Bach's *Violin Concerto in D minor* for Clara Schumann when she injured her right hand. The piece has been transcribed by a number of composers, including Larry Sitzky, from Australia who, after injuring his right hand and searching through the repertoire for left hand, decided to transcribe it himself rather than use Brahms' version.

A French left hand pianist, Charles Gros, gave successful recitals in London in 1899. William Coenen (1837-1918), who had the use of both hands, enjoyed fame for his left hand performances and published music in that area.[16]

Count Zichy (1849-1924) became history's first one hand pianist when, as a boy, he lost his right hand in a hunting accident. His music includes six studies (1878 Preface Liszt), *Sonata* and *Concerto in Eb major*, 1902. A cantata, songs, a ballet and opera are amongst his published works.[17]

Leopold Godowsky (1870-1938), after transcribing Chopin for left hand alone and writing other pieces, suffered a stroke at the age of 60 which paralyzed his right hand.

Hermann von Waltershausen (born 1882) lost his right arm and foot as a boy.[16]

Paul Wittgenstein (1887-1961) lost his right arm during World War I. To continue his concert career, in addition to his own compositions and arrangements, Wittgenstein commissioned works from composers including Britten, Hindemith, Prokofiev, Richard Strauss, Korngold and Ravel. Ravel wrote the *Concerto in D major* for Paul Wittgenstein who was overwhelmed by this difficult work but, after months of study, realized its greatness. Ravel, unable to perform the solo part as written, played it with two hands. The Ravel *Concerto* has been performed by many including Gary Graffman and Australian teacher and performer Stephen McIntyre.

When Harriet Cohen cut her right hand badly on broken glass, composer Arnold Bax wrote a left hand concerto to revive her confidence as her career was in danger of collapse. She performed this piece at the Cheltenham Festival on July 4th, 1950.[18]

Cyril Smith, a virtuoso pianist, lost the use of his left arm as the result of a second stroke. He and his wife, Phyllis Sellick, decided that since they both possessed a wide manual compass, it would be possible to play most piano duet music without having to make drastic alterations. After devising a three handed technique which allowed them to return to the concert platform, John Odom arranged a great number of pieces for them to play in this manner. A number of recordings of their performances are available.[19]

John Railton, a British concert pianist, suffered the loss of his left arm due to cancer more than twenty years ago. John began performing as a "three handed duo" with Kate Elmitt and their repertoire runs from Bach and Schubert to Gershwin and "Kitten on the Keys" as well as the works of Cyril Smith and Phyllis Sellick. When playing with one hand, John is fond of the Moskowsky *Études* and has a number in his repertoire.

Two noted American artists, Leon Fleisher and Gary Graffman, have performed repertoire for one hand due to injury. Performances by artists such as these should assist us in understanding the value of the one hand repertoire.

Miriam Hyde, a noted Australian composer and teacher, broke her arm before a performance at the Sydney Opera House in 1982. In order to perform, she wrote works for the left hand alone. She also wrote a collection of one hand music for Susan Bray, who was born without a right hand. However, before these pieces were printed, the publisher asked that they be modified for two hands. The pieces have now been published in my own collection, in their original one hand form.

Christine Patton, an Australian pianist who lost the use of her right hand in an accident, completed her F.T.C.L. with Trinity College, London, with a program of works for left hand alone. Her program as presented consisted of "Chaconne" (Bach/Brahms); "Sonata for Left Hand Alone" (Reinecke Op. 179); "Prelude and Nocturne" (Scriabin Op. 9 Nos. 1 and 2.); "Toccata and

Fugue" (Takacs Op. 56). Christine is now preparing a thesis for a Master's degree based on the piano repertoire for the left hand.

Simon Barare and Isadore Goodman are two famous performers who have played the Blumenfeld "Étude for Left Hand Alone Opus 36." The piece was dedicated to Godowsky and is rarely performed because of the tremendous technical demands required.

Using the piano as a medium for teaching music making skills, I have found that it improves gross and fine motor coordination, with carry over into other areas. Music can play an important part in the rehabilitation and well-being of disabled people, providing a foundation upon which they can grow and thereby improving their level of self and social acceptance.

REFERENCES

1   *Fidelio Club Magazine*, England, 1905.
2   Godowsky, L.: Piano music for the left hand. *Musical Quarterly*, July 1935, **21**, pp. 298-300.
3   Lewenthal, R.: Preface, *Piano Music for One Hand*. Melbourne, Australia: Allans Imperial Edition 21, Music Australia Pty, Ltd., 1984.
4   Thompson, J.: Foreword, *For The Left Hand Alone, Books 1 and 2*. Cincinnati, OH: Willis Music Co., 1955.
5   Steiner, E.: Foreword, *One Hand Only For The Young Pianist*. New York: Belwin, Inc., Rockville Centre, Long Island, 1962.
6   Schaum, J.: When, where to use the John M. Schaum left hand studies. In: *Left Hand Studies, Books 1 and 2*. New York: Belwin, Inc., Rockville Centre, Long Island, 1951.
7   Harris, S.: Foreword, *Piano Music for One Hand*. Melbourne, Australia: Allans Imperial Edition 21, Music Australia Pty, Ltd., 1984.
8   Sitzky, L.: Summary notes for a study on Alkan. *Studies in Music*, 1974, **73**(8), pp. 53-81.
9   Disabled Living Foundation: *Reference Sheet MP7*, Music Advisory Service, 380/384 Harrow Road, London W9 2HU.
10 Bailey, P.: *They Can Make Music*. London, U.K.: Oxford University Press, 1973, pp. 122-132.
11 Lewenthal, R.: The rich repertoire for one hand. *Clavier*, April 1978, **XVII**(4), pp. 15-18.
12 Strain, T.: *Bibliography of Piano Music for the Left Hand Alone*. Thesis, Kent State University, 1972.
13 Edel, T.: *Piano Music for the Left Hand Alone*. Thesis, Manhattan School of Music, May 1980.
14 Bonpensiere, L.: *New Pathways to Piano Technique: A Study of the Relationship Between Mind and Body*. Philosophical Library of New York, 1953.
15 Licht, Dr. Sidney: *Music in Medicine*. New England Conservatory of Music, Boston, MA, 1946, pp. 46-53.
16 Scholes, P.A.: *Oxford Companion to Music,* 10th Edition. London, U.K.: Oxford University Press, 1970, pp. 803-804.
17 Blom, E.: Zichy, Count. In: *Grove's Dictionary of Music and Musicians*. Fifth Ed. London, U.K.: Macmillan Press Ltd., 1975, Volume 9, p. 415.
18 Blom, E.: Bax. In: *Grove's Dictionary of Music and Musicians*. Fifth Ed. London, U.K.: Macmillan Press Ltd., 1975, Volume 1, p. 511.
19 Smith, C.: *Duet for Three Hands*. London, U.K.: Angus & Robertson, 1958.

ADDITIONAL SOURCES

Blom, E.: Bach, C.P.E. In: *Grove's Dictionary of Music and Musicians*. Fifth Ed. London, U.K.: Macmillan Press Ltd., 1975, Volume 1, p. 324.

Myers, R.H.: *Ravel – Life and Works*. London, U.K.: Gerald Duckworth & Co, Ltd., 1960, pp. 176-184.

Orenstein, A.: *Ravel – Man and Musician*. Columbia University Press, 1975, pp. 100-101.

Schonberg, H.C.: *The Great Pianists*. London, U.K.: Victor Gollancz, Ltd. 1969.

Sutherland, C.S.: *Arnold Bax*. London, U.K.: J.M. Dent and Sons Ltd., 1973, p. 103.

MUSICAL OPTIONS FOR UPPER-LIMB AMPUTEES

Joan E. Edelstein

The jolly god in triumph comes;
Sound the trumpets; beat the drums
John Dryden - *Alexander's Feast*

Musical participation is a delight which is accessible to all, including those with upper-limb amputation. Music opens vistas of self-expression and self-confidence while according players better coordination and overall physical improvement. Children and adults with amputation play many instruments, sometimes aided by simple modifications or variation from customary practice. Every category of instrument yields a multitude of options for the resourceful musician.

The discussion is intended, therefore to introduce the potential musician to the wealth of possibilities that await, together with likely means of realizing them. The suggestions should serve as a springboard for the music teacher to design performance methods and select literature ideal for the student with disability. The descriptions should also acquaint the clinician with the physical demands of standard and variant musicianship. Accordingly, numerous examples from each instrumental group are presented, with suggestions for performance by unilateral and bilateral amputees, below-elbow (BE) and above-elbow (AE), with and without prostheses.

WIND INSTRUMENTS

The unifying characteristic of all wind instruments, known as aerophones, is that sound is produced by air vibration, generally by blowing. Because the mouth of most upper-limb amputees is normal, many aerophones are playable. Brasses, notably the trumpet, horn, and trombone, are especially attractive. The trumpet is appealing for its association with marching bands, jazz, and even chamber music as newly popularized by crossover artists. Typical of special trumpeters is Tony who started playing when he was in the eighth grade so he could join the school band. Tony has left BE amputation, and began supporting the instrument with his amputation limb and fingering the valves with his sound right hand. The following year his terminal device was changed to a cable-controlled prosthetic hand, but he complained that the trumpet was unstable when he grasped with the hand, especially when marching. Last year he received a myoelectrically controlled hand which he uses to hold the instrument securely with the new hand's greater grasp force.

Valves on both the trumpet and cornet are designed for the right hand, but can be depressed with either hand by unilateral and bilateral BE and AE amputees. Prosthesis wearers secure the hook terminal device into a ring attached to the instrument. To prevent scratching the brass finish with the hook, the area adjacent to the ring should be covered with tape, or the hook can be shielded with rubber tubing or Plastisol coating. If the instrumentalist wears a hand terminal device, its glove affords protection of the shiny metal finish.

Without a prosthesis, the AE trumpeter stabilizes the instrument on a custom-made stand or wears an adapted neck strap. One bilateral BE musician sits so he can prop the bell on his leg; he pushes the valves with either or both amputation limbs, using both for valves 1 and 3 and either limb for any one or two adjacent valves. He plays fast enough to produce sixteenth notes.

More difficult to master, the French horn is another valved brass instrument suitable for amputees. Perseverance is rewarded, for reasonable competence places the hornist in great demand in band, orchestra, and chamber ensembles. Conventional performance assumes valve control with the left hand. Right BE amputees use the bare amputation limb in the bell, as done by professional hornists. A cupped cardboard or plastic fixture can be mounted in the bell to facilitate regulating the pitch and sound color with the bare limb. If the musician wears a prosthesis, a metal transposing mute can be helpful to close the bell so that pitch can be changed, as well as to produce a brassy sound. A left amputee can play in reverse, although balancing the horn will be cumbersome. For the beginner, the single horn in F is preferable, for it is lighter, easier to balance, and less expensive; however, the double (F and B flat) horn is customary for orchestral use. The thumb ordinarily presses the lever switching the instrument between the F and B flat horn, but any digit can serve. If the player develops a serious interest, an instrument with tubing coiled in reverse can be manufactured. Piston valves, rather than the customary rotary ones, are easier to manipulate with the right hand. The tenor and bass Wagner tubas are played in a fashion comparable to the horn.

Both the trumpet and horn are available in valveless, natural models, complementing the vogue for performing baroque music on authentic instruments. The player need only support the instrument with the terminal device or on the amputation limb or by a neck strap or floor stand, while producing harmonics and overtones by varying the position of the lips, teeth, tongue, and throat muscles to control the vibrating air column.

The baritone and alto horns, tuba, flugelhorn, mellophone, and valved trombone are traditionally right-handed instruments which can be played in reverse by unilateral right BE and AE amputees. Unilateral left amputees can manage the larger brasses, such as the euphonium, tuba, and, most conspicuous of all, the sousaphone. The marching tuba made of lightweight fiberglass is easier to stabilize than the conventional all-brass model. The more circular sousaphone is easier to transport in the marching band. The large brasses can be supported on the lap or on commercial chair stands. With a stand any unilateral left amputee, with or without prosthesis, can work the valves with the right hand.

Valveless brass instruments eliminate the problem of fingering. The slide trombone is particularly suited to unilateral amputees at any level who have 0 to 130 degrees elbow flexion on at least one side, as well as to bilateral BE amputees who wear prostheses. The unilateral amputee grasps the slide with the intact hand and supports the trombone with the terminal device. Right BE and AE amputees switch hands, holding with the right prosthesis and sliding with the intact left limb. Advanced bilateral BE trombonists, who support and slide with prostheses, can produce slide vibrato by subtle elbow motion, assuming that the prosthetic trimline does not impinge into the antecubital fossa. Repositioning the post or adding a commercial counterbalance to shift weight posteriorly will help the player support the weight of the instrument. Difficulty in assembling the trombone can be minimized by asking a friend to assist, or by removing prostheses to use the broader, more resilient surfaces of the bare amputation limbs, then redonning prostheses to play.

The bugle is another valveless instrument appropriate for amputees. It can be held and played by any unilateral amputee or a bilateral BE amputee with or without prostheses, or by a bilateral AE amputee wearing at least one prosthesis. The bugle is held by either the right or left limb, thus opening the fun of tooting in a fife-drum-bugle corps to limb-deficient children and adults.

While least appropriate for those with major amputations, aerophones such as the flute, piccolo, and those with reeds, including the oboe, English horn, clarinet, and saxophone are played by a few partial hand amputees. Loss of the right thumb, which ordinarily supports the instrument, but is not used for the keys is least difficult to accommodate. A hand opposition post plus a neck strap or the knees can support the instrument. A professional square dance caller with BE amputation holds a penny flute in his antecubital fossa and pipes merrily. Ingenious repairers have altered the key arrangements; for example, the keys of the saxophone can be placed in a double row near the top of the instrument for use by someone with a partial hand. The second row of keys is connected by rods to the appropriate positions. A similar adaptation can be made on the flute, particularly if it is the closed hole model. An active freelance oboist who sustained amputation of the little finger on the right hand has his woodwind keywork modified to alter the C/C sharp key and uses alternate fingering for other keys.

Soprano and alto recorders can be played by the musician missing one finger; however, both thumbs are needed for playing the conventional literature. A six-year-old bilateral BE amputee proudly displayed how he could play his plastic song flute. He supported it between his bare limbs and alternated two notes by covering and uncovering one hole, thus serving a quasi continuo function in his classroom ensemble. Another means of introducing instrumental music involved taping most of the holes in the recorder, so the one-handed musician can produce a limited scale by covering the remaining open holes as required.

On a simpler level the slide whistle, or Swannee whistle, can be played by unilateral amputees, and bilateral BE amputees wearing at least one prosthesis, for pitch is changed on this end-blown instrument by moving the slide in and out. One-handed pipes, sometimes called tabor pipes, popular in the eighteenth century when they were used with a drum, are another possibility.

Borrowing from the one-man band tradition, unilateral and bilateral amputees can purchase a rigid neck support for the harmonica to facilitate playing by moving the mouth along the instrument, rather than moving the instrument along the mouth. The holder must match the size of harmonica. The melodica is a type of harmonica often found in schools which suits all amputees. The player blows in one end of the melodica which is held by a friend or on a stand while depressing keys or buttons with the book, prosthetic hand, or bare limb. There is also a mouthpiece extension tube which allows the instrument to lie on the table. Guitar charts are readily adaptable to the soprano and alto melodica.

Unlike most other aerophones which are blown, accordions and similar instruments operate by manually controlled bellows which drive air over internal reeds. Individuals with one or more digits on both hands can play the concertina and melodeon. The strap at each end of the instrument may need alteration for extra stability. The ten buttons of the concertina are clustered for easier access, as compared to the linear array on the heavier, bulkier melodeon. The piano accordion ordinarily requires the right hand to press keys and the left, the buttons; however, the musician retaining at least one digit on the right hand can play in reverse, using the intact left hand on the keyboard and pressing buttons with the right finger(s). A shoulder strap suspends the accordion.

The organ is another aerophone which does not require the player to use the mouth. Keyboard adaptations, as subsequently described for the piano, apply to organ playing also. The pedalboard affords the organist a great selection of tones which augments notes played on the manuals.

PERCUSSION

Drums are the most familiar member of the membranophone category of instruments, encompassing those which sound when a stretched membrane, such as animal skin, is caused to vibrate, usually by being hit. Closely related in band and orchestral usage are the idiophones, instruments of sonorous material, such as the xylophone and cymbals. The numerous ways of sounding idiophones and membranophones makes them accessible to virtually all amputees. The instrumental category even includes tap shoes which are stamped against the floor by the dancer who creates a staccato pedal rhythm, and clog dancing as vigorously enjoyed in the Carolinas.

Michelle

Joan E. Edelstein

Michelle is an eighteen-year-old who was born with congenital absence of the left forearm and hand. She is facile enough with her prosthesis to play the snare drum, xylophone, and bells in her high school band, and is now majoring in music for special education. Another jazz and rock drummer wears bilateral shoulder disarticulation prostheses and creates complex rhythms by trunk and scapular motion. His special drumming limbs have rigid shoulder joints, elbow units locked at 90 degrees, and locked turntables. His drum sticks are notched to fit the hook tines; wide rubber tubing holds the sticks in place. In this manner he performs professionally on the trap set, snare and bass drums, timpani, gongs, chimes, and the rest of the battery.

Every subcategory of idiophones offers many rhythmic possibilities for amputees. Shaken instruments include rattles and colorful maracas. Their tapered handles may need padding with adhesive-backed polyethylene foam or enlargement with directly formed thermoplastic or simple covering with friction tape to make it easier to hold the instrument in the hook. The prosthetic glove generally provides sufficient friction and grasping surface, without any handle alteration. The novice will find the single maraca easy to play, and then can try a pair. As a prelude to using a standard maraca, the youngster can shake a soda can containing a few dry beans or buttons to learn simple rhythmic patterns. Jingle or sleigh bells are another simple shaken idiophone. They can be worn on wrist, upper arm, or ankle bracelets, or on a head band and shaken, or hung from a frame and struck.

Pitched percussion instruments are those which sound specific tones when struck, such as the xylophone, marimba, bell lyre, glockenspiel, and vibraphone. All are, or can be, mounted on stands, to eliminate the need for the player to support the instrument. Unilateral and bilateral BE and AE amputees are able to play them without changing the instrument. The xylophone, marimba, and vibraphone are customarily played while standing, necessitating good standing balance. In addition, the vibraphone player needs independent ankle action on one foot to depress the damper pedal. Beginners should try mallets of various weights, with wood, yarn wrapped and hard rubber heads. Standard xylophone bars are comparatively narrow, which requires facility to strike the correct one. Carl Orff diatonic and chromatic xylophones are designed for young players and are a good initiation for anyone whose grasp of the mallet or control is marginal, since individual bars may be removed for ease in learning. Advanced xylophonists use two mallets in the hand to create chords; the unilateral amputee can aspire to this technique. The bilateral amputee will find prostheses necessary to grasp the mallet; handle enlargement or grooving may be helpful.

Steel drums are other percussion possibilities which can be played with reasonable effect with either one or two beaters, with one or both held in the terminal device. The ping pong version of steel drum usually has 25 pitches for the melodic line, while the simpler bass pan has five, intended for accompaniment. A homemade version for the preschooler consists of an upended coffee can, in which the intact end is appropriately embossed.

Bell choirs where each participant rings hand bells of different pitches are open to any unilateral amputee. Advanced players hold two bells in one hand. One can hold a bell in the BE prosthesis, especially if the bell has a nonskid surface on an old fashioned wood handle, rather than the more common leather thong.

Chime bars are fascinating for new musicians, stimulating interest in melody and rhythm. Even a pair of bars, tuned to G and D, enable the percussionist to accompany "London Bridge," and three bars, E, D, and C, played by one child or a trio, form the accompaniment to "Three Blind Mice." Another primary idiophone is a tone block, whether smooth or corrugated. The unilateral amputee can grasp the tapered handle in the terminal device or support the block with the bare forearm. The bilateral amputee with prostheses will find the terminal device fits the handle easily, and the mallet or rhythm stick can be held in the other terminal device. Rectangular hollow hardwood blocks constructed with slits also resonate when tapped. Smaller blocks may have leather handles which can be suspended from furniture or held by another child, while the player strikes the block. The larger slitted blocks rest on the table or floor, making them ideal for those with multiple limb deficiencies, providing the mallet can be held in the antecubital fossa, terminal device, or mouth.

Claves, popular in Latin American music, are polished wood rods, 6 to 8 eight inches long. One is held in the cupped palm and struck by the other to produce a distinctive sound.

Simple rhythm sticks are sold in many sizes and colors, of different lengths and thicknesses. Some are hollow or grooved for unique sonic effects. The player grasps the stick in the terminal device and strikes or scrapes the other.

Cymbals and castanets sound when two similar parts are struck together. Wood or ivory hand castanets are held within the fingers and palm, ideal for the unilateral amputee. Tinkling metal finger cymbals are also held in the hand; the amputee can manage them easier than castanets because each cymbal has a strap which can be adapted to the contour of the hand. The attention commanded by crash cymbal in a marching band can be had by the unilateral BE amputee who has one cymbal secured to the prosthesis. For stationary use, single and double "hi-hat" cymbals on floor stands solve the problem of instrument support.

Friction instruments are sounded by rubbing. Glasses filled with various amounts of liquid and rubbed with a moistened finger or tapped or blown across the rim are a classic physics demonstration. Benjamin Franklin's "armonica", a graduated series of glass bowls just touching a water trough, can be played by a unilateral amputee with good dexterity in the sound hand. On a simpler level, primary graders like sand blocks for their swishing sound. They are made of wood blocks covered with fine grain sandpaper, with a handle which can be modified to fit the terminal device.

Scraped instruments have a notched or ridged surface against which a stick is drawn for a tapping effect. The washboard, a staple of country and western bands, need only be secured by the terminal device or bare forearm, while the player scrapes the fingers fitted with metal thimbles, or the terminal device across the surface, or uses a metal rod for the same purpose.

Plucked idiophones have flexible tongues attached to a frame or resonating chamber. Plucking the tongue produces sound. The dulcet African kalimba or sansa is fairly easy to find in novelty and music shops and lends itself to one-handed playing.

Most constituents of the orchestra battery can be handled by unilateral amputees. Tubular bells hanging in a frame are struck by mallets held in one or two terminal devices. Bronze tam-tams or gongs need only a well timed blow from a large mallet. Cymbals are sometimes brushed with a stick or wire brush which can be grasped in the terminal device; the cymbals are supported on stands. The triangle may be suspended from the stand, enabling a one-handed player to tremolo readily; the bilateral amputee would need to have the handle of the beater enlarged for secure grasp in the terminal device.

The drumhead is the distinguishing characteristic of membranophones which, like idiophones, usually must be hit to produce music. The head vibrates when beaten with one or both hands, wood sticks, padded beaters, or wire brushes, affording many choices for the musician. Various effects are achieved by striking or slapping the rim or sides of the drum. The pedal operated bass drum and "hi-hat" cymbals pose no problem for the seated amputee assuming good trunk balance and foot control. When marching, the drummer holds the sticks in the terminal device(s), getting quite a bang! A double headed drum stick enables the unilateral bass drummer to play while marching. For band participation, the prosthetic harness may need tightening. Some timpani also have a foot pedal to change pitch by adjusting tension of the drumhead; the player must be able to stand and move one foot independently.

The tambourine is a bright instrument for the unilateral amputee who can shake it to make the metal jingles ring, and slap the drumhead. It is a delightful point of emphasis for dancing, providing another physical experience for the physically challenged individual. Tambourines differ in frame dimension, so one should be selected to fit the player's hands. Some tambourines have a handle, making them easy to hold in the terminal device.

Technically in the same instrument family as drums, the kazoo is a musical toy which can be played by anyone with natural or prosthetic prehension sufficient to hold it to the mouth.

STRINGED INSTRUMENTS

Danny

Danny is a bank teller by day and a freelance professional guitarist evenings and weekends, with steady bookings at local night clubs. He has a congenital anomaly of the right forearm which terminates in a small nubbin just large enough for him to hold the pick. The guitar is the most popular representative of the chordophone family, comprised of instruments in which string vibration makes the sound. Alternate ways of holding the pick include using the terminal device, perhaps with an extra rubber band for greater grasp force in a voluntary-opening hook, or securing the pick to a snug bracelet on the forearm. The large felt pick has greater surface and provides more friction than smooth plastic models; for those with one or more digits, finger picks are appropriate. Above-elbow guitarists substitute shoulder motion for the minimum elbow and forearm action needed to move the pick. Left amputees simply reverse the strings and bridge, and for the steel-stringed guitar, the pick guard also. Commercial left hand guitars are another option, but are more expensive. Electric guitars generally have the controls and treble and bass pickup on the right side; for the left handed model, these are repositioned to the opposite side. The conventional strap aids in supporting the guitar as does the footrest ordinarily used on the right.

Other plucked and strummed chordophones adaptable for amputees are the banjo and ukulele, as well as the renaissance lute, mandolin, Greek bouzouki, Middle Eastern ud, Indian sitar, Russian balalaika, and Japanese samisen. A neck strap will keep most of these fretted instruments in place, and all can be reverse strung for left amputees. A cigar box ukulele is an economical introduction to the preschooler. Simply cut a 3 inch diameter hole in the lid and seal the box; drive three or four sets of nails at each end of the lid and stretch rubber bands longitudinally on the nails.

Performance on unfretted instruments, such as the violin and viola, is attainable if the player's committment to diligent practice is complemented by careful instrument selection and perhaps simple adaptations. The unilateral BE amputee holds the bow in the terminal device, possibly aided by modification of the stick, or can use a custom made bow holder which allows the bow to swivel. The potential violinist must have an elbow flexion range of 10 to 90 degrees on the bow arm and 70 to 90 degrees on the fingering side. Forearm pronation and supination are highly desirable to approximate standard bowing technique. Consequently, an individual with short BE or AE amputation would not be likely to tolerate the shoulder abduction and internal rotation needed to support the bow. A professional violinist who sustained right arm amputation developed another solution to the bow problem. He attached his bow to a chair and leaned his violin against the chair, moving the instrument, rather than the bow. The larger viola requires an elbow range of 20 to 90 degrees on the bow arm and 40 to 90 degrees on the fingering side. Supporting the instrument is aided by tightening the prosthetic harness. The violoncello and double bass are easier to stabilize on the floor, and the bow strokes are broader. The same type of bow holder is suitable for them.

Pizzicato is performed by the intact hand plucking near the pegs, rather than by the bridge. The right amputee can practice the standard Paganini exercises devised to strengthen the left hand.

For the left BE amputee, the violin and viola are reversed; the chin rest, bridge, strings, and possibly the fingerboard are readily adjusted to enable fingering with the intact right hand. Comparable reversals are accomplished with the cello and bass. The left amputee who achieves sufficient proficiency to play in an orchestra should be seated at an individual stand to avoid interfering with another section member bowing in the conventional direction.

Another group of chordophones suitable for amputees includes the zither, which has strings across the length of a resonating body. The modern concert zither has melody strings over a fretted fingerboard which is ordinarily played with the left hand; however, some zitherists press the strings with the bare amputation limb, one finger, or a rubber-tipped dowel, while strumming with the intact hand, or with a plectrum secured to the prosthesis or the forearm. The soprano and alto chordal dulcimer are similar to the zither; their twelve strings are grouped in four sets of three, each sounding a complete chord. The four stringed bass dulcimer can be played with one hand if the instrument is placed on a table. The psaltery and autoharp are other examples of the zither principle. They are designed to be plucked with the fingers or a plectrum fitted to the prosthesis, strapped to the forearm, or incorporated in a mouthstick for the bilateral amputee. The autoharp is an excellent instrument for musical debutantes who can control its dampers easily. The dampers prevent vibration of all strings except those needed for the desired chord, and are regulated by buttons which can be depressed by the tip of the unopened hook, the middle finger of the prosthetic hand, or the end of the bare amputation limb. The hand strums. The resulting chords are fine accompaniment to singing. Although autoharps are available in six and nine chord version, the twelve chord model is more rewarding. Initially one child can press the chord button while another strums. Guitar chords in sheet music are entirely applicable for the autoharp. Some songs, such as "Clementine," require only two chords, and many can be played with just three chords. The portability of the autoharp makes it useable by those in wheelchairs or in bed.

The dulcimer is another musical option for amputees, for the hammers needed to strike the strings can be secured in the terminal device(s). Felt-headed wooden beaters can be notched to improve grasp by the prosthetic hook.

Joan E. Edelstein

The piano is the most versatile of all chordophones. Other keyboard instruments, such as the organ, harpsichord, and clavichord, are also well within reach of individuals with upper-limb disorder. Unilateral amputees should be inspired by Paul Wittgenstein, the concert artist who sustained traumatic right amputation during World War I. Soon after his injury, he discovered left hand works by Haydn and Godowsky's arrangement of nineteen Chopin études. He arranged classical and romantic pieces and composed a school for the left hand. He later commissioned Ravel, Prokofiev, Strauss, Hindemith, and Britten to create literature which is still programmed in concert halls. More recently, the virtuoso Gary Graffman, coping with disuse atrophy of the intrinsic muscles in his right hand attributed to overuse of the long finger, revived Wittgenstein's literature.

On a basic level, elementary piano pieces for either hand are available from many music publishers and resourceful teachers can arrange many selections for satisfying unimanual execution. Duets and trios lend themselves to being played by two or three pianists, each using one hand. Some guitar and harp music can be played by one hand effectively. Compositions for the melodica are ideal for beginners. The Disabled Living Foundation, 380/384 Harrow Road, London W9 2HU, England, has a Music Advisory Service and publishes a list of music for one handed pianists, graded according to difficulty and classified as to whether for the left or right hand. For example, Bach's difficult "Chaconne in d minor" arranged by Brahms suits either hand. Kohler's moderately difficult "School of the Left Hand," opus 302, and Reinecke's "Sonata for the Left Hand" are classics. Wittgenstein's exercises and twenty-seven very difficult extracts from classical pieces can be executed by either hand.

The keyboard can be struck in various ways. It is very helpful for the beginner to feel the keys when playing, gaining sensory feedback and freedom of movement. A right BE amputee uses the bare limb to strike one key while the thumb of the intact left hand adds a second treble note, and the other left fingers play the bass line. The elbow may be used to strike keys; however, the wide elbow makes accurate playing difficult. White keys are depressed on the edge. Raised black keys can be managed, although G# is most difficult because of F# and A# on either side. Pieces in the keys of C, G, and F are easiest, for they use the fewest black keys. Another advantage of playing with the bare limb is that sightreading is easier because the pianist will not have to look at the keys frequently and risk losing the place in the score. Compositions with large intervals are more difficult because of the need to gauge large distances between keys. Thus the novice should have pieces with notes close together, to minimize glancing at the keyboard. One problem with performance techniques that overstretch or otherwise overuse the remaining fingers is that structural changes may develop. Swelling and tenderness indicate that practice time must be decreased and disciplined with regular breaks. Keyboard technique may also need revision.

If the pianist prefers to wear unilateral or bilateral prostheses, the medial finger of the hook can be shielded with a rubber arrowhead, ordinarily used for small game hunting. The arrowhead needs to be ground slightly to narrow its width to conform to the key. The lyre-shaped hook, manufactured only in adult size, can be blocked open to permit playing thirds, assuming both hook fingers are rubber-protected. Canted hooks are unsatisfactory for two note chords because the fingers do not lie on the same plane. Several custom made terminal devices have been invented to replace conventional models. One has two pieces of aluminum tubing affixed to the stud of a hook. The fingers are curved to span an octave when the hook is opened fully. The metal is weighted with lead and covered with rubber or resilient plastic to protect the keys. Another alternate terminal device is computerized for piano playing.

The middle finger of the prosthetic hand can be covered with a rubber bookkeeper's finger cot elongated with a 1/2 inch heavy rubber cylinder inside the cot to extend the finger enough for accurate, one-fingered, performance.

Above-elbow amputees lock the prosthetic elbow unit at 90 degrees flexion and control the keyboard action by shoulder motion.

Rubber-tipped dowels held in the axillae or by the rudimentary hands of those with longitudinal deficiency, such as phocomelia, or strapped to the upper arm, are other options. Some children with phocomelia play by sitting on a low stool so they can extend their small limbs to reach the keyboard with bare fingers. A few individuals use a mouthstick to interact with the keys.

Playing single notes makes appealing music because staccato production is achieved very well, and legato passages can be enhanced by the damper pedal. The piano action should be regulated to respond to the lighter touch afforded by the adapted striking methods. Another alteration of the piano designed to aid the player with upper-limb amputation is a commercial pedal actuator mechanism.

MECHANICAL AND ELECTRICAL INSTRUMENTS

Electronic keyboard instruments are economical options. The left amputee has little difficulty, for chord and style buttons are usually on the left side, allowing the right hand to play the keyboard. The right amputee plays by crossing hands. The compactness of these keyboards makes them practical for use on a wheelchair lapboard or in bed, and the panorama of sonic effects should satisfy musicians of every school. Exponents of the avant garde can try a hand at synthesizers, sold in a vast range of sizes and complexity, and amenable to a rapid unimanual control.

Old-fashioned entries to musicianship are provided by player and reproducing pianos. The fun of playing commercial piano rolls is open to unilateral amputees and bilateral amputees who wear at least one prosthesis. With minimal effort, the operator can be dazzled by performances of legendary artists emanating from the reproducer. The barrel organ, managed by turning a single crank, employs a surface similar to the piano roll whose perforations correspond to notes. The

Joan E. Edelstein

simple carillon is another living tradition. The unilateral amputee should have no difficulty pulling on the ropes attached to the bell clappers.

CODA

With the myriad of instrumental possibilities, the prospective player may correctly wonder, "Which one for me?" No easy answer follows, but, by answering a series of questions, the musician should be able to find the best prospects. Foremost, one must be attracted to the instrument – its timbre, musical style, general appearance, and perhaps concert artists or friends who serve as role models. An electric guitar holds more appeal for a rock devotee than does a violin; a small apartment may not accommodate a vibraphone.

Second, one should consider the upper-limb excursion required to maneuver across a keyboard, or toward and away from the torso with a bow or slide. Those who have difficulty standing should confine the search to instruments which can be played while seated; pedal operation narrows the field further. Playing an instrument poses additional physical challenges. How will the musician assemble and tune it? While the piano is immediately playable, most other instruments have to be removed from a case, pieces fitted together accurately, and delicate tuning adjustments made. The music teacher or family member will assist the neophyte, but it is preferable for the musician to opt for an instrument which promises independence, particularly if one plans to perform away from home or school. Some instruments require periodic attention during the course of playing; many wind instruments need occasional swabbing or release of a water key, and for the strings, bows entail rosining and tension adjustments. In addition to supporting the instrument, the self-sufficient musician must be able to manage the weight and bulk of the carrying case.

Other physical attributes of the musician bear scrutiny. Aural acuity is important for most string and wind instruments; one who cannot discriminate pitches accurately should choose an instrument, such as drums or piano, where this faculty is less critical. Respiratory status is a cardinal consideration for the wind player, as is the contour of the mouth and other oral structures.

Financial considerations cannot be ignored, including the price of a new, used, or borrowed instrument, the cost of any adaptations, and the teacher's fee computed in terms of the amount of study needed to gain satisfying proficiency. No one who begins lessons can predict the level of artistry which will be attained. The initial goal for all musicians, with or without upper-limb disability, should be personal enjoyment, not a professional career.

Alternatives to instrumental performance abound. A brilliant example was set by Schumann who injured the middle and ring fingers of his right hand with a mechanical finger strengthener he invented. He turned from concertizing to enriching posterity with his compositional genius. Computer programs for composition, transcription, and arrangement are on the market, and are well suited to anyone who has manual limitations. On another contemporary note, the pianistic artistry of Leon Fleisher hampered by carpal tunnel syndrome has transformed into perceptive conducting. Of course, manual dexterity is not a prerequisite for singing, in which amputees find and give great pleasure vocalizing in popular and classical ensembles and as professional and amateur soloists. Dancing is yet another route to musical involvement.

Harmony among imaginative music instructors, thoughtful clinical personnel, and eager children and adults with upper-limb disorders can create melodious pleasure. Conducting the movement toward greater musicality are the model program coordinated at Goldwater Memorial Hospital in collaboration with New York University, which introduces musical experience to chronic care patients, and the premier Programs for the Handicapped at Settlement Music School in

Philadelphia. They demonstrate that the number and character of one's limbs are not the sole criteria for engaging in the joy of musical participation.

If music be the food of love, play on
- William Shakespeare, *Twelfth Night*, Act 1, Scene i (1599)

BIBLIOGRAPHY

Alvin, J.: *Music for the Handicapped Child*. Second Edition. London, U.K.: Oxford University Press, 1965.

Association for Children with Artificial Arms: Fact Sheet 4: Sport/Leisure. Essex, U.K.: The Association for Children with Artifical Arms, undated.

Bailey, P.: *They Can Make Music*. New York: Oxford University Press, 1973.

Baines, A.: *Brass Instruments: Their History and Development*. New York: Charles Scribner's Sons, 1976.

Ballantyne, J.: Schumann's hand injury. *Brit Med J*, 1978, **1**, p. 1142.

Chadwick, D., Clark, C.: *Clinically Adapted Instruments for the Multiply Handicapped*. St. Louis, MO: MMB Music, Inc., 1980.

Coleman, J.L., Schoepfle, I.L., Templeton, V.: *Music for Exceptional Children*. Evanston, IL: Summy-Birchard Company, 1964.

Diagram Group: *Musical Instruments of the World*. New York: Bantam Books, Inc., 1976.

Dunning, J.: When a pianist's fingers fail to obey. *New York Times*, June 13, 1981.

Elliott, B.: *Guide to the Selection of Musical Instruments with Respect to Physical Ability and Disability*. Philadelphia: Moss Rehabilitation Hospital, 1982.

Erickson, L.: Keyboard fun for children with osteogenesis imperfecta and other physical limitations. *Inter-Clinic Inform Bull*, 1973, **12**, pp. 9-16.

Erickson, L.: Never say 'you can't do that' to an amputee! *Inter-Clinic Inform Bull*, 1974, **13**, pp. 13-14.

Erickson, L.: Piano playing as a hobby for children with problem hands. *Inter-Clinic Inform Bull*, 1972, **11**, pp. 6-17.

Erickson, L.: Unpublished manuscript.

Fry, H.J.H.: The physical injury (overuse) due to music making. *MEH Bull*, 1985, **1**, pp. 22-29.

Graffham, G.: Doctor, can you lend me an ear? *Med Problems of Performing Artists*, 1986, **1**, pp. 3-6.

Henson, R.A., Urlich, H.: Schumann's hand injury. *Brit Med J*, 1978, **1**, pp. 900-903.

Kennard, D.J.: *Access to Music for the Physically Handicapped Schoolchild and School Leaver*. London, U.K.: Disabled Living Foundation, 1977.

Kral, C.: Musical instruments for upper-limb amputees. *Inter-Clinic Inform Bull*, 1972, **12**, pp. 13-26.

Lederman, R.H., Calabrese, L.H.: Overuse syndromes in instrumentalists. *Med Problems of Performing Artists*, 1986, **1**, pp. 7-11.

Lee. M.H.M.: Music therapy for rehabilitation of the severely disabled: A model of excellence. *MEH Bull*, 1985, **1**, pp. 44-49.

Mailhot, A.: Musical instruments for upper-limb amputees. *Inter-Clinic Inform Bull*, 1974, **13**, pp. 9-15.

Nordoff, P., Robbins, C.: *Music Therapy in Special Education*. Second Edition. St. Louis, MO: MMB Music, Inc., 1985.

Reichard, C.L.: Blackburn D.B., *Music Based Instruction for the Exceptional Child*. New York: Love Publishing Company, 1973.

Riccardi, J., Vella, A.: *Elementary Piano for One Hand*. Boston, MA: Boston Music Company, undated.

Smithers, D., Wogram, K., Bowsher, J.: Playing the Baroque trumpet. *Scientific American,* 1986, **254**, pp. 108-115.

Timbelston, J.: Student project wins national design award. *Syracuse University News,* September 15, 1985.

University of California at Los Angeles: *Musical Instruments for the Limb-Deficient Child.* Motion picture, 1977.

ACKNOWLEDGEMENTS

Howard Erickson, Bruce Natalie, Gladys Thomas, and Ann Billing provided personal insights, and Melissa Coren, of the Sylvan Wind Ensemble, New York hornist, and Madeline Frand of the Chamber Music Society shared their professional expertise for this chapter.

MUSIC THERAPY USING COMPUTER MUSIC TECHNOLOGY

Joseph C. Nagler
Mathew H.M. Lee

INTRODUCTION

Music therapy is a process oriented modality of treatment that can provide a powerful means of self-expression.[1][2] Music as a healing art is a way for people to communicate with one another. In a therapeutic relationship, the patient and therapist are involved in an evolving continuum that helps to foster creativity and self-actualization through their collaborative creative input.[3] Many people display pronounced difficulty in expressing their emotions through words, creating music allows a more direct, and at times, a simpler means of self expression.[4]

The music therapy process in relation to the traditional verbal psycho-therapeutic model, reflects an outgrowth of the former from the latter.[5] In scrutinizing this relationship several parallels can be drawn and used to formulate a working model of treatment.[6] Historically, music therapy has employed traditional methodology and instrumentation to aid the client in achieving his/ her inherent musical potential.[7] The methods described in this chapter are a clear departure from the traditional instrumentation that has been utilized, while still maintaining and adapting the traditional methodology.

The therapeutic framework employed was derived from the humanistic school of psychology. Incorporating the music therapy methodologies of Nordoff and Robbins,[8] as developed by Hesser,[9] with the psychotherapy theories of Maslow[10] and Rogers,[11] a theoretical model was developed. This model postulates that all persons contain the inherent human potential towards positive growth and self-actualization. They can achieve this potential with therapeutic intervention. As Bugental[12] set forth in his five postulates of humanistic psychology, the potential of man is self-initiated and capable of change.

In our working model, the patient is guided through a treatment process that is directed and dictated by the patient's needs. The therapist develops a series of goals to help the patient successfully negotiate the obstacles that are facing him/her. The patient directs the course of events and the therapist is present in a supportive, non- directive manner. The therapist seeks to provide the patient with successful experiences throughout the therapeutic process. A successful experience can be defined as one in which the patient has been allowed ample and complete opportunity for self expression. Quantitative matters such as how many compositions are created or how "good " the music are not of importance.

What is of importance is the quality of the experience that the patient receives from his/ her involvement and interactions with the therapy and therapist. Client centered therapies are part of the humanistic therapeutic model.[13] In this model, the patient's human potential is the prime motivating force towards change. The therapist is working under the supposition that all people, regardless of physical or mental infirmities, are motivated towards achieving their true human potential and therefore self-actualization. The therapist's role is to provide the opportunity to the patient to attempt to achieve this potential.

Yet, the music therapy process can be altered by the presence of a physical disability or by a person who can not express him/herself adequately on a traditional musical instrument. This can become problematic for the therapist, limiting both the therapist's and the patient's creative repertoire. A therapist can offer the patient hand over hand assistance in manipulating the mechanics of a musical instrument, but does this with some compromise to the music making process. While there are many available methods of music making that are possible with assistance,[14] until recent developments, there were very few options available that allowed independent functioning by the handicapped person.

Traditionally, music therapists have altered musical instruments to meet the needs of the patient. By adapting the instrument to help compensate for the patient's lack of ability, the therapist has provided the patient an opportunity to create music. Unfortunately, these devices have been at best, compromises. The machines that have been created have been helpful in increasing the the range and depth of a musical interactions, but they lack many of the core elements that are necessary to create music.

To understand this issue, it is paramount to look at the pre-requisite skills that are necessary to create music. It is important to note at this juncture that our discussion removes the element of aesthetics that are normally associated with music. While aesthetics are an integral element of the music making process, it will serve our discussion better to eliminate qualitative judgements when discussing the physical creation of music. Therefore, at this point and time, we are only concerning ourselves with the phenomenon of the creation of sounds and silences moving through space and time at varying levels of loudness. If we accept this clinical definition of music, it is easier to understand the mechanics of what is involved with creating music.

The creation of music involves many activities occurring sequentially and at times, simultaneously. The person creating must decide on the musical information to convey, act on that impulse, transform that impulse into muscular energy and have his/her body engage in some activity that will cause a disturbance in the air surrounding the body. It is the disturbance of the air that will cause sound to emanate and express the musical intent of the person. Many devices are available to assist the person in the creation of sound, from the apparent simpleness of a drum to the complexities of a piano. What separates the different types of instruments is the range of sonic timbres that they have available and the complexity of the mechanical devices employed in creating sound.

COMPUTER MUSIC TECHNOLOGY

The introduction of computer music technology to the music therapy process is an exciting application of using computers in the therapeutic process. What at first glance may seem like an unnatural pairing of therapy and science is actually a quite complementary and compelling means of reaching a patient in the therapeutic process. A common perception of this application of technology is that it can be technocratic and devoid of the "warmth "of traditional instruments. It is the authors' experience that this is not a true or valid perception. As will be demonstrated later in the case study, a very satisfactory and humanistic experience can be achieved creating music with computer music technology.

The use of computer music technology in the music therapy process arose out of several needs that were facing clinicians at the time of the method's inception. First and foremost was the need to provide the patient with maximum opportunity to express him/herself musically: that is, without limitations of a handicapping condition or a "lack" of musical ability. Just as an "able bodied" person can create music freely and expressively by striking a drum, so too should a person with diminished physical capacities or an inability to express him/herself in a conventional manner be able to convey his/her musical intentions through interactions on an instrument.

The evolution of this machinery for therapy use has kept pace with the state of the art of the music technology. Within a time span of seven years, music technology for the general public has developed from a small group of hobbyists to one of the more dominant means of people creating music, both professionally and for personal enjoyment. The instruments created in this time frame have decreased in size and price so that they are accessible to many people who were excluded only a few years ago.

Within this same time period, the use of music technology for the music therapy process has developed from a series of case studies to a full course of study and treatment at one center. This chapter will discuss the evolution of this process, illustrate the process through a case study, and discuss the technical applications of system design and development.

MUSIC THERAPY AND TECHNOLOGY

Music therapy using computer music technology is a relatively new concept. The proliferation of personal computers and music technology that have become readily available to the general public has created a new means of creating music. Many institutions are already employing some of this technology in their programs. There have been a limited number of serious scientific inquires into how this technology can best be utilized. Recent studies conducted at Goldwater Memorial Hospital[15] have found this form of therapy to be beneficial in the music therapy process of a post-viral encephalitic musician. They have also found this technology to be useful in the treatment of post head trauma and aphasic patients.

In both studies the computer music system was designed to augment or supplant the physical deficits exhibited by the subjects. The goal areas were different for each patient, but there was the similar overall goal of allowing the patient the opportunity to independently create music without assistance. Prior to the implementation of these systems, this would not have been a realistic goal.

Additional studies have been conducted at Harvard's "Project Zero" exploring the role of computer technology in the development of musical skills in untrained children and adults. They have found, in part, that :

> An analysis of children's and adult novices' compositions provides powerful evidence of musical development without musical training... More surprisingly, on relatively simple composition tasks, there appears to be little difference between the products of trained conservatory students and adult novices when using the computer to compose.[16]

The technology employed in these studies is what is referred to as personal computer technology. Machines that were designed for business and home users are now being adapted for clinicians. This has not been an easy transition. The problems that have arisen with the technology are many. This has been documented recently as:

> The potential of the computer must always be described in light of its liabilities as well as its assets. For many tasks, computers are still clumsy, slow and even "stupid." For other tasks they are quite efficient... The computer can provide an entry into higher levels of artistic problem solving, especially for beginners.[17]

A significant technological development that has been pivotal in adapting this technology for music therapy use is the advent of the Musical Instrument Digital Interface (MIDI). MIDI has created a revolution in the way people are conceiving, creating and recording music. It is now possible for one person, working on his own, to create an entire finished piece of music using many different instruments, sounds and musical ideas. This is accomplished through the use of MIDI technology and computers. A MIDI system is one that allows Sequencers (devices that arrange musical events in space and time and different tempos and dynamic ranges), Synthesizers (devices that create music electronically) Samplers (devices that take the equivalent of an " audio snapshot" of a sound and then can play the sound back) and Signal processing (devices that alter the sound in space and time) to be linked together through a central computer.

MIDI is a system of transferring musical data from one point to another. It is a one way form of sending musical data to units that are capable of receiving the information. There are sixteen possible channels to transmit this data in four different modes. It is important to note that this system transfers only MIDI data; the audio output of these devices is a separate and distinct matter that requires amplification and speakers to be heard.

MIDI technology can be used to create a system for use in music therapy. When there is a physical handicapping condition, there are a myriad of different methods through which a disabled person can gain access to the control of a computer.[18] The method employed is commensurate with, and in direct response to the severity of the handicapping condition. That is, a patient with a limited range of motion will employ a method that is indigenous to his/her particular situation. The method utilized as a means of input into the computer needs to exploit all of the available resources of the person. The data input controls range from simple modifications of the computer[19] to complete alternate input systems.[20] There are many different means of interfacing the user with the computer. They range from simple adaptations of switches that control one or two functions of the computer, to complete systems that emulate the computers data entry system. These systems can use input from user created motion, the bio-electrical signals of the body, infra red scanning systems and spoken commands of the human voice. New and experimental methods that are currently being explored by the authors include the Biomuse[21] and the development of a voice controlled system of data input that will recognize the spoken words of the person using the system for commands.[22]

For the patient with a wider range of physical capabilities, there are many alternate musical instruments that negate some of mechanical difficulties found in traditional musical instruments. Yet for all of the many new and exciting opportunities offered to the patient by alternate instruments, creating music with them can be cumbersome and intimidating. Therefore, it is paramount for the therapist to allow this technology to remain as transparent as possible. That is, it can not be any more present in the process than any traditional instrument. If the means of entering the musical information are too demanding or are foreign to the naturalness of the music making process, the therapeutic goals will be compromised.

It is also important to allow the technology to diminish the learning curve involved in creating music. To create music in a traditional fashion requires that the person undergo a course of study in technique, theory and repertoire. Since our music is for therapeutic use, the main focus is on the music's ability to convey the thoughts and emotions of those involved in its creation. Both of these criteria can be accomplished in many different ways.

The computer music technology can be used to take on many of the more technical and physically demanding tasks involved in creating music or, the technology can be used to create a new class of instruments that will, unlike any of their traditional counter parts, be able to accommodate the users needs instead of the converse.

There are many commercially available alternate MIDI controllers that will suit this purpose. These devices allow MIDI data input by such diverse means as drum pads, to alternate systems that allow input from simple motions. As technology develops there will be many new and productive means of creating music through technology.

MUSIC THERAPY WITH COMPUTERS

When the power of music therapy is combined with the independent functioning potential of computer music technology, a new horizon for music making was created for a disabled person. The authors conducted a research project to explore the uses of computer music technology with a severely physically disabled person. The goal of the research project was to examine the practicality and effectiveness of the use of computer music technology for a severely physically handicapped person to create music. This study was undertaken as two complete and separate projects. The project that is first described took place in 1983. The second took place in 1986. The case study is presented in a descriptive narrative fashion to convey the development of the music therapy process in its entirety.

FIRST PROJECT:

This project began in early 1983. It was completed without the benefit of MIDI technology. Although MIDI had been introduced in late 1982, it was not until mid 1984 that many of the manufacturers of musical equipment began to explore its depth and power. Prior to 1984 the equipment was not suitable for this project. The patient, at the time of the study, was a twenty-seven year old, male. He was a professional musician prior to his illness. He had been hospitalized since the onset of viral encephalitis, which had left him a spastic quadriplegic with dysphagia, anarthria and pseudo-bulbar palsy. Before his illness, the patient, Mr. B., enjoyed the ability to play several instruments, although he lacked formal training in all areas of music. The instrument on which Mr. B. was most competent, is the guitar.

Due to the severity of his handicapping condition, the reintroduction of the guitar to Mr. B.'s music making process was not an alternative. He lacked the ability to hold, strum, or finger chord groupings on the fret board. Attempts at modifying a guitar to minimize the need for physical involvement and dexterity were not successful. These measures proved to be inadequate; attempts were viewed by Mr. B. as an unsatisfactory alternative to the instrument he had enjoyed playing. Mr. B. displayed a high level of resistance to interacting with the modified guitar.

Other conventional music therapy techniques such as group improvisation sessions, song writing workshops, and playing a keyboard with a stick controlled by his head movement had proven to be successful. Still, Mr. B. expressed a desire to create music without assistance, and on a level that he had been accustomed to as a professional musician. Mr. B. was aware of the potential uses of the available current technology, and was outfitted with a communications system that enabled him to communicate effectively and efficiently. The system, the Express-3 communications device, is manufactured by Prentkie Rhomich. This system allows the user to synthesize speech, print messages, and control a computer through the serial interface to the computer.

The introduction of a computer based speech system into his daily routine provided Mr. B. new opportunities of interaction with the world. It is through the use of this system that he was able to find a modality and means to interact with his therapists and his peers. His language skills remained undiminished from his illness, yet as evidenced by the ramifications of dysphagia, Mr. B.'s ability to produce speech was totally destroyed. There were no other possible alternatives for him to utilize for communication. Sign language, gesturing, and pointing were not possible due to his severe physical disability. The only movement possible for communication was his head motion, which at the time, was awkward and unrefined.

It became paramount to the speech therapists to enable the patient to secure the basic prerequisite skills that communication would require. After extensive research, it was decided that a system that would allow input in a random, scanning method would best serve the patient's

Joseph C. Nagler, Mathew H. Lee

needs. There is no need for the patient to physically manipulate the parameters of the unit. Instead, the device worn on the patient's forehead, and is self-manipulated through specific head movements. The device is pointed towards a receiving cell that allows the signal to be processed by the micro-processor which is housed within the unit. As shown in Figure 1, Mr. B. sat in his wheelchair with the Viewpoint Optical Indicator (VOI), which scans the receiving cells on the Express-3 unit.

Mr. B. developed a relationship with this system that is unique to his disabling condition. The system was able to complement the physical deficits that had previously isolated the patient. A strong bond formed between patient and machine. As evidenced in the following example of the patient's writing, the machine, labeled Mr. X. by the patient, has taken on its own identity, personality, and history.

" I am Mr. X. from a place called Ektnerp Hcimohr Ynapmoc. I am being operated by my best friend, Mr. B. We welcome you, even though I am doing all the talking. Mr. B. cannot speak and I can not hear. So he asked me to be his mental interpreter. We function as a team."[23]

This system enabled the patient to engage in many activities that were not previously available to him. As shown in the next example, Mr. B. has been able to effectively state his philosophy towards his condition through his creative writing workshop.

"No More, No More"

No more walk, no more talk – No more play everyday – No more kiss (smack!) like this – No more snugs and hugs – No more smoke without getting choke – No more sip, but that's hip – No more music to play you know, or even on a stage at a show – No more knife and fork in hand, I can understand. . . No more of the joyed life I left behind – No more, no more. . . No more drives in the car, going near and far – No more IRT, BMT or even IND – No more Eastern uh, huh! Or Delta – No more highrollers to skate with my date – No more of the joyed life I left behind, but I don't mind – It's not easy but I have "me"!. . . [24]

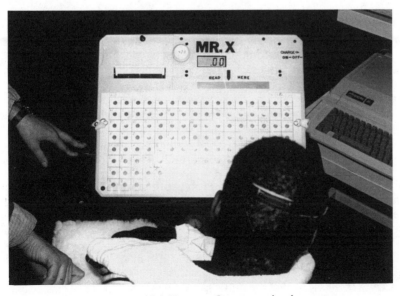

Figure 1. Mr. B. with Express-3 communications system

Treatment plans were formulated through a trans-disciplinary team of therapists. Criteria for assessing the areas to be addressed were set by analyses of Mr. B.'s current level of functioning, with consideration to his current psychosocial level.[25]

Discussion of the communication system's capability and capacity to interface with, and create a computer musical system, ensued. After analysis of the possibilities, it was decided at first, to utilize a system consisting of an Apple IIe computer, the Mountain Computer Music System, The Express-3, Music Theory Fundamental Software by MECC, Apple Keyboard Interface for the Express-3, Viewpoint Optical Indicator, and amplification of Mountain Computer Music System.

Procedure

The research project consisted of 20 ninety minute sessions with Mr. B. and the therapist involved in a direct, interactive relationship. The stages consisted of six sessions for Stage 1, and seven sessions each for both Stages 2 and 3. Both parties had access to the computer at any given time. Mr. B. interfaced with the computer through the serial output of the Express-3 to the Apple Keyboard Interface, which resided in expansion slot #3 of the computer. Residing in expansion slots #4 and #5 were the Mountain Computer Music System's main control boards. Both therapist and Mr. B. controlled data to the unit through commands which controlled the software.

The project underwent three stages of exploration. The stages were:

(1) music theory,
(2) controlling the computer music system,
(3) composition utilizing the computer system.

As shown in Figure 2, during the sessions, all components were in direct visual access of both Mr. B. and the therapist.

Stage 1

The first stage consisted of tutoring the patient in the elements of formal music theory. Mr. B. is an "intuitive" musician, that is, untrained in the traditional concepts and fundamentals of music. His training stems from a form of contemporary dance music where skills such as the ability to read or write music are not prerequisite to music making.

Several music theory software programs were employed in tutoring the patient in these remedial areas. These programs are designed to provide instruction in areas such as note naming, counting rhythm, aural and visual intervals, and key signatures. Mr. B. developed his skills in these areas through drill and practice with the music software. The therapist provided necessary assistance and interaction to aid him in mastering these skills.

Traditional instruments were employed in conjunction with the computer music instrument. This was done for further illustration, and to provide a common point of reference for him. The computerized sound textures emulated many traditional instrument timbres, but were a distinct departure from the instruments they were emulating.

Mr. B. aided the therapist in developing specific methods that would compensate for physical deficits that hampered the music making process. An example of this involved Mr. B.'s inability to vocally count the beat of the music measure he was playing. This became problematic as he was unable to use other methods such as tapping his foot or hand in time to the music. After several unsuccessful attempts to aid Mr. B. in counting the meter of the music, the patient suggested counting with his head gestures. This was done by using the Viewpoint Optical Indicator to enact the numbers cells on the Express-3 in accordance with the beat of the measure. This method proved successful in negotiating this problem.

Figure 2. Mr.B. with communication and computer music system.

As the process progressed, both Mr. B.and therapist developed an understanding of the limitations of the systems, and the patient's ability to work within that system. The patient displayed difficulty in changing from what had been an instinctive, intuitive process of music making to a formalized, structured process. There were distinct areas of resistance and confusion over the naming of music intervals. Difficulty was cited in controlling the parameters of the software program without delays between hearing and identifying musical intervals.

These problem areas manifested as a source of extreme frustration. This led to the patient's attempt to end three of the six sessions in this stage before the full ninety minutes allotted for each session. Mr. B was asked to consider spending the remaining time to discuss and work on the issue caused by his frustration, but he relayed that he was unable to continue, and needed to end the sessions.

His level of frustration diminished as he became more familiar with the system and a routine was established. As he grew more adept at using the computer music system, he began to create more music by himself during the week-long intervals between sessions. This additional work helped to expedite some of the learning process of the computer music system, enabling Mr. B. to move on to the next stage.

Stage 2

The second stage of his process entailed mastering the methods of manipulation and control of the computer music system. As with any musical instrument, there is a protocol of prerequisite skills and techniques necessary in order to facilitate the functioning of the instrument. Stage 1 had successfully prepared him for this introduction to the computer music system. There was adequate preparation in the areas of music theory, and familiarization of the communication system's interface with the micro-computer.

It was necessary to continue the training to include the command structure of the computer music system. The computer music system's structure is subdivided into three distinct parts: the music editor, the music player, and the music merger.[26]

The music editor allows the user to input data into the computer music system's memory for use later as part of a composition. The computer music system allows the user to sequence up to eight simultaneous musical sequences. These sequences can be single notes, or groupings of several notes together that comprise chords. The length of each sequence is determined by the amount of note events used in each sequence. The data that is input into each sequence is done in a mode referred to as "step time." The term step time refers to a method of inputting musical data in a modified, time related fashion. The data is entered in fragments, allowing the user to edit and modify any of the music events while creating the composition. The musical meter can be slowed down or suspended until played back. This method is analogous to placing a series of words together to create a phrase. It is not until the person reading the phrase connects all of the elements of the phrase together that the phrase is perceived as a phrase, and not a compilation of separate words. Data may also be entered into some computer music systems in "real time." Real time sequencing refers to a data entry method that allows the user to enter in a continuous manner that records the information as it occurs. Mr. B. employed the step time functions of the computer music system while engaged in this phase. This method of data entry allowed the patient easier access while mastering the music editor segment of the system.

The music player segment of the system allows the user to listen to the sequences that have been entered. Sequences that have been created in the music editor are stored within the computer's data storage system onto 5.25 inch diskettes. The sequences are titled, and are retrieved for use in creating larger series of phrases within the composition. The music player's role in this chain of events is to assign the sequence a musical "voice," that is, a sound that the computer music system has stored within its memory. The user can define the parameters of these sounds, controlling all aspects of timbre, volume, and other inherent characteristics.

Once this voice is assigned by the music player, it stores both the sequence and the voice together. The user then calls upon the titled sequence to hear the sequence. The third segment of the instrument, the music merger, compiles the sequences together so that they can be heard simultaneously. Up to eight sequences with three different sounds can be heard concurrently.

Mr. B. was able to create music using the three segments of the computer music system within the six allotted sessions. He appeared less resistant to this stage of the process than the previous stage. There was a marked improvement in the amount of music making accomplished without the therapist's interaction. Again, as in Stage 1, the patient assisted in creating methods that would improve his ability to interact with the computer music system. As shown in Figure 3, Mr. B. had all components within immediate visual access.

By the third session, he had committed many of the necessary command structures of the computer music system to the internal memory of his communication system. This aided in increasing his level of independent, autonomous functioning. There remained the need for another physically capable person to be present while the patient used the computer music system, in order to change the system's program and data diskettes as required.

He expressed the desire to enter a musical composition into the system during the fifth session. Because of the awkwardness of the system, we agreed that before he attempted to create his own composition, he would first input several compositions by other composers. In an attempt to demonstrate the systems capabilities the therapist suggested that he create music with two separate and distinct melody lines. We agreed to try "Invention #8" of J. S. Bach,[27] He input the musical data of the piece with great resistance, he did not enjoy the way the music sounded. We compromised and agreed to use more contemporary compositions, one of which was "Billy Jean" by Michael Jackson.[28]

This was accomplished by analyzing the song, and then assembling the composition into three pieces for entry into the computer music system. This composition proved to be a turning point for Mr. B. in his relationships with both the computer music system and the therapist. Hearing this song on the system provided the successful experience that Mr. B needed to validate this method as a means for creating music again. Prior to this experience, there was a degree of skepticism on his part. This helped to alter his perception of his new instrument.

It also provided the therapist the necessary material for transition into the third stage, for it enabled him to interact with the system in a clear, and musical manner.

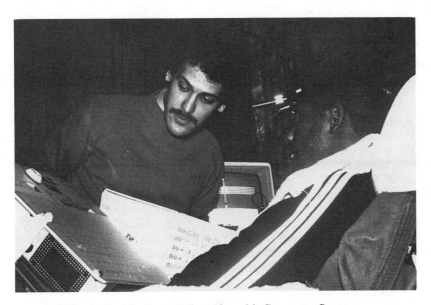

Figure 3. Mr. B. and Therapist with Computer Systems.

Stage 3

The third stage of Mr. B's process became the culmination of the work of the previous stages. In the final stages of the process, he began to engage in creating music without the need for direct interactions from the therapist. Mr. B. was now operating at a level of functioning that no longer necessitated tutoring or teaching any of the functionings of the system by the therapist. This combined with a mastery of the basic elements of music theory, and his own highly developed intuitive musical skills, provided all of the prerequisite skills needed to creative music making.

Mr. B. displayed an eagerness to participate in this stage that exceeded the level of the previous two. This was evidenced by a reduced level of resistance and an overall brighter affect. The first composition created by the patient was a improvisation which utilized the thematic structure of the M. Jackson composition which was input into the system at the close of Stage 2.

He used the ostinato bass pattern of the song to create his own improvisation. This was accomplished by sequencing the bass part with a musical voice that consisted of predominantly low pitches. Above this pattern, a sustained chord pattern was introduced. These two layers provided both a harmonic and a rhythmic structure for the composition to follow. After completing these two sections, a third line was added. This line, an improvisation, consisted of fragments of the harmonic material present in the other layers. By entering the data in a step time manner, the patient was able to experiment with different configuration of pitches and rhythms.

It was at this point in time that one of the greatest deficits of the system became apparent to both the patient and therapist. In creating music that was not predetermined in score form, as in an improvisation, there is no immediate form of sound that the machine produces as a feedback. As described in the earlier stages, the system must save all data on a diskette, assign a voice and then be recalled in order for the sound to be heard. When improvising, there is a need for a form of immediate gratification or feedback. This system proved incapable of fulfilling this requirement.

To a musician reliant upon his ability to hear the relationship between pitches in order to create, a serious problem is posed. Without the necessary feedback, the creative process is severely impeded. This became a point of frustration and resistance that remained present for the remainder of this final phase. Mr. B. expressed feelings of inadequacy and an inability to create within this medium. This was exacerbated by his continued resistance towards both the therapist and the computer music system.

Yet, despite his continued resistance, he was motivated to continue creating music, with additional assistance and support from the therapist and several staff members. Continued progress was maintained throughout this phase of development in regard to Mr. B.'s creative skills development. These skills improved as methods were established and developed to compensate for the deficits in the system. These methods continued to be a collaborative endeavor with both Mr. B. and therapist contributing to the resource of methods available to the music making process.

As in the earlier stages, traditional instruments continued to be employed. The piano and guitar were utilized to compensate for the deficits in immediate auditory feedback. The musical phrases that Mr. B. implemented into the computer music system were played by the therapist on traditional instruments. This method enabled him to experience the music he created without the processing delay.

The third stage concluded as Mr. B. displayed signs of mastery in the use of the computer music system in his music making process. In the fifth and sixth sessions, there appeared to be a marked improvement in his level of autonomous functioning, and an enhanced level of musical productivity. The process terminated in the seventh session with Mr. B. independently and successfully creating a short polyphonic composition.

PROJECT TWO

The results of the first project had demonstrated that this application of technology was a viable means of reaching a patient through music therapy. It was now possible to integrate newer, more powerful technology into Mr. B's equipment setup. By 1986, MIDI technology had developed to a point that was useful for the needs of this project. A small grant enabled the purchase of a MIDI system for Mr. B.

The system was again centered around an Apple IIe computer. This was decided for several reasons. The patient was familiar with the operation of the computer; all of the patient's augmentative communication equipment was compatible with the Apple IIe computer; it was affordable; and there were MIDI products available for the computer that were appropriate for the patient's needs.

The MIDI system consisted of a Casio CZ 1000 synthesizer, a Roland TR-505 Drum Machine, a Casio TB-1 MIDI Thru Box, and Dr. T's Keyboard Controlled Sequencer. All of these products were connected together in an appropriate fashion and then assembled on a cart so that Mr. B could view and interact the equipment easily.

The initial steps of this music therapy process were similar to the first stages of the first project. There was a sharp learning curve for Mr. B. to overcome in order to create music on the system. The interfacing of drum sounds and rhythms introduced many new sonic textures, but also several problems. There were software and hardware compatibility problems that prevented several musical tasks from being accomplished without an act of congress.

Again, as in the first project, the deciphering of the system and creating workable routines was a collaborative endeavor between the therapist and patient. As the learning curve diminished, the level of therapeutic interactions increased. The machinery had posed many obstacles that interfered with the therapy. Now that the machinery was less of an unknown quantity, the interactions were less strained and more conducive towards addressing the goal areas.

The goal areas that were being addressed in the project were :

(1) To allow Mr. B. to create music without assistance on a new level.
(2) To increase his vocational training in this medium so that he may resume his career as a composer.
(3) To develop a new means for self expression through the use of his music making equipment.
(4) To allow the patient new opportunities to explore his musical self in the music therapy process.
(5) To reduce the level of frustration and difficulty involved in the music making process.

Method

The methods used in this project were similar to the methods employed in the first project. Mr. B. and the therapist developed routines with the new equipment that enabled music making without assistance. He experienced difficulty in mastering the complex software used to sequence musical events. To help negate this, several pieces of music were transcribed and recorded into the sequencer for him to see and experience.

Mr. B requested transcriptions of several songs for his use in learning the system. Fragments of these songs later became the basis of improvisations and new compositions. This was accomplished by literally cutting and pasting rhythmic, melodic, and thematic elements of established pieces of music and then reconfiguring the pieces into new and different musical phrases.

This repertoire of songs and song fragments became the basis of the music that was employed in later sessions. With an established vocabulary of sounds and sequences readily available to both therapist and patient, the level of the therapeutic work increased. The removal of the barriers imposed by interacting with machines was not easy to overcome, yet there was finally a language in place that nurtured this interaction.

Overcoming this barrier became a turning point in the therapy. Improvisation was now possible, and with that, interaction on a different level. The Mr. B and therapist began composing spontaneously, feeding off of each other's ideas and nurturing them into musical statements. Mr. B. and the therapist began to perform together for other patients. Mr B. called the duo "The Disk Drives." One of these performances was chronicled briefly on the videotape *Rehabilitation, Music, and Human Well-Being*.[29]

Results

The results of these research projects have exceeded the original scope and projections originally planned. The patient has shown an increasing ability to utilize this medium as a productive modality of creative expression. The progress made in relation to the goal areas set for Mr. B. is as follows:

There was an increase in patient's level of creative expression throughout both projects. He was afforded an opportunity to renew his creative process through interactions with the therapist and the computer music system. Mr. B. was able to work within the framework of the computer music system's capabilities to create a successful product.

Mr. B. experienced an enhanced quality of life through involvement with this project. He was able to interact in a medium that had been unavailable to him since the onset of his illness. Prior to this experience, Mr. B. expressed serious doubts as to whether he would ever again create music. He experienced a reduced level of isolation and withdrawal. Prior to his experience with this research project, his history had reported withdrawal and isolation from the staff and peers. With the successful completion of this experience, there has been a sharp decline in the level of withdrawal and isolation present.

As a result of the projects, Mr. B. experienced an improved sense of self and of accomplishment. This was achieved through his successful mastery of music theory, the computer music system, and music composition. With each accomplishment, the patient's self-esteem and regard appeared to be increasing.

The results of this project have demonstrated to all those involved that the use of technology can enhance the music therapy process. As in the first project, Mr. B. experienced an increased level of creative expression through the use of this medium. He has not only created songs and compositions in the therapy process, but he has gone on to create songs and perform them in public as part of his hospital program. His sense of self appears to be greatly enhanced as a result of this experience. He is now producing music on a new and creative level. He has communicated to the therapist that his ability to make music again has changed his attitude towards his illness and his future. He now feels that he has options that were unavailable to him in the past.

The introduction of a MIDI system to his equipment has greatly reduced the frustration level of interacting with the equipment. While he may outgrow his present system in the foreseeable future, it is adequate for his needs at the present time.

The results of the projects described above, along with other clinical trials with different populations, has led the authors to believe that this is a viable means of therapy in need of further research to accomplish this. A center has been developed in New York City to investigate applications, methods, and theories of music therapy with technology. This center is a collaborative endeavor between the New York University Music Therapy Department, Goldwater Memorial Hospital and the Center for Electronic Music. The two sites of the center are Goldwater Memorial Hospital and the Education Building of New York University.

There will be no discussion of specific cases at this point; the model described is new and the research is incomplete as of this writing. Instead, what follows is a description of the center as it has been developed and is currently functioning. The center services several different patient populations, ranging from abused and neglected children to patients with chronic disabilities. A model of a session is as follows: The patient contracts with the therapist to create music in the music therapy room at a predetermined time for a session. The sessions range in time based on the patient's capabilities. He/she is then invited to interact musically. The only equipment that is visible to the patient is a MIDI controller and a master keyboard controller.

The controllers available to the patient include drum pads and percussion devices that transmit MIDI information, and traditional keyboard instruments. These are mounted in an appropriate fashion for the patient's method of data entry. All of the other equipment is obscured by thick curtains that surround the entire back half of the room.

The patient is invited to create music with the therapist. The focus of the session is on the "here and now." This means, focusing on what is happening at the present time, between the people involved in the interactions, regarding the creation of music. The music is both a metaphor and a means of communication. The patient is allowed the opportunity to use the MIDI controller to create music without assistance or compromise. The therapist is engaged in an interactive, relationship designed to foster the growth and development of the patient's musical self.

It is through the development of this "self" that the patient can then use music as a means of self expression and then as a tool towards self-actualization. It is important to note that the growth being discussed requires many levels of skills development that operate on a sharp learning curve. One of the primary goals of the therapist prior to engaging a patient into the therapy process is to limit and minimalize this learning curve for the patient. Again, the learning curve needs to be diminished to such a point that the technology becomes "transparent," so that it is not present as an obstacle. By way of analogy, there are many pianists who are not involved with the mechanics or physics of their instruments, yet they are able to communicate and express themselves on these instruments without any obstacles. An electronic musical instrument used in the therapy process needs to offer the same degree of "user friendliness." There is a fine balance that needs to be drawn between the opening of new vistas of music making and oversimplifying a powerful and complex means of creating music.

SYSTEM DESIGN

Through the use of new technology, patients explore the applications of MIDI technology in their music therapy process. The controllers allow musical data to be input into the computer without the use of computer keyboard, joystick, or mouse. The method that the devices use is through the conduction of energy on a touch sensitive pad. The devices can create separate zones that allow the user to input musical data by touching on that zone. The zones are pre-assigned to separate MIDI channels and can control any of the MIDI instruments assigned to them. Each zone can have the sensitivity range altered to match the level of patient's input.

Quantitative data can be drawn from the varying levels of input sensitivity that are required by the patient to enter the data into the computer. There can be one instrument sound with many distinct pitches, or many different instrument sounds with distinct pitches. There can also be various different combinations of the instruments on the different zones. The patient does not need any prerequisite musical skill to interact with the system. The system allows data entry to be accomplished by any touch. This will allow even some severely physically involved patients to interface with the system. The preferred method of data entry is through some hand motion, although nearly any limb that can do some level of refined motion can interface with the system.

The system consists of the MIDI instruments including samplers, synthesizers, drum machines, sequencers, signal processing and routing devices, amplification and speakers. The MIDI controllers are connected to a MIDI drum translator. This device takes incoming control voltages and converts them into MIDI data. The controllers provide the voltages through the touches of the user. Each of the drum translators inputs are receiving data from the controllers. The drum translator takes the entered data and converts the information back out as MIDI code. This information can be translated over sixteen distinct channels, either simultaneously, or in an individual assignment that can range from one to all sixteen channels. This information is sent over a network of cabling that is received by a MIDI patcher. The MIDI patcher then assigns the information to any of the synthesizers, samplers, or drum machines

Additional data is achieved through Pitch to MIDI conversions provided by a pitch extractor. This device monitors the vocalizations of the patient and enables the user to create synthesized textures and sounds through random vocalizations. By creating vocalizations, the patient is creating music that can later be shaped, molded, and converted into songs and therapeutic activities.

This is accomplished by taking the musical data that the patient created and sending it to a computer with a color monitor, on a large capacity hard disk, a printer, modem, and MIDI interface. This computer is used to record the information into sequences. This information is recorded by a sequencer and can be altered in terms of pitch, timbre, time, and construction. The information can be re-processed and configured into many different states. In addition, patient is interacting with the therapist and pre-composed music that the therapist and/or the patient has created. This music is played back to the patient in real time and is subject to the changes brought about by the MIDI information being created by the MIDI controllers. The therapist and patient can view the music in the form of music notation that the computer has printed out. Files can be transferred from center to center through a telecommunications link that is set up between the two sites.

SUMMARY

The goal of this chapter is to describe some of the applications of the use of computerized musical instruments in the music therapy process. The authors' explorations of this technology have demonstrated the possibilities of establishing this application as an effective means of treatment. It is our intention to inspire others, those who are interested in the use of this technology, to utilize this work as a springboard towards developing their own applications and methods.

As our understanding of our patients grows, along with the emergence of new and more "human"oriented technology, the barriers that have inhibited many from experiencing the joy of creating music will be lifted. When that day arrives, all those who wish to, can join in the song.

Joseph C. Nagler, Mathew H. Lee

REFERENCES

1   Boxill, E.: *Music Therapy for the Developmentally Disabled.* Rockville, MD: Aspen Systems Press, 1985.
2   Katsh, S., Merle-Fishman, C.: *The Music Within You.* Simon & Schuster, Inc., 1985.
3   Boxill, E.: *Music Therapy for the Developmentally Disabled.* Rockville, MD: Aspen Systems Press, 1985.
4   Gaston, E.T. (ed.): *Music in Therapy.* New York: Macmillan, 1968.
5   Wheeler, B.: Relationship between music therapy and theories of psychotherapy. *American Association for Music Therapy*, Summer 1981.
6   Ruud, E.: *Music Therapy and Its Relationship to Current Treatment Theories.* St. Louis, MO: MMB Music, Inc., 1980.
7   Goodman, K.D.: Music therapy. In: Arieti, Silvano, Brodie, Keith (eds.) *Handbook of Psychiatry.* New York: Basic Books, 1980, vol. 17.
8   Nordoff, P., Robbins, C.: *Creative Music Theapy.* New York: John Day Co., 1977.
9   Nagler, J.: In conversation with Barbara Hesser, 1985.
10 Maslow, A.: *The Further Reaches of Human Nature.* New York: Viking Press, 1971.
11 Rogers, C.: *On Becoming a Person.* Boston: Houghton Mifflin Co., 1961.
12 Bugental, J.F.T.: *The Search for Authenticity - An Existential Analytical Approach to Psychotherapy.* New York: Reinhart and Winston, Inc., 1963.
13 Wheeler, B.: Relationship between music therapy and theories of psychotherapy. *American Association for Music Therapy*, Summer 1981.
14 Chadwick, D., Clark, C.: *Clinically Adapted Instruments for the Multiply Handicapped.* St. Louis, MO: MMB Music, Inc., 1980.
15 Nagler, J., Lee, M.: Use of microcomputers in the music therapy process of a postviral encephalitic musician. *J Medical Problems of Performing Artists*, June 1987, pp. 72-74.
16 Scripps, L., Meyaard, J., Davidson, L.: Discerning musical development: Using computers to discover what we know. *J Aesthetic Education*, Spring 1988, 22(1), pp. 75-88.
17 Walters, J., Hodges, M., Simmons, S.: Sampling the image: Computers in arts education. *J Aesthetic Education*, Spring 1988, 22(1), pp. 99-110.
18 Bolton M.P., Taylor A.C., Soja, G.: Computer interface for the disabled (CID). *Med Biol End Comput*, September 1982, 20, pp. 645-647.
19 Casby, M.W.: Simple switch modifications for use in augmentative communication. *Language, Speech and Hearing Services in School*, July 1984, pp. 216-220.
20 Bolton, M.P., Taylor A.C.: A universal computer and interface system for the disabled (UNICAID). *J Miomed Ens*, October 1981, 3, pp. 281-284.
21 Knapp, R., Lusted, H.: A real-time signal processing system for bioelectic control of music. *Proceedings of the 1988 IEEE ICASSP*, New York, April 11-14, 1988.
22 Nagler, J.: In conversation with Don Slepian.
23 Nagler, J.: In conversation with Mr. B., 1985.
24 Mr. B.: Unpublished writing, 1985.
25 Broder, H., Hunton, G.: Preventative Psychotherapeutic measures for non-vocal clients. *J Rehab*, October-November-December 1982, pp. 24-27.
26 Mountain Computer System Operating Manual, 1980.
27 Bach, J.S.: Inventions for Piano, Number 8.
28 Jackson, M.: Billy Jean, Epic Records, 1983.
29 Lee, Mathew, H.M.: *Rehabilitation, Music, and Human Well-Being.* Goldwater Memorial Hospital, 1988.

MUSIC, EMOTIONS, AND HOSPITALIZED CHILDREN
Some Theoretical Considerations

Myrtha Perez

INTRODUCTION

Hospitalized children experience many emotions: fear of the unknown, fear of pain, loss of their familiar environment, and separation from loved ones. Although they are admitted for treatment of physical illnesses or disabling conditions, they may exhibit some imbalance in their abilities to think, feel and act. In the last 40 years, many studies have demonstrated the traumatic consequences that illness, hospitalization and treatment may have on the psychosocial development of children. The most complete review of this research can be found in Vernon *et al.*, *The Psychological Responses of Children to Hospitalization,*[1] and Richard H. Thompson, *Psychological Research on Pediatric Hospitalization and Health Care.*[2]

In order to counteract the adverse effects that hospitalization may have in the psychosocial development of children, a new professional has evolved in pediatrics, the Child Life Specialist. The role of the Child Life Specialist is to provide children with an opportunity for enjoyment, for learning about the self and about the environment, and for dealing with overwhelming emotions. Richard H. Thompson, *Child Life in Hospitals,*[3] gives a good account of the scope and diversity of the pediatric programs that Child Life Specialists have developed in the United States and Canada.

In meeting a child, the Child Life Specialist attempts to establish a trusting relationship. This relationship is built through consistent visits, belief in children's potentialities, and respect for their uniqueness. No two interventions are the same. No medium is used exclusively. To communicate with children's emotions, play and the expressive arts are the preferred tools of the Child Life Specialist. And among the expressive arts, music occupies a special place. Music speaks to the body, the mind, the soul. Music can be explained analytically by musical experts, but can be enjoyed by everyone. Most important, music conveys emotions, and is most effective in communicating with children.

I have been a Child Life Specialist at the Children's Memorial Medical Center in Chicago for over 17 years, and previously a professional musician on the European concert scene for 10 years. I am also an active participant in the Society for Clinical Philosophy founded by Dr. Hector Sabelli from Rush Medical School in Chicago; the Society ensures the union of psychology, biology, and physics with humanities to provide a theory for creative and comprehensive clinical care. This background has enabled me to develop unique techniques in the therapeutic use of music in Pediatrics.

Much can be said about the use of music as an agent for group communication and learning. However, I will address only the application of music as an individualized mode of intervention, and I will explore some theoretical reflections in light of this clinical experience.

CASE STUDIES

I want to present a few cases within the framework of four emotions: sadness, anger, anxiety, and joy. I will describe the individual sessions as they took place, and how music and play influence the children's moods, behavior, and identification of feelings.

Case 1: Sadness

Jane was an 18-year-old adolescent suffering from leukemia. She had been treated successfully for four years. However, during the last year, her chemotherapy had not been working out. In spite of many changes in the medical protocols for medication, she had not gone back into remission. I had known her for five years. In each of her admissions, we had a great time together. She had a devotion for poetry, as I have for music. She read me her beautiful poems, and I played music for her.

At this particular admission, she seemed different, paler, and quite withdrawn. In recent weeks, she had not been writing poetry as usual. The caring staff, unwilling to face the possibility of losing a loved patient began to pressure her to be "as cheerful as before." How could she? A bright 18-year-old knows what a long relapse means. She is entitled to feel sad, distant. What could I do? How could I show her some empathy? I was not in her condition. I really did not know what it felt like. Only music could connect with her feelings, or at least, meet her where she was, wherever that was. Knowing of her interest in classical music, I selected Ravel's *String Quartet,* and proposed that we listen to it together. She accepted with a pale smile.

First movement: intimate, sad, in suspense, like a fragile soul stretching into a line, hanging. One could be alone with this movement and not feel alone.

After a few minutes, she started to cry. Without a word said, holding hands, we listened.

The first movement evaporated, and the soft, bouncing life of the strings announced the second movement. There were no more suspense, thin air, or dark questions, but a sudden light, the reassuring repetitions of rhythmical patterns. We looked at each other. She smiled; I smiled. We never heard the third movement because she wanted to write!

When people are alone, in grief or in despair, music needs to be intimate, gentle, unobtrusive. It is hard to put into words the spiritual dimension that great musicians like Ravel can transmit.

Case 2: Anger

Joseph was a healthy six-year-old boy who fell from a three story building. He was brought to the hospital in critical condition, necessitating several surgeries including one on his brain. After a two-week battle for life in the Intensive Care Unit, he was transferred to the Neurosurgical Unit for further care. And he needed much of it.

Although he was stable and mentally alert, his jaw was wired, one side of his body was paralysed, he was tube fed, and his fractures were healing slowly. His physicians had a semi-optimistic prognosis for him to regain some movement after a long rehabilitation.

He was referred to me because of his long stay, and one of his nurses said, "You will love working with him. He is a delight, so cooperative!" I became worried for him. Usually, very cooperative children hold great frustrations inside.

From the beginning, music seemed to give him much pleasure. He would tap the rhythm of my songs on a drum with his only available hand, and I improvised songs for him, his mother, and his twin brother. At the end, he would motion for me to kiss him (by pointing to the communication board that I gave him), and he would kiss me by putting his stiff lips against my cheek. Even under these trying circumstances his social skills were remarkable.

However, as soon as he started to feel better and regain some energy, he became agitated, demanding, and irritable, especially with his mother, who felt very upset by it. With me, he was always in good humor because I did fun things with him.

His aggression towards his mother and the staff continued to escalate. I decided to approach him directly about his feelings. He had started to develop the ability to think concretely, and his intelligence, above average, had remained untouched by the accident.

Instead of using improvisations, I put words to "Are You Sleeping, Brother John?", and I sang:

> Are you angry? Are you angry?
> At your mom? At your mom?
> Tell your friend, tell your friend,
> Ding, dang, dong. Ding, dang, dong.

He shook his head: No. I answered back:

> I am not angry, I am not angry,
> At my mom, at my mom,
> Told my friend, told my friend,
> Ding, dang, dong. Ding, dang, dong.

I asked his permission to continue the song. He nodded: Yes.

> Who are you angry at?
> Who are you angry at?
> Tell your friend, etc.

He quickly pointed to his chest. And I sang:

> I am angry, I am angry
> At myself, at myself,
> Told your friend, told your friend, etc.

He nodded: Yes. And I sang:

> Why are you angry, why are you angry?
> At yourself, at yourself,
> Tell your friend, tell your friend, etc.

He pointed to his head. And I sang:

> I don't like it, I don't like it
> Hurt my head, hurt my head,
> Told my friend, told my friend, etc.

Then, Joseph smiled and gave me a hug with his one available arm. A very concrete, direct approach had dissipated the anger he felt, at least temporarily, and his behavior improved.

Case 3: Anger

John was a 13-year-old American Indian from Arizona, suffering from rheumatic fever, a condition brought about by bacteria which unfortunately had inflamed the membrane that lines his heart. Medication and absolute bed rest were the course of treatment.

John was very combative, and the staff had an awful time caring for him. After my nice introductory speech, he raised his foot and kicked me. Of course, I did not return to see him but he could hear the music that I made with other patients near by.

A week later, I received a call from his physician. The child's hostility had not subsided in spite of the psychiatrist's visits. His stage of agitation did not help his heart condition. A daily hour of play outside his room could help him deal with his frustrations, and calm him down.

John seemed mesmerized when he entered the room and heard the music of a Pueblo Indian dance. I had drums and clay on the table, and I began to follow softly the rhythm of the music.

He picked up a drum and started to do the same. Then, he changed the rhythm. I stopped the record, and I followed his lead. We created a whole gamut of rhythmical combinations and intensity patterns. This process was one of responsiveness to, and affirmation of John's contributions while sharing my own.

Through the extraordinary power of music, we became friends. I had recognized his uniqueness as a person, and his culture as being different from my own. In fact, his family was very militant in the American Indian community. He started to see me as a human being, not as an enemy, and he was able to gradually develop better patterns of behavior and communication with others.

Case 4: Anxiety

Martin was a 5-year-old black child with kidney failure who necessitated dialysis treatment. His hospitalizations were usually due to infections which required for him to sometimes be in isolation.

Martin was extremely anxious, especially when his mother was not with him. Those were the times of my visits. He enjoyed playing drums and bells. He would smile at me but he would not sing, constantly keeping an eye on the door.

One day he seemed particularly lethargic, and nothing I did seemed to interest him. I thought he might like to hear a Spiritual Song. But at that precise moment, I could not think of any particular one, and decided to improvise a song "in the style of a Spiritual": warm, expressive voice, low register, jazzy rhythm. Within seconds, he started to sing a song and beat the rhythm with his hand on his leg as if it were an imaginary drum, and with much enthusiasm.

I learned later from his mother that Martin's grandmother used to sing with him when he was living in Tennessee. Through the great magic of music, he was able to bring his grandmother back into awareness in the most pleasurable fashion. From that time on, he enjoyed singing many songs with me, recorded or invented. His anxiety during his mother's absence decreased. Perhaps, I became a sort of family member, a reassuring presence.

Case 5: Joy

Stephanie was an 11-year-old girl with a hormonal imbalance which precipitated a psychotic episode. Her condition necessitated medication and close observation. Her psychiatric complication was considered – hopefully – a temporary episode which could be monitored in the medical unit.

She was unresponsive, and made no eye contact. For a week I came to visit her, but I had no response. I became tired of talking to no avail, and I started to speak Spanish. To my surprise – she was not a Hispanic child – she answered, "Uno, dos, tres." Later, I learned that she had taken Spanish lessons in school.

When her physical condition permitted it, I took her for daily sessions. Spanish music did not get a response. I played with finger paints, and she slowly went from one finger to two, but her demeanor remained unchanged: very unexpressive, with an occasional "hola" in Spanish, or brief eye contact.

One day I tried to elicit some bodily sensations by playing very sensual music, Ravel's *Bolero* by the French National Orchestra. We began finger painting, and I started to move my head and shoulders suggesting some movement. She began to stand and sit alternatively, until suddenly, with a burst of energy, she stood up and began to dance. I followed her, and we choreographed a wonderful dance together, laughing at each other, and enjoying the movement a great deal.

The child's hormonal problems had a real impact on her emotions, and music has the ability to connect emotions to the body. The obsessive repetitions of the *Bolero* gave her the opportunity to exercise and release much physical energy. The joy of feeling her body in harmony with the music was a remarkable experience for this child who continued to enjoy daily movement explorations with Bizet's *Carmen*, Strauss's waltzes, and jazz. She started to talk and to be well quite rapidly. Her communication skills became normal by the time of her discharge from the hospital.

DISCUSSION

The vignettes of music sessions presented here raise important points for discussion: (1) the theoretical base that one selects, (2) the methodology that one employs, (3) the consideration given to alternative theoretical views.

The Theoretical Base

One of the great dilemmas that music presents for a theoretical discussion of its clinical application is the fact that music has a global influence on the person. Physical, emotional, social, and spiritual aspects of human life can be touched and influenced by music. Is there a unifying theory on which the clinical use of music is based? With certainty, the answer is "no." Should efforts in the future be directed toward one model of understanding, or should the field be open to different approaches which may possibly cooperate with each other? Perhaps this last question may be answered in a more positive fashion. If the interest of music therapists leads them to the exploration of many possibilities, with an openness to views different from their own, we may be able to cooperate with each other and enrich the field. In the meantime, we all make choices.

It is evident that my theoretical orientation has been inspired by a theory derived from humanistic psychology which uses a process approach, and has been largely influenced by phenomenological and existential theories. Carl Rogers was a humanist psychologist who developed the client-centered concept in therapy. This concept is characterized by two principles: (1) the therapist is not an observer but a participant, (2) the therapist perceives the client as a person, not as an object for study.[4]

This respect for the client proposed by Carl Rogers is taken a step further by child-centered play therapists Clark Moustakas and Virginia Axline. The child-centered play therapy philosophy "is not mainly concerned with techniques and skills but rather with the kind of relationship which enables children to grow emotionally, and to gain faith in themselves as feeling individuals. The basic attitudes toward children are faith, acceptance, respect, and a complete belief in the child's potentialities," says Moustakas.[5] For Axline, "the relationship that is created between the therapist and the child is the deciding factor in the success or failure of the therapy. And structuring is the word used for building up the relationship."[6] In *Child Life* philosophy, the relationship is essential for the intervention, and the "structuring" is called "developing trust."[7] Both theories approach children with acceptance and confidence in their ability to understand themselves and others.

There is also a parity of relationship and creative interaction in the practice of "Clinical Philosophy" which is based on the new theory of Process developed by Hector Sabelli.[8] Sabelli's theory of process or flux derives from the philosophies of Heraclitus[9] and Lao Tzu,[10] and links them to modern physics, biology, and the social sciences. One of the main concepts of Process Theory is Monism, or the triune composition of processes: energy, matter, and information. These three elements achieve oneness by being in constant flow and undergoing mutual transformation. When applied to human interactions, the flow of energy is present in physical, spiritual, and social behavior; the matter or structure constitutes the anatomical and biochemical elements of the person, and information is represented by the consciousness of emotions or thoughts felt or exchanged. In the cases presented here, the three elements of processes – behavior/spirit, body, emotions/thoughts – were activated by the creative interaction between therapist and patient and by the effect that music had on all three elements.

Another dynamic aspect of these cases presented is the unexpected expression of contrasting emotions that led to new awareness. In "Clinical Philosophy", contrasting emotions are expected, and the patient is helped to uncover them. This process is based on the theory of the union of opposites and attempts to lead the patient to the understanding of harmonious or conflicting aspects in her/his life. Conflict is seen as desirable because it may lead to awareness and change. Music is also a process that moves in space and time, and may express feelings of peaceful harmony or passionate conflict. Music reveals the creative life of the human spirit, which is best manifested through spontaneous thoughts or actions. Spontaneity plays a major role in the approach proposed here. The author who has written extensively and positively about the role of spontaneity and co-creativity in the therapeutic process is the psychiatric Jacob L. Moreno, the founder of *Psychodrama* .[11] *Psychodrama* is a technique of group therapy based on spontaneous acting and role reversal in which the person acts as the other with whom she/he is in conflict, in order to see the world from the other person's eyes.

If the use of music and the creation of a dynamic relationship between therapist and patient are the basic elements of music therapy, as proposed here, its theoretical formulation will have to examine "process" and "creativity" as central concepts.

The various principles and techniques discussed above seem to encompass process and creativity, and coincide with the approach used in the cases presented. But for a better understanding of these observations and where they may lead, it is necessary to analyze the methodology that I have employed.

Methodology

Goals, techniques, and musical materials are the essential components of the methodology. The environment can play a significant role in the therapeutic impact of the intervention. But in a hospital, the medical condition of the patient has priority, and the therapist needs to adapt to the various locations the patient may be in.

A. GOALS

1. The first goal of the creative process described here is the *encouragement* of the child and the *involvement* of the therapist to create the flow of energy leading to a trusting relationship. Music transforms the bodily and psychic energy within the person and between persons creating a sense of connectiveness, an ideal first step toward the development of trust.

2. The second goal is the *understanding of contradicting emotions* (case 5), and of the *conflicts* aroused by a high intensity of feelings, and confused or diminished cognition (cases 1 and 2). The second point has been discussed by R. Bolig and T. Gnezda who see young hospitalized children as being "infused with affect." Bolig and Gnezda also define their major therapeutic goal as helping children reestablish equilibrium between feeling and thinking.[12] For this, and for the understanding of contradicting emotions, music is a very powerful ally.

3. The third goal is *co-creativity* between patient and therapist. Co-creativity seems important because it leads either to harmony (cases 3 and 4 in which the children developed peaceful interactions with others or within themselves) or to change (case 2 and 5 in which the children became aware of contradictory emotions that led them to restructure their behavior or thinking). The process of co-creativity is based on the two preceding goals. The therapist needs to be open to it, and to avoid predetermining the path the patient may choose.

4. The fourth goal is the *dialectic of body and spirit* that leads to health and wellness. It is important for the sick or handicapped person to become aware of "the other part," of the healthy self, that may be buried under symptoms or feelings of helplessness. Thanks to the flow of music and the co-creative relationship, the spirit is engaged in a dynamic interaction with the body. The asymmetry between illness and health may then be transformed by a feeling of well-being, by the enjoyment of being One in body and spirit, by the awareness of the capacity to respond or create.

B. TECHNIQUES

Techniques can be classified as directive or nondirective.

The *nondirective technique* is the base of child-centered play therapists who permit children to take the lead in the relationship and be themselves in order to feel free to express feelings. The therapist interprets the expressed feeling and reflects it back to the child in a mirror-like effect with the hope that it will lead to emotional clarification and growth.

This approach has been used in music therapy by eminent therapists such as Paul Nordoff and Clive Robbins.[13] They have promoted spontaneous improvisation as a dynamic modality by which therapist and child become co-creators.

In the *directive technique* preferred by behaviorists, the therapist takes the lead in suggesting a mode in interaction. Depending on the case, age and situation, the suggestion may be very subtle, direct, or openly confrontive (case 5).

The nondirective purists may consider the directive approach invasive of children's right to explore themselves at their own pace. The nondirective technique may be possible in private practice or residential settings, where treatment may last a long time. In acute care hospitals, the time available with the patient is very limited, and a directive approach may be a desirable choice.

Because directive and nondirective techniques have made different contributions, I use both. Both have biases. A nondirective therapist may not be aware of how much direction he/she is providing by setting the environment in a certain fashion. Conversely, a directive therapist underestimates the contributions made by the child's spontaneity. Both techniques can serve the philosophy of trust, acceptance, and respect for the child. There are times when a nondirective approach is more effective (case 1); there are other times when the patient responds better to music expressing a contradictory emotion (case 5), or when reflection of feelings may stand in the way of a dynamic interaction between therapist and patient (case 3).

Although children are always different and challenging, clinical experience suggests the need for freedom; freedom for the therapist to be spontaneous in selecting a mode or an interaction; freedom to lead or to relinquish leadership; freedom to be somewhere in-between, as a partner.

C. MUSICAL MATERIALS

Musical materials should be made available according to the children's physical and emotional status, their taste, and that of the therapist.

If the relationship is the core of the intervention, the likes and dislikes should be shared equally. It enhances the scope and the quality of the experience for both the therapist and the child. This becomes more difficult when working with adolescents who have developed a taste for an exclusive type of music. A variety of materials, techniques, and above all, a parity in the relationship may open the adolescent to unexpected discoveries such as writing a poem and jointly creating its music.

Much could be said about techniques for "developing trust" or warming up to the relationship, and for "closing off," or preparing for departing from each other. For the sake of this discussion, it seems more important to take a look at other theoretical views as a frame of reference.

Alternative Theories

Because reality is so complex, no theory can successfully describe all its aspects, and serious consideration should be given to alternative views. T.C. Chamberlain, a Chicago geologist at the turn of the century, and more recently J.R. Platt,[14] championed this method of multiple hypotheses. Differences in methodology have occurred since early human history. But opposing and complemental methods have probably played a major role in scientific progress and in human relations.

There seem to be some points of contact between the techniques described here and some musical applications of psychoanalytical theories. Both may use musical improvisations to lead the patient to personal insights, to master a coping goal, or to integrate functions. But the expressiveness of feelings in psychoanalytical theory is seen as a discharge of painful emotions, or "catharsis," for the resolution of disabling conflicts.[15]

This is a big point of disagreement. Feelings are always in flux, dancing with different steps. They never stay very long in the same place unless they get fixed by some conflicting forces, unable to maintain the internal flux. Even after an intense expression of feelings, or "catharsis," a person will experience a wide array of emotions, expressed or not. The emotions discharged are not always painful. It is, then, questionable that conflicts may be resolved through expressivity alone.

In addition, the word resolution suggests an ending of the process. In fact, a strong expression of feelings may mark the beginning of a new awareness.

Even more questionable is the application of behavioral theories to music therapy. The idea of using music as a reinforcer of behavior, as C. Madsen suggests,[16] is in conflict with the person's right to select music suited to their taste, and to choose to listen or not. Music is, after all, intrusive. It enters the body through its auditory system, and may influence pulse rate, respiration, and blood pressure. To leave the control of the musical experience to the behavioral therapist is demeaning to the patient. And above all, this technique presupposes that behavior represents specific emotions or cognition that can be manipulated by external means. In fact, behaviors often do not transmit what the person feels or thinks, and sometimes they transmit the opposite. It is doubtful that behavior therapists may be able to control the sensations and alterations that music can have in the physical and psychosocial status of the patient.

Summary

Therapeutic interventions using music as a medium utilize techniques derived principally from humanistic psychology, but also from psychoanalysis and behaviorism. My goals and techniques parallel some of the principles derived from humanist psychology of adult and child-centered therapies, psychodrama, and clinical philosophy.

The exploration of Moreno's concepts in psychodrama and philosophy of creativity[17] may lead music therapists and child life specialists to interesting discoveries. Although psychodrama uses only theater as a medium, it touches on all aspects of life through the creative process. It may be enriching to music therapists to learn the psychodrama techniques and incorporate music with them. On the other hand, the concept of role reversal, practiced by psychodramatists, is used by child life specialists as a basic technique for "medical play" in which the child plays the role of doctor, nurse, technician, or whomever at the time is "the enemy." These links need to be further explored.

The nondirective techniques of the child-centered play therapists have been a source of inspiration and guide for me for many years.

The new theory of process and the clinical philosophy techniques learned from Sabelli and his associates have been helpful in understanding the importance of "the other emotion," the opposite of what patients show through their behaviors, self-expression, or concerns. Also, this theory provides a scientific basis for the role of creativity as a necessary ingredient in the process of evolution and change. And change is, indeed, the main goal of therapeutic interventions.

It would be presumptuous to think that these techniques for the use of music have not been employed before. What is perhaps new is the examination of their theoretical framework on the basis of relational and creative processes. This represents an approach distant from the application of behavioral and psychoanalytical theories which are deterministic and past-oriented. In fact, human processes are partially determined by many factors, for instance, sex, age, and genetics, and are partially open. If matter, energy, and information are constantly in flux and transforming each other, it would be possible to think that some unexplainable changes in the condition of patients, for good or for worse, may occur when the asymmetry of health and illness received positive or negative charges; and that these emotional, physical, intellectual, or sensorial charges of energy, being One, influence the asymmetric pattern of illness and health in one direction or the other. Thus, a medium of communication with the patient, such as music, allows various aspects of life to be activated, connected, and recreated (see diagram).

The encompassing nature of music requires a comprehensive view of process. It is hoped that this attempt may be an open door to new possibilities, and that further studies of musical application to therapy will be conducted to better understand the philosophical and theoretical base of music as a tool in clinical practice.

Children's illness, pain, separation from loved ones, and lack of appropriate stimulation can be their worst enemies. But children have not yet blocked the flow of energy that opens the imagination, the body, and the spirit to new experiences. They need the opportunity to share their creativity. And to share the creative process with a child is to co-create the world.

Let us hope that through the power of music we will strive for a better understanding of the humanity in us and in others in order to provide a higher quality of comprehensive care to the sick and the handicapped.

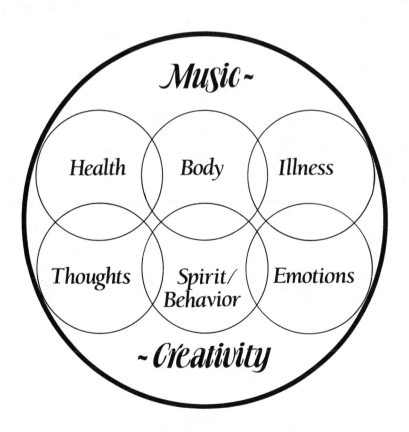

Dynamic and Comprehensive
Processes

REFERENCES

1   Vernon, D., Foley, J., Sipowicz, R., Schulman, J.: *The Psychological Responses of Children to Hospitalization and Illness*. Springfield, IL: Charles Thomas, 1965.

2   Thompson, R.H.: *Psychosocial Research on Pediatric Hospitalization and Health Care*. Springfield, IL: Charles Thomas, 1985.

3   Thompson, R.H.: *Child Life in Hospitals*. Springfield, IL: Charles Thomas, 1981.

4   Rogers, C.: *On Becoming a Person*. New York: Houghton Mifflin, 1961.

5   Moustakas, C.: *Children in Play Therapy*. New York: Ballantine Books, 1953, p. 2

6   Axline, V.M.: *Play Therapy*. New York: Ballantine Books, 1953, p. 74.

7   Thompson, R.H.: *Child Life in Hospitals*. Springfield, IL: Charles Thomas, 1981, pp. 7-8.

8   Sabelli, H.C.: *Union of Opposites: A Comprehensive Theory of Natural and Human Processes*. Lawrenceville, VA: Brunswick Publishing Corporation, 1989.

9   *Heraclitus*. Commented and edited by Philip Wheelwright. Princeton, NJ: Princeton University Press, 1959.

10 Lao Tsu: *The Way of Life*. Translated by Witter Bynner. New York: A Perigee Book, 1944.

11 Moreno, J.L.: *Psychodrama*. Vol. I. Beacon, New York: Beacon House, 1946.

12 Bolig, R., Gnezda, M.T.: A cognitive-affective approach to child life programming for young Children. *Children's Health Care*, Winter 1984, **12**(3), pp. 122-129.

13 Nordoff, P., Robbins, C.: *Therapy in Music for Handicapped Children*. London, U.K.: Victor Gollanz Ltd., 1971.

14 Platt, J.R.: Strong inference. *Science*, 1964, **146**, pp. 347-353.

15 Ruud, E. *Music Therapy in its Relation to Current Theories*. Oslo: Musikforlag, 1978 and St. Louis, MO: MMB Music, Inc., 1980.

16 Madsen, C., Madsen, C.: Music as a behavioral modification technique with a juvenile delinquent. *J Music Therapy*, Sept. 1968, **3**, pp. 72-77.

17 Moreno, J.L.: The creativity theory of personality: Spontaneity, creativity, and human potentialities. *Arts & Sciences*, New York University Bulletin, Jan 24 1966, **66**(4), p. 21, 22.

WHEELCHAIR DANCING

PART ONE

Corrie van Hugten

I am very glad to have the opportunity to contribute something about wheelchair dancing and to tell why wheelchair dancing is so important in my life.

Before I became ill and had to use a wheelchair, I had been working as a dance teacher for about fifteen years as well as teaching preschool children. Being in a wheelchair, I thought that it would be impossible to do enjoyable things as before - all the happy events of dancing: balls, championships, etc. were gone.

Eight years ago, after she had seen wheelchair dancing in England, a Dutch dance teacher told me about it and we went to see it together. I became enthusiastic at once! Not only was it possible to dance with a wheelchair, but there were far more possibilities than I saw in England. In the beginning, I worked with a few participants in the place where I live. In addition, Ondine, who is a physical therapist, and I began a course for instructors. We now have 75 groups of wheelchair dancers in the Netherlands and more than 300 instructors! We have developed possibilities for all disabled people: those with more or less abilities; those with electric wheelchairs; etc. Most importantly, we try to give all people the pleasure of moving to music. Couples composed of two wheelchair users, or a wheelchair use with a standing partner can dance together. We have possibilities for people lying in bed or simply sitting on a chair. Wheelchair dancing gives us the same good feeling as what is called "normal" dancing. All people feel music in the same place, not in their feet or wheels, but somewhere deep inside.

Of course, dancing is very important for young disabled children since there are a lot of activities in which these children can not participate such as cycling and other types of sports. With dancing, disabled children easily learn not only the happiness of movement, but also can experience what they can do with their bodies and their wheelchairs. While dancing, children learn directions such as forward and backward, left and right, and learn to do things with other children as well. Dancing can be a very good way of helping children find their place in life.

I enjoy dancing as much now as I did twenty years ago and, with the very quick development of wheelchair dancing, I am busier than ever. My life is full of activities and nice happenings. I enjoy wheelchair dancing and will try to have as many people as possible enjoy it to help fulfill their lives.

PART TWO

A Fairy tale
about a woman who with and in spite of her handicap brings
joy and relaxation to many people who are wheelchair bound

A short story by Ondine de Hullu

Lynden, August, 1986.

Once upon a time. . . . That's how a fairy tale should begin. Surprisingly, they still exist in this world full of trouble, violence and pain. As a rule, fairy tales are fantasy tales and they are about ancient times. The good always overcomes and "all's well that ends well." One can hardly imagine fairy tales happening today. No, fairy tales crowded with elves and princes are from a long, long time ago – very nice for children, but they don't happen anymore . . . or do they?

Once upon a time, there was an early childhood school teacher named Corrie. She was dedicated to her job as head teacher of an early childhood school and in the evening she assisted her uncle in a dance school. Every minute of her life was filled with great enthusiasm. Corrie took care that her children were happy and that they had a good time at school. In addition, she had enough energy left to be actively engaged in dance, giving lessons, participating in contests and congresses, traveling nationally and internationally with the dance team, etc. Music and dance were very important in her life, a life in which she enjoyed every moment. It was like a fairy tale, until a disease made walking impossible for Corrie! Working and dancing came to an end and so did the fairy tale. Or did it?

No, it didn't. One day, after years of hospitalizations, pain, sorrow, rehabilitation, hope and disappointment, a good fairy appeared. She was disguised as a dance instructor and carried a big old briefcase filled with papers, empty cigar boxes with scribbling all over them, and many other things. From this briefcase the good fairy juggled a gift for Corrie: wheelchair dancing!

Corrie considered the gift thoroughly: people in wheelchairs moving in time to the music, using their wheelchairs instead of their feet for making figures; people who dance and have fun like able bodied people – a world of new opportunities was opened for her. Would she be able to pick up her old hobby again? Would it really be possible to dance again? Things like that happen only in fairy tales, don't they?

In a short time, Corrie learned everything there was to know about wheelchair dancing. The good fairy did warn her though that it wasn't a simple thing to introduce something as novel as dancing in a wheelchair and that it would take a lot of courage and persistence. Corrie willingly accepted the challenge and began to work with enormous energy. She wanted to give as many disabled people as possible the opportunity to enjoy moving in time with the music. In the first dance class she began with careful experimentation, drawing on her experience as a teacher as well as her patience and imagination.

Very slowly, wheelchair dancing began to expand – creating, trying, talking, demonstrating, being written about here and there in a newspaper – step by step wheelchair dancing became better known.

A lot of people were opposed to it at first. A woman in a wheelchair claiming that people in wheelchairs could dance? No – something had to be wrong with her brain as well as with her legs! But, once people had seen it, often watching with tears in their eyes, they had to admit that it was possible to dance in a wheelchair. The happy faces of the participants convinced even the most skeptical spectators. Not only were the able bodied distrustful at first, but even handicapped people themselves had to get used to the idea! Fortunately, Corrie wasn't just another therapist telling them what was right for them. The fact that she was disabled and had herself experienced what wheelchair dancing could mean, and with her inspiring charisma, changed the hopeless into cheerful people dancing in wheelchairs! Even Corrie's former dance teacher colleagues realized that wheelchair dancing was a reality and began to help with its further development.

During the "years of the disabled," attention was paid to integration, sports with the disabled, etc. – wheelchair dancing also benefitted from the growing attention. The teacher training that had started during this time provided new teachers who could start wheelchair dancing groups in their own communities. The number of wheelchair dancers was expanding more and more. The ball was rolling and Corrie had never been busier. All kinds of dances – ballroom dancing, folk dancing, Latin-American dancing, rock and roll – had to be adapted for wheelchair dancing. Not only did adjustments have to be found for the severely disabled, but also for disabled people with more possibilities as well. Contacts with foreign countries were established, people in wheelchairs now had the opportunity to take dance lessons every week, to participate in national events and contests, to give demonstrations and even to travel abroad to festivals of wheelchair dancing. In nursing homes and holiday centers for the disabled, wheelchair demonstrations provided many happy hours for people to enjoy themselves.

When it seemed to Corrie that the hard work, the pain or the envy of some people became too great to bear, she was always encouraged again when she saw the happy faces of the disabled dancing in their wheelchairs.

Corrie's life was full again with dancing and music. In cooperation with a few prominent professional dancers, the technical side of wheelchair dancing was further developed and Corrie had the opportunity to give demonstrations with them on television as well as at important national and international dance events. Every week, with lessons to different groups of wheelchair dancers, education, demonstrations, study and further development there wasn't a single minute in Corrie's life which wasn't utilized.

A woman whose life had once seemed to be at an end was living an active life again. A life of hard work and happiness which had come to a sudden end had returned. A dream come true – a disabled woman who became a great success on many evenings, was treated like a princess, and many people also shared her happiness.

In this world where it seems there is no place for fairy tales – a fairy tale came into being!

A fairy tale, in most cases, ends: "and they lived happily ever after," so this should be the end of this fairy tale: "Corrie, and all the people to whom she has brought happiness through wheelchair dancing, lived happily every after." I sincerely hope so!

Editor's note: For specific directions, see Donna Douglass *Accent on Rhythm*. St. Louis, MO: MMB Music, Inc., 1985, pp. 3-21.

FOUNDATION OF WHEELCHAIR DANCING OF THE NETHERLANDS

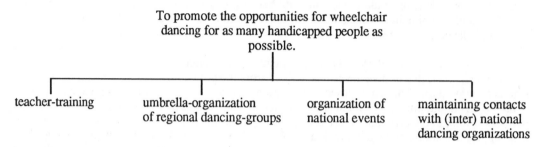

Objective:

To promote the opportunities for wheelchair
dancing for as many handicapped people as
possible.

| teacher-training | umbrella-organization of regional dancing-groups | organization of national events | maintaining contacts with (inter) national dancing organizations |

Teacher-Training

Content:
- dealing with handicapped people
- knowledge of dancing
- didactics and methods
- organization

Wheelchair Dancing

Forms:
- two wheelchair dancers make a couple
- combination-dance
- formation
- moving in time with music

Wheelchair Dancing-Groups

Locations:
- dance-schools
- nursing homes
- neighborhood organizations
- sport organizations for handicapped
- associations of participants
- activities for elderly people

THE LEGALIZATION OF MUSIC AS A FORM OF TREATMENT FOR THE MENTALLY AND PHYSICALLY DISABLED

Peter F. Jampel

INTRODUCTION

With his features bloated and distorted almost beyond recognition, Philip Marlow's only healthy means of escape from his misery was through music. As Philip lay confined to a hospital bed, memories of his beloved father's beautiful voice singing in the local English pub brought a look of fond remembrance to his eyes.

This movie written by Dennis Potter and aptly titled *The Singing Detective* details the experience of a novelist suffering from crippling arthritis and psoriasis. For him the memories of music in his family provided the one pleasurable link to both of his parents. His tormented relationship with his mother, whose adultery he witnessed and whose life ended in suicide, had few redeeming qualities. One that did stand out though was the way Philip remembered her playing the piano.

Music has never been more vividly used as such an integral means of coping with upper despair. The clues for Marlow's recovery were sung in the detective's voice. The handsome crooner of his novel could sing in the face of mayhem. In his voice there was hope. And hope was his only chance of fighting the debilitative effects of his illnesses.

There is a strong psychosomatic component to psoriasis. Deriving pleasure from making or listening to music for one so physically limited can provide a basis on which constructive therapeutic engagement can occur. Considering this patient's positive associations with music in his past, a music therapist would have a likely advantage over strictly verbal techniques. This is an illustration of the rationale for music therapy that can be used in the treatment of disabling mental and physical disorders. Yet Mr. Marlow would not likely have had available to him the services of a music therapist. Seeing how it can be applied and sanctioning its use are stages far apart. How close music therapy has come to being a sanctioned form of treatment for mental and physical disorders will be discussed here.

This chapter will attempt to assess the level of professional recognition that the field of music therapy has attained. The historical context in which to view this analysis will include a discussion of constitutional rights of the mentally ill and the right of the handicapped child to an appropriate education. How voluntary programs operate in terms of music therapy practice will follow. Licensure, civil service, and Workmen's Compensation Law as it applied to musicians and music therapy as a compensable form of treatment will conclude the discussion.

THE RIGHT TO PSYCHIATRIC TREATMENT

A new problem arose in the 1950s with the widespread use of neuroleptic medications in psychiatric institutions: How to treat people who had been considered untreatable? Treatment approaches like music therapy were profoundly affected as a new, treatable patient was literally created. For many schizophrenics, lifelong confinement was no longer deemed necessary or humane. Medication could stabilize their illnesses but offered no cure. As more effective treatment became available, the constitutional rights of the mentally ill gained attention.

Society's attitude today is substantially different from what it had been in early United States history when the most benign form of care for the mentally ill was provided through subsidized custodial care. The vast majority of such persons "were simply restrained in poor houses, almshouses or jails."[1] The primary concern of the few states that did provide institutional care was that of humane confinement. Attempting to treat them was quite secondary.

Indefinite confinement of mental incompetents is a recent development. Protecting society from those convicted of anti-social acts is undisputed. The ability to confine someone who is potentially dangerous to others or to himself has been more difficult to determine. The state assumed this power as it expanded its interpretation of the Nineteenth Century doctrine known as *parens patrie*. This allowed the state to assume guardian power of the incurably insane.

When psychiatric medications no longer made perpetual care necessary, the concept of meaningful treatment became a constitutional question. In 1972, the United States Supreme Court considered this issue in the case of O'Connor v. Donaldson, 422 US 563, 45 L Ed 2d 396, 96 S Ct 2486. The court affirmed that there were indeed minimal treatment standards for psychiatric patients and that perpetual confinement constituted a denial of due process under the Fourteenth Amendment. Mr. Justice Stewart in writing the majority opinion held that the state may not confine someone against his will unless that person poses a danger to himself or to others. Providing the mentally ill with a better living environment than they may be able to maintain for themselves is not sufficient reason for custodial confinement. He asserted that some form of rehabilitative treatment is the right of those involuntarily held. The loss of due process can be justified only when substantive treatment is offered.

This ruling altered treatment in state psychiatric hospitals as new approaches were tried in reaching this previously unreachable population. The hiring of interdisciplinary treatment teams became more commonplace. Voluntary accrediting agencies reflected these changing staffing patterns as they revised their manuals. Thus such relatively obscure professions as music therapy took on a more prominent role in mental health treatment.

VOLUNTARY ACCREDITING AGENCIES

Voluntary accrediting programs operate in a delicately balanced state of conflicting interests. These programs are designed to insure that health care facilities "provide quality services to the general public."[2] Their approval means that an institution has met up to nationally established standards of practice. Without it, Medicaid, Medicare or other insurance payments may be withheld. It could also result in the revocation of a facility's operating license by the state department of health.

These financial realities determine the kinds of pressures brought to bear upon the accredition agencies decisions in developing treatment standards. Insurance companies which try to keep health care costs down may limit the extent of national standardization. Regional standards are usually less demanding and thereby less costly. Hospitals have similar interests in keeping costs down and they too prefer softer regional treatment practices. These are very large and influential players.

Professional associations often lobby on the other side to promote greater specificity of standards which they hope will result in expanded professional opportunities for their members. These groups often oppose each other in their efforts to influence accrediting programs.

The Joint Commission on the Accreditation of Hospitals (JCAH) was born out of the efforts of the American Medical Association, the American Hospital Association and the American

College of Surgeons. The Hospital Accrediting Program was the first such program formed by JCAH. By 1965, its mushrooming acceptance had brought about similar programs monitoring nursing homes, psychiatric facilities, ambulatory health care facilities, and programs for the mentally retarded and developmentally disabled. Surveying of hospice care began in 1983.

Each accrediting program keeps itself current on the standards of practice in its own area of specialization through the advice of those professionals employed in their facilities. Being represented on one of these Professional and Technical Advisory Committees (PTAC) is an important symbol of professional recognition. The operating manual in each program details necessary services, standards of practices, and those qualified to render them. The recommendations of the PTAC is crucial in revising standards.

Music therapy is presently listed as an activity in only one of JCAH's manual, the *Consolidated Standards Manual of the Accrediting Program for Psychiatric Facilities* (AP/PF). In Chapter 30 under Rehabilitation Services, the 1987 manual mentions the use of music, art and dance therapy as possible rehabilitation services. Efforts to include the creative arts therapies in the *Accreditation Manual for Hospitals* under services for the chronically mentally ill have not been successful thus far. Specific language on psychosocial services in general hospitals will be reintroduced in future PTAC meetings. The critical determinant in gaining inclusion is evidence of existing widespread use of that treatment modality in accredited facilities. So far this has been demonstrated only in the six hundred psychiatric facilities that JCAH surveys.

The National Coalition of Arts Therapy Associations (NCATA) represents all of the creative arts therapies to the AP/PF PTAC. NCATA is represented by the American Occupations Therapy Association (AOTA) which sits on this committee. The two Recreation Therapy associations are also represented by AOTA's seat. NCATA has been actively cultivating an alliance with these two organizations in their efforts to gain greater influence with JCAH.

The Commission on Accreditation of Rehabilitation Facilities (CARF) is another voluntary accrediting agency. Despite a creditable representation in their facilities, music therapists are not represented on their governing board. A similar situation presently exists with the Accrediting Council for Services of Mentally Retarded and Other Developmentally Disabled Persons (AC MRDD). Music Therapists are frequently employed in their facilities but have no direct or indirect representation in their decision making bodies.

MENTAL RETARDATION SERVICES AND SPECIAL EDUCATION

The Kennedy administration was instrumental in focusing attention on the needs of the exceptional child. This culminated two administrations later in two events of landmark proportions for those who work with this population. The term "Qualified Mental Retardation Professional" (QMRP) first appeared in the *Federal Register* on January 17, 1974. This title spelled out the necessary qualifications for professionals working with the mentally retarded in all Intermediate Care Facilities (ICF/MR). Trained music therapists were not permitted to qualify.

The passage of the Education for All Handicapped Children Act of 1975 or Public Law 92-142 committed this country to educational plans designed to the individual needs of special education students. To accomplish this, new educational resources had to be located and marshalled to provide meaningful services to the mentally retarded.

The purpose of regulating the qualifications to become a QMRP was "to insure consistency in developing and coordinating the resident's individual rehabilitation plan by trained professional possessing experience in the field."[3] Those permitted to become QMRPs are privileged to assume administrative and supervisory positions. This translates in the state of Illinois to a $40,000 a year job.

Controversy raged over the qualifications necessary to become a QMRP from the beginning. There were those who wanted competency to be the determinant while others (who succeeded) felt that only certain disciplines should be included. Music therapists have gained extremely limited access to these positions. In California, Louisiana, and Oklahoma music therapists have been accepted as QMRPs but only if they also hold degrees in education.

This may change soon depending on what the Department of Health and Human Services does in its first comprehensive revision of standards for ICM/MR's since 1974. There is a proposal before it now that would permit music, art, and dance therapists to become QMRP's. This process is in its final determination phase called "the stage of highest consideration" and could be enacted in any of several forms. The National Association for Music Therapy (NAMT) is closely monitoring this situation (verbal communication, Gfeller, 1987.)

The fortunes of music therapists have fared considerably better in special education since the passage of PL 92-142. Under the provisions of this act, music, art and dance therapy can be named as related services when the Individual Education Plan (IEP) so stipulates. A teacher, parent, school principal or school psychologist may make the request. Music therapy is considered a related service in forty-two states, but locating qualified professionals is difficult in certain locations. Naming a creative arts therapist as a related service does not occur frequently.

Considerable efforts have been made in Florida to increase the level of visibility of music therapists through aggressive cooperation with parent and teacher groups. They have succeeded in being named more frequently in IEP's than in any other state.[4] The precedent of being named in one school district's IEP does seem to carry weight in the decisions of neighboring communities.

Additionally, PL 89-313 allocates funds to the education of all formerly institutionalized children. The use of music therapy as a related service with this population is particularly high. The salient issue here is the right of all handicapped children and their parents to gain access to appropriate services. The degree to which music therapy is named seems to depend upon how familiar and available these services are.

LICENSURE

Professions such as physicians and nurses obtain licenses to practice. Social workers are certified that they have obtained the necessary qualifications for that title and that no one may use that title who does not meet those qualifications. Music therapists seek this latter form of title legislation. Presently it is perfectly legal for anyone to call himself a music therapist regardless of training, competence or compliance with any standards of ethical conduct. Licensure is a form of public protection against the rendering of services by incompetent and unethical practitioners.

If a music therapist were to behave in an abhorrent manner either ethically or clinically, they would be subject only to the disciplinary actions of their national association. If the charges were upheld, that person's certification/registration could be revoked. Yet that same individual could the very next day call himself a music therapist and practice with legal impunity.

Since no state in the union has as yet passed a bill that would limit the scope of practice of music therapy to music therapists, other titled professions may practice music therapy but not vice versa. A few creative arts therapists have qualified for other titles. Such is the case in California where trained music therapists who have taken the necessary coursework have been certified as marriage and family counselors. In Texas and Ohio, music therapists have met the qualifications to be called professional counselors. New York is the first state to introduce a title bill into its state Senate which would restrict the use of the term "creative arts therapist" (S7411, introduced by Sen. Donovan to the Committee on Education, March 7, 1988). Music therapy has been named in Massachusetts as a qualified subspecialty for the title of Professional Counselor. Efforts are underway in Michigan, Rhode Island and Virginia to draft similar legislation. There have also been several instances of reciprocal recognition of a title that a music therapist has obtained from one state to another.

The protection of the consumer "not the status or economic interests of a profession" is the primary basis for licensure.[5] Such legislation requires the training programs of the profession to meet established guidelines for minority participation. Referral criteria to and from other professions is often required as well.

The experience of other professions which have acquired title protection points to the usefulness of developing a national certification examination. The recent emergence of the Certifying Board for Music Therapy CBMT meets that need. The drawback with CBMT stems from the fact that it certifies bachelor's and master's level applicants without differentiation. The trend towards master's level training as the base level necessary for title protection is clear. Art, dance and drama therapy all certify on the master's level and seem better positioned than music therapy in this regard.

CIVIL SERVICE

Career opportunities in state civil service can be considered a barometer of a profession's mature development. Such opportunities are enhanced when JCAH decides to mention that field in one of its manuals. Reimburseability by an insurance company is another positive factor in promoting career development in civil service.

On the federal level, music therapists who work for the Veterans Administration qualify to start at the GS-6 level under the Recreation Creative Arts Therapist title (GS 638 Series) (U.S. Office of Personnel Management, 1980). One's level of responsibility influences the grade level one may obtain. Opportunities exist for creative arts therapists to be promoted to administrative and supervisory positions. The more their professional judgement is relied upon in this system the higher the level of responsibility they are given.[6]

It is different in state civil service as one's title dictates one's responsibilities. Despite the fact that music therapists are integrated into the civil service systems of forty-six states, only 19% of these people work under the title of music therapist. They are often hired under other titles, the most common being as activities, recreation or rehabilitation therapists.

A major obstacle to improved career opportunities for music therapists is that Medicaid does not reimburse for this service. Few private insurance companies cover this service in their plans. If this were to change as a result of, for instance, increased passage of licensure bills, then those who shape career ladder development could well be moved.

MUSIC THERAPY AS A COMPENSABLE FORM OF TREATMENT FOR MUSICIANS WHO QUALIFY UNDER WORKMEN'S COMPENSATION LAW

Perhaps the last exclusive domain of psychiatry is in the treatment of psychiatric disabilities under Workmen's Compensation Law (WCL). A mental health service other than psychiatry becomes compensable only when a physician refers his patient to that particular service. An individual who seeks out his own non-MD psychotherapist would be ill advised if he wished to be compensated for that service by the state insurance fund.

The issue for music therapy as it pertains to WCL is entirely theoretical at this point but I think worth making. Does music therapy offer any particular advantage in treating, for instance, stress related disorders suffered by musicians? A clinically documented response to this question is beyond the scope of this discussion but music therapists who work with those suffering from the severe manifestations of performance anxiety do get remarkable results. If a solid case were to be made to the treating psychiatrist that such debilitating anxiety disorders could best be treated by music therapists who understand the inherent stressors of the creative process more fully, then perhaps this question could move past the conjectural stage.

Musicians are presently covered under WCL when they are regularly employed by theaters, nightclubs, etc. and suffer accidents while on the job. Those working as independents are not covered. In the United States no legal test has ever arisen regarding the compensability of overuse injuries suffered by musicians. These neuromuscular disorders are classified as occupational diseases in several Scandinavian countries. The definition of an occupational disease as it has been interpreted in Goldberg v. 945 Marcy Corporation (276 N.Y. 313 [1938]) and subsequently Detenbeck v. General Motors Corporation (309 N.Y. 558 [1958]) would both seem to affirm a positive outcome for inclusion of these types of injuries.

WCL has only recently allowed psychiatric illnesses to be considered compensable. When allowable, it must arise out of a traumatic occurrence. For a psychological injury to be regarded as a disease two conditions must exist: that the injured employee is not idiopathic, i.e., vulnerable to that singular hazard, and that the work hazard must be a natural and inherent factor of that job. Active pre-existing psychological disorders that make a worker susceptible to occupational stresses work against claims for psychiatric disability. Dormant psychological conditions do not jeopardize such claims (Hennige v. Fairview Fire District *et al.,* 1984).

The stress inherent in giving live performances may be sufficient to qualify as psychiatrically disabled those who suffer from disabling forms of performance anxiety. A strong argument can be made that these injuries are commonplace enough to be viewed as occupational hazards and not the result of the idiopathic tendencies of those who suffer from them. If psychiatry recognized music therapy as most capable of providing psychotherapeutic services to such patients then music therapy could become compensable. This, however, depends on music therapists convincingly documenting their work with this patient group in order to get the referrals.

CONCLUSION

There is no certainty, of course, that music therapy will attain the recognition that ensues when one's field arrives at the level of a profession. The traditional professions of medicine, law, theology and engineering have had to grudgingly accept the arrival of psychologists, social workers and others into their ranks. So perhaps new fields are likely to follow.

This society has assumed greater and greater levels of responsibility for its sick and disabled. By doing so the fundamental freedom of the mentally ill, particularly those released after years of institutional care, has been called into question. The actions of the City of New York in rounding up and detaining the homeless mentally ill will probably be settled by the courts. It is in this atmosphere of pyramiding legal questions and health regulations that music therapy needs to define itself as distinct and essential. *The Singing Detective* did not seem to know what his song was about. Perhaps with the help of a music therapist he could have discovered this.

REFERENCES

1 Burger, C.J., Stewart, J.: O'Connor V. Donaldon, 422, US 563, 45 L. Ed 2d 396, 95 s Ct. 2486. 1972. P. 411.

2 Scalengthe, R.: The accreditation process and its impact on music therapy practice. *Fiscal, Regulatory and Legislative Issues for the Music Therapist*. NAMT, 1986, p. 22.

3 Davis, W.B.: QMRP's: What they are and how current legislation will affect the music therapist employed in ICF/MR facilities. *Fiscal, Regulatory and Legislative Issues for the Music Therapist*. NAMT, 1986, p. 18.

4 Hughes, J., McComb, P.G.: Music therapy in the public schools: Developing a network of support at the state level. *Fiscal, Regulatory and Legislative Issues for the Music Therapist*. NAMT, 1986.

5 Wheeler, B.L.: Licensure: The present climate for credentialling. *Fiscal, Regulatory and Legislative Issues for the Music Therapist*. NAMT, 1986.

6 Reuer, B., Gfeller, K.: Civil Service job lines for the music therapist. *Fiscal, Regulatory and Legislative Issues for the Music Therapist*. NAMT, 1986, pp. 44-45.